OIL POWERS

VICTOR MCFARLAND

OIL POWERS

A History of the U.S.-Saudi Alliance

Columbia University Press / *New York*

Columbia University Press
Publishers Since 1893
New York   Chichester, West Sussex
cup.columbia.edu
Copyright © 2020 Columbia University Press
All rights reserved

Library of Congress Cataloging-in-Publication Data

Names: McFarland, Victor, author.
Title: Oil powers : a history of the U.S.-Saudi alliance / Victor McFarland.
Description: New York : Columbia University Press, 2020. |
Includes bibliographical references and index.
Identifiers: LCCN 2019056209 (print) | LCCN 2019056210 (ebook) |
ISBN 9780231197267 (cloth) | ISBN 9780231197274 (paperback) |
ISBN 9780231552073 (ebook)
Subjects: LCSH: Petroleum industry and trade—Saudi Arabia. |
United States—Foreign relations—Saudi Arabia. | Saudi Arabia—Foreign
relations—United States. | United States—Foreign economic relations—
Saudi Arabia. | Saudi Arabia—Foreign economic relations—United States.
Classification: LCC E183.8.S25 M38 2020 (print) | LCC E183.8.S25
(ebook) | DDC 327.730538—dc23
LC record available at https://lccn.loc.gov/2019056209
LC ebook record available at https://lccn.loc.gov/2019056210

Cover image: Getty Images © Dirck Halstead

CONTENTS

CONTENTS

ACKNOWLEDGMENTS

t is a pleasure to thank the many friends and colleagues who helped this book come together. While working on *Oil Powers*, I was fortunate to make my academic home at Yale University, the Miller Center at the University of Virginia, the Dickey Center for International Understanding at Dartmouth College, the Charles Warren Center for Studies in American History at Harvard University, and the University of Missouri.

Funding from Yale University, the University of Missouri, the Gerald R. Ford Presidential Library, and the Society for Historians of American Foreign Relations (SHAFR) supported my archival research. Those travels took me to libraries and archives in the United States, Saudi Arabia, and beyond. I am grateful to the staff at the Center for Research Libraries in Chicago, the Dolph Briscoe Center for American History at the University of Texas, the Federal Reserve Bank of New York (with special thanks to Jay Sager), the Rockefeller Archive Center in Sleepy Hollow, Georgetown University, the Gerald R. Ford Presidential Library in Ann Arbor, Harvard University, the Institute for Palestine Studies in Beirut, the Institute of Public Administration in Riyadh, the Jimmy Carter Presidential Library in Atlanta, the John F. Kennedy Presidential Library in Boston, King Abdulaziz University, King Saud University, the University of Jordan (with special thanks to Afnan Rafeeq), Lafayette College, the National Archives and Records Administration in College Park, the National Center for Documentation and Research in Abu Dhabi, the Organization of Petroleum Exporting Countries in Vienna, the Organization of Arab Petroleum Exporting Countries in Kuwait City (with special thanks to Omar Karameh), Princeton University, the Richard Nixon Presidential Library in Yorba Linda, and the Ronald Reagan Library in Simi Valley.

I could not have conducted research in Saudi Arabia without the support of Prince Turki al-Faisal, Naila al-Sowayel, Ibrahim al-Hadlaq, and the staff of the King Faisal Center for Research and Islamic Studies in Riyadh, as well as Mohammed Al Fahad and Majid Al-Moneef at the Ministry of Petroleum and Mineral Resources. Thanks to Abdulaziz Al Fahad, Saeed Badeeb, and Hassan Husseini for their hospitality and their insights into Saudi history, and to Daniela Olivier, Hamed Tabrizi, Michael Farquhar, and Nadav Samin for our shared adventures in the kingdom.

I am grateful to the former U.S. and Saudi officials and others who agreed to be interviewed for this book. Special thanks to William Quandt for being exceptionally generous with his time and for helping me to understand what happened behind the scenes in the Nixon and Carter administrations.

I received valuable advice on work in progress from the organizers and participants of workshops, seminars, and conferences with the American Historical Association, the American Political Science Association, Ca' Foscari University of Venice, the Seminar on Twentieth Century Politics and Society at Columbia University, the Dickey Center at Dartmouth College, the Warren Center at Harvard University, the International Studies Association, the Middle East Studies Association, the University of Missouri, the Abu Dhabi Institute and the Remarque Institute of New York University, SHAFR, the Maison de la Recherche of Sorbonne University, the University of Tübingen, the Miller Center at the University of Virginia, and Yale University.

My academic advisors, John Lewis Gaddis, Abbas Amanat, and Beverly Gage, guided this project from the beginning. I am also deeply indebted to David Painter and Salim Yaqub for their generous mentorship and support over the years.

Many other colleagues, teachers, and friends read and discussed this project with me. They included Sultan Alamer, Marino Auffant, Fritz Bartel, Amanda Behm, Jadwiga Biskupska, Rosie Bsheer, Daniel Chardell, Dag Harald Claes, Jeff Colgan, Guillemette Crouzet, Christina Davidson, Michael Farquhar, Kevin Fogg, Jeffrey Friedman, Joe Fronczak, Giuliano Garavini, Nils Gilman, Gretchen Heefner, Ryan Irwin, Rose Kelanic, Paul Kennedy, Josh Kertzer, Sulmaan Khan, Kevin Kim, Jenny Lind, Doug Little, Fred Logevall, Chris Low, ShawnaKim Lowey-Ball, Erez Manela, Emily Meierding, Chris Miller, Ed Miller, Jennie Miller, Mike Morgan, Sam Moyn, Marta Musso, Aaron O'Connell, Lindsey O'Rourke, Ken Osgood, Daryl Press, Paul Sabin, Daniel Sargent, Kathryn Schwartz, Kristina Shull, Jeremi Suri, Laura Thaut Vinson, Bob Vitalis, Jessica Wang, Odd Arne Westad, and Bill Wohlforth. Special thanks to Chris Dietrich, Molly Geidel, Nathan Kurz, and Saje Mathieu for going above and beyond the call of duty in their thorough reading of the manuscript and their detailed and insightful comments.

Kevin Kim and Daniel Sargent generously shared material they had collected on their own trips to the archives. Molly Bradtke, Oksana Levkovych, and Natascha Otoya gathered critical sources at the Library of Congress, the Guildhall Library in London, and the Georgetown University Library. Amro Alansari, Mohammed Alaskari, Duaa Alhou, Ali Almajed, Eissa Almoteiri, and Laith Hujab helped transcribe Arabic documents into electronic formats. Their help was invaluable, especially with older newspapers whose smudged and blurry text was a challenge even for native speakers. All translations, and any resulting errors, are my own.

I am grateful to Dick Doughty at *Saudi Aramco World* and Sharon Seymour at the Sausalito Historical Society for sharing images from their collections.

Thanks to the editors and staff at Columbia University Press (including Stephen Wesley, Christian Winting, and Kat Jorge) and to Susan Ecklund and Helen Wheeler at Westchester Publishing Services for their expert work in preparing the manuscript for publication. I also appreciate the careful reading and valuable feedback from three anonymous reviewers.

My parents encouraged my love of history, and supported me during the long path from the beginning of my research to the finished book.

Most of all, thanks to Emily Gustafson. She helped with this project in a thousand different ways. Without her guidance, encouragement, and love, it would never have been possible.

A NOTE ON ARABIC TRANSLITERATION

This book uses the most common English versions of Arabic names and words, particularly when those spellings are preferred by the individual or organization in question. When standards have changed over time, I use the current version in the main text and the original spelling in direct quotations and references. For example, Saudi Arabia's main Red Sea port and longtime diplomatic capital appears as "Jeddah," the spelling now preferred by the Saudi and U.S. governments. The U.S. State Department formerly used the spelling "Jidda," so cables from the U.S. embassy in Saudi Arabia to the department's headquarters in Washington, DC are labeled "Jidda to State."

When transliterating Arabic into English, specialists use diacritical marks to represent the original spelling as precisely as possible. For the sake of accessibility, I avoid the use of those marks in quotations that appear in the main text, along with names, newspaper titles, and common words. For longer Arabic quotations and the titles of books and articles, I use spellings based on the transliteration system employed by the *International Journal of Middle East Studies*.

OIL POWERS

Saudi Arabia with present-day borders.

INTRODUCTION

Jeddah, 1974

I n the summer of 1974, Jeddah hummed with activity. Despite the blistering heat, the port city on Saudi Arabia's west coast swarmed with cranes and bulldozers working around the clock. Jeddah was expanding in all directions, fueled by a tremendous economic boom. Just months before, the price of oil had soared as the Arab petroleum-exporting states cut production and imposed a temporary embargo on the United States. With the embargo now over and the kingdom's oil revenues skyrocketing, money and goods were pouring in from all over the world. A line of cargo ships extended far out into the Red Sea waiting to dock at Jeddah's hopelessly overcrowded port.

Oil brought new wealth to Saudi Arabia. It also attracted the attention of the United States. On June 14, 1974, a giant fleet of American aircraft descended onto Jeddah's airport. President Richard Nixon arrived in Air Force One, accompanied by Secretary of State Henry Kissinger and dozens of aides, Secret Service guards, and support staff. A separate transport hauled Nixon's custom armored limousines. Two chartered airliners brought 122 photographers and journalists, including some of the most famous names in American news: Walter Cronkite, Dan Rather, and Connie Chung. It was the first time a U.S. president had ever visited Saudi Arabia, and the

U.S. embassy in Jeddah was astonished by the sight. The State Department official Hume Horan marveled at the presidential fleet: "There were maybe 500 in his delegation and 20 aircraft from the U.S. government there on the hard top, a sort of U.S. pilgrimage to Arabia! We thought the Peninsula might slip below the Red Sea under the weight of this American armada!"[1]

Saudi Arabia's King Faisal met Nixon on the tarmac. They walked past the Saudi honor guard as the evening sun glinted off the swords and gold-embroidered uniforms of the soldiers, before boarding a motorcade headed to a nearby royal palace. Just months before, Faisal had led the oil embargo against the United States. Now, both men were determined to put that episode behind them. They shook hands for the cameras and spoke glowingly about their "constructive and fruitful cooperation" and the long "unbroken friendship" between their two nations (figure 0.1).[2]

FIGURE 0.1 Richard Nixon and King Faisal, Riyadh, June 1974. To the left is Crown Prince Khalid. To the right is famed U.S. State Department interpreter Isa Sabbagh. In the crowd behind them are prominent U.S. and Saudi officials, including secretary of state Henry Kissinger, deputy national security adviser Brent Scowcroft, and ambassador James Akins, along with the princes Abdullah, Fahd, and Sultan. Courtesy of the Richard Nixon Presidential Library and Museum, National Archives and Records Administration.

Nixon and Faisal put the final stamp on work that had already been done earlier that month by Kissinger and Prince Fahd, third in line for the Saudi throne. The secretary of state and the prince concluded a pair of landmark deals that accelerated U.S.-Saudi economic and military cooperation. They were delighted to see their initiative confirmed by their nation's leaders. As Nixon and Faisal shook hands, Kissinger and Fahd stood behind them, grinning.

Nixon and Faisal would soon be out of power. Facing certain impeachment, Nixon resigned from office just two months after his meeting with Faisal. The Saudi king was assassinated by one of his relatives less than a year later, in March 1975. Their legacy, however, would endure. During the following years, Saudi and American leaders consolidated their alliance. Saudi Arabia invested billions of dollars in U.S. financial markets, bought huge quantities of American goods, and promised to keep oil prices down. The United States sold the kingdom advanced weapons, provided technical expertise, educated the children of the Saudi elite, and pledged to protect Saudi Arabia from its enemies. Their alliance reshaped the Middle East and left a lasting mark on both nations. This book is the story of how that alliance was built.

* * *

The first step in understanding the U.S.-Saudi alliance is admitting that it exists. U.S. and Saudi leaders have always been careful to deny that they have an alliance, insisting that it is merely a "security partnership" or a "special relationship."[3] Technically, they are right. The United States and Saudi Arabia do not have a formal treaty agreement to defend each other from attack, like the one between the members of the North Atlantic Treaty Organization (NATO).

By any commonsense definition, though, the United States and Saudi Arabia are obviously allies. For decades, it has been clear that the United States would protect Saudi Arabia—including, if necessary, by force. That commitment was proven in the 1990–91 Gulf War, when the United States sent more than half a million troops to defend the kingdom from Iraq. The United States has armed and trained the Saudi military, refueled Saudi aircraft, and provided data that guided Saudi military strikes against adversaries from Iran in the 1980s to the Houthi rebels in Yemen after 2015. Saudi Arabia has shared intelligence with the U.S. military, hosted thousands of American troops, and helped the United States launch two invasions of Iraq from Saudi soil. If that is not an alliance, then what is?

U.S. policymakers have chosen to avoid the domestic backlash and public oversight that would come with a formal treaty relationship. Treaties with foreign powers must be ratified by the Senate, but Congress—and the American people—have often been skeptical of close U.S.-Saudi relations.[4]

Riyadh, too, has hidden the extent of its alliance with Washington. In 1979, the Saudi foreign minister Saud al-Faisal was asked about his country's military cooperation with the United States. He flatly denied that an alliance existed. "We do not enter into alliances [ahlaf]," Saud al-Faisal said, except with other Arab and Muslim countries.[5] Such dissembling came at a cost. When Saudi Arabia asked the United States to intervene in the Gulf War, half a million U.S. troops suddenly arrived in the kingdom. The Saudi people had never been informed that their nation depended so completely on U.S. military protection. That realization infuriated the regime's critics, including Osama bin Laden, and planted the seeds of future conflict.

U.S. and Saudi elites obscured their alliance because they feared opposition from their own people. As early as the 1940s, many Americans saw the Saudi regime as too backward, bigoted, and despotic to be an American ally. Arab nationalists in Saudi Arabia and elsewhere in the region denounced the kingdom for betraying its fellow Arabs and partnering with Israel's chief patron. Religious conservatives feared that their nation was being contaminated and secularized by American influence. And leftist Saudis accused the U.S. government and the oil company Aramco of plundering the nation's wealth and propping up the authoritarian Saudi regime.

During Nixon's visit, the royal family deflected such criticism by emphasizing its nationalist credentials. The government-linked newspaper *Al-Riyadh* reminded its readers that Faisal had led the embargo against the United States just a few months earlier. "We started the oil war," *Al-Riyadh* declared, "to restore an uprooted people"—the Palestinians—to their homes. Until Jerusalem was returned to its rightful inhabitants, *Al-Riyadh* vowed, "we will not back down." Faisal himself warned there would be no peace in the region until Israel restored the rights of the Palestinians and withdrew from the Arab territory it had seized in 1967.[6]

The Saudi government worried that such reminders might not be enough to quiet public opposition. The regime's security forces kept spectators away from Nixon's motorcade route. American journalists noticed that soldiers and police outnumbered ordinary civilians along the roadway. Despite Faisal's loudly proclaimed sympathy for the Palestinian cause, his regime could be much less sympathetic to actual Palestinians. The security forces tracked down and questioned all Palestinian immigrants in the area, in case they posed a threat to Faisal and his American visitors.[7]

The U.S. delegation was unsure what sort of welcome they could expect from Saudis outside the royal palaces. The administration gave them private instructions not to stray beyond approved parts of Jeddah. The Americans were to watch what they said to local citizens, and under no circumstances mention that after they left Saudi Arabia, they were scheduled to visit Israel.[8] Back at home, not all Americans were pleased to see Nixon currying favor with Saudi Arabia, either. Many, including some leading members of Congress, had not forgotten that Faisal had declared an oil embargo against the United States less than one year earlier.[9] In the face of such opposition, U.S. and Saudi leaders maintained their alliance by shielding it from public scrutiny and accountability.

* * *

When U.S. and Saudi leaders *did* admit they had an unusually close relationship, they often claimed they had no choice in the matter. They described the ties between Washington and Riyadh as the inevitable consequence of basic geological and economic facts. They argued that Saudi Arabia had oil, and the United States needed it, so they were forced to work together despite their political and cultural differences. In October 1974, the Lebanese newspaper *Al-Anwar* interviewed Prince Fahd. By that point, the oil embargo had been over for seven months, and U.S.-Saudi economic cooperation was expanding rapidly. Why, *Al-Anwar* asked, was Saudi Arabia working so closely with the United States, investing its oil earnings in American markets and buying American goods rather than sharing the money with its Arab brothers? Fahd dismissed the question. It was "only natural" (*min al-tabi'i*), he said, that Washington and Riyadh should have a close relationship, since "the United States is the largest oil consumer and Saudi Arabia is the largest producer" in the world.[10]

U.S. officials stressed similar themes, pointing to Saudi Arabia's importance as an oil producer. Even when they claimed to be uncomfortable with the relationship, they argued that it was locked into place by circumstances outside their control and decisions made by their predecessors. In 1963, during a proxy war in Yemen between Saudi Arabia and Egypt, Faisal asked the United States to send an air force squadron to defend the kingdom against Egyptian bombing raids. The Joint Chiefs of Staff were reluctant to step into the middle of an Egyptian-Saudi conflict. The national security adviser McGeorge Bundy admonished them: "I gather the Chiefs also wonder whether this flea-bitten part of the world is one where we should get involved. I'm afraid we are involved here long since—even though it may have been a mistake in the first place. But remember oil."[11]

At that time, the United States had dominated the global oil industry for more than a century. American petroleum made the United States into the prototype of a high-energy, motorized society and fueled Allied victory in both world wars. The lavish use of oil, in machines from air force jets to presidential limousines and the big cars of ordinary consumers, epitomized American power. Most of the largest oil companies in the world—including the owners of the Arabian American Oil Company (Aramco), the consortium that ran Saudi Arabia's oil fields—were American-owned. The United States still produced most of the oil it needed from its own domestic sources. It even had surplus production capacity that it could tap in an emergency.

During the early 1970s, that surplus disappeared. The United States became increasingly dependent on imports. Simultaneously, the balance of power in the whole global oil market shifted as Saudi Arabia and the other producers took more control over their own resources and demanded higher prices for their oil. That transformation was underscored by the oil crisis of 1973–74, when U.S. consumers waited in long lines for scarce gasoline. It was a traumatic experience for Americans who believed that giving up their energy self-sufficiency meant losing national sovereignty and global influence. Saudi Arabia, it seemed, had replaced the United States as the world's leading oil power.[12]

All three presidents of the 1970s—Richard Nixon, Gerald Ford, and Jimmy Carter—spent the decade promoting various ideas for regaining "energy independence." In practice, though, they recognized that their plans offered no panacea. The alliance with Saudi Arabia offered an alternative way of ensuring the continued supply of petroleum even as U.S. production dwindled. Nixon alluded to that concern—and the fact that oil had become so expensive—at his dinner with Faisal in 1974, when he joked that Air Force One would need Saudi fuel to make it to its next stop. "Your Majesty," Nixon said, "I just want to make clear, we, of course, will pay the world price."[13]

* * *

It would be a mistake, however, to assume that America's need for Saudi oil made the U.S.-Saudi alliance inevitable. When American leaders pursued closer ties with Saudi Arabia, disregarding concerns about democracy, human rights, and religious freedom, they claimed to be motivated by a clear-eyed view of the facts. Those facts sometimes turned out to be mistaken. Exaggerated fears of oil scarcity were a powerful influence on U.S. energy policy in the 1970s. Many U.S. officials worried that global oil supplies were quickly running out, leaving Saudi Arabia as the one remaining country that still had large reserves to spare. The pessimistic forecasts were incorrect, and oil prices would plunge during the 1980s as a supply glut overwhelmed demand.[14]

Advocates of the U.S.-Saudi alliance also overstated the risk that the United States would lose access to Saudi oil if it did not back the Saudi regime. They overestimated Saudi Arabia's ability, and desire, to stop producing oil if U.S. leaders failed to heed Saudi wishes.[15] Hawkish officials conjured up dangers, like a Soviet move into the Persian Gulf after the 1979 occupation of Afghanistan, which never materialized. And they constantly fretted about the survival of the Saudi monarchy, which proved far more durable than most outside observers predicted. This is not to suggest that such fears were never real; only that they rested on a debatable reading of the evidence, one that U.S. and Saudi elites used to reinforce their own policy preferences.

Even the role of Saudi oil was more complicated than it first appeared. Other countries like Muammar Qaddafi's Libya, Baathist Iraq, and the Soviet Union also controlled large oil reserves, but none of them enjoyed anything like Saudi Arabia's privileged relationship with the United States. U.S. leaders believed that Saudi oil was more valuable than Libyan, Iraqi, or Soviet oil not only because there was so much of it, but also because they believed that Saudi Arabia wanted to help the United States.

Saudi Arabia was remarkably successful at persuading American leaders that it was the most responsible member of the Organization of the Petroleum Exporting Countries (OPEC). The Saudi regime argued that among the world's leading oil producers, it alone was willing to limit oil price increases, foregoing short-term profits to help the global economy and protect the anticommunist world. Those Saudi claims were questionable, but they found a ready audience among American policymakers, who were dismayed by the rapid increase in oil prices during the 1970s and desperately wanted an ally inside OPEC.[16]

U.S. leaders also approved of the way Saudi Arabia spent its oil revenues. When Nixon arrived, Jeddah's docks were filled with American-made cars, appliances, and other goods. Students from wealthy Saudi families studied at American universities. The Saudi government hired consultants from places like Harvard, the Stanford Research Institute (SRI), and the Ford Foundation to oversee the kingdom's development plans. Saudi demand for the most advanced U.S. fighter jets, tanks, and missiles was so limitless that it dismayed many of the Pentagon's advisors in the kingdom, who feared that the kingdom could never operate and maintain such an array of equipment. And at the peak of the oil boom in the 1970s, when the money was piling up too fast to spend, Saudi Arabia deposited much of the surplus in U.S. banks.

The opportunities available for American companies were enormous. They were on full display during Fahd's visit to Washington, DC in June 1974 when the Saudi embassy threw a gigantic party for Henry Kissinger and 1,400 other guests, including representatives from Chase Manhattan, First National City Bank, Exxon, and Lockheed.[17] The royal family often stressed its commitment to doing business with U.S. corporations. During Nixon's visit to Jeddah later that month, Crown Prince Khalid told Kissinger that even though the aviation world was abuzz with the news of the supersonic Concorde that Britain and France were developing, Saudi Arabia still preferred to buy American. "Boeing," he said, "is the best aircraft."[18] Khalid, who suffered from heart trouble, would later order a custom Boeing 747 with the world's only flying surgical operating room.

Other Saudi funds went to fight Marxism and support allied political forces beyond the kingdom's borders. Riyadh sent billions of dollars to bolster anticommunist regimes in Egypt, Jordan, and elsewhere, delighting U.S. officials, even if some money went to groups like the Palestine Liberation Organization (PLO), which the United States viewed less favorably. The Saudi regime combined its financial resources with the promotion of conservative Wahhabi Islam, which it used as a weapon against its political rivals. Working together, Washington and Riyadh succeeded in pushing Soviet influence out of much of the greater Middle East and permanently weakening the Arab left. The cost included the rise of militant political Islam, long-lasting civil wars, and the crumbling of state authority in countries, like Afghanistan and Yemen, where Saudi Arabia bankrolled violent insurgencies.[19]

* * *

The U.S.-Saudi alliance had a profound impact on Saudi Arabia. Revenue from oil production transformed the kingdom. Aramco and other firms like Bechtel built much of the kingdom's physical infrastructure, including petroleum refineries, highways, railroads, and the electrical grid. With new wealth came better nutrition, hospitals, and schools, and corresponding improvements in life expectancy, infant mortality, literacy, and other measures of human welfare. Despite Saudi Arabia's image as an ultra-traditional society, a reputation reinforced by the government's emphasis on Islamic morality, some aspects of Saudi life gradually liberalized. A few high-profile changes, like the abolition of slavery in the 1960s, were trumpeted by the regime and its defenders as proof of the monarchy's enlightened leadership.[20]

9

One aspect of Saudi life that did not change, however, was the royal family's political dominance. Many outside observers, including U.S. officials, predicted that eventually the royals would cede much of their power to commoner technocrats. In practice, though, U.S. policy favored the leading members of the Saudi dynasty. American leaders believed that close ties with the royal family offered the best chance for influencing Saudi foreign policy and securing lucrative commercial opportunities. The king and the senior princes used their ties with the U.S. government to enhance their own power, giving them control over enormous arms contracts and other resources. As a result, the royals, and their allies among the business community and other Saudi elites, reaped the biggest rewards from the oil boom of the 1970s. Far less fortunate were dissidents, labor activists, and workers who came from the marginalized Shia community or from overseas.[21]

U.S. leaders defended their ties with the royal family by pointing to common interests in fighting communism and other enemies. They argued that the Saudi regime was reforming and modernizing the kingdom. And they fell back on old stereotypes about Arab culture, suggesting that autocracy was the natural state of Middle Eastern politics.[22] When Fahd visited Washington, DC, in 1974, Nixon told him that the United States had no interest in democratizing the rest of the world. Nixon reassured Fahd that as far as he was concerned, "all countries, as for example Saudi Arabia," could "maintain their own systems without outside interference from anyone." When the Saudi foreign minister Omar Saqqaf told Kissinger that many Saudis were impatient to modernize their kingdom, Kissinger cautioned that the royals should move "slowly enough to keep your political structure."[23]

* * *

The U.S.-Saudi alliance changed the United States, too. It encouraged corporate consolidation, the financialization of the economy, and the growth of executive power. Over time, Saudi Arabia became more like the United States, but the United States also became a bit more like Saudi Arabia.[24]

The largest U.S. corporations made the biggest profits in Saudi Arabia. Saudi oil production was controlled by just four American companies, the predecessors of Chevron and ExxonMobil, who had the exclusive right to operate in the main oil-producing region of the kingdom. They enjoyed a privileged relationship not only with the Saudi government, but also with the U.S. government. They shared intelligence with the Central Intelligence Agency (CIA) and coordinated their activities with the State Department and the Pentagon. That status helped shield them from legal oversight at home, leading the Harry Truman administration to veto a criminal antitrust case that could have broken them up into smaller companies.

Even beyond the oil sector, Saudi Arabia was a difficult market for most American firms to enter. It was challenging to transport labor and supplies over thousands of miles, and sometimes even harder to secure the cooperation of the Saudi government. The largest corporations, like Bechtel, Lockheed, and Boeing, had the resources and the political connections to do business in the kingdom. Their smaller rivals could not compete.

The high oil prices of the 1970s created a more volatile and inegalitarian U.S. economy, less dependent on manufacturing and more dependent on finance. U.S. government leaders sought to attract Saudi investment to the United States by promising special exemptions from public and congressional oversight. The secrecy requirements were so strict that even the CIA had to be reprimanded when it published data on Saudi funds. Billions of Saudi "petrodollars" flowed to the U.S. Treasury and the mortgage lender Fannie Mae, foreshadowing the role of foreign capital in financing U.S. deficit spending and the housing bubbles of later decades.[25] These arrangements underlined the rise of a new economic environment involving gigantic flows of capital across international borders, with even the world's most powerful nations competing to attract investment by offering perks, like secrecy and anonymity, once pioneered by small offshore banking hubs.[26]

During the late 1970s, Saudi Arabia encouraged a dramatic shift in U.S. monetary policy. At that time, the United States was experiencing rapid inflation and the value of the dollar was sliding. Those trends threatened Saudi Arabia because the kingdom had invested billions in the United States, and priced its oil in dollars, so a decline in the dollar threatened both the kingdom's revenues and its accumulated reserves. Riyadh demanded that the United States reduce inflation and boost the value of the dollar. In 1978 the Jimmy Carter administration took a series of painful steps to defend the dollar, with the Federal Reserve Bank boosting interest rates sharply even though doing so increased the risk of a recession. In 1979, the new Federal Reserve chairman, Paul Volcker, adopted an even more extreme approach, sending interest rates soaring and throwing millions of Americans out of work in order to control inflation. That move, too, was preceded by Saudi pressure for the United States to stabilize the value of the dollar.[27]

* * *

The clearest Saudi influence on the United States was in the realm of foreign policy. The kingdom pushed a previously skeptical U.S. government to join Saudi anticommunist initiatives in the Horn of Africa, Yemen, and Afghanistan. U.S. leaders valued Saudi cooperation on oil, financial affairs, and regional security so highly that maintaining Saudi confidence in the United States—even if that meant intervening in places where U.S. officials did not agree that any clear national interest was at stake—became an end in itself for American policy makers.

Saudi Arabia's effort to sway U.S. foreign policy was aided by the kingdom's especially close relations with the White House and the rest of the executive branch. Congress was more skeptical of the U.S.-Saudi alliance. The Saudi regime was endlessly frustrated by congressional complaints about the kingdom's human rights record, along with legislative resistance to U.S.-Saudi arms sales and other deals. The royals faced no such constraints on their own power at home and had little patience for legal niceties in Washington, DC.

Nixon probably understood their feelings. When he visited Jeddah, the Watergate scandal was entering its final phase, and Nixon was trying desperately to stave off impeachment. His visit to the Middle East was a welcome escape from Washington. There were no special prosecutors or investigative committees in the kingdom, and Nixon must have felt at least a touch of envy for Saudi leaders who never had to deal with a critical press, legislature, or Supreme Court.

The White House played up its ties with the Saudi regime, sometimes sounding as if it was collaborating with Saudi Arabia not only against foreign enemies, but also against the U.S. Congress. Nixon and Kissinger tried to convince the Saudi leaders that if Nixon were removed from office, the kingdom would lose its best friend in the United States. During the 1974 visit, Kissinger told Saqqaf that the administration was under attack "by the Jews" and suggested that Democratic senators who criticized Nixon's foreign policy were doing so on Israel's orders.[28]

Faisal agreed. Implying that Watergate was a Jewish plot, he told Nixon privately that he found it "painful to see all these intrigues against the President and his Secretary of State" just as Nixon and Kissinger were putting pressure on Israel to make peace with its Arab neighbors. "It cannot be coincidental," Faisal concluded darkly. Speaking to the press later that day, the king declared that "anybody who stands against you, Mr. President," was an enemy of "tranquility and peace in the world," and asked Americans "to rally around you, Mr. President."[29]

Faisal could not save Nixon from prosecution. He could, however, help the president bypass other kinds of legal oversight. In the wake of the Vietnam War, Congress was trying to reassert its authority over foreign policy. Meeting Faisal in Jeddah, Nixon complained that there were congressional limitations on sending U.S. arms to their mutual friends in Egypt and Pakistan. He suggested that Saudi Arabia take up the task instead, warning Faisal that "this whole subject should be held in strictest confidence."[30] During the following years, Saudi Arabia bankrolled joint covert operations and foreign aid initiatives, contributing to the growing power of the U.S. presidency as it bypassed congressional restrictions on funding.

Saudi Arabia was still the junior partner in the alliance. It could influence U.S. policy, though, because Saudi and American elites thought they shared a set of common interests. U.S. banks wanted a deregulated financial system, economic policy makers like Volcker wanted to tackle inflation, hawkish officials wanted a more aggressive approach toward the Soviet Union, and the White House wanted to limit congressional authority over foreign policy. They all found that Saudi preferences coincided with their own, and saw Saudi influence as a way to advance their agendas.

The U.S.-Saudi alliance entrenched executive and royal power in both countries, enriched big corporations, and pushed both countries to the right.

It paved the way for a militarized U.S. foreign policy in the Middle East and decades of armed intervention, including the 1991 and 2003 invasions of Iraq and the post-9/11 "War on Terror." The ties between Washington and Riyadh had such a profound impact because they were the product of decades of hard political work by leaders on both sides. To understand how they built their alliance, we will turn back to the first Saudi royal visit to the United States in 1943, when Faisal was still a young prince.

1

WHEELS OF EMPIRE

I n September 1943, a group of Saudi officials led by Prince Faisal boarded an American military transport plane in Jeddah. Over the next week, they completed a remarkable journey, touching down in the Sudan, Ghana, St. Helena, Brazil, Venezuela, and Florida, before reaching their final destination: Washington, DC. On the way, the pilot took the plane low over the Venezuelan oilfields on the Caribbean coast, joking to the Saudis that the view should remind them of home. The trip was a spectacular demonstration of the new possibilities of worldwide air travel. It also showed the global spread of American military power. Faisal's trip was made possible by a network of U.S. bases, airfields, and refueling stations that now extended around the world. Abdullah Balkhair, Faisal's translator, marveled at the reach of "the US military, which was everywhere during the war," sending cars and jeeps to meet the Saudis even at the most remote tropical airstrips.[1]

The visit was a new experience for both Americans and Saudis. When Faisal arrived in Washington, the State Department was so unaccustomed to hosting Saudis that it found itself without a Saudi flag to fly over the Blair House, the official guest residence for foreign leaders. An urgent order went out for a new flag, which was hastily sewn and delivered just in time.[2] U.S. leaders had never paid much attention to Saudi Arabia, but now they were increasingly taken by its potential as a future source of oil, an engine of profits for American companies, and a site for military facilities.

Oil fueled America's rise to superpower status in the 1940s. No other nation had the petroleum and the infrastructure to move people, goods, and weapons across such distances and on such a gigantic scale. The war also encouraged the rise of U.S. executive authority in alliance with private industry, as the president assumed vast new war-making powers and corporations won huge defense contracts.

Faisal's visit was made possible by the partnership between the U.S. federal government and private business. The Saudi delegation traveled around the country on a tour sponsored by the U.S. State Department and American corporations, including Standard Oil of California (Chevron), the Texas Company (Texaco), and the construction giant Bechtel. Every stop in the tour demonstrated the scale of oil-fueled U.S. industrial and military power. In New York City, the Saudis were driven in Mayor Fiorella La Guardia's own automobile, escorted by fourteen motorcycle police with sirens blaring to clear the way. They visited the Grumman factory on Long Island, where they saw warplanes being constructed and flew in an amphibious aircraft. Members of Faisal's party rode a private train car to Chicago and received a limousine tour of the city, then resumed their rail journey to New Mexico and Arizona, where they toured the local attractions by automobile. At the Grand Canyon, Faisal and his half-brother Prince Khalid thrilled local children by giving them rides in borrowed jeeps. In California, the Saudis inspected oil refineries and the gigantic Kaiser and Bechtel-McCone shipyards, where Faisal would later return on his second trip to the United States in 1945 (figure 1.1).[3]

Faisal and his companions were impressed with American technical achievements, and they were eager to use American resources to enhance the power of their own regime. When they returned to Washington, DC, and met with State Department officials at the beginning of November, they agreed on an expansion of U.S. involvement in the kingdom, including a major new oil refinery. They also asked the United States to send Saudi Arabia medical supplies, radio equipment, water pumps, and other machinery. Faisal was particularly impressed with the irrigation technology he

FIGURE 1.1 Saudi delegation on the oil tanker SS *Paloma Hills* at the Bechtel-McCone Marinship yard, Sausalito, California, 1945. From left are Hafiz Wahba and the princes Fahd, Faisal, Muhammad al-Faisal, and Nawwaf, along with Bechtel president Stephen Bechtel and Marinship president Kenneth Bechtel. Courtesy of the Sausalito Historical Society.

had seen in the Southwest. Most of all, the Saudis wanted automobiles, including trucks and buses to carry Muslim pilgrims to Mecca and Medina. The princes were so impressed with American vehicles, they wanted to buy fourteen passenger cars for their personal use and have them shipped back to Saudi Arabia.[4] Saudi and American leaders agreed: in the twentieth century, power came from oil and the machines that burned it.

The U.S.-Saudi relationship was a new phenomenon in 1943, and so was the Saudi kingdom itself. When Faisal was born in 1906, his father ruled little more than the land immediately surrounding his capital, Riyadh. Over the next three decades, he built the modern Saudi kingdom through a combination of diplomacy and violent force. The automobile played a critical role in that process. Cars transported the first Saudi king Abdulaziz, his court, and his troops, knitting his far-flung domains into a single, increasingly centralized realm.[5] They also served as a visible symbol of royal wealth and prestige. Contrary to common perceptions, state-directed Saudi modernization and the rise of oil as a source of political and economic power preceded, rather than followed, the beginning of Saudi oil production. Before the first oil wells were drilled, Saudi Arabia was already being transformed by the power of gasoline, as automobiles enabled a new form of centralized state-building.

THE ORIGINS OF THE SAUDI DYNASTY

The Al Saud began as the rulers of the minor farming settlement of Diriyah in Najd, the region at the center of the Arabian Peninsula. The Al Saud were one of many families that fought for power in this chaotic environment, each controlling a small oasis settlement and its immediate surroundings.[6] Their fortunes changed in the 1740s when the Saudi leader Muhammad ibn Saud joined forces with Muhammad ibn Abd al-Wahhab, a religious reformer who believed that Islam had been corrupted by harmful innovations.[7] Ibn Abd al-Wahhab called for a return to the pristine Islam of the prophet Muhammad and his earliest followers. Muhammad ibn Saud pledged to support the religious teachings of Muhammad ibn Abd al-Wahhab, whose descendants became the Al al-Sheikh ("the people of the Sheikh"), a family that still supplies many of the kingdom's senior clerics. In return, Muhammad ibn Abd al-Wahhab swore political allegiance to Muhammad ibn Saud.[8]

Over the next half-century, the Saudi-Wahhabi alliance conquered most of the Arabian Peninsula.[9] The Al Saud imposed Wahhabism on their territories, while Wahhabi clerics provided ideological justification for Saudi rule. Ever since, critics have denounced Wahhabism as a violent faith spread by the sword. In the 1980s, the dissident Khalifa Fahad wrote that Muhammad ibn Saud made his alliance with Muhammad ibn Abd al-Wahhab not for spiritual reasons "but for the sake of worldly power," while Wahhabism legitimized "destruction, killing, and looting in the name of Islam and the Quran." The legitimate clerics of Najd "were all against Wahhabi ideas," falling silent only after their towns were conquered.[10] To its followers, how-ever, Wahhabism had many attractions. It promised theological certainty, simplicity, and fidelity to the holy texts of Islam, along with an end to the constant conflict in Najd by redirecting violence outward toward lands not yet under Saudi rule.

In the early nineteenth century that expansionist impulse led the Al Saud to disaster, bringing them into conflict with the Ottoman Empire and its vassal, the Egyptian leader Muhammad Ali. An Egyptian army defeated the Saudis in 1818, capturing the Saudi ruler Abdullah ibn Saud, sending him to Constantinople to be executed, and destroying Diriyah so thor-oughly that only ruins were left standing. A second, smaller version of the Saudi emirate rose later in the nineteenth century, based in Riyadh, but it collapsed due to internal conflict and war with the Rashidis, a rival Najdi dynasty that captured Riyadh and expelled the Al Saud in 1890–1891. The young Saudi prince Abdulaziz, a teenager when Riyadh fell, went into exile in Kuwait and planned revenge against the Rashidis.

THE MODERN SAUDI STATE

In 1902, when Abdulaziz was still only in his midtwenties, he sneaked into Riyadh with a few dozen of his closest followers and killed the Rashidi governor of the city. Abdulaziz and his successors would later celebrate that moment as the beginning of the modern Saudi state. Over three de-cades of intermittent warfare, Abdulaziz built a new Saudi kingdom. In 1913, he conquered al-Hasa along the shores of the Persian Gulf, acquiring the richest oil fields in the world, although no one realized it at the time. After World War I, Abdulaziz captured the Rashidi capital of Hail in the north, along with part of the region of Asir in the south, near the Yemeni border. The biggest prize was the Hijaz on the Red Sea coast, the home of the holy cities Mecca and Medina. It was ruled by the Hashemite dynasty, but Abdulaziz defeated them and drove them into exile. By the mid-1920s, the rough outlines of the current Saudi state were coming into view.

Abdulaziz welded his kingdom together out of separate regions with distinct histories and cultures. Al-Hasa and Asir included many Shia, often persecuted by Wahhabis who did not see them as true Muslims. The Hijaz was the destination of the hajj, the Muslim pilgrimage to Mecca, and centuries of pilgrimage and trading connections with the rest of the Muslim world made it more cosmopolitan and ethnically diverse than Najd. After Abdulaziz conquered Mecca and Medina, taxing the pilgrims and using the revenues to bolster his own power, many Hijazis resented their region's loss of independence. Even the Saudi heartland of Najd was populated by Bedouin tribes and small farming villages that were accustomed to managing their own affairs and resisted Abdulaziz's imposition of centralized authority.

The Al Saud and their allies celebrated Abdulaziz's defeat of his enemies, claiming that national unification brought an end to tribal warfare and political chaos. The Saudi scholar and government official Abdullah ibn Abd al-Mohsen al-Turki wrote that prior to the rise of the Saudi state, "Raiding, looting, and robbing people of their means of existence was a way of life for many of the tribes that lived in the Arabian Peninsula, and there was no safety to be found in the land of the two holy cities—neither for their inhabitants, nor for pilgrims to the House of God." Under Abdulaziz "the hand of the state was so strong that it changed the behavior of the entire society" and brought peace to the land.[11] Opponents of the regime, however, saw its creation as a brutal act. The dissident historian Khalifa Fahad argued that the kingdom of the Al Saud was "erected not by popular consent, or by means of persuasion, but with force and domination, over heaps of bodies and oceans of blood."[12]

Abdulaziz deployed that violence with the help of the Ikhwan, or "Brotherhood," a group of Bedouin warriors who adopted Wahhabi Islam. Their heyday was brief, around 1913–1929, but they played a pivotal role in creating Abdulaziz's new kingdom. The Ikhwan took the lead in the conquest of the Hijaz and earned a fearful reputation by sacking the city of Taif with such brutality, killing hundreds of civilians, that Medina and Jeddah subsequently surrendered on the condition that Abdulaziz not allow the Ikhwan inside their walls. Once the conquest of the Hijaz was completed, the Ikhwan demanded that Abdulaziz continue the jihad to spread Wahhabism to other lands.

That demand conflicted with Abdulaziz's desire for a closer relationship with Great Britain, the leading imperial power in the Middle East. In 1915, Britain sent Abdulaziz one thousand rifles and a modest financial subsidy to recruit him as an ally in World War I. In exchange, Abdulaziz agreed to consult with London before dealing with any other foreign powers, and he recognized British control over the small sheikhdoms of the Persian Gulf—what are now Kuwait, Bahrain, Qatar, the United Arab Emirates, and Oman. During the 1920s, he also negotiated borders between Najd and the British protectorates of Kuwait, Iraq, and Transjordan to his north.[13] His acceptance of a frontier negotiated with a non-Muslim imperial power put Abdulaziz on a path toward confrontation with the Ikhwan.

The Saudi-Iraqi frontier cut across the traditional grazing lands of Najdi tribes who moved depending on the season. The region's former imperial rulers, the Ottomans, had never tried to exert full control over the remote border region, instead paying local tribes and power brokers to keep the peace. The British were different. They built a line of forts along the frontier, a strategy dependent on oil-powered military technology. Reinforcements coming by camel and horse might take weeks to reach a fort under attack, but trucks and armored cars could arrive much faster. The British also launched punitive air raids against the tribes, killing many women and children.[14]

A group of outraged Ikhwan met Abdulaziz in 1928 and demanded that he go to war against Britain. "The borders," they declared, "were drawn through the desert unlawfully." They denied that Abdulaziz had any right to give up Muslim territory and insisted that the British forts be removed. The Ikhwan also accused Abdulaziz of breaching the boundary between Islam and the realm of unbelief by allowing foreign inventions into Arabia, including automobiles and the telegraph, which the Ikhwan viewed as sorcery.[15]

Abdulaziz sent the Ikhwan home with a vague promise to resolve their complaints about the border. By early 1929, however, with the British forts still in place, many of the Ikhwan were in open rebellion. Abdulaziz gathered his loyal armies and prepared to put down the rebellion. The Ikhwan were badly outmatched against the king's better-equipped army. At the

Battle of Sabilla in March 1929, the royal forces used hidden machine guns to rout the Ikhwan. Abdulaziz then crushed the remaining rebels in a series of smaller engagements later that year.[16]

THE PAX WAHHABICA

The defeat of the rebel Ikhwan marked Abulaziz's acceptance of international borders and the European-dominated international order in the Middle East. In many places, the precise frontiers of the kingdom still had to be negotiated. The borders with Iraq and Kuwait included large neutral zones that were not partitioned until the late twentieth century. The borders with the British protectorates on the Persian Gulf were even vaguer; they ran through such remote and sparsely populated territory that Saudi Arabia and Britain did not even try to agree on a precise boundary. In the meantime, maps often simply left those areas blank. To the southwest, Abdulaziz fought a series of conflicts with Yemen, and the Saudi-Yemeni border remained disputed for decades. Nevertheless, Abdulaziz had eliminated his most threatening group of rivals whose political identity was based on tribal affiliation or the Islamic religion rather than membership in a state whose borders had been negotiated with a non-Muslim power.

Abdulaziz found that borders could enhance his control over his kingdom. They let him charge custom duties and other taxes, including the fees on pilgrims to Mecca that provided his main source of income. They also let him defeat armed challenges to his rule. Abdulaziz used automobiles, armored cars, and British weapons against the last groups of rebellious Ikhwan in 1929. The rebel leader Faisal al-Dawish fled to the British protectorate of Kuwait—a sign of his desperation, considering the Ikhwan's usual opposition to contact with non-Muslims. Al-Dawish found no sanctuary in Kuwait; the British put him on an airplane and handed him over to Abdulaziz, who imprisoned al-Dawish for the rest of his life.[17] In 1932, when a group of tribesmen crossed from Transjordan to aid a group of anti-Saudi rebels in the Hijaz, Abdulaziz and the local British authorities jointly sealed the Saudi-Jordanian border and cut the rebels off from their supplies. They were easy prey for the Saudi forces, which used automobiles and armored cars to crush the rebels.[18]

In place of the Ikhwan's absolute boundary between the world of Islam and the world of unbelief, Abdulaziz offered a vision of religious and national boundaries that could be managed for the Muslims' own benefit, according to rules that he laid down. Abdulaziz denounced the uncritical adoption of Western ways—what he called "Frankification" (*al-tafranj*), using an old Arabic word for Europeans. This "Frankification," Abdulaziz said, "is a tendency to imitate the Franks in their social lives, including the evils of their modern civilization." Muslims should not adopt Western ways of life if it meant "losing our religion and our faith." True progress consisted not of blind imitation but of taking only what was useful from the Western world. Unlike the Ikhwan, Abdulaziz welcomed technological innovations like automobiles and radios; he argued that by holding fast to Islamic law, the kingdom could adopt foreign inventions without compromising its religious values. The king declared: "Muslims can keep their morals, tastes, customs, spiritual aspirations, and national identities, while at the same time drawing selectively from the material sciences they need in this life."[19]

Abdulaziz also exploited the talents of people from outside his kingdom. Some of his most influential advisers were from other parts of the Arab world. At the 1922 Uqair conference, when the king negotiated the Najdi border with Iraq and Kuwait, and angered the Ikhwan, his interpreter was the Arab American writer Ameen Rihani, who had been born in Lebanon but spent his youth in New York City. The Egyptian Hafiz Wahbah and the Syrian Yusuf Yassin also played important roles in managing the kingdom's foreign affairs. Many other Arab immigrants served as doctors, engineers, and other professionals, supplying technocratic expertise that was hard to come by in Arabia itself. They had the additional advantage, from the king's point of view, of standing outside the existing tribal and familial networks in the kingdom, so their loyalty was to Abdulaziz alone.[20]

Other advisers came from beyond the Arab world altogether. The most famous was Harry St. John Bridger ("Jack") Philby, a British imperial official sent to Arabia who disagreed with his own government's policies, resigned his position, and joined Abdulaziz's court instead. Philby converted to Islam and took the name Abdullah, married a Muslim wife, and left his old family in Britain, including his son Kim, later to become notorious as the chief of British counterintelligence during the Cold War and a spy for the Soviet Union. Abdulaziz also invited technical experts from the United States to develop clean water supplies, including the businessman Charles Crane and the engineer Karl Twitchell, foreshadowing the later arrival of American petroleum geologists.[21]

Alongside the strengthening of external frontiers came the elimination of internal boundaries and the consolidation of Abdulaziz's domains into a single unit. Najd and the Hijaz were combined into the Kingdom of Saudi Arabia on September 23, 1932, a date that the regime later commemorated as "Saudi National Day."[22] That political message was incorporated into the name of the state itself, which—almost uniquely among the nations of the world—was derived from the royal family.[23] After 1932, a new Saudi national identity was superimposed on older attachments to tribes, individual towns, and specific regions like Najd and the Hijaz. Since the 1930s, the unification of the kingdom and the accumulation of oil wealth have blurred many of the old boundaries. Highways and railroads have eased travel between the regions. Job opportunities in the major cities of Riyadh, Jeddah, and Dammam have attracted people from all over the kingdom, along with millions of immigrants from abroad, creating a new, mixed population. Decades of indoctrination by schools and the state-supervised media have encouraged the rise of a more homogeneous national identity. This process of unification, however, was only possible because of Abdulaziz's forcible incorporation of separate regions into a single state. As their flag reminds Saudis, their kingdom was founded by the sword.

Eliminating the old tribal boundaries and imposing new international borders was a violent and traumatic process for the people whom Abdulaziz conquered. The Bedouin traditionally saw their land as a collective inheritance that could not be sold or given away. The poet Ibn Batla of the Dawasir tribe declared:

One lesson our forefathers drilled into us: "Hold onto the borders!"
Compared to this everything else pales into insignificance.
Losses for the sake of our ancestors' legacy are light to bear.[24]

For the Bedouin, maintaining their territories was both a duty to their forefathers and an economic necessity. Good grazing land and water supplies were limited, and the tribes supplemented their income by raiding, charging tribute on the settled farming towns, and demanding tolls from travelers who passed through their land. Abdulaziz destroyed that economic system by confiscating tribal land, suppressing raids and vendettas, and imposing Islamic religious law and his own rulings in place of traditional Bedouin practices.

The new legal order was ultimately backed by force. In another of Ibn Batla's poems, he fumes to an enemy that he would fight them, avenging an insult in the old style, if only they did not both have to fear the wrath of the king in Riyadh.[25] Abdulaziz claimed a monopoly on violence in his kingdom, an idea that was alien to the traditional Bedouin ethos. The Saudi scholar Abdulaziz Al Fahad has written about one Bedouin raider, Dghaylib ibn Khnaysir, who was renowned for killing eighteen of his enemies during the final years of tribal fighting around the turn of the twentieth century. King Abdulaziz ended tribal raiding, and Dghaylib, to his great disappointment, died peacefully as an old man in the 1950s instead of falling in battle. When other Saudis reproached the elderly Dghaylib for committing murder and suggested that he would go to hell, Dghaylib responded that God would never punish him for killing a mere eighteen men when Abdulaziz had killed thousands. He did not believe that there was any moral difference between killing done by an individual and killing done by the state. Al Fahad writes that Dghaylib "was one of the last men to profess and practice such a sensibility."[26]

Abdulaziz stamped out tribal raiding and punished any who resisted. To accomplish that goal, he needed to project force across his far-flung lands. Oil, and the machines it powered, would help him do that.

PAVING THE WAY OF THE STATE

The unity of the new state was reinforced by a transportation revolution that was both political and technological. Abdulaziz's suppression of the

Bedouin made the kingdom's roads safer, while the arrival of the automobile shrank the distances that had kept different parts of the Arabian Peninsula isolated from one another. Contemporary observers were quick to grasp the extent of the changes under way. Philby wrote enthusiastically about the "Pax Wahhabica" that had changed "the Arabian nomad into a settled agriculturalist" and ensured that pilgrims and other travelers could visit any part of the kingdom "by motor-car or by camel, without risk of molestation."[27] Philby was so bullish on the market for automobiles in Saudi Arabia that he went into auto sales himself and secured a special license to import Ford cars from the United States.

The most notable auto enthusiast in the kingdom was Abdulaziz. On their way to confront the Ikhwan in November 1929, the king, his lieutenants, and his bodyguards drove in a caravan of at least 30 automobiles.[28] By 1935, Abdulaziz's collection had grown to the point where he now toured his kingdom and went on hunting trips in caravans of 150 to 200 automobiles.[29] During the following decade, the king and his government imported a gigantic fleet of cars, including 1,450 purchased from Philby.[30]

In the late 1930s the Arab-British writer and diplomat George Antonius wrote admiringly of Abdulaziz "as he motors from one end of his empire to another" while his radio operators kept the airwaves humming with news of his latest travels. Less than a decade earlier, the Ikhwan had been in open revolt against the king, condemning him for using automobiles and electric communications. After crushing their rebellion, Abdulaziz could ignore such objections. The same was true of the Bedouin who had once charged tolls (*khuwa*) on travelers in their territory. Abdulaziz sped right through the old tribal boundaries, advertising his total victory over the Bedouin; as Antonius wrote, they were so thoroughly cowed that the word *khuwa* "has dropped out of the tribal vocabulary." The king was remaking Saudi Arabia according to his own design, as "the old caravan routes are being made fit for motor traffic, and already the traveler can drive in comfort from the Red Sea to the Persian Gulf."[31]

The Saudi government argued that the automobile was not foreign sorcery, as the rebel Ikhwan had claimed, but a tool in the service of Islam. It pointed to the growing use of automobiles in the holy cities. Antonius wrote: "In barely ten years, the transport of pilgrims has become entirely mecha-

Desert Sheiks Ride in Autos to Mecca

AMERICAN-MADE motor cars were the steeds of wild sheiks in the capture of Mecca by Ibn-El-Saud, sultan of Nedjed. Fleet as are the racing dromedaries and the Arabian horses of purest pedigree, the Wahabi tribesmen have found that there is nothing like the auto to cross the desert in a hurry, unless it be airplanes. Mecca is now in the control of the Wahabis (or "puritan" Moslems). The car shown is bearing staff officers of Ibn-Saud.

FIGURE 1.2 Prince Faisal and companions in Mecca shortly after the Saudi conquest of the Hijaz. *Windsor Star* (Windsor, Ontario), November 14, 1924.

nised, and the one hundred thousand or more who come to the Hejaz annually travel to Mecca and Medina on petrol."[32] Motorcars carried pilgrims from the port of Jeddah to the holy cities, those who fell ill were driven to clinics and hospitals, and the government stockpiled emergency gasoline reserves so the pilgrims would never be stranded.[33] A 1931 report from the U.S. State Department estimated that out of 953 automobiles in the Hijaz, 678—more than two-thirds of the total—were dedicated to carrying pilgrims to the holy cities.[34]

Modern cars needed modern roads to carry them. The streets of the Hijaz had been designed for foot and animal traffic, not automobiles. They were narrow, twisting, and dusty, prompting complaints from the government press. In 1927, *Umm al-Qura* wrote that Mecca belonged to all Muslims around the world, making it especially shameful that its streets were in poor condition. The newspaper denounced the previous Hashemite and

Turkish administrations for neglecting the situation and failing to enforce rules on keeping the roads clear of obstructions. *Umm al-Qura* noted that one of the most important Meccan streets had once been "almost straight" but had been narrowed and twisted by later additions. Shopkeepers often set out temporary cloth shelters in front of their stores, but soon enough the shelters became permanent. It amounted to an "assault on the roads," but thankfully, the newspaper explained, the Saudi government was demolishing the cloth shelters, making the road straight again, and restoring "consistency in the buildings and streets."[35] Two years later, *Umm al-Qura* was still dissatisfied, writing: "Everyone knows that everything in the Hijaz is neglected and needs renewal." The newspaper again blamed the Hijaz's previous rulers, the Hashemites, and praised Abdulaziz for starting an array of construction projects to haul Mecca into the motor age: improving the streets to keep the dust down, widening the roads, and demolishing old buildings that blocked traffic and made the city look disorderly and unpleasant.[36]

The new roads sped pilgrims and merchants on their way, serving God and filling the royal coffers. For Abdulaziz, those two goals were identical, since pilgrimage fees were his largest source of income. Improving Mecca's roads also made the city easier to govern. When *Umm al-Qura* published its editorials in 1927–1929, Mecca had been under Saudi rule for only half a decade. It was still an occupied city, suspected of harboring opponents of the Al Saud and overseen by armed representatives of the king. Replacing Mecca's warren of old alleyways with broad streets allowed the government's increasingly motorized forces to keep the city under surveillance and respond more quickly to potential challenges.[37]

The arrival of the automobile provided new opportunities for the extension of state control over the pilgrimage and the Saudi people. In 1926 the government announced new regulations on the cars that shuttled pilgrims between Jeddah and Mecca. Automobiles involved in the pilgrimage traffic had to be registered with the state and pay a fee based on the number of passengers they could carry. They had to have headlights and taillights and follow the speed limit. If they were involved in an accident and were not removed promptly from the road, they would be impounded. With these technocratic regulations came a reminder of royal privilege; the government insisted: "When His Majesty's car passes by, every driver must stop his car on the side of the road until His Majesty has proceeded."[38]

THE ROAD TO THE OIL CONCESSION

Abdulaziz's use of the automobile and other Western technology won American praise. During the 1920s, U.S. journalists lauded Abdulaziz's early efforts to bring cars to the kingdom, make the hajj safer for pilgrims, and build hospitals.[39] Writing for the *New York Times* in 1928, Joseph Levy praised the king's efforts to improve roads, sanitation systems, and the port at Jeddah, as well as introducing "far-reaching reforms in the administrative methods" of government.[40] Even before the two countries were bound together by mutual commercial and strategic interests, they were linked by a shared belief that the Saudi monarchy was modernizing a backward land.[41]

Saudi adoption of the automobile also encouraged the first U.S. commercial and diplomatic ties with the kingdom. In December 1929, Philby urged the United States to extend official recognition to Abdulaziz's regime. He argued that the kingdom's steady progress "on modern lines" had much to do with its "active trade with America, which now sends us one direct ship a month laden with motor cars and their various accessories." Philby stood to profit, since he was the registered agent for Ford, Firestone Tires, and other American companies in the Hijaz. In June 1930, the U.S. automotive trade commissioner for the Near East visited Jeddah and recommended the establishment of a U.S. consulate, noting that American companies were already doing a thriving trade with the Hijaz consisting "chiefly of automobiles and accessories, kerosene, pumps, and machinery." Ameen Rihani, the Arab American confidant of Abdulaziz, wrote in 1931 that because of ongoing Saudi development projects, including highway construction, "there are big prospects for American enterprise" in this "virgin market of great possibilities."[42] In November 1933, the United States took the advice of Philby, Rihani, and other supporters of Abdulaziz, entering into formal diplomatic relations with the new Kingdom of Saudi Arabia.[43]

As Abdulaziz's state-building efforts picked up speed, his revenue needs also grew. The Great Depression, however, dramatically reduced the number of foreign Muslims who could afford the expensive trip to Mecca. Between 1929 and 1933, the number of pilgrims plunged from 148,000 to 20,500.[44] Through the hajj, Saudi Arabia was now so integrated with the global economy that a stock market crash in distant New York City could trigger a chain of events that sent the kingdom toward bankruptcy. But if economic danger could arrive from overseas, so could opportunity. When the flow of pilgrims was at its lowest level in 1933, the badly cash-strapped Abdulaziz signed a deal with the Standard Oil Company of California (Socal) granting the American corporation the right to explore for oil in the eastern part of his kingdom. In exchange, Socal agreed to pay 5,000 British pounds in gold to the king every year, with ten times that amount to follow if oil were discovered, along with a small royalty per ton of oil produced. At this point, Abdulaziz was so desperate for short-term financial relief that his government demanded 50,000 pounds in loans from Socal within the first year and a half, to be paid out of the kingdom's still-hypothetical oil revenues.[45]

Within months, geologists working for Socal's local subsidiary, the California Arabian Standard Oil Company (Casoc), were in Saudi Arabia exploring for petroleum. To find oil, they first had to burn it. The geologists covered hundreds of miles of remote territory with automobiles brought from the United States: first a set of 1933 Ford cars, and later a growing array of trucks and four-wheel-drive vehicles. They also relied on Abdulaziz's military protection. The Americans arrived only four years after the suppression of the Ikhwan revolt. If the Casoc geologists had arrived just a few years earlier, they would have found themselves in the middle of an active war zone. The major cities of the kingdom were still surrounded by thick walls and gates that were locked at night, a reminder of the age, barely past, when hostile armies and Bedouin raiding parties might attack without warning. The geologists were always accompanied by armed soldiers and guides provided by the government. Many of those guides were drawn from Bedouin tribes that had once been autonomous but now served the king.

The Bedouin still remembered the days of tribal independence and raiding that prevailed before the rise of the Saudi state. Camping in the desert with the Americans, they liked to tell stories about the old times, reciting poems about the achievements of their ancestors. One night around the campfire in 1938, the Casoc geologists Tom Barger and Jerry Harriss joined in by recounting the white Americans' wars against the Indians, "the American Bedu," including Daniel Boone's escape "swinging across a river gorge on a grapevine" and Custer's last stand. One of their guides was Khamis ibn Rimthan, a member of the Ajman, a Bedouin tribe who were crushed in battle by Abdulaziz. What happened to the American Bedouin, he asked, after the Battle of Little Bighorn? Barger drew "a large and a small circle in the sand: before the war their land was like this, after like this." Ibn Rimthan understood. "Yes," he said, "that is what happens to the Bedu in Arabia when they make war with the government."[46]

Much of the land that Abdulaziz seized from the tribes became royal property. It was an important source of state power and personal enrichment for the Al Saud, as land that was once collectively owned by the Bedouin was now under the control of the king, to be distributed as he saw fit. Saudis with close ties to the government, especially members of the royal family itself, received enormous tracts to subdivide and sell at a profit. As Riyadh and the kingdom's other cities grew, property on their outskirts skyrocketed in value, and those lucky or well-connected enough to own that land reaped colossal gains. The Al Saud used their political power to become the kingdom's biggest real estate speculators, and land grants became one of the most important mechanisms for the redistribution of state wealth to the royal family and its allies. The royals became so notorious for the barbed wire they strung around formerly open land, reserving it for their own use or keeping it vacant as it appreciated in value, that critics gave them the mocking nickname Al-Shubook: "The Fences."[47]

OIL AND THE AMERICAN STATE

Like the Al Saud, many early American leaders were avid land speculators. Westward expansion, the violent dispossession of Native American tribes, and the conversion of land into private property created opportunities for well-connected elites to buy up vast tracts of land, invest in transportation infrastructure, and exploit natural resources. The oil industry was no exception. The first major American oil discovery was made in western Pennsylvania in 1859, followed by discoveries in California, Texas, Oklahoma, and other southwestern states a few decades later, within living memory of the time when those areas were settled by Anglo-Americans and brought under the authority of the United States. As early as 1866, the U.S. government saw the great potential for oil's role in the American economy. The Treasury Department reported on the possibilities for "petroleum as a source for national wealth," a product "so recently unknown to our commerce, and now of such vast importance."[48]

By the late nineteenth century, the industry was dominated by John D. Rockefeller's Standard Oil trust. Standard Oil benefited from implicit government support as it absorbed its competitors or drove them into bankruptcy, while avoiding antitrust prosecution for years after it had become an effective monopoly.

The executive branch of the U.S. government also backed Standard Oil's expansion abroad. Rockefeller's company produced so much oil that even with the steady growth of domestic demand, a large surplus was still available for export. Rockefeller wrote: "One of our greatest helpers has been the State Department in Washington. Our ambassadors and ministers and consuls have aided to push our way into new markets to the utmost corners of the world."[49] American exports reached all the way to the Arabian Peninsula. A U.S. diplomat reported in 1879: "Even the sacred lamps over the Prophet's tomb at Mecca are fed with oil from the wells of Pennsylvania."[50]

Oil fueled the rise of U.S. power in the early twentieth century. The United States was the world's largest oil producer by far, and even after Standard Oil was broken up in an antitrust suit in 1911, its successor companies—Standard Oil of New Jersey (Exxon), New York (Mobil), California (Chevron), and others—remained among the biggest companies on the planet. The importance of oil, and the new leverage it gave the United States as a military power, became obvious during World War I. Some of the most important machines used in the war—airplanes, dirigibles, submarines, and tanks—were fueled by oil. Behind the front lines, gasoline-powered trucks were vital for moving troops and supplies. Even before the

United States entered the war, the Allies had already become dependent on American oil; Britain, for example, imported 92 percent of its petroleum in 1915, with the United States as its biggest supplier.[51] Germany and its allies, by contrast, had no access to oil from overseas and suffered from serious fuel shortages by 1918.[52] Oil was only one of the American resources, including food, capital, and manpower, that were critical to the Allied war effort, but it had great psychological significance as the fuel for a new generation of mobile weaponry.

Fear of those weapons helped convince the United States to go to war. Oil-fueled machines expanded the zone of combat, endangering people far from the battlefield. Allied propaganda focused on German U-boats and the threat they posed to innocent civilians. Advocates of U.S. entry into the war also warned Americans that they were no longer protected by the Atlantic Ocean. One famous poster featured New York City in flames as German biplanes flew overhead and a U-boat prowled the harbor.[53] Such fears were exaggerated, since no German aircraft had the range to bomb New York, but they still caught the American imagination. Interventionists claimed that when war machines could cross the skies and the oceans, the only way to make the world "safe for democracy" was to eliminate military threats even if they were thousands of miles away. Oil power made an expanded American role in world affairs seem both feasible and necessary.

AUTOMOTIVE POWER

After World War I, the United States became the first nation in the world where automobile ownership expanded beyond the rich to include middle-class and even working-class Americans. The American state encouraged that trend and saw its authority grow along with the new, car-centric society. During World War I, as U.S. automobile enthusiasts saw the importance of motor transport in modern combat, they demanded a massive increase in road construction as a war preparedness measure. Long-distance automobile trips at the turn of the century could be harrowing experiences, with muddy roads, bridges unable to bear a car's weight, and hundreds of miles of road with no gasoline stations.[54] In 1915, one of the main lobbying groups, the National Highways Association (NHA), printed a map of its proposed highways and compared their importance to that of the Panama Canal. In case the connection between automobiles and empire was not clear enough, the NHA distributed hood ornaments featuring an eagle clutching a globe in its talons, turning cars into rolling symbols of American power.[55]

After 1918, the U.S. Army threw its weight behind the highway lobby. The army's Motor Transport Corps was led by General Charles Drake, a decorated veteran of the Philippine-American War and World War I. In 1919, Drake ordered a motorized army convoy to cross the country from Washington, DC, to San Francisco. The roads were so bad, especially in the West, that the convoy had to carry its own equipment to repair roads and bridges. It took nearly two months to make the trip. A young Dwight D. Eisenhower was a member of the expedition. He later titled his memoirs about the 1919 convoy "Through Darkest America," emphasizing the colonial aspect of exploring those parts of the United States not yet civilized by the highway.[56] In his report on the mission, Drake argued that "a comprehensive system of national highways" was "a defensive military necessity." It would also complete the work of westward expansion, letting the United States "colonize and develop the sparsely settled sections of the country."[57] The convoy helped automobile boosters make the case for much greater government spending on roads, and highways spread across the United States during the subsequent years.

As the U.S. government encouraged the spread of roads across the country, it expanded its power to regulate the new, automobile-dependent American society. American law enforcement agencies soon used more cars than similar agencies in any other country. The police car became perhaps the most ubiquitous symbol of state power, and traffic stops brought more Americans into direct contact with law enforcement than ever before. They also disproportionately targeted African Americans and other disadvantaged groups, reinforcing social inequality even as automobiles also gave some African Americans an alternative to racially segregated public transit. The automobile allowed the U.S. government to police the country's borders much more closely. The country's frontiers were so long and crossed such remote territory that they were difficult to cover by foot or horseback. The U.S. Border Patrol was founded in 1924, just as automobiles were becoming common, and from the beginning, its agents relied on cars, trucks, and aircraft. It became one of the most heavily motorized law enforcement agencies in the world.[58]

The growth of the American automobile industry accelerated the rise of the United States as a global power. American car companies dominated the market at home and abroad, accounting for more than 70 percent of world car exports and spreading U.S. economic and cultural influence across the globe.[59] Henry Ford was the most famous industrialist of his time. The Soviet Union and Nazi Germany both sought Ford's advice, and the great dystopian novel of the era, Aldous Huxley's *Brave New World*, imagined human civilization remade along Fordist lines with Ford himself revered as a godlike figure.[60] The reputation of Ford Motor Company reached the Arabian Peninsula years before the U.S.-Saudi oil relationship began, as St. John Philby recognized when he sought a license to import Ford cars into Abdulaziz's kingdom.

WORLD WAR II

World War II and oil created new opportunities for the United States to expand its global reach. The rise of air power convinced many Americans that the Atlantic and Pacific oceans no longer kept the country safe from attack. Franklin Roosevelt warned: "Any possible attack has been brought infinitely closer than it was five years or twenty years or fifty years ago," given "the amazing speed with which modern equipment can reach and attack the enemy's country."[61]

In reality, the immediate military threat to the United States would have been quite limited even in the event of Axis victory in Europe and Asia. Germany and Japan simply did not have the means to launch mass attacks on the Western Hemisphere. U.S. leaders were more concerned about the long-term economic and political difficulty of surviving as a democracy if the main U.S. allies and trading partners in Europe were to fall. The specter of direct Axis attack on the United States, however, was a potent argument for interventionists in their efforts to sway the American public. The rapid German conquest of France in 1940 and the Japanese attack on Pearl Harbor in 1941 seemed to prove the interventionists right. They argued that the Atlantic and Pacific Oceans no longer protected the United States, and that only an offensive strategy could keep Americans safe.[62] The United States had to create a global order that acknowledged the new possibilities for long-distance warfare, commerce, and travel created by oil-powered machines. As the publisher Henry Luce wrote in his essay "The American Century" (1941), the United States had to seize "the right to go with our ships and our ocean-going airplanes where we wish, when we wish and as we wish."[63]

The resources available to the Axis powers fell far short of their ambitions. Germany produced almost no oil of its own, forcing it to rely on scarce Romanian petroleum and synthetic fuel made from coal. Late in the war, even those inadequate supplies were increasingly disrupted by Allied attacks, and the Wehrmacht suffered crippling fuel shortages. Despite the fearsome reputation of the panzers, most of the German army still used horses for transportation. Japan faced similar problems. Even before the war began, the United States imposed a de facto oil embargo on Japan. With no major petroleum deposits in its home islands, Japan seized the oil fields of the Dutch East Indies in 1941–1942. Its navy, however, was unable to protect the shipping lanes to Southeast Asia. By the end of the war, Japan's oil imports were almost completely cut off, and its air and naval units were practically immobilized.[64]

During World War II, no other nation could match American oil power. The United States produced roughly twice as much oil as the rest of the world combined. Those resources enabled motorized warfare on a scale that had never been seen before. The Petroleum Administration for War (PAW), a new government body established to supervise fuel supplies, reported that U.S. military gasoline consumption during World War II was one hundred times higher than during World War I. The army and navy operated six hundred times as many automobiles as American forces had used in 1917–1918, while the number of U.S. military aircraft rose 1,250 percent in just four years from 1941 to 1945. By the end of the war, oil accounted for two-thirds of the tonnage of U.S. military supplies sent overseas. One PAW official called it "the greatest of all munitions." Not only the U.S. military but also the armed forces of allies like Great Britain depended on American oil to fuel their armed forces.[65]

THE DAWN OF THE U.S.-SAUDI RELATIONSHIP

When World War II began, Saudi oil did not yet play a major role in the rising global order dominated by the United States.[66] The Saudi oil fields had only been discovered in the late 1930s, and their production capacity was still quite modest. They were also isolated from secure shipping routes and were considered vulnerable to Axis attack, so production was shut down during the war.[67] Casoc warned the Roosevelt administration in April 1941 that the Saudi government's financial situation was "desperate," since war meant a temporarily halt to oil revenues and pilgrimage fees. Casoc and the British government advanced some funds to Abdulaziz, but he also sought financial support from the United States. After considering the offer, Roosevelt wrote to an aide: "Will you tell the British I hope they can take care of the King of Saudi-Arabia. This is a little far afield for us!"[68]

American entry into the war dramatically changed the U.S. view of Saudi Arabia. No part of the world was now considered too far afield for the projection of American power. U.S. officials soon began looking at the kingdom as a possible site for military facilities, especially for air transport.[69] They secured overflight rights from Abdulaziz and eventually won permission for the construction of a large airbase at Dhahran, the headquarters of the Arabian American Oil Company (Aramco), as Casoc was renamed in 1944. The airbase was finished too late to play any role in the fighting, and the U.S. military doubted its importance for postwar strategy, but it symbolized the growing U.S. role in the kingdom and provided a valuable facility for Aramco and Trans World Airlines (TWA).

The war also encouraged U.S. interest in Saudi Arabia's future oil production. In 1944, the consultant Everett Lee DeGolyer visited the Persian Gulf with a team from the PAW. His conclusion was dramatic: "The center of gravity of world oil production is shifting from the Gulf-Caribbean area to the Middle East—to the Persian Gulf area." DeGolyer noted that "the proven and indicated reserves of this area" were already "comparable with those of the United States." Almost unbelievably, though, these huge reserves had been found with only 150 exploratory wells. In the United States, oil companies and independent entrepreneurs drilled more than 3,000 wildcat wells each year. DeGolyer's conclusion was that as vast as the already-discovered reserves of the Gulf were, even larger oil fields remained to be found in the region. In fact, DeGolyer warned, there was so much oil in the Gulf that it threatened to overwhelm existing demand and create a glut in the world market that could last for at least fifteen years.[70]

Even compared with the rest of the Gulf, Saudi Arabia stood out. The State Department petroleum adviser Charles Rayner reported that Saudi Arabia had the largest potential of all Middle Eastern oil producers. Another advantage, he noted, was that the Saudi concession was "entirely American owned."[71] During World War II, the Roosevelt administration tried taking a direct government stake in the Saudi oil fields by purchasing the concession from Socal and the Texas Company. The administration backed down, partly because of opposition from other oil companies and their congressional allies who feared competition from a U.S. government entity supplied with cheap Saudi oil. But although the concession remained in private hands, the U.S. government expanded its ties with Riyadh to maintain American control over Saudi oil resources.[72]

The new U.S. relationship with Saudi Arabia was cemented by the extension of technical and financial aid, demonstrating the global reach of American logistics. The Roosevelt administration made Saudi Arabia eligible for lend-lease aid in 1943 even though the kingdom had not joined the war against Germany. The United States sent millions of dollars in assistance, largely in the form of gold and silver that was physically transported to the kingdom on American ships and aircraft. The aid also included an agricultural mission to develop Saudi irrigation, including the geologist Karl Twitchell and representatives from the Department of Agriculture's Albuquerque office and the Indian Bureau of the Department of the Interior, on the thinking that the desert Southwest was the best model for Saudi conditions. The Interior representative was dispatched to the western United States to scour Indian reservations for used agricultural machinery that might be shipped to Saudi Arabia. He was unsuccessful, but other irrigation equipment was soon sent to the kingdom.[73] The Saudi government especially wanted motor vehicles, with the first direct U.S. lend-lease aid to the kingdom consisting of several dozen trucks, with many more to come.[74]

Washington increasingly displaced London as the main provider of equipment and financial support to the Saudi monarchy. The U.S. ability to move people and goods around the world was a vital ingredient in that shift. When Faisal's party asked the State Department to ship private automobiles from the United States in November 1943, U.S. officials noted that transportation would be difficult. After all, German U-boats were patrolling the Atlantic, sinking every merchant vessel they could find, and cargo space was at a premium everywhere in the world. Even so, the State Department proposed shipping two cars, one each for Prince Faisal and Prince Khalid. That the United States could even consider sending private automobiles halfway around the world for the personal use of foreign dignitaries, in the middle of World War II, demonstrated America's unrivaled transportation capabilities fueled by oil.[75]

THE DIPLOMACY OF OIL POWER

On his way back from the Yalta Conference in February 1945, Franklin Roosevelt met Abdulaziz on board the USS *Quincy*, a cruiser anchored in Egypt's Great Bitter Lake. It was the first meeting between U.S. and Saudi heads of state, and would be endlessly celebrated and mythologized by both nations in later years.[76] The meeting was kept secret from the Saudi people; even the members of Abdulaziz's court were kept in the dark until the king's motorcade departed his palace in Jeddah and drove straight to the city pier. The translator at the meeting was William Eddy, an Arabic-speaking U.S. diplomat and intelligence officer who would later work for both Aramco and the CIA, helping establish a long tradition of behind-the-scenes diplomacy and blurred lines between public and private affairs in U.S.-Saudi relations.[77]

Roosevelt and Abdulaziz got along famously, bonding over their shared status as national leaders. The presence of an American warship in Egypt was a reminder of the global projection of U.S. power during World War II, an impression the navy reinforced by demonstrating the ship's antiaircraft guns and depth charges and showing a documentary film about the USS *Yorktown*, a famous aircraft carrier in the Pacific theater. Roosevelt also offered Abdulaziz direct access to the mobility provided by American technology, giving the king, who walked poorly because of old age and battle wounds, one of his wheelchairs and a DC-3 airliner complete with an American pilot.[78]

The one sour note was disagreement over Zionist immigration to Palestine, to which Abdulaziz fiercely objected. Roosevelt tried to change the subject, suggesting that American irrigation technology would turn the Saudi desert into productive farmland, but Abdulaziz grimly replied that he "could not engage with any enthusiasm in the development of his country's agriculture and public works if this prosperity would be inherited by the Jews." Roosevelt offered a vague promise that "he would do nothing to assist the Jews against the Arabs," a pledge that would later become the focus of great controversy after the United States recognized Israel's independence in 1948. By then, Roosevelt had passed from the scene; he was visibly ill during his meeting with Abdulaziz and had less than two months to live.

On April 14, 1945, Prince Faisal attended Roosevelt's funeral in Washington, DC. He was on his second visit to the United States, this time to represent Saudi Arabia at the United Nations (UN) conference in San Francisco and tour other parts of America. Once again, the U.S. government, along with Bechtel, Aramco, and other private corporations that subsidized the tour, put American oil power on full display. Faisal's party visited oil fields and refineries in Texas and witnessed an "air review" of U.S. warplanes at the Corpus Christi Naval Air Station. In Detroit, they toured the mammoth Chrysler Arsenal turning out M-26 Pershing tanks, demonstrating the ability of the U.S. auto industry to convert its factories to war production. The Saudis flew on a chartered TWA Boeing Stratoliner, a luxury plane formerly used for transporting high-ranking U.S. government officials. Reporters marveled at the plane's deluxe furnishings. Even when not in the air, the Saudis stood out. At the UN conference, a columnist noted that the Saudis rode in a private limousine while most of the other countries' delegates were packed into four buses, looking "like four loads of tourists."[79]

Average U.S. citizens had no access to the kind of transportation now available to the Saudi royals. As one columnist put it, Faisal and his companions "behaved the way most Americans wished they could."[80] Air travel was out of reach to all but the wealthy. The *Santa Fe New Mexican* pointed out that many of the people who turned out to greet Faisal had never even seen a Boeing Stratoliner, let alone flown in one. Americans had trouble even driving ordinary automobiles. In 1945, wartime gasoline rationing was still in effect for American civilians. Some wealthier drivers bought additional fuel on the black market, but the less privileged had no such recourse. Faisal and his party, however, were able to disregard such limits. Their planes and limousines burned vast quantities of gasoline without their owners having to worry about rationing. The Saudi royal family had become honorary members of an American elite distinguished by its access to the power of oil.

PERSONAL CONNECTIONS

Faisal's visits to the United States, and the meeting between Roosevelt and Abdulaziz, marked not only the consolidation of the U.S.-Saudi partnership but also its emergence as a contentious topic in American politics. The Saudi delegation received an enthusiastic welcome from the Arab American community and American institutions that dealt with the Arab world. They visited Princeton University, where they were hosted by Philip Hitti, a pioneering Lebanese American historian who had helped make Princeton an early center for Arabic and Islamic studies in the United States. Princeton was training several dozen students in Arabic for the U.S. military. One of the trainees delivered a speech in Arabic, praising "the noble language of the Koran" and telling Faisal how impressed the Princetonians were "by the epoch-making reforms which His Royal Majesty your father has introduced into Saudi Arabia, which is his creation."[81] In New York City, the Saudi princes met with George Kheirallah, the head of the Arabian Society, other Arab Americans, and Arab diplomats in the United States.[82]

On his 1945 visit, Faisal encountered Arab American communities throughout the United States. In New Mexico, he was welcomed in Arabic by Raymond Shaya, a Santa Fe alderman originally from Lebanon. Shaya had worked to maintain knowledge of the Arab culture in the local immigrant community. He started a school to teach Arabic, and he and his wife, Zelma, ordered Lebanese spices and other ingredients via New York so they could have authentic Levantine food. Shaya was thrilled to host the Saudi princes at his home. His daughter JoAnn remembered him being "elated" at the chance to represent Santa Fe and translate for the visitors, while she was "completely in awe of their attire," never having seen such a group in traditional Saudi robes. The visit "was the talk of the town for a long time."[83]

In New York, Faisal attended a ceremony at the Waldorf Astoria featuring Elia Abu Madi, a prominent Lebanese American poet, and other Arab Americans.[84] In Detroit, he was welcomed by the local Committee of Arabic-Speaking Americans and spoke at a banquet with eight hundred guests, including Arab American religious officials and other community leaders.[85] Prince Mohammed even had a romantic tryst with a local Arab American woman, Mary Mohammed, who flew to New York to reunite with the royal party after they left Detroit. Faisal forbade his brother from continuing the relationship, and Prince Mohammed denied that the liaison had ever happened, although it was widely reported in the press and confirmed by multiple witnesses.[86]

During the 1940s, the U.S.-Saudi relationship began to extend beyond the commercial and diplomatic realm to include a wider array of personal connections. The first Saudi to attend college in the United States was Ali Alireza, the scion of a prominent Jeddah merchant family that took over the Ford automobile import business after St. John Philby. Alireza studied business and petroleum engineering at the University of California at Berkeley. He married an American woman, Marianne Likowski, after they met in a paleontology class. When Faisal arrived in San Francisco for the United

Nations conference, he ordered Alireza to drop out of college and join the Saudi diplomatic service. Faisal wanted someone on his staff who spoke fluent English and understood the United States. After the San Francisco conference, Ali, Marianne, and their four-year-old daughter, Hamida, sailed to Britain with Faisal on the *Queen Mary*, and from there to Saudi Arabia.[87] Thousands of Saudis would later follow Alireza's path, studying in the United States and filling the ranks of the kingdom's economic and political elites. They included Faisal's sons Saud and Turki, who went to Princeton, which had impressed Faisal during his 1943 visit, with Saud eventually becoming Saudi Arabia's foreign minister and Turki becoming the head of intelligence and later the ambassador to the United States.[88] Those educational and cultural ties helped consolidate the U.S.-Saudi partnership during the following decades.

EARLY OPPOSITION

Other Americans saw danger in the emerging U.S.-Saudi relationship. The most prominent critics were American Zionists. By the 1940s, the kingdom was already widely known for barring Jews from its territory and opposing Jewish settlement in Palestine. During Faisal's 1943 visit to Arizona, rumors suggested that his true mission was not to see the Grand Canyon and irrigated farms, as the State Department claimed, but to lobby against Zionism.[89] In 1944, Rep. Emmanuel Celler (D-NY) denounced U.S. aid to Saudi Arabia. He complained that Abdulaziz had done nothing for the war effort and had no legitimate need for the weapons that the Roosevelt administration was sending to the kingdom. Celler warned that the arms might be used to attack the Jewish settlers in Palestine, making his remarks one of the first examples of what would become a persistent critique of U.S. military aid to Saudi Arabia: that Saudi Arabia would transfer American weapons to the Palestinians or other enemies of Israel. Celler suggested that U.S. foreign policy was being manipulated by "American oil interests" to protect their own investments in the Gulf.[90] Rep. Samuel Dickstein (D-NY) condemned the Roosevelt administration's "appeasement policy" toward

Abdulaziz and read into the record a New York newspaper editorial accusing the forces of "oil imperialism" of sentencing "millions of Jewish postwar refugees to continued poverty and persecution in Europe."[91]

Critics of the partnership with Riyadh warned that it threatened to undermine democracy in the United States itself. They feared that the Roosevelt administration was making secret agreements with Saudi Arabia, bypassing congressional and public oversight. In 1943, Rep. John Coffee (D-WA) noted that during Faisal's visit earlier that year, "no one knows what agreements were entered into by the United States." Coffee suggested that former oil company executives filled the Roosevelt administration, some of them still drawing salaries from their old companies, while other prominent officials like the Middle East envoy Patrick Hurley and the assistant secretary of state Dean Acheson had business ties with the oil industry.[92] After Roosevelt's meeting with Abdulaziz in February 1945, rumors circulated that the president had agreed to oppose Jewish settlement in Palestine, prompting members of Congress to denounce Roosevelt's "secret commitments" and "covenants."[93] Such attacks were part of a broader set of worries about the growth of the U.S. national security state during World War II, creating a huge new bureaucracy and war-making apparatus closely linked with some of the largest and most powerful corporations in the country.

* * *

During Faisal's 1943 visit to the United States, one U.S. newspaper called the Saudi delegation the "royal filling station salesmen."[94] The joke was an early example of a common stereotype about Saudi Arabia: that it was fundamentally different from the United States and other countries because it was a "petrostate" totally dependent on oil production. That idea obscured how much the United States and Saudi Arabia had in common. If any country was the world's "filling station" in 1943, it was the United States, fueling the Allied war effort and producing twice as much oil as all other nations put together. The United States had pioneered a new kind of society based on petroleum. By the 1940s, that way of life was spreading to other countries across the world, including Saudi Arabia. Faisal's tour was part of that process, a chance for the U.S. government and American corporations to demonstrate automobiles, aircraft, water pumps, and other oil-fueled machines that the Saudi royals could bring to their own country.

The vision of modernity that Faisal and his companions encountered was about more than technology. It was also about political and economic power. World War II drove a massive expansion of executive authority in the United States, as the president assumed control over an enormous military and foreign policy establishment. Executive power was bolstered by a close partnership with private corporations, which built the weapons and extracted the natural resources that underpinned the U.S. war effort. That partnership made Faisal's visit possible, as his delegation was hosted by the State Department in partnership with Aramco and other private companies. A close linkage between executive and corporate power was attractive to the Saudi regime, which had already built a political system based on unconstrained royal authority and practically nonexistent lines between the public interests of the state and the private interests of the elite. Oil entrenched Saudi royal power, first in the form of automobiles that helped Abdulaziz knit his kingdom together, and later in the form of oil revenues. By the end of the war, the seeds of an alliance had been sown between the U.S. executive branch, American corporations, and the Saudi royal family, all of which used oil to enhance their authority.

That alliance, however, still faced major obstacles. Saudi Arabia was not yet a major priority for most U.S. government leaders. The growing relationship between Washington and Riyadh was driven more by private interests like Aramco and Bechtel, and a few mid-ranking officials like William Eddy. Tensions between the United States and Saudi Arabia over Zionism were already apparent. And critics in the U.S. Congress and media were becoming uneasy about the close relationship developing between the executive branch, private corporations, and the Saudi kingdom. Over the next two decades, those tensions would mean a bumpy road for the developing U.S.-Saudi alliance.

2

ROADS TO PROFIT

In June 1966, a motorcade of chauffeured cars rolled up to Kykuit, the lavish Rockefeller family estate in Pocantico Hills, New York. Inside were King Faisal and his entourage. They had driven up from the Waldorf-Astoria in Manhattan, the same hotel where Faisal had stayed on his first visits to the United States in 1943 and 1945. Faisal's host was David Rockefeller, the grandson of John D. Rockefeller and the president of Chase Manhattan Bank. Over lunch, Faisal and Rockefeller met privately with more than three dozen oil executives, bankers, and academics. Faisal delighted his audience by telling them about the virtues of the free-enterprise system and the progress it was bringing to Saudi Arabia.[1]

Faisal's visit underlined the growing web of connections between U.S. and Saudi elites. The Rockefellers were the leading American oil dynasty, just as the Al Saud were the leading Arab oil dynasty. The oil industry had interlocking ties with the largest American banks like Chase Manhattan, the traditional Rockefeller family bank. David Rockefeller was not only its president but also its largest shareholder. Chase handled the finances of Aramco, which was mostly owned by successor companies to the Standard

Oil empire. Other American companies, like the construction giant Bechtel and various defense contractors, also had special relationships with the oil industry and the Saudi government, and they profited directly from the U.S.-Saudi relationship.

As the Cold War developed, the commercial ties between Washington and Riyadh were reinforced by shared ideology. Anticommunism and hostility to the Arab socialism of Egypt's president Gamal Abdel Nasser bound the two countries together. Just before arriving in New York, Faisal met President Lyndon Johnson in Washington, DC. "As long as I am in office," Johnson promised the king, "I will not permit your country to be gobbled up by the Communists." Johnson said that the United States had already suffered 170,000 casualties in Korea, Vietnam, and other battlefields against communism. Faisal reassured Johnson that Saudi Arabia was just as anticommunist as the United States, telling the president that the Saudis "deeply appreciate the sacrifices and the efforts expended by the U.S. on behalf of humanity."[2]

Faisal's visit also demonstrated the continuing challenges to the U.S.-Saudi alliance. At a news conference, the king declared: "Jews support Israel and we consider those who provide assistance to our enemies as our own enemies." New York's mayor John Lindsay promptly canceled a welcome dinner for Faisal and ordered city officials not to greet Faisal when he arrived at La Guardia Airport. Protesters picketed in front of the Waldorf-Astoria, waving signs calling Saudi Arabia a "dictatorship" and asking: "Is Arab oil worth the blood of millions?"[3] Even New York governor Nelson Rockefeller, David's brother, snubbed the king by canceling his planned meeting with Faisal.[4]

Such complaints were nothing new. For more than two decades, American Zionists, labor activists, and other critics had denounced Saudi Arabia for its repressive policies and argued that the United States should not support such a brutal regime. Congress featured heated debates over arms sales to the kingdom. The main complaints included Saudi Arabia's opposition to Israel, its ban on Jews entering the kingdom, and its tolerance of slavery. Critics of the U.S.-Saudi relationship warned, as early as the 1940s, that it was corrupting the American government by engaging in secret diplomacy with the White House and encouraging disregard for congressional authority and public opinion.

Those critics saw the malign influence of the American oil industry at work, arguing that acquiescence to Saudi tyranny abroad was linked to the growth of untrammeled corporate power at home. Only the largest American corporations had the resources, and the political connections, to do business in Saudi Arabia. The leading oil companies, including the four parent companies of Aramco, were protected from domestic oversight by their status as close partners of the U.S. national security state. The companies engaged in a range of anticompetitive practices to protect their hold on the market. When Truman's Justice Department tried to prosecute them for antitrust violations, they were saved by their close relationship with the State, Defense, and Interior Departments, which argued that prosecuting the companies, or even revealing the details of their anticompetitive arrangements, would endanger U.S. national security. The U.S.-Saudi economic relationship aided corporate consolidation in the United States by channeling revenue to firms that already dominated their industries, shrouding their operations in secrecy, and shielding them from antitrust enforcement.

Critiques of the U.S.-Saudi alliance were not limited to the United States. Saudi labor activists challenged racial segregation and unequal working conditions at Aramco, only to be met with severe repression. After the Saudi government refused to nationalize Aramco or cut off oil shipments to the United States after the Truman administration recognized Israel in 1948, dissidents like the left-wing activist Nasir al-Said accused the Saudi regime of betraying the Palestinians and choosing the United States over the rest of the Arab world. Such critiques acquired a sharper edge during the Saudi rivalry with Gamal Abdel Nasser's Egypt, as Nasser portrayed the Saudi royal family as a reactionary puppet of the United States. Even Saudi officials, like the oil minister Abdullah Tariki, thought that Aramco was exploiting the kingdom and taking a disproportionate share of oil profits. Faisal's rise to power in 1962, however, heralded the defeat of the Saudi left and the consolidation of the U.S.-Saudi alliance around shared commercial interests, Cold War ideology, and opposition to Nasser's Arab nationalism.

THE UNITED STATES, SAUDI ARABIA, AND ZIONISM

The emerging U.S.-Saudi relationship proved its durability by surviving the disagreement between the two countries over Israel's founding in the late 1940s. American sympathy for Zionism dismayed Saudi elites, not least because it complicated their efforts to strengthen ties with the United States. Abdulaziz's Palestinian adviser Izzidine Shawa warned that the Arab world was losing its "good opinion of the United States" because of Harry Truman's support for Zionism. Hinting at potential danger to the Saudi oil concession, Shawa declared: "The United States has great commercial interests in the Near East and she had a great many friends there and if she is not careful she is going to lose all of these friends."[5]

Despite such warnings, the United States voted in favor of a UN plan for partitioning Palestine in November 1947 and recognized Israel almost immediately after the Jewish state declared independence in May 1948. Abdulaziz told Truman that U.S. support for Zionism would be a betrayal of Roosevelt's promises to Saudi Arabia and "a deathblow to American interests in the Arab countries." After the United States supported partition, Prince Faisal lamented that all his work to build a stronger U.S.-Saudi partnership, beginning with his first American visit in 1943, had now been "reduced to ashes." If he were in charge of Saudi foreign policy, Faisal said, he would have broken off relations with the United States altogether.[6] In January 1949, Faisal told a Saudi audience that the Arabs were no longer fighting the Jews alone, but also "the brutal colonial states." He marveled that the United States and the Soviet Union both supported Israel, even though they agreed on nothing else.[7]

Truman administration officials worried that the United States might lose access to Middle East oil. Secretary of Defense James Forrestal wrote that if the United States backed Israel, Detroit "would have to design a four-cylinder motorcar," smaller and more efficient than the six- and eight-cylinder cars most Americans preferred at the time.[8] Abdulaziz warned Aramco that "he may be compelled, in certain circumstances, to apply sanctions against the American oil concessions" because of the force of Arab public opinion.[9] Saudi Arabia, however, never took that step. Crown Prince Saud proudly told the United States that the kingdom had resisted pressure from other Arab countries to break relations with the United States and cancel the Aramco oil concession.[10]

Saudi Arabia loudly proclaimed its support for the Arab cause in Palestine, but its real contribution was minimal. The kingdom contributed only a small quantity of weapons and supplies, along with a tiny detachment of soldiers.[11] Other Arabs, and even many Saudis, were upset at the kingdom's failure to do more. Nasir al-Said organized a protest in 1947 demanding that the Saudi government cut off oil shipments to the United States and other allies of Israel. He later denounced the royal family for abandoning the Palestinians and choosing to help Aramco and the United States instead of its fellow Arabs.[12]

Nasir al-Said was right that the Saudi government prioritized its relationship with Washington over Arab solidarity. Saudi Arabia pressed the United States for arms and military assistance, not for use against Israel but for protection against other Arab countries, especially the Hashemite monarchies in Jordan and Iraq. The Al Saud claimed that the Hashemites wanted to recover their old territories in the Hijaz that Abdulaziz had conquered in the 1920s. The Hashemite threat was a recurring theme in Saudi meetings with U.S. officials throughout the 1940s.[13] In April 1948, with war raging in Palestine, Abdulaziz told a visiting team of U.S. military officers that he wanted American help creating a mechanized Saudi army. "If the Americans are really my friends," he suggested, they should help him at least as much "as the British are helping the Hashemites." Yusuf Yassin, the Saudi deputy foreign minister, told the U.S. delegation: "You should think of Saudi Arabia as your own territory in elaborating your defense plans."[14]

The American team recommended an ambitious military program for Saudi Arabia. The commander of the survey, General Richard O'Keefe, privately conceded that the kingdom did not need a large army, and probably had little to fear from its neighbors. He argued, though, that the army would be a "steadying influence" to support Crown Prince Saud's rise to power once Abdulaziz died. In addition, O'Keefe said, the Saudi army would boost Saudi regional influence and "would be a useful force for our purposes in the event of war with Russia." The price tag was far more than Saudi Arabia could afford at the time, and O'Keefe's recommendations were never implemented.[15] The United States did, however, issue its first official commitment to Saudi Arabia's security when Harry Truman told Abdulaziz in 1950 that the United States supported "the independence and territorial integrity of Saudi Arabia." Any threat to the kingdom, Truman wrote, would be "a matter of immediate concern to the United States."[16] The United States also began a military training mission in Saudi Arabia that would become a cornerstone of American efforts to strengthen the kingdom's armed forces.

PROFITING FROM THE
U.S.-SAUDI RELATIONSHIP

By supporting the Saudi regime, the U.S. government upheld a political and economic order in the kingdom that offered profitable opportunities for American firms. In 1943–1945, U.S. lend-lease aid to the Saudi monarchy took some of the financial pressure off Aramco, which had been lending money to Abdulaziz to compensate for the loss of oil and pilgrimage revenue during World War II. The U.S. military built a large airfield at Dhahran that in practice was mostly used not by the U.S. Air Force but by Aramco and civilian airlines, giving private businesses a first-class air transport facility subsidized by the government.[17] When Standard Oil of New Jersey (Exxon) and Socony-Vacuum (Mobil) bought part of Aramco in the late 1940s, violating a previous agreement they had made with French and British oil firms, the U.S. State Department helped smooth over the dispute to ensure that the deal went forward.[18] The so-called Fifty-Fifty agreement brokered by the Truman administration in 1950 was another example of government support for Aramco's owners. It increased the share of revenues that Aramco paid to the Saudi government but compensated Aramco by allowing the company to deduct the payments from its U.S. tax bill, subsidizing the Aramco-Saudi partnership at the expense of the American taxpayer.

One of the most valuable services the U.S. government gave the oil companies was protection from antitrust enforcement. The global oil market was dominated by a small group of Anglo-American companies, the so-called Seven Sisters, including the predecessors of today's ExxonMobil, Chevron, BP, and Shell. The Seven Sisters controlled not only Aramco but all the largest oil concessions in the Middle East, where oil was far cheaper to produce than in the United States. There was so much oil in the ground that the Seven Sisters worried more about surplus than scarcity. If they expanded their production capacity too quickly, they would create a massive glut of oil and send prices plunging. To prevent that outcome, the companies organized an interlocking set of jointly owned subsidiaries like Aramco, effectively giving themselves a collective veto over their counterparts' production plans and restricting worldwide output. The result was less competition and higher prices.[19]

During the Truman administration, the Federal Trade Commission (FTC) and the Department of Justice accused the companies of forming an illegal "world petroleum cartel" and recommended immediate criminal prosecution. The Seven Sisters, however, were protected by the U.S. national security state. The Departments of State, Defense, and the Interior argued that the Seven Sisters served U.S. interests by keeping the world's biggest oil fields in American hands, preserving U.S. influence in the Middle East, and ensuring the flow of oil to Cold War allies.[20] They also argued that the oil companies represented the United States abroad, and that accusing the Seven Sisters of criminal conspiracy would undermine U.S. policy in the Cold War by damaging the reputation of "American enterprise and the American system" overseas. As a result, the State, Defense, and Interior Departments warned that not only should the Seven Sisters be spared from prosecution, but the government should bury any information uncovered by the FTC suggesting that the companies had broken with the law. Harry Truman sided with the companies and declared that since "the national security was at stake," the criminal prosecution of the Seven Sisters would be downgraded to a civil case. Truman claimed that he made his decision reluctantly, and only after the intervention of General Omar Bradley, the chairman of the Joint Chiefs of Staff.[21]

The giant oil fields of the Middle East favored the emergence of a few huge companies that collaborated with each other, preventing overproduction from swamping the market. The political context of the global oil industry favored consolidation, as well. An enormous consortium like Aramco could build close ties with the U.S. and Saudi governments more easily than a smaller company. Aramco coordinated its activities with the State Department, shared facilities like the Dhahran airfield with the U.S. military, and provided cover to CIA agents in the kingdom. Truman's decision suggested that the secrecy and blurred lines between public and private interests involved in such arrangements were starting to influence the domestic American political economy as well as U.S. commercial involvement overseas.

Other American corporations benefited from Saudi business, including the airline TWA, Chase Manhattan Bank, and the construction firm Bechtel. TWA used the Dhahran airfield and managed the fledgling Saudi national airline. Aramco regularly lent funds to the perpetually cash-strapped Saudi government, but only on the condition that the money be handled through Chase Manhattan. When the Saudi government wanted to transfer some of the funds to a Swiss bank instead, Aramco and Chase forced the king to back down.[22] Bechtel built much of the physical infra-structure in the kingdom, including a major railroad project finished in 1951. Crown Prince Saud personally drove the golden spike that completed the railway.[23] The close relationship between Bechtel and the Saudi royal family was underlined by the gift of two Arabian horses by Abdulaziz and his finance minister, Abdullah Sulaiman, to Barbara Bechtel, the teenage daughter of the corporation's president, Stephen Bechtel, who had hosted Prince Faisal on his visits to Bechtel's Marinship shipyards in 1943 and 1945. At enormous expense, the horses were flown from Dhahran to Miami and sent by train from there to California. Abdulaziz's gift was a dramatic demonstration of the possibilities created by postwar air travel, Saudi wealth, and the ties between Bechtel, a family-run business, and Saudi Arabia, a family-run country.[24]

The success of companies like TWA, Chase, and Bechtel was another example of the U.S.-Saudi business relationship encouraging corporate consolidation in the United States itself. They were all among the largest companies in their respective industries, and enjoyed unusually strong connections with the U.S. government. TWA was an unofficial flag carrier of the United States. The chairman of Chase Manhattan during the 1950s was John J. McCloy, the former assistant secretary of war and U.S.

high commissioner for Germany. Bechtel had risen to prominence after helping build the Hoover Dam and winning enormous defense contracts during World War II. John McCone, the cofounder of the Bechtel-McCone operation that ran Marinship during the war, would later become director of the CIA. Only such large, well-connected companies had the resources to enter the Saudi market and secure U.S. government backing for their activities. The profits they made abroad helped solidify their power at home.

OIL WEALTH AND THE SAUDI POLITICAL ORDER

The U.S.-Saudi economic relationship empowered Saudi elites as well as American elites. The Saudi royal family advertised its role in the kingdom's economic development to legitimize its control over the country. In 1950, Prince Faisal declared that the regime was committed to "the spread of knowledge, the expansion of cities, and the provision of health facilities," along with infrastructure including dams, roads, airports, and telephone lines.[25] Much of that infrastructure was built by U.S. firms like Bechtel, whose projects, like the Riyadh–Dammam railroad, became some of the most visible symbols of the regime's accomplishments.

As they had done since the 1920s, Saudi leaders argued that development served the cause of Islam. In 1947, Saud announced that the monarchy was building new facilities at Jeddah, the traditional entry point for pilgrims from overseas; new water pipes for Mecca; and "new roads for cars," including one to the pilgrimage site of Mount Arafat. He told pilgrims at the Grand Mosque of Mecca that the government would provide cold water and ambulances if they fell ill.[26] The most notable Islamic construction project was the expansion of the Grand Mosque beginning in the mid-1950s, ordered by Saud and carried out by the contractor Muhammad bin Laden, an immigrant from the Hadhramaut region in what is now Yemen.[27] Bin Laden made a fortune from the mosque renovations and other contracts with the Saudi government, and his family became one of the wealthiest in the kingdom. The Bin Ladens, like the other leading Saudi business dynasties, enjoyed close ties with the Al Saud and thrived in an environment where the line between public and private interests was almost nonexistent. Muhammad bin Laden was unusual in being a self-made man who worked his way up from the status of common laborer. Many other great merchant families in the kingdom, like the Alirezas of Jeddah, were already part of the commercial elite before oil was discovered.[28]

Oil wealth was shared very unequally in Saudi Arabia. The Saudi workers who built Aramco's infrastructure and maintained the oil facilities were poorly paid and subjected to racial discrimination. The best facilities at Aramco were in the "American camp," while Saudis, Indians, and other non-white workers were housed in much less comfortable conditions. As Aramco's operations expanded after 1945, dissatisfaction with the unequal working conditions became stronger. Rising political consciousness among the work-force was encouraged by the presence of Lebanese, Syrian, and Egyptian immigrants, many of whom were hired by Aramco or the Saudi government as schoolteachers, clerks, and other educated workers. They were accustomed to organized politics and anticolonial activism in their home countries and played an important role in the growth of labor activism in Saudi Arabia.[29]

U.S. and Arab critiques of the oil industry reinforced one another. Dur-ing the late 1940s, a U.S. Senate committee chaired by Owen Brewster (R-ME) investigated the oil industry and accused Aramco of greatly over-charging the U.S. Navy for oil during World War II.[30] The news reached Saudi Arabia, where Aramco complained that the Saudi government was being influenced by "the attacks being made on the Company by the United States press, the Brewster Committee, and by columnists." One dismayed Aramco official wrote his colleagues about an article in the Egyptian daily *Al Misri* in June 1948, which noted the Brewster Committee's investigation into the naval fuel scandal. Arab Americans who followed the story, *Al Misri* wrote, were asking themselves why Saudi Arabia and the other Arab oil producers did not nationalize their oil fields. Instead, they let the profits flow to "the Oil Companies, whose capital is Jewish and whose profits go to Jews."[31] Such anti-Semitic rhetoric was a common theme in Arab criticism of the United States at a time when the first Arab-Israeli war was under way in Palestine.

Saudi discontent with the discrimination and unequal pay at Aramco inspired a series of major strikes in 1945, 1953, and 1956. The Saudi government expressed some sympathy with the workers' demands. In 1945, Abdulaziz told the U.S. ambassador William Eddy that "some of my people have been spoken to as no man should speak to a dog." The Saudi finance minister Abdullah Sulaiman and the deputy foreign minister Yusuf Yassin visited Dhahran in spring 1948 and told Aramco that the Arab housing needed to be upgraded and eventually merged with the American housing, undoing the existing racial segregation. When the workers became more assertive, however, the government cracked down, subjecting the ringleaders to beatings, imprisonment, and exile. In 1956, the king issued a royal decree banning further strikes. He had no intention of allowing the emergence of a labor movement that could serve as a focus for opposition politics.[32]

Aramco cooperated with the Saudi government to defuse the threat of labor activism. The company began offering better pay, housing, and education opportunities to its Arab workers, but only after it became clear that labor discontent threatened Aramco's privileged position in the kingdom. One 1948 Aramco document suggested channeling higher wages and benefits to "top Arab employees" in case other oil companies tried to enter the kingdom and poach Aramco's best workers. While offering some concessions to labor, Aramco also benefited from the Saudi government's brutal repression of political resistance. Much of that work was carried out by Saud ibn Jiluwi, the famously harsh governor of the oil regions. The Aramco executive Baldo Marinovic later recalled: "This Amir Bin Jiluwi was an absolute terror. He was feared by the whole population of the Eastern Province. I mean, he had no hesitations in having people beheaded or hands chopped off. But at the same time, he was very fair and highly respected."[33] The State Department blandly noted that after the 1956 strike, "Bin Jiluwi arrested many of the leaders and reportedly tortured a few." The department concluded that the amir's measures had been "effective" enough to satisfy Aramco.[34]

Ibn Jiluwi was a distant relative of the Saudi monarchs and a son of one of Abdulaziz's companions who helped capture Riyadh in 1902. His appointment was a reminder that al-Hasa was ruled like an internal colony, with its governors appointed by the king and much of its oil wealth redirected to Riyadh, hundreds of miles away. Even the traditional name al-Hasa was replaced in Saudi administrative parlance by "the Eastern Province" (al-Mintaqa al-Sharqia), redefining the region's identity in terms of its relationship to Riyadh. The fact that much of the local population was Shia, viewed with disdain by the Wahhabi elite of Najd, only added to their disempowerment. The dissident publication *Jaheem al-Hukm al-Saudia* (The hell of Saudi rule) accused the Saudi government of plundering al-Hasa's wealth, noting that although the oil was "extracted from their land," the Shia received only "crumbs" in return.[35]

In his novel *Al-Tih* (The wilderness), published in English as *Cities of Salt*, the exiled writer and economist Abdelrahman Munif vividly described the way oil development overturned al-Hasa's traditional society and played havoc with the region's ecology.[36] Munif's view of pre-oil village life was tinged with nostalgia, but he did not advocate a return to the past. Munif was a petroleum economist who believed that oil could help lift the Arab world out of backwardness and underdevelopment. His real target was not oil development but the way that oil wealth enabled political tyranny. In Munif's later novel *Al-Akhud* (The trench), set in a fictionalized version of midcentury Saudi Arabia, a U.S. adviser calmly praises the regime for crushing all opposition. The art of government in a petro-state, the American explains, is simple. It "required just two methods, or at least one: incentive and force." Money would motivate the regime's supporters, and force would take care of "the others, dissidents, those who were never satisfied with anything."[37]

SAUDI ARABIA AND THE COLD WAR

The Saudi regime's willingness to crush the left-wing opposition made it a natural Cold War ally of the United States. In 1951, Abdulaziz told a U.S. general: "If you could find a Communist in Saudi Arabia, I will hand you his head."[38] The Cold War also strengthened the importance of Saudi oil in the eyes of U.S. policymakers. During the 1940s and 1950s, the United States imported very little Middle Eastern oil. Most American oil consumption was still met by domestic sources, Canada, and Venezuela. The most important exception was the U.S. military, which used Saudi oil to supply U.S. forces overseas. When Abdulaziz visited Dhahran in 1947, he was received on board the USS *Cimarron*, a naval tanker getting fuel for U.S. forces in East Asia (figure 2.1).[39]

Aramco's most important market was Western Europe, where oil consumption rose sharply after the end of World War II. Beginning in 1948, the massive infusion of U.S. aid under the Marshall Plan paid for European countries to import oil from the Middle East. More than 10 percent of all Marshall Plan aid was spent on oil, more than on any other commodity. Cheap oil helped meet the plan's goal of bolstering European resistance to communism by speeding economic recovery. It undermined the European left by providing a source of energy that did not depend on the coal industry, whose mines were a center of left-wing labor organizing. By strengthening European dependence on oil, the Marshall Plan also helped the Anglo-American oil companies by encouraging the growth of huge new

FIGURE 2.1 King Abdulaziz (*seated*) on the navy oil tanker USS *Cimarron* during his visit to Aramco headquarters in Dhahran, 1947. Courtesy of the Naval History and Heritage Command.

markets. The American left understood that the oil industry was one of the biggest winners from the program, with Progressive Party presidential candidate Henry Wallace attacking the Marshall Plan as a giveaway to the oil companies and other large corporations. Such critiques made little headway, as the Marshall Plan consolidated the Cold War ties between Europe, the United States, and the oil industry, and leftists like Wallace were discredited by accusations of sympathy for communism.[40]

The Seven Sisters understood that their market position was supported by U.S. power, and that they would benefit from supporting U.S. Cold War strategy even at the expense of short-term profits. Standard Oil of New Jersey (Exxon) warned that if the companies increased prices for Middle East oil, they would "hamper the economic recovery of countries being aided by the U.S. Government." Lower prices would mean giving up immediate revenue, but they would be "an investment in future sound and satisfactory relationships." A 1947 memorandum from the Socal-Texaco subsidiary Caltex agreed, arguing that a price increase in the face of "Europe's desperate need for petroleum" would hurt the industry's political position not only in Europe but also in the United States.[41] The postwar oil market was not a free market. It was an oligopoly that blurred the lines between public and private interests, where the Seven Sisters functioned as unofficial agents of U.S. and British foreign policy and made many of their business decisions based on politics as much as economics.

U.S. officials were uneasy about the growing dependence of the United States and its allies on oil from the Middle East. The Truman administration's desire to defend American access to the region's oil was an unspoken motivation for the Truman Doctrine of 1947, which extended U.S. aid to Greece and Turkey.[42] Most U.S. defense policymakers, however, concluded that the United States lacked the military forces and logistical capabilities to stop a Soviet invasion of the Persian Gulf. After a contentious debate, the Truman administration decided that it should not try to defend the Gulf in the event of full-scale war. Instead, it developed plans to destroy Aramco's oil installations and deny Saudi oil to the Soviet Union.[43] For the next three decades, U.S. leaders would generally assume that they would be unable to defend Saudi Arabia against a determined Soviet attack, and they accepted that U.S. military capabilities in the Gulf would be quite limited.

Only at the end of the 1970s would they revisit that conclusion and begin investing in a network of bases and transport routes to project American military power into the region.

THE GROWTH OF AMERICAN OIL CONSUMPTION

With U.S. policymakers unsure they could maintain access to Middle East oil, there was an obvious incentive for the United States to limit its reliance on imported petroleum. The U.S. government could have reduced American oil demand by taxing gasoline and other fuels, encouraging denser urban development, and promoting smaller cars. Instead, the opposite happened. The federal and state governments built an ever-growing network of roads to carry automobile traffic, while railways and public transit were increasingly neglected. Starting in the 1930s, agencies like the Federal Housing Administration, the Home Owners' Loan Corporation (HOLC), and the Federal National Mortgage Association (FNMA, or Fannie Mae) offered subsidized mortgages to American home buyers, while the 1944 GI Bill provided additional subsidies for returning veterans. Americans could also deduct mortgage interest from their tax bills, a lucrative perk that renters did not enjoy. The result was a massive stimulus to private home ownership, speeding the development of energy-hungry suburbs and draining resources from denser urban neighborhoods served by public transit.[44] During the 1950s, Dwight D. Eisenhower oversaw the construction of a national network of roads, defended on national security grounds and billed as "Defense Highways," that further accelerated suburbanization and drained funds from railways and mass transit. The highway lobby successfully drew on the long association between American motorization, national prestige, and military power to frame road building as a patriotic duty.[45]

Rising American oil consumption was also driven by racial inequality. Starting in the early twentieth century, African Americans moved to northern cities as part of the Great Migration.[46] White Americans left urban neighborhoods that were becoming more racially diverse and moved to suburbs that were often segregated, whether by law, restrictive covenants and other private agreements, or informal social pressure. The federal government actively encouraged that shift. In the infamous practice of "redlining," the government deliberately favored white suburban areas and denied mortgage subsidies to urban neighborhoods with large nonwhite populations. The HOLC even refused benefits to white districts that were too close to black districts. The result was continuous pressure for cities to sprawl outward, making them more car-dependent, while older, denser neighborhoods were starved of resources.[47]

Racial politics sped the decline of public transit in the United States in the midcentury period. Some of the most important episodes of the mid-twentieth-century civil rights movement involved public transit, including the 1955–1956 Montgomery bus boycott and the 1961 challenge to bus segregation by the Freedom Riders. During the 1950s and 1960s, de jure segregation of public transit was eliminated. In many cases, however, whites responded by simply abandoning public transit and turning to private automobiles instead. In Atlanta, black riders were first allowed onto city buses in 1957. So many whites stopped using the system that, by 1960, a clear majority of riders were black (at a time when the city was still two-thirds white).[48] Even in northern cities, affluent whites increasingly associated public transit with crime and poverty, seeing private car ownership as a badge of middle-class status. Such trends fueled not only social inequality but also higher energy consumption in the United States.

The postwar decades witnessed the curious spectacle of the U.S. government worrying about the country's growing dependence on Middle East oil and trying to limit foreign imports, while government policies simultaneously undermined those efforts by encouraging a massive, sustained increase in American oil demand. That contradiction was never seriously examined by U.S. policymakers. Oil seemed cheap and plentiful enough that, for the time being, policymakers could ignore hard questions about rising energy consumption.

THE NATIONALIST CHALLENGE

Although the world oil market was in surplus, Saudi oil already provided an important margin of safety for the oil companies if production was disrupted elsewhere. In 1951, the new Iranian prime minister Mohammad Mosaddegh nationalized the British-owned Anglo-Iranian Oil Company. In response, the Seven Sisters boycotted Iran's oil exports and replaced them with oil from other countries, including Saudi Arabia. With the Iranian economy slumping, Mosaddegh's popular support declined until he was overthrown in a military coup sponsored by the United States and Great Britain in 1953. Although the details are still classified more than sixty years later, Saudi Arabia's Dhahran airfield may have been used as a transit point for U.S. supplies as part of the covert operations against Iran.[49] Mosaddegh's fate was a powerful warning to any other oil-producing country that thought about challenging the companies, which could draw on the support of their home governments and the surplus production capacity of Saudi Arabia.[50]

Another challenge to the existing political order in the Middle East came from Gamal Abdel Nasser, the Egyptian leader who seized control after a 1952 coup. Nasser soon became the most popular leader in the Arab world, particularly after he nationalized the Suez Canal and faced down a joint British, French, and Israeli attempt to seize the canal in October 1956. Although it sided with Nasser during the Suez Crisis, the Eisenhower administration soon concluded that he threatened American interests in the Middle East. Nasser's brand of Arab nationalism inspired opponents to conservative regimes throughout the Middle East.[51] U.S. officials worried that Nasser could interfere with Western access to Arab oil. His nationalization of the Suez Canal provided a precedent for nationalizing oil supplies in the future, especially since Nasser urged the Arabs to use oil as a tool in their struggle against Israel and Western imperialism.[52] When Eisenhower ordered the military to support the conservative government of Lebanon against Nasserist forces, he told his vice president, Richard Nixon, that Nasser threatened "vitally needed petroleum supplies" and that, if he took over the region's oil fields, Nasser would have "the income and the power to destroy the Western world."[53]

Seeking allies against Nasser, the Eisenhower administration turned to Saud, who had succeeded his father, Abdulaziz, as the king of Saudi Arabia in 1953. Eisenhower hoped that Saudi Arabia could be a conservative counterweight to Egypt. He welcomed Saud on a high-profile visit to Washington, DC, in 1957. Saud was nowhere near as popular as Nasser, however, and Saudi Arabia, with its small population and limited military forces, was not prepared to compete with Egypt for regional influence. U.S.-Saudi ties were also strained by a series of disagreements. Saudi Arabia tried to partner with the Greek shipping magnate Aristotle Onassis to transport Saudi oil on his tankers, but the deal was blocked by Aramco's legal objections. Another problem came from Saudi Arabia's claim to sovereignty over Buraimi, an area near the border with the British client states of Abu Dhabi and Oman. The dispute was especially heated because the area was thought to hold lucrative oil resources. In 1955, Britain sent troops to secure Buraimi, while Saud threatened that if Saudi Arabia could not resolve the problem at the UN, he would use any means necessary "to restore that part of our country." Aramco supported the Saudi government and drafted legal briefs backing the Saudi position. The Eisenhower administration, however, was irritated by the Saudi-British conflict and mostly stayed out of the dispute.[54]

AMERICAN OPPOSITION TO THE ALLIANCE

The U.S.-Saudi relationship was also troubled by American criticism of the kingdom as a reactionary, despotic backwater. Activists, journalists, and members of Congress slammed the Eisenhower administration for inviting Saud to visit Washington in 1957. Testifying before the House of Representatives, Rabbi Philip Bernstein, the chairman of the American Zionist Committee for Public Affairs, denounced the administration for its willingness to welcome "an arbitrary feudal monarch of a backward country." Rep. George McGovern (D-ND) condemned the decadent practices of Saud's court, declaring that the Saudi royal family embodied "everything that is alien to our tradition of liberty and equality." He denounced the administration for inviting a leader "whose hands drip with blood just because there is oil on those same hands." When Saud arrived in New York City, Mayor Robert Wagner refused to greet the king and vetoed any official welcome ceremony for the Saudi delegation.[55]

Much of the criticism focused on Saudi discrimination against Jews, along with the willingness of Aramco and the U.S. government to support that policy. The Pentagon barred Jewish personnel from serving at the Dhahran airfield, prompting fierce protests from Jewish war veterans. The navy also surreptitiously aided the long-standing Arab boycott by including a clause in shipping contracts that threatened the charters of ships barred from Arab ports because they did business with Israel.[56] Aramco, too, refused to hire Jewish personnel, even in its New York offices. The New York State Supreme Court ruled in 1959 that Aramco had to stop asking its employees about their religion, but the company continued its discriminatory policy until the early 1960s.[57] Because Jewish groups and Democrats were so incensed by U.S. executive capitulation to Saudi Arabia's discriminatory policies, the 1960 Democratic Party platform included a statement condemning international agreements that allowed religious discrimination against American citizens.[58]

Other critics focused on Saudi Arabia's brutal labor policies. The International Labor Organization in Geneva and the AFL-CIO denounced the Saudi government's repression of workers. Lester Holtzman (D-NY) complained: "For the life of me, I cannot understand the attitude of our officials in rolling out a red carpet welcome for this tyrant. No quantity of oil, no airbase, no other consideration is worth it." He read into the record a newspaper column by Victor Riesel in the *New York Daily Mirror* condemning the torture and killing of labor activists in Saudi Arabia. The Saudi monarchy had a "quick labor cure," Riesel wrote. "Strike—and you die."[59]

Some of the most intense criticism focused on slavery in Saudi Arabia. The UN reported that despite Saudi promises to outlaw the slave trade, at least five thousand people were trafficked to Saudi Arabia and Yemen every month. An investigation by the French embassy in Jeddah uncovered a slave-trading operation backed by the Jeddah municipal government, which allowed the slaves to be housed in the city jail until they were distributed to their new masters. Many Africans were tricked into coming to Saudi Arabia on the pretext that they were performing a pilgrimage to Mecca, only to find themselves sold into slavery on their arrival. Other Africans came as the servants of other pilgrims and were sold as "living travelers' checks" to pay their employers' travel costs.[60]

When Eisenhower invited Saud to visit in 1957, many Americans were furious. The *Baltimore Afro-American* ran a letter arguing that it was a crime "to welcome the royal slave owner into the house where Lincoln signed the Emancipation Proclamation." Others criticized African American leaders for not doing more to protest the slave trade. The American Jewish Congress slammed Rep. Adam Clayton Powell (D-NY), who represented Harlem, for praising Saud and his father, Abdulaziz, and a supporter of the National Association for the Advancement of Colored People (NAACP) wrote the *New York Amsterdam News* accusing the NAACP of bowing to State Department pressure by remaining mute on Saudi slavery.[61]

Despite the outcry, the U.S. government put little pressure on Saudi Arabia to end slavery during the 1950s. When Britain took the issue to the UN in 1956 and proposed inspecting ships headed to Saudi Arabia to confirm that they were not smuggling enslaved people, the United States refused to support the proposal.[62] When Congress questioned State Department officials, they minimized the horror of the slave trade, repeating excuses once used to defend American slavery in the nineteenth century. Raymond Hare, the former U.S. ambassador in Jeddah, told a Senate committee that "these so-called slaves" were "rather privileged people very often." Hare claimed that enslaved children were raised with the master's children as if they were siblings. The current ambassador George Wadsworth agreed, arguing that Saudi slaves "are treated as members of the family and take pride in the service."[63]

THE SAUDI-EGYPTIAN RIVALRY

The Saudi monarchy's reactionary politics were no obstacle to its alliance with the United States, but they outraged critics closer to home—especially Arab nationalists and leftists who looked to Gamal Abdel Nasser for inspiration. The Saudi response to Nasser was complicated by an ongoing power struggle between King Saud and Crown Prince Faisal. Over the course of the 1950s, Saud alienated Faisal and other senior princes by promoting his own sons to positions of authority at the expense of his half-brothers. In March 1958, he was implicated in a plot to assassinate Nasser and sponsor a coup in Syria, which had just merged with Egypt to form the short-lived United Arab Republic (UAR). The UAR government exposed the plot, humiliating Saud. Dismayed, the other leading royals stripped Saud of his authority over day-to-day governance and transferred it to Faisal. The crown prince tried to patch up Saudi relations with Nasser. He also promoted several reformist commoners in the Saudi government, most notably the oil expert Abdullah Tariki.[64] Like almost all the senior royals, however, Faisal remained fundamentally conservative and authoritarian. U.S. officials initially worried that Faisal might be anti-American compared with Saud, but the CIA director Allen Dulles reassured Eisenhower's cabinet that Faisal's anticommunism made him a reliable partner.[65]

In December 1960, Saud temporarily reclaimed power and sidelined Faisal. Seeking an alliance with the progressive forces in the kingdom, he appointed several reformers to the cabinet. Prince Talal, the most prominent liberal in the royal family, became finance minister. Abdulaziz ibn Muammar, an activist who had clashed with Aramco in the mid-1950s, was an important adviser, and Tariki became the kingdom's first oil minister. Tariki, Ibn Muammar, and other reformers hoped to limit the arbitrary power of the royal family and turn the kingdom into a constitutional monarchy.[66]

Tariki also wanted Saudi Arabia to take more control over its oil industry. He had studied geology at the University of Texas and married an American woman, but he suffered racial discrimination both as a student in the United States and in Aramco's facilities in Saudi Arabia. Over time he became increasingly critical of Aramco. Working with Venezuela, Iran, and other oil producers, Tariki cofounded the Organization of the Petroleum Exporting Countries (OPEC) in September 1960. The Seven Sisters had recently cut their payments to Saudi Arabia and other oil exporters. OPEC was designed to prevent a repetition of that experience, forming a united front to stop the companies from playing one oil producer against another. Eisenhower dismissed OPEC, remarking: "Anyone could break up the Organization by offering five cents more per barrel for the oil of one of the countries." The oil companies took OPEC more seriously, worrying that it might reduce their control over the market. Tariki himself saw OPEC as only the beginning; he hoped that Saudi Arabia could eventually take partial ownership of Aramco and secure a greater share of the profits.[67]

American leaders were concerned about these new developments in Saudi politics. Aramco disliked Tariki, seeing him as a dangerous radical. U.S. government officials also took a dim view of Saud. They considered him less intelligent than Faisal, ignorant of modern methods of government, and prone to waste the country's resources on extravagant personal spending.[68] That critique was particularly influential in the Kennedy administration. Robert Komer, the top Middle East expert on Kennedy's National Security Council, dismissed Saudi Arabia under Saud as a "great, oil-rich non-country with a medieval regime and an incompetent king who is a drunkard."[69] Some of Kennedy's leading advisers doubted that the Saudi monarchy would survive and saw Nasserism as the future of Arab politics. A 1961 U.S. National Intelligence Estimate (NIE) concluded that "militant nationalism will continue to be the most dynamic force in Arab political affairs." By contrast, the NIE warned, "The long term outlook for the conservative and Western-aligned regimes is bleak."[70]

Not wanting to tie itself too closely to Saudi Arabia, the Kennedy administration stepped up U.S. aid to Egypt and sought better relations with Nasser. The policy shift dismayed the Saudi regime. Saud complained that the United States was favoring Egypt over Saudi Arabia. He tried to convince the United States that Nasser was unworthy of U.S. aid, protesting: "This man is a communist."[71] Saud's actions only alienated Kennedy further. In a letter to the new president soon after he took office, Saud infuriated Kennedy by questioning his grasp of Middle East affairs and accusing the United States of encouraging Israeli aggression.[72] Saud also abruptly ended the U.S. lease of the Dhahran airfield in March 1961, irritating Washington by failing to coordinate the announcement with the United States.[73]

The Kennedy administration began looking forward to the end of Saud's reign. It did not expect to wait long, as Saud was a heavy drinker whose health took a sharp turn for the worse in late 1961. He was rushed to the Aramco hospital in Dhahran after he started bleeding from the mouth and suffered cardiac complications. His illness was concealed with a cover story about leg pains, but Saud was no longer healthy enough to retain control over day-to-day governance.[74] He brought Faisal back into the cabinet, pleasing U.S. observers.[75] The U.S. ambassador Parker T. Hart wrote that Saud had a "warm heart" but a "limited intellect." Hart argued that Saud badly needed the advice of Faisal, who was "highly intelligent" and had great political "skill and subtlety." Moreover, Hart emphasized, "Faisal believes in America." He had "entrusted his sons to it for education," sending his children Saud and Turki to Princeton.[76] Komer agreed, telling national security adviser McGeorge Bundy that Saud was "a simple-minded type." Although U.S.-Saudi relations had been going through a rough patch, Komer reassured Bundy that they just had to wait "until the King drinks himself to death. Then Feisal (who's twice the man) will straighten matters out."[77]

The leading progressives were soon removed from the Saudi government. Talal left the cabinet in late 1961 and was subsequently forced into exile in Beirut and Cairo, where he headed the dissident "Free Princes" faction and called for a constitutional monarchy.[78] Tariki was fired in March after he accused Faisal's brother-in-law Kamal Adham of corruption. He was replaced by the lawyer Ahmed Zaki Yamani. The U.S. consulate in Dhahran reported that although Aramco was careful to say little publicly, behind closed doors its executives were probably giving a "whoop" of "delight" to see Tariki gone. They were confident that Yamani would be much easier to work with. Aramco decided to hand Yamani a few easy victories in their first negotiating sessions to make him look good and ensure that he would not be "labelled a company stooge."[79]

U.S. PRESSURE FOR REFORM

While Kennedy administration officials like Komer were glad that Faisal had returned to the government, they still had their doubts about the future of the Saudi monarchy. They worried that the regime was not delivering enough economic progress to satisfy the Saudi people, leaving the monarchy vulnerable to challenges from Nasserists and other leftists. In June 1962 they encouraged a private mission to Saudi Arabia headed by Albert J. (A. J.) Meyer, a Harvard economist. The Meyer team praised Faisal for getting the kingdom's finances in order but warned that the regime was not moving fast enough with its economic development program. Faisal was impressed with the team, and the U.S. embassy gave him an official copy of Meyer's report to guide the regime's economic planning.[80]

Privately, the Meyer team was more pessimistic about the regime's prospects. Meyer's personal notes stated that among senior Saudi leaders, "enthusiasm for development" was only "occasionally present" and was often motivated only by fear of Nasser.[81] A confidential attachment to the report, for U.S. government eyes only, noted that younger, educated Saudis were heavily influenced by "pro Nasser revolutionary ideas" and impatient with the slow pace of progress. Even if the regime did step up its development efforts, it might just be digging its own grave. As modernization proceeded and "the destruction of the Bedu economy goes inevitably onward," the traditional social foundations that supported the monarchy, including tribal authority, would be dismantled. Once the process was under way, there would be no stopping it. The team warned: "The kingdom seems to be mounting a toboggan at the top of the chute" and not might survive the ride.[82]

The Meyer team concluded that the United States should hedge its bets. It should "avoid public alignment" with "the forces of the establishment" and be ready to deal with any future Saudi government if the regime fell. The report also noted that "few nations have had as bad a press abroad as Saudi Arabia." The State Department was only too aware of that problem. It tried to avoid publicity for the Meyer mission. In a confidential briefing for Meyer's team, it warned them that if they recommended U.S. financial aid for Saudi Arabia, it would probably be impossible to get congressional approval because of the kingdom's discrimination against Jews. Meyer suggested that the U.S. government officially keep its distance from the Saudi regime, while supporting private institutions like American universities and consultants who could assist Saudi development and polish the royal family's international reputation.[83]

The Kennedy administration agreed that Faisal needed to do more to meet his subjects' aspirations. The State Department warned Faisal that the

U.S. commitment to the royal family was not a blank check; it was "contingent upon progress and reform in Saudi Arabia." U.S. officials often repeated that message to Faisal over the following months. They did not, however, argue in favor of full-blown democracy, or political reform for the sake of the Saudi people. Instead, they tried to convince Faisal to allow just enough reform to satisfy popular demand for change and deflect challenges from the left. As Komer put it, "Deliberate, controlled internal reform is the best antidote to Nasserism."[84] The United States also pressed the Saudi regime to end slavery and the kingdom's ban on visas for Jewish visitors, two policies that had provoked constant criticism in the United States. Hart told the Saudi minister Ibrahim al-Sowayel that Saudi Arabia needed to do more to reduce the "chronic attacks from our Congress" and the American public.[85]

THE YEMENI CIVIL WAR AND FAISAL'S RISE TO POWER

The U.S.-Saudi relationship and the kingdom's internal politics reached a turning point in late 1962. In September, an Egyptian-backed military coup overthrew the Yemeni monarchy and established a nationalist republic. A civil war between the Yemeni republicans and royalists broke out and soon became a proxy conflict between Nasser and Faisal. Egypt sent thousands of troops to support the new regime, while Saudi Arabia gave money and weapons to the royalist resistance.[86]

The war marked a serious escalation in the Saudi-Egyptian rivalry. In response to Saudi support for the royalists, Egyptian bombers humiliated the Saudi military by flying over Jeddah, in full view of the city's population, too high and fast for the Saudi air force to intercept them. Several Saudi pilots defected and took their planes to Egypt to join Nasser. In response, the Saudi regime grounded its entire air force.[87] The CIA reported in mid-October that leading businessmen and members of the royal family were panicking. Worried that a nationalist coup might overthrow the monarchy at any time, they started liquidating their assets and moving their money out of the country.[88] The regime was so afraid that it filled Riyadh with plainclothes security officers disguised as taxi drivers, while Saudis caught listening to Nasser's radio station, Voice of the Arabs, were summarily arrested. Jeeps constantly patrolled the royal palace grounds at night to guard against attack.[89] The executives of Tapline, the Aramco pipeline subsidiary, told the State Department they were preparing to evacuate American women and children at the earliest possible sign of a revolution. They asked for U.S. paratroopers to rescue Tapline workers if the Al Saud fell.[90]

In that frantic atmosphere, the senior royals decided that Saud had to be removed from power. Led by Prince Fahd and his full brothers, the so-called Sudairi Seven, they stripped Saud of his authority and made Faisal prime minister and king in all but name.[91] The move came while Faisal was out of the country, less than two weeks after a meeting between him and John F. Kennedy in Washington, DC, on October 5. Ever since, rumors—especially popular on the Saudi left—have suggested that the United States backed the coup against Saud. The evidence is inconclusive. After his lunch meeting with Kennedy, Faisal asked to talk with the president for half an hour with no other Saudis present. Isa Sabbagh, a renowned Palestinian-born U.S. diplomat who enjoyed a close relationship with Faisal, served as translator. The declassified memorandum of conversation says only that Kennedy and Faisal discussed U.S. aid for Saudi road building, U.S. naval visits to Saudi ports, arms sales, and the Saudi refusal to grant visas to Jewish Americans.[92] Aramco or CIA officers in the kingdom might have supported the royal family's move against Saud, but most of the relevant documents remain secret.[93]

After taking power, Faisal announced a ten-point reform program that included promises to protect Islamic values, promote economic development, build new infrastructure, bolster the welfare state, and end slavery. The plan referred vaguely to a new "basic law" that would define the relationship between the government and the people, falling short of a written constitution that would satisfy Saudi progressives.[94] When U.S. officials pressed him for more political liberalization, Faisal was unsympathetic. In December 1962, U.S. Ambassador Parker Hart told Faisal that he needed "quick and dramatic reforms including some popular representation by degrees in government." Faisal made no response.[95] Several months later, Sabbagh suggested that the crown prince allow the dissidents Prince Talal and Abdullah Tariki to return from exile. Faisal brushed off the suggestion, dismissing Talal as "an irresponsible, foolish playboy" and saying that "you Americans seemed to have had an exaggerated appreciation of Tariki," who was dangerous and would do no good if brought back to the kingdom.[96]

U.S. officials saw Faisal as a clear improvement over Saud, but they were dissatisfied with the limits of his reform program. Hart reported that the Saudi regime was having trouble maintaining public loyalty because of "continued limitations on innocent public amusements" by the widely disliked religious police and the regime's costly, unpopular involvement in Yemen's civil war. Even fiscal discipline, supposed to be Faisal's strong suit, was lacking. "Princely waste and extravagance" remained a serious problem. Senior royals received large subsidies hidden in the state budget. Faisal proposed eliminating them but failed to follow through in the face of objections from Fahd and the other Sudairi princes. Hart warned that while Faisal's ten-point program had been favorably received, the public was now getting impatient. The U.S. consulate in Dhahran estimated that 85 percent of the local population were either politically apathetic or actively disloyal to the regime, and that one would be "hard pressed to find anyone in Al-Hasa" who truly liked the Al Saud.[97]

With those doubts in mind, the Kennedy administration initially tried to distance itself from the conflict in Yemen. Over fierce Saudi objections, the United States recognized the new Yemeni republic. The administration ordered some U.S. aid and naval units to the region to reassure Faisal, but the Joint Chiefs of Staff were reluctant to get involved. Komer was also skeptical, telling Kennedy: "It's one thing to defend Saudis against aggression. It's another to declare we choose the kings over the bulk of the Arab world; that would be the real way to lose our oil."[98]

American oil companies pressed Kennedy to do more. Kermit Roosevelt, an ex-CIA agent who had worked on the 1953 coup in Iran and other covert operations in the Middle East, was now employed by Gulf Oil. He lobbied the administration to back Faisal against Nasser.[99] U.S. officials eventually decided that American petroleum interests did require the United States to intervene, prompting Bundy's comment to Maxwell Taylor, the chairman of the Joint Chiefs of Staff: "Remember oil."[100] The growing hostility between Egypt and Saudi Arabia made it difficult for the United States to remain neutral. Egyptian air force units bombed Saudi Arabia and air-dropped weapons into the Saudi desert for retrieval by local revolutionaries. Faisal demanded U.S. protection. The Kennedy administration, still hoping to avoid an open break with Nasser, negotiated a Saudi-Egyptian disengagement agreement to de-escalate the conflict in Yemen. In order to win Faisal's assent, however, Kennedy agreed to deploy a squadron of U.S. fighter aircraft to the kingdom in "Operation Hard Surface." Officially, it was only a training mission, but its real purpose was to demonstrate U.S. support for the Saudi regime.

Hard Surface was almost called off because of Saudi discrimination against Jews. The U.S. Air Force initially planned to exclude Jewish personnel from the mission, since the Saudi regime would not issue them visas. After Rep. Emmanuel Celler (D-NY), a longtime critic of the Saudi regime, learned of the plan, the Pentagon reversed course. Celler announced in a radio interview that Jews would be allowed into Saudi Arabia after all. Sen. Hubert Humphrey (D-MN) hailed the news, denouncing Saudi "warped national prejudices" and the Pentagon's willingness to tolerate such discrimination. The story was picked up by Cairo's Voice of the Arabs, which mocked Saudi Arabia for relying on Jewish protection. Faisal immediately revoked permission for the deployment. The problem was only papered over after Faisal assured Hart that he did not really care whether Jews were present, as long as the issue could be hushed up.[101] The Saudi government secretly waived the rule for Jews in the kingdom "on a transient basis," and the Kennedy administration leaned on the American Jewish Committee and other lobbying groups to keep the affair quiet.[102]

The U.S. squadron, with a total of more than five hundred personnel, was deployed to Saudi Arabia. The air force had no intention of getting into a shooting war with Egypt, and the mission's restrictive rules of engagement limited the chances of any real fighting. Nevertheless, the Saudi regime understood the symbolic power of the deployment. It asked the first Hard Surface fighters to fly low over the city of Jeddah in full view of the Saudi public. The Saudi deputy foreign minister Omar Saqqaf met Parker Hart to watch the planes arrive. As they roared overhead, an excited Saqqaf shouted in Hart's ear: "Tell them to break the sound barrier!" Hart explained that if the planes went supersonic, the shock waves would break windows all over the city and anger the local citizens. Even at slower speeds, however, the planes made quite an impression.[103] They signaled that the United States was extending its protection over the kingdom.

After Kennedy was assassinated in November 1963, Lyndon Johnson became president and largely abandoned the U.S. rapprochement with Nasser. Increasingly preoccupied with the war in Vietnam, Johnson had little patience with Nasser as the Egyptian leader moved closer to the Soviet Union and stepped up his criticism of the United States. In place of Kennedy's neutral stance on the Yemeni civil war, Johnson tilted toward Saudi Arabia. Pro-Israel forces in the United States, although traditionally critical of Saudi Arabia, limited their objections during this period. Nasser's Egypt, with the largest and most advanced armed forces in the Arab world, had emerged as the most serious military threat to Israel, and Saudi Arabia seemed less threatening by comparison. The kingdom even became a de facto ally of Israel against Nasser, although the Saudi regime would never have admitted it. Saudi sponsorship of the royalist insurgency in Yemen tied down thousands of Egyptian troops, undermining Nasser's ability to fight Israel when the next Arab-Israeli war broke out in 1967.

The new, closer relationship between Washington and Riyadh was consolidated through the largest U.S.-Saudi arms sales to date. After Egyptian bombing raids exposed the limits of Saudi Arabia's air defenses, the kingdom bought more than $100 million in surface-to-air missiles from the American company Raytheon. Saudi Arabia also purchased British missiles and jet interceptors, while the Johnson administration encouraged Britain to reuse the profits from the Saudi deal to buy American aircraft. The Saudi deals not only benefited U.S. arms contractors but also empowered Prince Sultan, the new Saudi defense minister and one of the Sudairi brothers who helped put Faisal in power, by boosting his ministry's budget and providing new opportunities for personal profit.[104]

The deals enriched a small but growing group of middlemen and consultants who represented American arms manufacturers in Saudi Arabia. They included Kermit Roosevelt, the former CIA agent who later represented Gulf Oil and Northrop, and Adnan Khashoggi, the son of King

Abdulaziz's personal doctor, who used his family's connections at court to become the kingdom's leading arms dealer. One of Khashoggi's earliest contracts with the Saudi government was for American-made Kenworth trucks, used to haul supplies to the royalist rebels in Yemen. Already by the mid-1960s, Khashoggi had developed an unsavory reputation that made some American firms reluctant to do business with him. Even so, Northrop, Lockheed, and other leading U.S. arms manufacturers relied on Khashoggi to open doors at the Saudi court, letting him take a substantial cut of their contracts with the Saudi government until he became embroiled in a major corruption scandal during the mid-1970s.[105]

THE IDEOLOGICAL ALLIANCE

The commercial ties between the United States and Saudi Arabia were reinforced by ideological affinities. As the Yemeni civil war dragged on, Nasser and Faisal grew ever more openly hostile to each other. In 1964, Faisal and his allies formally deposed Saud and sent him into exile, making Faisal king. Nasser accused Faisal of seizing the throne with American aid, calling him a "client" of the United States and a traitor to the Arab people.[106] Faisal denounced Nasser's doctrine of "Arab socialism" as un-Islamic, declaring that, in Saudi Arabia, "We don't believe in socialism, we don't believe in communism, we don't believe in any doctrine other than Islamic law."[107]

Faisal's attacks on socialism delighted U.S. officials. At a meeting of U.S. national security officials in 1964, Earle Wheeler, the chairman of the Joint Chiefs of Staff, remarked that "Saudi Arabia could prove to be the key to the entire peninsula," and that Faisal's "approach in developing free enterprise," with assistance and military protection from the United States, "will be a good example" to the other states in the region. CIA director John McCone, a founder of the Bechtel-McCone firm whose Marinship operations Faisal visited during World War II, agreed with Wheeler. He praised the "enormous progress" accomplished in Saudi Arabia, "both physically and culturally."[108]

FIGURE 2.2 Government-sponsored demonstration in support of the Saudi regime during the Yemeni civil war and the Saudi confrontation with Gamal Abdel Nasser. Jeddah, April 20, 1963. Jim Pringle/AP/Shutterstock.

Faisal had American help in his ideological battle against Nasser. When he gave a speech in Dammam to denounce Egyptian involvement in Yemen, Aramco declared a holiday, gave its employees the day off, and bused people to the rally. More than thirty thousand attended. The audience included John Horner, the local U.S. consul, who sat next to Faisal and praised the king's "political awareness" and "oratorical gifts."[109] The Saudi regime later organized similar rallies in other cities (figure 2.2).

Faisal's hostility to Nasserism opened the door for a larger U.S. role in shaping Saudi development. For years, many Egyptian advisers had served in the kingdom, working in Saudi government agencies and teaching in Saudi schools, but the regime expelled hundreds of them after the outbreak of the Yemeni civil war. Some of the Egyptians were replaced by advisers from the Ford Foundation, the largest U.S. philanthropic organization, which had been built with the wealth that Henry Ford accumulated by founding the Ford Motor Company. In its overseas operations, it often worked in parallel with the Rockefeller Foundation and the U.S. government. One sign of those close ties was the appointment of McGeorge Bundy, the former U.S. national security adviser, as president of the Ford Foundation in 1966.[110]

The Ford Foundation arrived in the kingdom in October 1964 and began a new program to recruit Saudi officials "who were receptive to change," those "with sparkling eyes and inquiring minds." The foundation sent them abroad for education, training them in American administrative methods and supporting their rise up the bureaucratic ranks after they returned to Saudi Arabia. Ford Foundation leaders congratulated themselves on their creation of a tightly knit network of Saudi officials who cooperated closely with each other, even across the lines that divided different branches of the Saudi bureaucracy—a sort of government within the government. The Ford Foundation worked to bolster the Saudi regime, which it described as a "benevolent monarchy" that ran the country according to the principles of "free enterprise."[111]

The Ford Foundation's actions were in keeping with the strategy that A. J. Meyer had recommended: let philanthropic groups, universities, and other private institutions work closely with the Saudi regime, while the U.S. government maintained greater distance—at least in public. In private, however, U.S. officials made it clear that they were committed to helping Faisal. Assistant Secretary of State Phillips Talbot argued in 1964 that Faisal was the "driving influence" behind Saudi "reform and development," and that the kingdom's stability depended on Faisal remaining in power. Talbot wrote: "United States policy aims at strengthening and preserving the Faysal regime." Three years later, the State Department concluded that, as good anticommunists, "the House of Saud has been one of our best friends in the Middle East." If the royal family lost its grip on the country, "a violent overthrow of the monarchy would, in all likelihood, destroy our position of primacy in Saudi Arabia and open the door to the establishment of Communist bloc presence and influence."[112]

* * *

By the late 1960s, shared commercial interests, anticommunism, and hostility to Nasser had brought the United States and Saudi Arabia closer together. U.S. officials who had once seen the Saudi monarchy as a corrupt, outdated institution now believed it was vital to protecting American interests in the kingdom. This shift came at a time when the United States was not yet importing much oil from Saudi Arabia or elsewhere in the Middle East—with U.S. overseas military forces (especially in Vietnam) as the main exception. Instead, the primary U.S. concern was protecting the large American investment in the Saudi oil industry and keeping the Al Saud as Cold War allies. The U.S. government remained somewhat skeptical about the Saudi monarchy, and would not completely throw in its lot with the Al Saud until the oil boom of the 1970s. Nevertheless, by the late 1960s the U.S.-Saudi partnership was closer than ever before.

There were signs, however, that Saudi Arabia would find it difficult to balance its relationship with the United States and its ties with other Arab countries. The tension between those two goals came into the open during the controversy over the deployment of Jewish personnel as part of Operation Hard Surface in 1963, as well as Faisal's trip to New York three years later. The Saudi-Egyptian feud helped Israel by diverting thousands of Egyptian troops to Yemen, but it also led Cairo and Riyadh to engage in a growing war of words to prove their anti-Zionist credentials. Nasser complained that Faisal was more afraid of the revolutionary Arab forces in Egypt and Yemen than he was of Israel, and argued that Faisal's call for Islamic solidarity was merely a distraction from the need for joint Arab resistance to Zionism. Faisal taunted Nasser that if he really wanted to fight Israel, he should ask the UN to withdraw its peacekeepers from the Sinai, so the Egyptian army could fight Israel instead of the Yemeni royalists.[113] The need for every Arab state to prove its commitment to the fight against Zionism would pose a major challenge to the Saudi regime in 1967, when a new war between Israel and its Arab neighbors threatened to drive a wedge between Washington and Riyadh.

3

IGNITION

L ate on the night of June 6, 1967, King Faisal strode into the Riyadh horse-racing stadium. It was packed with a crowd chanting slogans against Zionism. Israel had just launched a surprise attack against Egypt, Jordan, and Syria, and its forces were advancing on every front. The media in Egypt and other Arab countries blamed the United States and Great Britain for supporting Israel, fueling anger at the United States even in countries like Saudi Arabia that were not directly participating in the war.

Political assemblies were rare in the kingdom. Faisal tried to mobilize his subjects against Nasser during the 1960s, but he retained his traditional distrust of mass politics. The monarchy feared that a more assertive population would threaten its hold on power. The regime never built anything in Riyadh like Tahrir Square in Cairo or Martyrs' Square in Beirut, public spaces where people could gather and demonstrate. The racetrack could hold a large crowd, but it was in al-Malaz, an affluent neighborhood well outside central Riyadh, and was built as a private facility for the royal family. The rally's location reminded Saudis that they could express their political views only on terms set by the regime.[1]

Lower-ranking officials spoke first, promising that the Saudi armed forces were "ready to fight the battle of honor and dignity for the liberation of Palestine" and carry out a "great cleansing" operation against Israel. By the time Faisal reached the podium late in the evening, the crowd was already roaring. "We must teach Zionism and colonialism a lesson," Faisal declared, shouting: "To the jihad, nation of Muhammad, people of Islam!" The king vowed that Saudi Arabia would fight not only Israel but "any country that supports the Israeli Zionist aggression against the Arabs in any way."[2]

When the Saudi government newspaper *Umm al-Qura* reported Faisal's speech, it concealed the rally's chaotic intensity. The crowd became so agitated that Faisal grew alarmed and cut the event short. The Saudi dissident Nasir al-Said wrote that the audience surrounded the king and clutched at his cloak, forcing Faisal's bodyguards to clear a way out of the stadium with their batons. As the king left, the crowd shouted: "Oil, oil . . . cut off oil from America, Britain, and Israel! Faisal, cut off the oil!"[3]

Faisal's conflicted attitude toward the crowd, stoking its anger but recoiling when the listeners took his words to heart, mirrored the kingdom's ambivalent response to the 1967 war. The royal family loudly announced that it was ordering Saudi troops to the front, but it sent only a token force that arrived too late to join the fighting. Saudi Arabia joined an Arab oil embargo against the United States and Britain but secretly sent fuel to the U.S. military, boosted production only a week after the cuts began, and publicly criticized the embargo until the other Arab states agreed to resume oil shipments in September. When Aramco workers went on strike, demanding an oil cutoff, protesting U.S. support for Israel, and destroying property at American facilities in the kingdom, the regime hesitated at first, then sent its security forces to crush the demonstrations.

Today, the 1967 embargo is largely forgotten. The United States and other non-Arab oil producers had enough surplus production capacity to make up the shortfall, ensuring that the cutoff had little impact on individual consumers. The events of 1967, however, paved the way for the oil crisis of the following decade. Behind the scenes, officials in the United States and other oil-importing countries were shaken by the threat of the 1967 embargo. It drove a wedge between America and its Western European allies, who were more dependent on Arab oil and less closely tied to the Anglo-American companies that dominated the global oil market. They scrambled to make their own arrangements with Middle Eastern oil producers, suggesting that any country that nationalized its oil industry could find willing customers in Europe. The resulting strains in the Western alliance, and the accompanying psychological shifts in the global oil market, would have major consequences during the following decade.

The 1967 war also revealed important political tensions in Saudi Arabia. Since the early twentieth century, the Saudi monarchy had built a nation-state at the expense of older forms of political organization like independent towns and Bedouin tribes. By 1967, the Saudi state was much more firmly established than before, but it still had to compete with alternative forms of political identity like Pan-Arabism and Pan-Islamism. The unfinished nature of the Saudi state-building project led the regime to seek American aid, especially in building up its security forces to control the Saudi borders. At the same time, the persistence of other loyalties to the Arab world and to Islam complicated Saudi Arabia's cooperation with the United States.

Riyadh argued that Saudi nationalism under royal leadership was compatible with Arab and Islamic solidarity, but the 1967 war forced a set of painful choices between the kingdom's conflicting political ideals. The Saudi monarchy hoped to weaken Gamal Abdel Nasser's regime in Egypt and preserve its own relationship with the United States, but supporting the collective Arab and Islamic cause meant backing Nasser and opposing Israel's patron, the United States. Those tensions lay behind the apparent contradictions of Saudi policy in 1967, and they led the Saudi regime to equivocate whenever possible, seeking to demonstrate its anti-Zionist credentials even as it continued to work with the United States.

The United States, too, had an ambivalent attitude toward Saudi Arabia. U.S. officials acknowledged the importance of Saudi oil and the profits that it represented, and they valued the Saudi regime as a reliable anticommunist partner. They worried, however, that the Saudi government was spending too much money on its military, buying weapons systems it did not need and could not maintain, tolerating unseemly levels of corruption, and failing to develop a modern bureaucracy. The United States doubted the staying power of the Saudi monarchy, particularly since no one knew how much longer the aging King Faisal would remain on the throne. U.S.

leaders were confident, however, that even a revolutionary Saudi regime would continue to sell oil to any willing buyer. The survival of the royal family was not necessary to guarantee the continued flow of petroleum to the United States and its allies. That attitude would change dramatically after the balance of power in the global oil market shifted in the early 1970s. The late 1960s were the last period when U.S.-Saudi relations were not a leading priority for American policy in the Middle East, but they were also a harbinger of the changes to come.

THE 1967 WAR AND OIL EMBARGO

As Arab-Israeli tensions escalated during the late spring and early summer of 1967, Iraq invited the oil ministers of other Arab countries to a conference in Baghdad. Together they would develop a common oil policy to support the frontline states, led by Egypt, that were on the verge of war with Israel. The ministers would need to overcome a deep ideological rift between Saudi Arabia and Arab nationalist states like Iraq and Egypt. Saudi Arabia and Egypt had been waging a proxy war in Yemen for the last half decade. Egypt's president Gamal Abdel Nasser portrayed Faisal as an American puppet, while Faisal accused Nasser of abandoning Islam and aligning Egypt with the atheist Soviet Union.[4] Despite such divisions, the ideal of Arab unity remained a powerful force in Arab politics. When Aramco's vice president Robert Brougham asked the Saudi oil minister Ahmed Zaki Yamani why Saudi Arabia would support Egypt, its bitter rival, Yamani replied: "We are all Arabs."[5] Yamani accepted the Iraqi invitation and attended the oil ministers' conference in Baghdad on June 4, while Faisal promised that in the event of war, Saudi Arabia would be "at the forefront of her Arab sisters in the use of all economic weapons in the battle, including oil."[6]

The Saudi government also promised that Saudi Arabia would send its armed forces to fight Israel. Even before the war began, Faisal announced that he was mobilizing the kingdom's army. At the June 6 rally at the Riyadh racetrack, the king and other Saudi leaders pledged that their armed forces were ready to serve "at the forefront of the fighting ranks on the bor-der" with the Jewish state. *Umm al-Qura* printed a series of cables that military officers, tribal sheikhs, and other notables sent to Faisal, vowing to fight "under your guidance and the banner of Islam" so they could liber-ate "beloved Palestine."[7]

The reality was less impressive than the rhetoric. Saudi Arabia deployed only a single brigade to the war. It was sent to southern Jordan, far from the fighting, where it remained for the next several years. U.S. intelligence reported that while the deployment gave the Saudi military "some sense of participation in the struggle with Israel," it was merely a token act. The CIA even suggested that the royal family wanted its troops in Jordan because it doubted their loyalty. If they were out of the country, they were too far away to carry out a coup.[8]

Not all Saudis were willing to wait for their government to act against the United States. As the rally participants dispersed late at night after Faisal's June 6 speech, some of them smashed the windows of a local Ar-amco office. The following day, Aramco workers in the Eastern Province walked off the job. Students tried to prevent the loading of U.S. Navy tank-ers at the port of Ras Tanura, while striking workers and other local resi-dents protested at the offices of Aramco, the U.S. consulate, the U.S. Mili-tary Training Mission, Trans World Airlines (TWA), and other American institutions. The protesters targeted symbols of the privileged status enjoyed by Americans in the kingdom, taking down the U.S. flag at the Dhahran consulate and running up a Saudi flag instead. They also saw American cars as emblems of U.S. power, smashing the cars' windows, lighting the vehi-cles on fire, and vandalizing a local Chevrolet agency.[9]

The protests were a reminder of the inequality within Saudi Arabia. The Shia of the Eastern Province received only a small share of the region's oil wealth and suffered from discrimination by the Wahhabi elites in Najd. They were often at the forefront of opposition activity in the kingdom. Other dissidents included non-Saudi Arabs in the local workforce, who lacked the benefits of Saudi citizenship. Both Aramco and the Saudi government tried to discredit the opposition by stressing the presence of foreigners in its ranks. Aramco pointedly noted that the Eastern Province protesters in June 1967 included workers from Yemen, Syria, Lebanon, and elsewhere.[10]

During the demonstrations at the Aramco compound, U.S. employees sheltered in a gymnasium while the company demanded help from the Saudi government. Aramco officials and American diplomats were disturbed that, at first, Saudi security forces were nowhere to be found. They suspected that some Saudi military and police officers were involved in the protests themselves. Hoping to defuse public anger, Aramco asked Yamani to denounce the rumors that the United States and Britain were helping Israel in the war, but Yamani refused to make such a statement.[11] Eventually police arrived, and their commander dispersed the demonstrators on the Aramco compound by firing a few shots into the air. On June 9, four days into the war, the regime deployed the Saudi National Guard, its most trusted internal security force, recruited from Bedouin tribes known for their loyalty to the monarchy. By that point, the protests had already died down, but the National Guard troops took positions around the Aramco facilities to ensure they were not targeted again. Both governments downplayed the incident to preserve their relationship. The Saudi government assured the United States that the king was "most apologetic," and that the leading protesters had been thrown in prison. President Lyndon Johnson wrote to Faisal and expressed concern about the "mob action" in the kingdom, but he promised not to embarrass Faisal by drawing further attention to the issue.[12]

In its oil policy, the Saudi government walked a fine line between solidarity with its fellow Arabs and its relationship with the United States. After the war began, Saudi Arabia announced that it was cutting its oil production and stopping exports to the United States and Great Britain.[13] At the same time, Riyadh privately downplayed its confrontation with the United States, claiming that it was only joining the embargo to placate its own people. The U.S. ambassador Hermann Eilts remembered Faisal telling the United States: "I don't want to do this, but I have to because of domestic pressures."[14] A Venezuelan official confided that "from the earliest days of the Arab-Israeli crisis, the Saudis openly told the diplomatic corps," including the Venezuelan ambassador to the kingdom, "that of course they would permit oil shipments to go to the West, despite the announced embargo."[15]

On June 11, Yamani stage-managed a confrontation with Aramco to bolster his Arab nationalist credentials. An Iraqi delegation was in the kingdom to urge harsh measures against U.S. oil interests, including nationalization. Yamani organized a meeting with the Iraqi and Kuwaiti oil ministers and a group of Aramco executives and U.S. diplomats. A day in advance, Yamani warned Brougham that, in front of the Iraqi minister, Yamani would castigate the United States for supporting Israel. Yamani listed the points that Brougham should make in response, including offering to use Aramco's influence in the United States to plead on the Arabs' behalf. After the meeting took place, an impressed Brougham reported that it had gone almost exactly according to Yamani's script.[16]

The Saudi government wanted to smooth over its disagreement with the United States partly because the United States was not yet very vulnerable to a cutoff of foreign oil. The domestic American oil industry still had ample surplus production capacity it could tap to cover the deficit. Non-Arab oil producers, especially Venezuela and Iran, were also eager to increase their own production and take market share from the Arabs. The embargo forced the oil companies to carry out a complicated rearrangement of oil shipments around the world, but the United States and other importers weathered the shortfall without any real hardship for individual consumers. Unless they followed the news closely, Americans would never have known that an embargo was under way.[17]

The biggest danger to the United States was not the loss of oil for civilian use but an interruption to U.S. armed forces overseas. During the Vietnam War, American planes, ships, and tanks burned fuel at a stupendous rate. Half of the total tonnage of U.S. military supplies shipped to Southeast Asia consisted of petroleum products, and almost all that oil came from Saudi Arabia and Bahrain. Three-quarters of the production of the Saudi refinery at Ras Tanura went to the U.S. Navy. If Faisal had wanted to put maximum pressure on the United States, he could have cut off oil sales to the Pentagon. Saudi Arabia, though, prioritized its alliance with Washington over solidarity with its fellow Arabs. Faisal allowed Aramco to keep supplying the U.S. military as long as the arrangement was kept secret. As part of the deal, Saudi oil barges resupplied U.S. Navy vessels in the Red

Sea during the middle of the night so they would remain unseen. The Pentagon breathed a sigh of relief, noting that even with Saudi cooperation, the 1967 war had "posed the most severe test of the DoD [Department of Defense] petroleum system in recent years." The military's oil supply network was "delicately balanced" and could not tolerate "prolonged interruptions." Only the quick resolution of the 1967 crisis prevented a real disruption of the American war effort in Vietnam.[18]

The embargo and production cuts meant a serious loss of revenue for Saudi Arabia, and the kingdom waited only a week before raising its production levels again.[19] The kingdom initially retained its ban on direct shipments to the United States and Great Britain. By the end of June, however, the Saudi oil minister Ahmed Zaki Yamani was publicly campaigning to resume sales to those countries. He argued that by depriving the Arab oil producers of badly needed earnings, the embargo was hurting them more than it was hurting the United States. Arab nationalist states like Iraq and Syria denounced Yamani's proposal and accused him of bowing to American pressure.[20]

Saudi Arabia was reluctant to lift the embargo without support from the other leading Arab countries, which it finally obtained at the end of August during a conference of Arab leaders in Khartoum.[21] Syria refused to go along, but Egypt and Jordan both gave their blessing. Saudi Arabia, in turn, offered them hundreds of millions of dollars of financial aid, giving Faisal the political cover he needed to resume oil shipments. The king cynically told an American diplomat that he saw the subsidies as "a tax the Kingdom was paying to avoid a halt in production."[22]

Egypt's new financial dependence on Saudi Arabia marked a reversal in fortunes between the two countries. Between the mid-1950s and mid-1960s, Nasser was by far the most powerful leader in the Arab world. Egypt's crushing defeat by Israel in 1967, however, badly damaged Nasser's authority. Meeting with Ambassador Eilts on June 9, the Saudi foreign minister Omar Saqqaf did not bother hiding his satisfaction. Saqqaf gloated that there was a "good chance Nasser is finished" and had lost his prestige, "hopefully for good."[23] Egypt's defeat meant an expensive program to rebuild its military, reinforcing its need for Saudi aid and giving the kingdom more leverage over its old rival. At the Khartoum Conference, Nasser not only approved the end of the oil embargo but also agreed to withdraw Egyptian forces from Yemen, handing Saudi Arabia a victory it had been seeking for years.[24]

THE CONSEQUENCES OF THE EMBARGO

Saudi leftists and Arab nationalists were dismayed by the royal family's performance during the 1967 war. The former Saudi oil minister Abdullah Tariki, exiled to Beirut after being dismissed by Faisal in 1962, was one of the most prominent critics. He argued that "right-wing Arabs" like the Saudi royal family were so subservient to the West that they betrayed their Arab brothers. The Arabs would be unable to defend themselves and liberate Palestine, Tariki explained, until they nationalized their oil industry, seized control of Aramco and other foreign companies, and learned to use oil as an "economic and political weapon."[25] Nasir al-Said was even more disgusted with the Saudi royal family, accusing them of sacrificing the Arab cause for their own interests, conspiring with Israel to start the 1967 war as a way to weaken Nasser, and shipping oil to the U.S. military while it protected the Jewish state.[26]

Most U.S. policymakers agreed with Tariki and al-Said that 1967 was a major defeat for the Arab oil producers. They saw the embargo's failure as proof that the "oil weapon" was overrated. For the next several years, until conditions in the global oil market changed during the early 1970s, U.S. officials generally assumed that a targeted embargo would be useless. They believed that as in 1967, the oil companies could simply redirect non-Arab oil to the United States while sending Arab oil to other importers. A complete halt of Arab production would be more serious but could not be maintained for long, since the Arabs would never be able to endure the resulting loss of revenue. U.S. officials counted on the Arab world remaining split between nationalists and conservatives, preventing joint action against the United States.[27]

The events of 1967, however, should not have been so easily dismissed. They were a prelude to the coming upheaval in the global oil market. Even an unsuccessful Arab embargo was enough to reveal deep strains between the major oil-consuming nations. Three related factors drove a wedge between the United States and the nations of Western Europe. First, the Europeans were more dependent on Arab oil than the United States and had more to fear from a cutoff. Second, the Middle Eastern oil industry was dominated by the "Seven Sisters," the largest Anglo-American companies, while continental European competitors were mostly excluded from the richest oil-producing areas. Many Europeans distrusted the Seven Sisters, while the companies, and their home governments in Washington and London, feared that France and other European countries would try to expand their involvement in the Middle East at the expense of the Anglo-American corporations. And third, France and other European countries began distancing themselves from Israel and improving their relations with the Arab world during the late 1960s, just as Washington was increasing its own support for the Jewish state.

Those divisions came into view in 1967. During the prelude to the war, Nasser blockaded Israeli shipping in the Strait of Tiran. The Johnson administration proposed an international flotilla to challenge the blockade, but the Pentagon official Townsend Hoopes warned that France, Britain, and Canada were all reluctant to join the United States. The prospect of Arab retaliation frightened them. Britain, for example, worried about losing its oil revenues and the large Saudi and Kuwaiti deposits in London's financial markets. Later, when the United States tried to organize a joint response to the embargo, both France and West Germany balked. They feared that associating themselves with the United States would invite Arab retaliation and threaten their access to oil. Paris and Bonn came on board in July, but their delay in joining a united consumer front signaled that the U.S.-European alliance might crack under the pressure of a cutoff as each nation scrambled to secure its own supplies.[28] Such doubts would later haunt Secretary of State Henry Kissinger and other U.S. leaders during the 1973–1974 embargo.

The fragility of the consumer alliance became apparent to the Arab oil producers in 1967, giving them a hint of their potential long-term power even as their embargo failed in the short term. France tried to exploit the crisis to advance its own interests at the expense of the United States and Great Britain. The prominent American columnist Joseph Alsop accused two leading French oil companies of secretly offering to work with the Arab producers if they nationalized the operations of the Anglo-American companies. The French government indignantly denied Alsop's claims. In a secret briefing, however, the CIA director John McCone confirmed that Alsop was right. The French, along with other European companies and governments, were "making carefully guarded overtures to all of the oil-producing Arab countries, pointing out that should the latter be forced to take over American oil properties, they can depend on the Europeans for assistance." McCone warned that the situation was very different from the Iranian nationalization crisis of 1951–1953, when the Seven Sisters had organized an effective boycott against Iran. Now the consumers were too fragmented to maintain a united front, and any nation that nationalized its oil could easily find assistance from France, Italy, and other nations looking to expand their access to crude supplies.[29]

That realization set the stage for the producers to take more control over their resources in the 1970s. On July 2, 1967, Yamani told Brougham that he had once thought Aramco might keep its concession in Saudi Arabia for another "thirty odd years." The 1967 war and U.S. support for Israel, however, had dramatically accelerated that timetable. Yamani said that Aramco now had "closer to four years."[30] Yamani's prediction was not far off. The Saudi government would take partial ownership of Aramco in 1972, leading to complete nationalization at the beginning of the 1980s.

The events of June 1967 had a profound, but complicated, impact on later Saudi foreign policy. The Saudi government learned that while the oil consumers were not as united as they once were, conditions were not yet ripe for an open confrontation. Saudi Arabia also learned that once it declared an embargo in alliance with other Arab states, it would not be able to resume oil shipments unilaterally without appearing to betray the Arab cause. As a result, Riyadh would be more cautious about declaring an embargo in the future. The kingdom, however, had been reminded of the political risks involved if it appeared to be standing on the sidelines while other Arab nations led the fight against Israel. Those contradictory forces would pull Saudi Arabia in opposite directions during the next Arab-Israeli war in 1973, leading to a long period of indecision before the kingdom once again cut off its oil exports to the United States.

DEFENDING THE BORDERS OF ISLAM

While the Saudi retreat on the embargo in 1967 seemed to prove that the kingdom would choose its relationship with the United States over solidarity with its fellow Arabs, the war also fueled Saudi opposition to Zionism and exacerbated Saudi tensions with the United States. Israel's conquests included East Jerusalem, the home of the Temple Mount, the Al-Aqsa Mosque, and the Dome of the Rock. King Faisal, who carefully cultivated his image as a defender of Islam, protested the loss of the Muslim holy sites. On June 13, 1967, only three days after the fighting ended, Faisal asked the United States to force Israel to give up the territory it had just seized. He later indicated that he was open to some adjustment of Israel's borders if neighboring states like Jordan agreed, but Faisal remained inflexible on the question of Jerusalem. The king promised that Saudi Arabia would use any means necessary to block a peace treaty that failed to restore full Arab control over the holy sites. "Even if Jordan and Egypt agree, we will not," Faisal told a U.S. envoy. "We will declare Jihad. We may die, but it will be with honor."[31]

Some U.S. officials (especially diplomats posted to the Arab world, the so-called Arabists), along with the international oil companies that had the most to lose in the event of a U.S.-Saudi split, had long believed that the United States should limit its support for Israel in order to preserve ties with Saudi Arabia and the rest of the Arab world. They were unable to sway senior policymakers, however, and U.S. policy shifted toward Israel after 1967. The war dramatically boosted Israel's reputation in the United States. Many Americans came to admire Israel as a fighting democracy that knew how to win quick, decisive victories, a sharp contrast with the United States during the Vietnam War. Evangelical Christians also increasingly supported Israel, seeing its victories as the miraculous fulfillment of biblical prophecies that described the return of the Jews to the Holy Land. By contrast, popular American stereotypes stressed Arab fanaticism and military incompetence.[32]

U.S. foreign policy mirrored the shift in public opinion. The 1967 war seemed to prove Israel's value as a Cold War ally, a nation with the strength to defeat Soviet-armed states like Egypt and Syria. Encouraged by pro-Israel members of Congress like Senators Henry "Scoop" Jackson (D-WA) and Jacob Javits (R-NY), the U.S. government increased its support for Israel. Washington tacitly accepted Israeli occupation of the territories conquered in 1967, overlooked Israel's secret nuclear program, and began offering Israel more sophisticated weapons. The most controversial arms deal involved the F-4 Phantom, a state-of-the-art aircraft that formed the backbone of America's own fighter squadrons. Previous U.S. administrations had always refused Israeli requests for such advanced weapons, but after 1967 that policy of restraint was abandoned. The outgoing Johnson administration approved the sale over fierce Arab objections, and the first Phantoms were delivered to Israel in September 1969. More followed over the next several years.[33]

Saudi Arabia joined the rest of the Arab world in protesting U.S. arms sales to Israel. In 1970, the minister of defense Prince Sultan warned that the sales were provoking popular fury against the Saudi regime. Sultan asked the U.S. ambassador if he truly understood the "depth of anti-American feeling in this country." The only reason such anti-Americanism was not more visible, Sultan explained, was because the regime was so quick to suppress it. The anger of the Saudi people was like "embers under the coals" that could flare up at any time.[34] Sultan came close to invoking the unspoken bargain the Al Saud offered the United States: *We protect you by keeping our own people in check. If we fall, you will regret it.*

U.S. diplomats in Saudi Arabia privately agreed with Sultan. Immediately after the 1967 war, the U.S. ambassador reported that many Saudis believed the United States had helped Israel defeat the Arabs.[35] A 1969 National Security Council (NSC) study warned that the Saudi-U.S. relationship was close but fragile, since it depended "largely on the personal disposition of King Faisal, a handful of senior officials, various public security agencies, and public media systems." Outside the highest levels of government, "public sentiment opposes U.S. and is probably simply biding its time to show this."[36] A year later, the embassy noted the rising anger against the United States in Saudi Arabia, caused in part by the highly publicized U.S. arms sales to Israel. Shouted insults, minor physical confrontations, and other kinds of harassment directed against Americans were becoming more common, and they were making "an already jittery American community" even more nervous about its safety.[37]

Saudi leaders often told American officials that they were constrained by popular opinion. Arab sentiment both inside and outside the kingdom was so anti-Zionist, they explained, that even if they wanted to take a more moderate line on Israel, they could not defy their own people. The Saudi government, though, was not merely a passive follower of public opinion. It actively encouraged popular anger against Israel.

One U.S. diplomat gently teased Faisal that while the Jeddah book market was constrained by strict government censorship, readers had their pick of anti-Semitic literature. He mentioned that the *Protocols of the Elders of Zion*, an infamous forgery purporting to describe a Jewish plot to control the world, was available in multiple languages. Faisal readily admitted that his government was distributing the *Protocols*. The world, he explained, needed to be alerted to the enormity of the Zionist threat.[38] Another senior U.S. diplomat remembered that Faisal had a bookshelf filled with copies of the *Protocols* outside his office so every visitor could take one, embarrassing the embassy whenever members of Congress came to see the king.[39]

Saudi anti-Zionism reached beyond the kingdom's borders. Riyadh sponsored an array of global Islamic institutions, like the Muslim World League (MWL), that acted as conduits for Saudi influence. During Faisal's rivalry with Nasser in the mid-1960s, the king promoted Islamic solidarity as an alternative to secular Arab nationalism. Immediately after the 1967 war, the MWL declared that Muslims around the world had a religious duty to liberate Jerusalem from Israeli occupation.[40] Over the next several years, the MWL kept up a regular stream of resolutions and publications denouncing Israel. Its secretary-general, the veteran Saudi intellectual and civil servant Mohammed Sorour al-Sabban, wrote an open letter to Lyndon Johnson warning that U.S. support for the Jewish state was "a serious threat to American interests in the Islamic world" and was turning the region into "a scene of wars and bloody strife."[41]

In 1969, Faisal sponsored a new group called the Organization of the Islamic Conference to coordinate the foreign policies of all Muslim states. He argued that only a united Muslim world could wrest Jerusalem from Israel's grip and ensure the safety of the Muslim holy places. Faisal denounced "peaceful solutions" to the Arab-Israeli conflict as nothing but a "mirage." Further negotiations and appeals to international law would be pointless, according to the king, since Israel was "contemptuous of all UN resolutions" and respected only "the logic of force."[42]

Faisal bolstered those efforts with his own global travels. In 1970 he toured Malaysia, Indonesia, and Afghanistan. Faisal appealed to Muslims in those countries to fight communism and Zionism, which he described as parts of a vast conspiracy to attack Islam.[43] Public diplomacy was a way for Saudi Arabia to project its influence abroad, despite its lack of large military forces and other traditional instruments of power. Faisal's strategy allowed the kingdom to exploit the kinds of power it did have, like the religious prestige that came with control over the holy cities of Mecca and Medina. In the long run, however, that strategy had serious costs. By portraying compromise with Zionism as a betrayal of Islam, the Saudi government encouraged forces that would later threaten the monarchy itself. It also exacerbated its great challenge: how to retain popular support while simultaneously keeping its partnership with Israel's protector, the United States.

DEFENDING THE BORDERS OF THE KINGDOM

Despite American support for Israel, the Saudi regime sought American help against communism and left-wing Arab nationalism. The U.S. ambassador Hermann Eilts reported in January 1970 that "the Saudis are currently obsessed" with the fear of "encirclement by leftist states, all of which they regard as Soviet catspaws." That category included Egypt, Syria, Iraq, North and South Yemen, Sudan, and Somalia, surrounding the kingdom on three sides. In October 1970, Eilts's successor, Nicholas Thacher, commented that Saudi fears of communism gave the Saudi regime "a heightened awareness" of its "dependence on the United States, in the final analysis, for its own external security."[44]

Riyadh wanted to acquire American weapons, but the United States was not always willing to oblige. Sultan asked the United States to sell advanced F-4 Phantom jets to Saudi Arabia, while he simultaneously denounced the sale of the same aircraft to Israel. U.S. officials balked at the idea. They warned that the Phantom was too expensive for Saudi Arabia, that the Saudis did not have the technical capability to maintain such sophisticated aircraft, and that any such sale would arouse fierce opposition from the Israeli government and its allies in Washington. Saudi Arabia was not considered important enough to merit the sale of first-rate American arms. For the time being, the kingdom was forced to buy the Northrop F-5, a smaller, cheaper American fighter intended for sale to developing countries.[45] In addition to combat aircraft, the Saudi government had a long shopping list of other weapons and American training and advice for nearly every branch of the Saudi military. The United States was rarely willing to meet those requests in full.

Saudi arms deals with the United States served political as well as military purposes. By demonstrating American support for the kingdom, they suggested that potential aggressors against Saudi Arabia would risk American retaliation. They also boosted the kingdom's prestige by proving its ability to defend its remote frontier areas. After the British withdrew from the South Yemeni protectorate of Aden in 1967, a Marxist regime—the People's Democratic Republic of Yemen (PDRY)—rose to power. In November 1969, PDRY troops crossed the Saudi border and seized control of the village of Wadiah, killing several members of the Saudi Frontier Forces. A few days later, the Saudi military retook Wadiah with air support from U.S.-made F-86 aircraft. Wadiah was a tiny place devoid of any great economic or strategic significance. The real importance of the battle was symbolic. A defeat could have embarrassed Riyadh and reinforced the impact of South Yemeni propaganda, inspiring left-wing dissidents at home. The Battle of Wadiah was a chance for the Al Saud to demonstrate their ability to project power to the furthest reaches of their kingdom.[46]

If Saudi Arabia was determined to enforce its own sovereignty, it was less fastidious about the sovereignty of South Yemen. The Saudi government began funding and arming South Yemeni tribesmen and anti-government exiles, paying them to launch raids into the PDRY and overthrow the regime in Aden. The raids made the South Yemeni countryside a more chaotic place, but they never came close to toppling the PDRY. They also provoked a major increase in Soviet aid to South Yemen. Although it did not succeed, the Saudi effort to undermine the PDRY illustrated one of the kingdom's favorite strategies: using oil revenues to fund a tribal in-surgency, the sort of approach that the kingdom had already used in North Yemen in the 1960s and would later employ in Afghanistan against the Soviet Union in the 1980s.[47]

The Saudi regime believed that it had to prove its ability to defend its borders because they were still partly undefined, especially to the south and east. In some cases, political disputes had blocked agreement—even with fellow Gulf monarchies like Abu Dhabi. The de facto boundaries had been imposed from outside by imperial powers, especially Great Brit-ain, and had never been officially accepted by the kingdom. The land-scape also played a role. The Saudi boundary with South Yemen and Oman ran through the vast Rub al-Khali desert. The difficulty of survey-ing such terrain, combined with the fact that it was largely uninhabited and held few resources of any importance, meant that the countries on both sides had never bothered to draw a precise border. Maps often left those frontiers blank or arbitrarily drew a vague dotted line through the empty spaces (figure 3.1).

By the late twentieth century, however, land that was once considered worthless might now hold important petroleum resources. Saudi Arabia was alarmed to learn that Abu Dhabi was permitting oil exploration near a dis-puted part of the Gulf coast.[48] The kingdom wanted the territory for itself, planning to use it for a pipeline from the newly discovered Shaybah oil field to the Gulf.[49] When Saudi Arabia and Abu Dhabi held talks on their bor-der dispute, the delegations were led not by their foreign ministers but by their oil ministers.[50] The same was true of the agreement that partitioned the neutral zone between Saudi Arabia and Kuwait.[51]

Oil provided not only an incentive to control distant places but also the ability to reach them. Remote desert areas could now be crossed by four-wheel-drive vehicles and aircraft, giving new opportunities to smugglers and immigrants as well as the states trying to stop them. Beginning in the 1920s, the United States had developed its own Border Patrol into a highly motorized police force. Wanting to benefit from American expertise in that field, Saudi Arabia sought U.S. training and equipment for the royal Fron-tier Forces and Coast Guard to control movement across the kingdom's borders.[52]

FIGURE 3.1 The undefined frontiers of Saudi Arabia, as seen on a U.S. Central Intelligence Agency (CIA) map from the mid-1960s. The southern and eastern borders are unmarked, the northern borders include large neutral zones (N.Z.), and even the borders that *are* shown come with the disclaimer: "Boundary representation is not necessarily authoritative." Courtesy of the CIA Freedom of Information Act Electronic Reading Room.

The Saudi military buildup was hindered by the regime's unwillingness to let its armed forces become too powerful. The royal family was always more concerned about an internal coup than an external invasion. It remembered that other Arab monarchies in Egypt, Iraq, Yemen, and Libya had fallen to their own military officers rather than to foreign attackers. To prevent coup plotters from cooperating, the Saudi government deliberately fragmented its armed forces; some units were under the Ministry of Defense and Aviation, while others were with the National Guard or the Ministry of the Interior. These different organizations had separate chains of command and could not easily work with one another. In fact, the National Guard was expected to fight the regular army in the event of a coup. Military units were scattered around the country and barred from entering major cities like Riyadh. The monarchy was so determined to hamstring its armed forces that it often refused to issue them with live ammunition and fuel for their vehicles, distributing those supplies only during emergencies. Those measures could have spelled disaster in any fight with a competent foreign adversary, suggesting the overwhelming priority that Riyadh placed on coup-proofing measures even at the expense of military readiness.[53]

As a result, Saudi requests for advanced American arms were about internal politics as much as national defense. Expensive, high-technology weapons systems like fighter aircraft posed a smaller risk of a military coup compared with large groups of professional soldiers. The fragmentation of the Saudi military, with the regular army and air force under Sultan's command, the National Guard under Abdullah, and the Interior Ministry forces under Fahd, also gave each of the princes an incentive to seek arms contracts that would expand their budget, increase their prestige, and provide jobs for their supporters. As minister of defense and aviation, for example, Sultan distributed coveted fighter pilot jobs to members of the royal family. They became the "flying princes," an important base of support for Sultan and his air force. The most famous of them, Sultan's own son Bandar, later became ambassador to the United States and head of Saudi intelligence.[54]

THE MONARCHY'S UNCERTAIN FUTURE

The kingdom's revenues were not big enough to match its military ambitions. The subsidies to Egypt and Jordan beginning in 1967 strained the kingdom's finances, forcing the government to impose budget cuts and a temporary "jihad tax."[55] The move was highly unusual; the kingdom usually relied on oil revenues instead of taxing its own people. By arguing that paying the new tax was a kind of jihad, the Saudi government advertised its solidarity with other Muslim countries and reassured Saudis that their financial sacrifice was for an important cause.

Even with the jihad tax, the U.S. embassy predicted a large Saudi government deficit for 1970 and noted Riyadh's struggles "to meet its mounting defense costs in an era of relative recession and budget stringencies."[56] To fill the gap, the interior minister Prince Fahd asked the United States to fund the expansion of the navy, the Coast Guard, and the Frontier Forces, while deferring payment on some equipment already purchased by the kingdom.[57] Direct U.S. aid to Saudi Arabia, however, was hard to sell to Congress. Critics objected that the kingdom had plenty of money, especially considering that it was subsidizing other Arab countries while they rebuilt their militaries to face Israel. When a U.S. military official told Rep. Leonard Farbstein (D-NY) that the United States was training Saudi military officers, Farbstein asked sarcastically: "Saudi Arabia is a pretty rich country, is it not?" He could not understand why any kingdom "where the head of the government can spend money as profligately as he does" would need the American taxpayer to cover its military costs.[58] Mindful of such criticism, the Nixon administration arranged for the U.S. Export-Import Bank to offer some credit to Saudi Arabia, but deflected Fahd's request for more direct assistance.[59]

U.S. policymakers worried that Saudi Arabia was spending too much on its military. A 1969 U.S. intelligence report concluded that "there is no immediate serious external threat to Saudi Arabia." In fact, the monarchy's preoccupation with foreign policy was diverting its attention from another and potentially more important problem: "the internal dissident threat" posed by "leftist revolutionaries."[60] As the kingdom spent more money on arms, it had less for economic development. In 1969–1970, the Saudi defense budget rose by 20 percent to more than $500 million, almost 40 percent of the total government budget, while development spending fell 7 percent to $357 million.[61] Concerned by the trend, the United States sent a team to study the kingdom's defense requirements. The team leader, General Osmund Leahy of the U.S. Army, reported that "Saudi military expansion appetites" needed a "rather severe whittling down." U.S. officials had to convince Saudi Arabia "that it is poorer than its military planners realize."[62]

That belief was shared by civilian leaders in the Saudi government itself. Anwar Ali, the head of the Saudi Arabian Monetary Agency (SAMA), the Saudi central bank, privately met Ambassador Thacher and warned that the kingdom was already having trouble paying its bills. Going over the kingdom's recent weapons purchases and military spending plans, Ali told Thacher that he just "could not understand why [Saudi Arabia] needed all this." Ali suggested that in exchange for debt relief, the United States should force Riyadh "to sharply limit future defense spending."[63] It was remarkable to see a Saudi official asking the United States to restrain his own government. Ali, though, probably thought he had no choice. His political position was tenuous; he was a nonroyal and a foreigner, having moved to the kingdom from Pakistan. The biggest arms requests were coming from senior princes like Sultan and Fahd, who were far too powerful for Ali to confront directly. Instead, he tried to go around them by meeting directly with Thacher. Although U.S. officials sympathized with such concerns, they never seriously tried to limit Saudi defense spending. When forced to choose, they always prioritized their relationships with the royal family over those with commoner technocrats like Ali.

That attitude seemed remarkably shortsighted when set next to the U.S. government's own assessments of the Saudi political situation. The State Department reported that "corruption, some of it in high places, is a major problem."[64] Some of the most senior Saudi leaders were notorious for their willingness to take bribes and skim money from state contracts under their supervision. Public anger at government mismanagement was growing. Ambassador Eilts wrote: "The growing middle class of educated 'elite,' and even the proliferating urban 'mass,' chafe at the lack of social liberalization, the stagnation of domestic political reform, the corruption in high places, the increasingly 'police state' nature of the Kingdom, and its isolation from the mainstream of modern Arab society." He concluded that the "present domestic discontent, inflamed by outside political ideologies, and the regime's inept reaction to it, do not augur well for the long range survival prospects of the present ruling order."[65]

The Saudi regime responded to popular dissent by cracking down on its political opponents. After it learned of a possible coup plot in mid-1969, the royal family's confidence was shaken, and U.S. officials concluded that it was more worried about the "incipient internal security threat than it cares to admit." The regime arrested six hundred suspected dissidents.[66] They were mostly army and police officers, but they also included civilians like Salih Ambah, the dean of the College of Petroleum and Minerals in Dhahran. Ambah disappeared into the Saudi prison system in 1970 and was not seen again until he was released without explanation in 1972. Ambah was a close associate of the oil minister Ahmed Zaki Yamani. Rumors suggested that Yamani himself might be taken by the secret police, since he was thought to have reformist views and had recruited leftist teachers to work in the kingdom. An Aramco representative found Yamani "frantic" at the possibility, canceling his scheduled meetings and scrambling to shore up his political position.[67] In the end, Yamani was not arrested, but the fact that even one of the most prominent Saudi officials was terrified of falling into the hands of the secret police vividly demonstrated the climate of fear in Saudi Arabia.

Some U.S. officials worried that the regime was losing its grip on the country, but those concerns were less widespread than during the Saudi-Egyptian confrontation of the early 1960s. The United States believed that Faisal's campaign of repression was effective. The State Department reported that the wave of arrests beginning in 1969 had neutralized the opposition.[68] The United States was also more committed to the survival of the monarchy, fearing what might come after Faisal left the scene. A 1970 National Intelligence Estimate concluded: "If the ruling family were overthrown, the successor regime almost certainly would be radical, militantly anti-Israeli, and markedly anti-American."[69]

* * *

By the end of the 1960s, the Saudi government had outlasted the Nasserist challenge. Egypt's crushing defeat by Israel in 1967 weakened Saudi Arabia's most important rival. Egypt became dependent on Saudi financial aid, withdrew its army from Yemen, and no longer threatened to topple the Saudi monarchy. Nasser's death in September 1970 was another stroke of good luck for King Faisal, as Nasser's successor, Anwar Sadat, distanced Egypt from the Soviet Union, retreated from Nasser's socialist economic policies, and strengthened Egyptian ties with Saudi Arabia.

Saudi power, however, was still limited. The subsidies to Egypt strained the Saudi budget, and the kingdom was forced to institute unpopular new taxes to make up the difference. The Saudi military was so weak that the regime feared even third-rate adversaries like the Marxist regime in South Yemen. The royal family was so uncertain of its soldiers' loyalty that it refused to issue them fuel and ammunition except during emergencies. Saudi Arabia compensated for its weakness by seeking U.S. support, including arms sales and the implicit promise of protection against the kingdom's neighbors. Despite continued disagreement over Israel, the Saudi government remained committed to its alliance with the United States, and even undermined its own oil embargo in 1967 by shipping oil to the U.S. military. Individual Saudi leaders tried to use American resources to enhance their own power. Fahd, Sultan, and others sought large purchases of American arms to expand the size and budget of the ministries they controlled, while the central banker Anwar Ali asked the United States to restrain his colleagues' spending.

U.S. officials abandoned many of their earlier doubts about the Saudi regime. They saw it as an ally against communism and Arab nationalism, and an important source of profits for the U.S. oil industry. Saudi Arabia was still, however, not a high priority for the most senior U.S. policymakers. They paid little attention to events in the Persian Gulf, which they saw as a strategic backwater compared with the Cold War battlegrounds of Europe and East Asia. They were also confident that since the world oil market remained in surplus, political instability in Saudi Arabia posed no real threat to the world's oil supplies. No matter who ruled in Riyadh, U.S. leaders assumed, Saudi Arabia would keep the oil flowing because it needed money even more than consumers needed oil. As the CIA reported in 1969, no "Saudi regime—even a revolutionary one—would be willing to risk oil revenues in an attempt to embargo the U.S."[70] Beginning in 1970, however, that optimistic view would be threatened by a remarkable transformation of the global oil market, one that would dramatically alter the relationship between Saudi Arabia and the United States.

4

MACHINES IN MOTION

n February 1973, King Faisal spoke in Jeddah. It was the city his father, Abdulaziz, had conquered half a century before, and where Faisal had served as viceroy when he was a young prince. Now, as king, Faisal was returning to announce the next step in Jeddah's development: the completion of a huge new port. The steel equipment, concrete piers, and expanses of bare pavement were a sharp contrast to the ornate coral homes of the old city just two miles away. To Faisal, though, the port had its own kind of beauty. It shone with the promise of wealth for the kingdom, power for the Al Saud, and glory for the Muslim faith.[1]

Faisal praised the private contractors and Ministry of Transportation officials who had worked on the project, although he claimed to be unhappy that the ministry had named it the "King Faisal Port." It would have been better, Faisal suggested, to have honored his father instead of himself, since Abdulaziz had first dreamed of a new anchorage at Jeddah many years before. Or perhaps the facility could be called the "Islamic Port." As the gateway to Mecca, it was designed "to receive as many hajj pilgrims as possible from among our Muslim brothers in the world." Faisal's words were a fitting expression of Saudi ideology: the glorification of Abdulaziz as the kingdom's founder; the synthesis of monarchy, capitalism, and the modern state; and the belief that Islam could, and should, coexist with rapid economic development. Faisal conjured a vision of oil-fueled machines moving in service of both God and profit, with bulldozers and cranes demolishing the old city and building a new one, making space for ships carrying valuable goods as well as pious Muslims on their way to the holiest place on Earth.

Saudi Arabia was in the initial stages of a tremendous economic boom. The kingdom's oil production was increasing as Aramco built new physical infrastructure like oil wells and pipelines. At the same time, an even more fundamental shift was taking place in the oil industry's political infrastructure. All over the world, oil-producing nations were seizing more control over their own natural resources and raising the price of petroleum. Saudi Arabia emerged as the biggest beneficiary. In 1970, the kingdom was still having trouble paying its bills, and Saudi leaders were asking the United States for financial aid. Just three years later, Saudi revenues were soaring, and American officials were trying to attract Saudi money to the United States. Although often remembered as a product of the 1973–1974 oil shock, the Saudi economic boom started before the October 1973 embargo and production cuts. The events of 1973–1974 accelerated trends that were already under way.

The United States was on a very different path. American oil production peaked in 1970 and started a long decline, while domestic consumption continued to grow. As a result, American dependence on foreign oil rapidly increased. Over the next three years, government officials, corporate executives, and other experts warned that the United States was entering an "energy crisis." Fierce political battles broke out over energy pricing, exacerbated by a deep divide between oil-producing states like Texas and oil-consuming states like Massachusetts. The Nixon administration's most important policy response to the crisis was the imposition of oil price controls, a counterproductive move that left the country unable to adapt to changes in the world oil market. By late 1973, the United States was far more vulnerable to oil supply disruptions.

U.S. leaders hoped that the rise of Saudi Arabia would provide a silver lining to the oil crisis. American businesses and their allies in the U.S. government saw a rich opportunity in the kingdom's economic growth. The port

FIGURE 4.1 New Chevrolet pickup trucks arriving at the port of Jeddah during the 1970s. B. H. Moody/*Saudi Aramco World*/SAWDIA.

at Jeddah was soon crowded with American cars, trucks, and other goods on their way to newly wealthy Saudi consumers, while U.S. financial firms competed to attract Saudi investments (figure 4.1). Those commercial ties went along with a deeper political relationship, as the Nixon administration hoped that the kingdom would be an important ally in the Middle East.

The United States and Saudi Arabia, however, were still divided over the question of Israel. That disagreement was nothing new, but the 1967 Israeli conquest of East Jerusalem, seizing control over sites holy to Muslims as well as Jews, fueled Saudi anger and underlined the religious dimension of the conflict. The only pessimistic note in Faisal's speech at the Jeddah port was his denunciation of "World Zionism," whose forces were carrying out "attacks on our country and our holy places and our brothers" in Islam. Faisal asked "all Arabs and Muslims" to unite against their Zionist enemies.[2] At that moment, the United States was increasing its own support for Israel, providing it with financial aid and advanced weaponry. This clash over Israel was a major challenge for both Washington and Riyadh, even as they strengthened their alliance in other areas.

THE TRANSFORMATION OF THE OIL MARKET

Beginning in 1970, the world oil market went through a dramatic shift as the producers took more control over their own resources and secured a series of major price increases. The change came about in part because of the delayed impact of the 1967 Arab-Israeli war and the accompanying embargo. The Suez Canal became the new front line between Egyptian and Israeli forces, closing to shipping and remaining off limits even after the ceasefire. The closure of the canal shut off the most important transit route from the Persian Gulf oil producers to their primary markets in Western Europe. It accelerated a transition toward a new generation of "supertankers," whose increased size made them more efficient and compensated for the increased time and cost of sailing around Africa. Supertankers threatened to reduce the economic and strategic importance of the Suez Canal, leading the Palestine Liberation Organization (PLO) to describe them as imperialist tools meant to weaken the Arab world by redirecting shipping outside the region.[3] Ships of that size, however, took years to build; they offered no short-term fix. By mid-1970, the world's shipyards capable of building supertankers were fully booked for the next several years. Shipping capacity was strained even further by a May 1970 accident that damaged Tapline, the pipeline that carried Saudi oil to the Mediterranean, forcing that oil to be put on tankers instead. Shipping rates more than doubled.[4]

The turmoil created new opportunities for oil producers, especially Libya. Since it was located on the Mediterranean, its oil could be shipped directly to Europe and was unaffected by the Suez Canal closure. During the 1967 embargo, the temporary halt of Libyan exports unsettled European consumers and gave Libya a hint of its potential leverage. Libyan oil was also in demand because it was low in sulfur, making it "sweet" crude, in the industry's jargon. Like Americans, Europeans were becoming more sensitive to environmental issues at the beginning of the 1970s, and they were willing to pay a premium for cleaner fuels.[5] A final Libyan advantage was political. The Libyan oil fields were divided into many small plots operated by separate companies, including independent firms that were more vulnerable to government pressure than a giant consortium like Aramco.

In 1969, the conservative Libyan monarchy was overthrown in a military coup led by the young officer Muammar Qaddafi. The new regime immediately stepped up efforts, already begun by the previous government, to extract more revenue from the foreign oil companies. Since France and other European countries had broken ranks with the United States in 1967 and pursued separate deals with the oil producers, U.S. officials doubted that the Europeans would stand firm in the event of another oil cutoff. In May 1970, the U.S. delegation to the Organization for Economic Cooperation and Development (OECD) reported that "as we saw first in 1967," there was a "clear danger" that the European oil consumers would "act against U.S. international companies if deliveries fell off substantially." The continental Europeans had long resented the Anglo-American companies' dominance over the industry and might leap at the opportunity to make their own direct arrangements with the producer countries.[6] With U.S. spare capacity sharply declining, the United States was also less able to help the Europeans in the event of a supply disruption. As a result, the U.S. government encouraged the companies to compromise with Libya rather than risk a confrontation that could fracture the Western alliance.

In late 1970, the companies conceded to the Libyan demand for higher prices. Their acquiescence stood in sharp contrast to previous confrontations between oil producers and consumers, especially the 1951–1953 Iranian nationalization crisis when the companies boycotted Iranian oil and the U.S. and British governments helped engineer the overthrow of Mohammad Mosaddegh. The Libyan breakthrough had an immediate psychological impact on oil producers and consumers alike. Qaddafi had proved that it was possible to take on the companies and win. Soon the other producers were also seeking more government control over their oil industries.[7] The extent of the changes under way became obvious in early 1971, when the oil producers won large price increases through a pair of agreements signed in Tripoli and Tehran. By July 1972, the U.S. National Security Council (NSC) concluded that "the past few years have seen a decisive shift in the balance of power away from the oil companies and consuming countries and in favor of the producing states," since "key Middle East states are able to play the companies (and the consumers) off against each other, where formerly it was the Arabs who could be so manipulated."[8] Producers like Libya and Kuwait started to limit their production, finding that in the new era of rising prices they could earn enough revenue while still keeping more oil in the ground for future use. As consumer demand continued to increase, the result was growing pressure for higher prices.

THE DOMESTIC ROOTS OF U.S. DEPENDENCE ON FOREIGN OIL

One cause of the shift in the global oil market was that by 1970, the long golden age of American oil production was coming to an end. After rising for more than a century, domestic production peaked and began to fall.[9] The shift marked a dramatic reversal from longtime trends. For decades, Texas had been the center of the American oil industry. Its surplus capacity, controlled by the Texas Railroad Commission (TRC), provided a critical margin of safety in responding to supply disruptions.[10] By the beginning of the 1970s, however, Texas had nothing left to spare. In February 1970, Texas governor Preston Smith told Nixon: "I understand that some feel we have adequate stand-by capacity in this country now. I happen to be Governor of the State that's supposed to have the bulk of that stand-by capacity. I am saying to you, *you had better not count on it.*"[11] In March 1971, spare capacity fell to zero, and the TRC authorized 100 percent production for the first time in decades. Byron Tunnell, the chairman of the TRC, said: "Texas oil fields have been like a reliable old warrior that could rise to the task when needed. That old warrior can't rise anymore."[12]

Texan spare capacity had helped the United States withstand previous shortages, like the 1951–1953 Iranian nationalization crisis and the 1967 Arab-Israeli war. With that cushion gone, the United States and its allies were now far more vulnerable to any cutoff of foreign oil. Already in January 1970, the U.S. delegation to the OECD warned the other members that they could no longer rely on American oil in a future crisis like the 1967 embargo, an announcement that deeply alarmed the Europeans and encouraged the companies and their home governments to back down from their confrontation with Libya.[13]

The decline in U.S. production was relatively modest. It fell from 11.3 million barrels per day (mbd) in 1970 to 10.9 mbd in 1973, a decline of about 3 percent. That still left the United States the world's biggest producer by a large margin.[14] A more serious problem was the rapid growth in U.S. oil consumption. From 12.6 mbd in 1967, it rose almost 38 percent to 17.3 mbd in 1973. The average American consumed more than three gallons of crude oil per day, roughly twice the rate in other wealthy, industrialized countries like Britain, France, and Japan. The reasons for such voracious demand were not hard to find. Americans owned bigger cars and drove more than people in other countries. There was more suburban sprawl in the United States, and public transit was less effective. Americans were more likely to live in large, detached houses that took more energy to heat, cool, and illuminate than the smaller dwellings popular in the rest of the world. Some observers traced those differences to geography, since America was a bigger country with a more dispersed population. Others pointed to American culture, including a supposed attachment to wide open spaces and a "love affair" with the automobile.[15]

Those explanations obscured the role of deliberate policy choices and political power in making the United States an oil-dependent society. The U.S. government could have done a great deal to limit American oil consumption. Spending on federal highway aid dwarfed the amount allocated to mass transit.[16] European countries charged much higher taxes on gasoline, discouraging excessive driving and the use of large automobiles, but the United States never followed their lead.[17] The U.S. government declined to impose any mandatory fuel economy standards on American cars, leaving them larger and heavier than most European and Japanese automobiles of that era. American passenger cars averaged less than 13.5 miles per gallon in the early 1970s.[18] Oil companies also played a role in maintaining widespread automobile dependence. Standard, Shell, Texaco, and other petroleum industry interests helped defeat Proposition 18 in California, which would have allowed diversion of gas tax revenues to fund mass transit.[19]

Resistance to car-centric urban planning was growing by the beginning of the 1970s. Local activists, often from minority communities, protested freeway construction plans that leveled urban neighborhoods and displaced their residents.[20] The writer and urban theorist Jane Jacobs attacked urban renewal schemes that prioritized cars over people.[21] Public transit supporters won approval of new rail systems in Washington, DC (Metro) in 1968 and Atlanta (MARTA) in 1971.[22] Nevertheless, the antiurbanism that led many Americans to abandon cities and public transit systems continued and even intensified during the 1970s. New York City's fiscal struggles became a national scandal, and images of graffiti-covered New York subway cars served as one of the most notorious symbols of urban decay in the United States.[23] Two largely white suburban counties outside Atlanta rejected MARTA, despite overwhelming support from public officials, forcing the new system to stop at their county lines and leaving the suburbs dependent on automobiles.[24] Countless similar choices made at the local level continued to spur the growth of freeways and suburbs and accelerated the country's growing dependence on foreign oil.

Those decisions sat uneasily with rising concern about the environment and the depletion of natural resources. Books like Paul Ehrlich's *The Population Bomb* (1968), the Club of Rome's *Limits to Growth* (1972), and E. F. Schumacher's *Small Is Beautiful* (1973) suggested that the Earth's capacity to sustain human civilization was being exhausted.[25] Similar fears were evident in science fiction, including the 1973 film *Soylent Green* that depicted a dystopian future of overpopulation, starvation, and extreme energy shortages.[26] Environmental concerns were so widespread that Richard Nixon, although a Republican, supported initiatives like the creation of the Environmental Protection Agency (EPA).[27] In 1971, Nixon even suggested "pricing energy on the basis of its full costs to society" (including environmental pollution), a potentially radical proposal that foreshadowed later calls for a carbon tax.[28]

Nixon, however, never tried to implement that suggestion. Aware of the political risks of tampering with delicate energy policy arrangements, especially after an abortive effort to remove oil import quotas in 1969–70, he was unwilling to raise the price of energy to American consumers. Nixon's only specific conservation proposals in 1971 were small, inoffensive ideas: tightening insulation standards for federally insured houses, and making data on the energy use of appliances more readily available to consumers. His energy policy focused on expanding supply, including nuclear power, rather than restraining demand.[29] Even though Nixon and other U.S. leaders were coming to appreciate the costs of excessive energy consumption, they were reluctant to bear the political costs of trying to change an energy-intensive society that was the product of decades of policy choices. Those choices were not easy to undo.

The costs of profligate U.S. energy use began to become obvious around 1970, well before the Arab embargo of 1973–1974. Some cities suffered electricity brownouts. Consolidated Edison ran low on generating capacity in New York City and pleaded with customers to conserve energy, while thousands of government workers were sent home early and subway service was curtailed.[30] By 1970–1971, commentators were beginning to describe the various challenges as a single national "fuel crisis" or "energy crisis."[31] In July 1971, the *New York Times* ran a three-part series on the topic, declaring that the energy crisis stemmed from "a bewildering, seemingly unresolvable dilemma"—the impossibility of reconciling abundant energy and environmental protection—and suggested that it was "likely to persist for years, perhaps for as long as the industrial-technological civilization that has made modern America a model for many other nations continues to proliferate in its present form."[32]

Rather than raising energy prices in response to the growing shortages, Nixon did the opposite. In August 1971, he announced a sweeping new package of wage and price controls as a way to fight inflation and outflank his Democratic opponents who had been calling for similar measures.[33] The move was part of a dramatic reorientation of U.S. economic policy that also included a surcharge on imports and ending the dollar's convertibility of gold, designed to halt the flow of U.S. gold reserves abroad.[34] Oil was included in the price controls almost as an afterthought, but Nixon's decision to fix oil prices at their mid-1971 level would prove the most consequential of all his energy policy decisions. As world prices rose, domestic oil prices were kept artificially low. That subsidized consumption and discouraged production—precisely the opposite of what Nixon should have done if he wanted to boost America's energy self-sufficiency. U.S. dependence on foreign oil steadily increased. Out of necessity, the import quotas were gradually loosened until April 1973, when Nixon abolished the program and opened the United States to unlimited imports.[35] As the number of foreign tankers arriving at U.S. ports grew month by month, American anxieties about an oil cutoff grew along with them.

THE PRODUCERS TAKE CONTROL

The rapid growth in U.S. demand added to the pressure on the global oil market, strengthening Libya and other oil producers in their negotiations with the companies. No nation benefited more from that shift than Saudi Arabia. Although the kingdom was less aggressive than Libya, Iraq, and other leftist and nationalist states in forcing new terms on the companies, it took advantage of the situation they created. In December 1970, the Saudi government increased the tax rate on Aramco to 55 percent. The dollar value of the change was not as important as its symbolic significance; the Saudi government was now taking the initiative, confident in its ability to impose terms on Aramco.[36] In contrast to the situation just a few years earlier, the companies could no longer easily find alternative sources of oil if they lost their Saudi production. Meeting the Esso director George Piercy in January 1971, Saudi oil minister Ahmad Zaki Yamani told him: "George, you know the supply situation better than I. You know you cannot take a shutdown."[37]

Saudi Arabia took the lead in demanding "participation," partial government ownership over the local operations of the foreign oil companies. Yamani proposed the idea of participation in June 1968. At first it went nowhere, but after the Libyan breakthrough of 1970 the producers' hand was strengthened, and the companies came to see participation as a less dangerous alternative to outright nationalization. The other OPEC states allowed Yamani to act as their spokesperson on the issue. Yamani argued that if the companies failed to compromise with him, they would be forced to deal with other, more radical countries like Iraq. His efforts led to an agreement between Saudi Arabia and the companies in December 1972, in which the Aramco partners agreed to a gradual government buyout of their operations leading to a 51 percent stake by the beginning of the 1980s.[38]

While prices were rising and Saudi Arabia was taking a greater share of the resulting revenues, Saudi oil production was also growing rapidly. It more than doubled from 3.2 mbd in 1969 to 7.6 mbd in 1973. During the same period, Saudi revenues for every barrel of Arabian Light crude went from 99 cents in 1970 to $1.70 by early 1973. The combination of more production and a higher price meant a stunning increase in Saudi oil revenues, which more than quadrupled from $949 million in 1969 to $4.331 billion in 1973.[39] Government revenues rose nearly 70 percent between 1970 and 1971 alone.[40]

THE SAUDI BOOM

The flood of oil money instantly ended the previous era of austerity. The U.S. ambassador concluded that Saudi Arabia's budgetary problems were now over; the kingdom could now "look forward almost indefinitely to very plentiful financial resources."[41] The Saudi minister of planning Hisham Nazir was "simply delighted" with the additional revenues at his command.[42] The widely disliked jihad tax was abolished, and spending was increased across the board. Transportation infrastructure was a high priority. The new port at Jeddah was only one example; huge sums were spent on the kingdom's other major ports at Dammam and Yanbu, new airport facilities at Jeddah and Riyadh, and thousands of miles of new roads. Other projects included schools and hospitals, telecommunication systems, and desalination plants.[43] Saudi business leaders were in a buoyant mood, as the spending increases and tax cuts boosted their profits. The U.S. embassy reported in 1971 that "the level of commercial activity should exceed anything seen heretofore."[44] Those expectations were correct; the Saudi economy soared, growing more than 20 percent every year between 1970 and 1973.[45]

The Saudi leadership stressed that oil wealth was more than simply an economic asset; it had political, military, and religious significance. Faisal hailed the "progress and development in our economy, our industry, and our productivity," which, "with the blessing of Almighty God," was serving "the religion, the Islamic community, and the nation."[46] Development was a holy mission, strengthening Muslims and enabling them to face their enemies. Faisal pointed out that Saudi funds went to the governments of

Egypt and Jordan and the militants of the PLO, who needed it to buy weapons for use against Israel.[47]

The Saudi focus on development was shaped by the conviction that the Muslim nations were economically weak and needed to catch up with the industrialized world if they hoped to defend themselves. Saudi leaders drew on stereotypes of sinister Jewish bankers to explain what they were up against. Speaking to a gathering of Muslim diplomats in Jeddah, the Saudi foreign minister Omar Saqqaf emphasized the power of modern finance in world affairs. He announced that "the enemies of Islam" had "reached their current position of material strength, vast and brutal, through the buildup of money and the harnessing of all its sorcerous energy to serve their evil goals." Muslims needed to learn from their foes, Saqqaf argued, by creating an international Islamic bank that would give them the financial strength already enjoyed by their adversaries.[48]

Although the monarchy depicted Saudi economic growth as a victory for Islam, that growth also generated large profits for non-Muslims. Saudi Arabia was heavily dependent on imports for everything from manufactured goods to food. In 1973, more than three-quarters of Saudi imports came from the major industrialized countries, especially the United States.[49] U.S. government and business leaders were quick to see the commercial opportunities opening up. Just before Faisal's visit to Washington, DC, in May 1971, Secretary of Commerce Maurice Stans told Nixon that U.S. firms were eager to sell the kingdom equipment for telecommunication systems, air traffic control, water desalination, petrochemical plants, construction services, and, most of all, weapons. He asked the president to pitch the Northrop F-5 fighter to Faisal, commenting that "this would be a very substantial transaction for Northrop Corporation" and handwriting a personal note to Nixon explaining that the sale "would help employment in California, immediately."[50]

The rush to tap into the new Saudi wealth struck some U.S. policymakers as a bit unseemly. Hal Saunders of the NSC objected to Stans's request, noting that the Saudi government was already planning to buy the F-5s, and "special pleading" from the president was unnecessary. While U.S. diplomats in the kingdom were supposed to promote the commercial interests of American firms, they looked with disdain at some of the salespeople pitching dubious schemes and products to the Saudis. Once word got out about the Saudi boom, the gold rush was on. The U.S. diplomat Hume Horan recalled that "our first-string, first-rate military-industrial giants, such as Bechtel," came to the kingdom, but so did "people who came to them offering to sell them snow mobiles and God knows what." During the 1970s, "every four-flushing mountebank in the world was at their door."[51] Horan's comments suggested not only the intensity of the scramble for Saudi wealth but also the way that the biggest American companies, like Bechtel, were implicitly endorsed by the U.S. government. James Akins, the State Department's oil expert and future ambassador to the kingdom, wrote that "the sky over Riyadh today is black with vultures with great new get-richer-quicker plans under their wings." Akins found the scramble for profits dangerous as well as crass, worrying that after being cheated one too many times by American "charlatans," Saudis would lose their confidence in the United States and cut their oil production.[52]

Akins and his colleagues were anxious to preserve the U.S. relationship with Saudi Arabia because they believed the kingdom held immense power over global oil and financial markets. Although Saudi production grew rapidly in the early 1970s, experts thought Aramco was still only scratching the surface of its capabilities. Aramco executives privately told U.S. government officials and other important visitors that "it would be perfectly feasible" to produce 20 mbd, a figure publicly confirmed by Saudi oil minister Ahmad Zaki Yamani in 1973.[53] At the beginning of the 1970s, Saudi Arabia was producing less than 4 mbd, and the United States, the largest producer in the world, was making just over 11 mbd; 20 mbd, then, would be almost twice as much oil as any country had ever produced in history. Other estimates were even more spectacular. Saudi government representatives told a group of U.S. congresspeople in July 1972 that if the kingdom wanted, it could reach 25 to 35 mbd by 1985.[54] These jaw-dropping figures were never achieved, but they indicated the ambitious plans for Saudi oil production. U.S. officials and oil company executives saw the kingdom as by far the greatest source of capacity left in the world, an indispensable asset in meeting future energy demand.

The problem, from the U.S. point of view, was that the Saudi government already had more than enough revenue to meet its short-term spending needs. If the kingdom kept expanding its oil production, most of the earnings would need to be invested rather than spent. But with oil demand growing and prices going up, keeping oil in the ground might be a better investment than stocks and bonds, especially since in the industrialized world, inflation was rising, the Bretton Woods system of exchange rate management was breaking down, and financial markets were increasingly nervous. The U.S. embassy reported that with Saudi oil increasing "in value at 8–10 percent a year," the kingdom would be foolish to "convert such an asset into money that actually depreciates in value at present rates of return." Looking skeptically at the 20 mbd estimates for Saudi production by the end of the decade, the State Department official Eugene Bird concluded that there was "little reason after 1978 or 1979 for Saudi Arabia to continue to pull oil out of the ground at anywhere near the rates being projected."[55] Oil consumers, though, were counting on that oil. If Saudi Arabia capped its production short of 20 mbd, the world's energy future would become very uncertain.

THE RISE OF SAUDI FINANCIAL POWER

Even with the more modest production levels of the early 1970s, rising from 3.9 mbd in 1970 to 7.7 mbd in 1973, Saudi earnings were already piling up at a rapid rate.[56] The kingdom ran a budget deficit of 2 percent of GDP in 1969, but by 1973 that had been transformed into an astonishing 43 percent surplus.[57] Unable to spend the money quickly enough, the Saudi government was accumulating currency reserves at a rate of $150 to $200 million every month, a figure expected to get much larger as the decade went on. Bird predicted that the Saudi Arabian Monetary Agency (SAMA), the kingdom's central bank, would "become the largest single financial investment house in the world before 1980." He wrote that Faisal had still not fully realized how rich his country had become, and that "one can only speculate what the King in his counting house will do when he suddenly realizes that he is the modern Midas on a scale never before known."[58]

U.S. government and business leaders sensed both danger and opportunity in Saudi Arabia's emergence as a financial power. They thought the kingdom lacked the expertise to manage the massive reserves it was accumulating.[59] U.S. banks and other financial institutions believed they could provide such knowledge, earning hefty profits on fees and consulting services. Bankers like David Rockefeller at Chase Manhattan and Walter Wriston at First National City Bank had been cultivating ties with Saudi Arabia for decades. In the 1970s, they were joined by many others. American business leaders courted Saudi officials like Ahmad Zaki Yamani at conferences and private gatherings, where the Saudis mingled with the highest levels of the American business elite.[60] They believed in the power of money—and the people who controlled it—to transcend political and cultural barriers.

U.S. policymakers thought that managing Saudi investments was more than a way for American banks to increase their profits; it would also serve the U.S. national interest. If Saudi Arabia and other oil exporters kept their money in highly liquid, short-term investments, "petrodollars" would lurch around the world, damaging the global economy by causing sudden swings in equity markets and currency values.[61] U.S. officials hoped to encourage a longer-term Saudi investment strategy that would bolster economic stability. They also believed that by providing the kingdom with safe, profitable investments, they could convince Riyadh that pumping oil now and investing the proceeds was better than keeping it in the ground.[62]

By the early 1970s, critics were beginning to worry about Arabs buying up American businesses and acquiring excessive influence over the American economy. U.S. policymakers, however, argued that Saudi investment would benefit the United States. The State Department reported in 1972 that Saudi Arabia and other oil producers "are becoming important sources for financing economic activity in our own country and other industrial nations."[63] George Shultz dismissed concerns about "Arab oil money," pointing out that it still made up only a small portion of the investment capital in the United States. In any case, he argued, Arab investment was a good thing; it represented "a highly advantageous mutual bargain" between the United States and the oil producers that was "worked out, as the best bargains usually are, largely in the market place." Shultz argued that it would improve the U.S. balance of payments and help the United States compete with Europe and Japan.[64]

THE THREAT OF THE OIL WEAPON

The growing commercial ties between U.S. and Saudi elites were challenged by Arab critics who pointed to America's support for Israel. In 1970, the PLO demanded that foreign "oil interests in the Arab world" be used as leverage against "the imperialist nations led by the United States of America."[65] The more radical, left-wing Popular Front for the Liberation of Palestine denounced Saudi Arabia for siding with the United States and demanded the use of oil as a weapon.[66] The dissident former Saudi oil minister Abdullah Tariki wrote in 1972 that "the enemy of the Arab nation and Islam is the United States of America" and argued that only the threat of losing access to Arab oil would change America's policies in the Middle East.[67] Even the National Assembly of Kuwait, a conservative Gulf state usually on good terms with Saudi Arabia, passed a resolution in January 1973 arguing that the Arab oil producers should be prepared to cut off oil to the West as soon as the next Arab-Israeli war began.[68]

Faced with such pressure, the Saudi regime tried to bolster its credentials as a supporter of the Arab cause against Israel. It bankrolled Fatah, the militant group led by Yasser Arafat that formed the core of the PLO. The Saudi government continued to support Fatah even after members of the Black September Organization (BSO), a PLO splinter group, attacked the Saudi embassy in Khartoum in March 1973 while it was hosting a diplomatic reception for the U.S. ambassador and other guests. The BSO militants killed the ambassador, his chief deputy, and a Belgian official before releasing their other hostages.[69] The U.S. government viewed Fatah as a terrorist organization and told King Faisal that it was closely linked with the BSO, but Faisal refused to cut off aid to Yasser Arafat.[70] Just two months after the Khartoum attack, the governor of Riyadh, Prince Salman, presided over the opening of a new Fatah office in Saudi Arabia and pledged the royal family's full support for the Palestinian movement.[71]

The royal family hoped that such ostentatious displays would deflect attention from the way it treated Palestinians within its own borders.[72] No matter how long they lived in the kingdom, most of them had little hope of attaining Saudi citizenship. The same was true of Yemenis and other immigrants to Saudi Arabia. The regime's distrust of non-Saudi Arabs was so great that Palestinians, Yemenis, Egyptians, Jordanians, Syrians, and Iraqis were barred from even setting foot in Ras Tanura, the home of the kingdom's main oil shipping terminal. That was true even if they were naturalized citizens of another Arab state, like Abu Dhabi, that enjoyed good relations with Saudi Arabia. Simply having been born in Palestine was enough to put them on the regime's watch list and disqualify them from working in the most important oil installations.[73]

Faisal publicly criticized the United States for its pro-Israel stance even as his government relied on U.S. weapons, technical assistance, and other aid. "Unfortunately," Faisal explained to a Lebanese newspaper in July 1973, "I have to tell you that Zionism controls the U.S. Congress and the U.S. government as well." The king, however, was careful to temper his words. He argued that the Arabs should not lose hope in the American people. Since "it is not in their interest to stand by Israel," Faisal said, eventually the Americans would come to their senses.[74]

Faisal privately warned Aramco executives in May 1973 that their company would suffer if the United States continued to support Israel. Faisal was amazed, he said, at America's failure to recognize that its own interests in the Middle East lay with the Arabs and not with the Zionists. He asked Aramco to lobby the U.S. government and noted that "a simple disavowal of Israeli policies and actions" would go a long way. Faisal told the executives that they needed to explain to the U.S. government that "time is running out," and inform the American people of facts that were being obscured by the Zionist "controlled news media." The companies took Faisal's message to officials from the State Department, the White House, and the Department of Defense, but they later reported that government leaders were unsympathetic and thought Faisal was "calling wolf when no wolf exists except in his imagination."[75]

On June 21, 1973, Mobil Oil placed an advertisement in the *New York Times* arguing that because of American oil consumption, "like it or not, the

United States is dependent on the Middle East just to maintain our present living standards in the years ahead." Saudi Arabia could cut off oil to the United States, the advertisement warned, "because we will need the oil more than Saudi Arabia will need the money." The only solution, Mobil concluded, was for the United States to broker an Arab-Israeli peace and prevent another war in the Middle East.[76] On July 26, Otto Miller, the chairman of Standard Oil of California, sent a letter to the three hundred thousand shareholders and employees of his company arguing that "the United States should work more closely with the Arab governments to build up and enhance our relations with the Arab people" and asking for more "understanding on our part of the aspirations of the Arab people, and more positive support of their efforts toward peace in the Middle East." Miller's letter triggered immediate protests and calls by pro-Israel groups to boycott Socal.[77] The companies believed, however, that the protests helped their political position in Saudi Arabia. The Saudi media reported the controversy as proof that the companies' messages had struck a nerve and inspired fear in the Zionist lobby.[78]

When the oil companies' efforts appeared to be having little effect, Faisal took his message directly to the American people. In July 1973, he told a *Washington Post* reporter that American support for Israel was threatening Saudi cooperation with the United States.[79] That August, Faisal gave an interview to NBC television, telling his audience that while Saudi Arabia would prefer to keep shipping oil to the United States, "America's complete support of Zionism against the Arabs makes it extremely difficult for us to continue to supply the United States with oil, or even to remain friends with the United States."[80]

MIXED MESSAGES

While some Saudi officials reiterated Faisal's warnings, others undercut their own government's position. In April 1973, Yamani suggested that Saudi Arabia might find it difficult to keep increasing oil production if the United States did not do more to resolve the Arab-Israeli conflict, comments that were publicly reported by the *Washington Post*.[81] Yamani's statement was quickly contradicted by a curious back-channel message delivered in Faisal's name, but originating with Prince Fahd and probably delivered via the CIA. The message declared that Saudi Arabia's commitment to maximum oil exports was "permanent and unchanging, just as is our friendship with the United States." Even more remarkably, the message continued: "I would never expect the United States to modify its commitments to Israel; I would never expect you to discontinue your provision of armament and war materials to Israel, or your political and diplomatic support; that would be completely unrealistic." Important details of the exchange are still classified, but it seems to have been an attempt by Fahd to reassure the United States that no oil production restrictions were being considered. Yamani, apparently rebuked by his superiors, soon backtracked and claimed that his previous comments had been misquoted by the *Post*.[82]

Other reassuring messages came from Fahd, Sultan, and the Saudi intelligence chief Kamal Adham in July 1973. Fahd explained that Saudi Arabia had "declared and undeclared" policies when it came to oil and other sensitive issues; although Saudi leaders might criticize the United States publicly, his country's "undeclared policy will be to continue to provide the United States with the petroleum it requires." In return, Saudi Arabia expected U.S. help against Iraq and South Yemen, along with progress on an Arab-Israeli settlement. Sultan, too, admitted that Saudi Arabia sometimes had to demonstrate its independence from the United States, but that "it should be a jointly-accepted condition of our partnership" that Washington and Riyadh agree to overlook embarrassing positions taken by each other. "The highest levels of leadership on both sides must cooperate in this," Sultan explained, "because we understand the whole situation as lower levels of government cannot."[83]

Sultan and Fahd wanted a collaborative relationship between U.S. and Saudi policymaking elites, established over the heads of their own citizens and even over the rest of their own governments. These backchannel messages were not merely secret; they bypassed the Saudi Foreign Ministry and the U.S. State Department. The U.S. memorandum that accompanied the messages from Fahd and Sultan speculated that Faisal, "in his increasing senility and irascibility," would make rash public statements that would "prejudice the special Saudi-American relationship which Fahd and Sultan, in particular, believe is critical to the long-term survival of the Sa'udi regime." The princes also feared that commoner advisers close to the king, especially Yamani and Saqqaf, would undermine U.S.-Saudi relations by threatening an oil cutoff. Fahd and Sultan wanted to reassure the United States that "even if the King is tactless and indiscreet in his public attitudes, the American reaction will be tempered by the knowledge that the next generation of Saudi leadership is going to be more cooperative."[84] It remains unclear whether Fahd and Sultan were truly acting against Faisal's wishes, or if the exchanges were part of a coordinated strategy, one that let the regime publicly threaten the United States to shore up its nationalist credentials while senior officials secretly told Washington not to take the threats too seriously.

Even King Faisal himself downplayed the threat of an embargo. In August 1973, Faisal and his son Saud al-Faisal, the deputy oil minister, cautioned against the idea. "If we cut off oil," Faisal asked, "then where do we get the money we need?" He stressed that oil money paid for arms and militant operations against Israel; losing that revenue would set back the Arab cause. Asked about the "oil weapon," Saud al-Faisal responded: "What do we mean by the word weapon? Is oil a cannon, to be fired once?" No, he explained; oil had to be used carefully, or it would hurt the Arabs more than their enemies. The time was not yet right for the use of the oil weapon, since the United States was not expected to be heavily dependent on Arab oil until the late 1970s. "If we were to implement a decision to cut off oil today," Saud al-Faisal argued, "America is the last country that would be harmed."[85]

The mixed messages from Saudi Arabia kept the U.S. government in a state of uncertainly. Some American officials believed that the United States was extremely vulnerable to an Arab oil embargo. The most famous warning came from the State Department's oil expert James Akins, whose 1973 article "The Oil Crisis: This Time the Wolf Is Here" predicted that an embargo would inflict "severe damage to our economy, possibly amounting to collapse."[86] Other experts, like the MIT economist Morris Adelman and the policy analyst Robert Hunter, claimed that an embargo would be impossible to enforce, since in a unified global oil market, supplies could simply be shifted around to make up for the loss of production from any one part of the world.[87] Confused by the conflicting reports, the Nixon administration remained unsure about the threat until it finally materialized in October 1973.

* * *

By 1973, a combination of factors, including the growth in oil consumption, consumer anxiety after the 1967 embargo, the closure of the Suez Canal, and an emboldened OPEC, had shifted the balance of power in the world oil market. The United States became more dependent on foreign oil and more vulnerable to a supply disruption. Even before the October 1973 embargo, the United States was already suffering from shortages of gasoline and other fuels, inspiring talk of an "energy crisis." U.S. officials believed that rising oil prices and growing concerns about resource scarcity had made Saudi Arabia and the other Arab oil producers far more influential in world affairs. Even Treasury secretary George Shultz, who had hailed the possibilities for economic cooperation with the oil producers, was irritated by their new assertiveness. "I must say they swagger these days," Shultz told reporters in September 1973. "I don't appreciate it particularly."[88]

Economic ties between the United States and Saudi Arabia offered new opportunities for profit to U.S. and Saudi elites, but they also created new vulnerabilities. By late 1973, the economic health of the United States was increasingly dependent on events overseas. An array of machines moving around the world had laid the groundwork for the coming oil shock. Cars, aircraft, and other vehicles burned ever-increasing amounts of oil, straining the available supplies. Tankers shuttled between the Persian Gulf and ports around the world, linking the fate of American, European, and Japanese consumers with the politics of the Middle East. Even the United States, although still a major oil producer, increasingly relied on imports to meet domestic demand. In early October 1973, the final piece fell into place as Egyptian and Syrian tanks, aircraft, and other weapons were readied to attack Israeli forces in the occupied Sinai Peninsula and Golan Heights. On the afternoon of October 6, those machines would also be set in motion, starting a war that would trigger a new Arab oil embargo against the United States and throw the world oil market into turmoil.

5

THE CUTOFF

On February 19, 1974, Secretary of State Henry Kissinger telephoned Joseph Sisco, his assistant secretary of state for Near Eastern affairs. They were in the middle of sensitive negotiations to defuse the Arab-Israeli conflict, but Sisco was not yet in the office. When, Kissinger asked, was he planning to show up? An exasperated Sisco explained that he was late because he had waited an hour to refuel his car that morning. The gas line had stretched around the block twice. Senior officials like Kissinger were chauffeured in government cars, but Sisco reminded his boss that other Americans did not enjoy that luxury. "Getting gasoline," he explained, "is a small problem if you are not Secretary of State."[1]

Four months earlier, the United States had launched a massive airlift to resupply Israel in its war against Egypt and Syria. In retaliation, Saudi Arabia and the other Arab oil producers reduced their exports and imposed an embargo on the United States. The embargo itself was mostly symbolic, but the production cuts sent oil prices skyrocketing worldwide. A cumbersome U.S. system of price controls and regulations made the situation worse, throwing the American energy market into chaos. Energy shortages spread across the country, and millions of Americans worried if they would have enough fuel to drive their cars or heat their homes.

Richard Nixon was locked in conflict with Congress over the Watergate scandal that would soon end his presidency. The legislative branch was also engaged in a broader effort to reclaim its influence, passing the War Powers Act to restrict the president's authority to launch new military operations, and beginning a series of investigations into misdeeds by the CIA and other executive agencies. In that context, the use of limousines and jet aircraft by administration officials struck some members of Congress as an egregious symbol of unchecked executive power. Rep. Charles Rangel (D-NY) argued, "The Presidency, accompanied as it is in movement by a fleet of jetliners, helicopters, limousines, and yachts, is entirely too wasteful of our precious energy resources." Sen. William Proxmire (D-WI) introduced an amendment to limit the use of limousines, asking: "How can any responsible Government official in good conscience insist on being driven around Washington in gas guzzling monsters when this Nation needs every gallon of gasoline it can get for essential purposes?" Sen. Henry "Scoop" Jackson (D-WA) agreed, adding that when he was commuting to the Capitol and was passed by administration officials in their chauffeured cars, "I get sick, seeing some of these characters in this town driving around in that manner."[2]

While the embargo underlined the tensions between Congress and the president, it also gave Nixon a chance to reassert his authority. Until 1973, most Americans saw the energy crisis as a domestic problem, one that involved questions about economic regulation and environmental protection that fell under congressional control. The embargo let Nixon reframe the energy crisis as a national security issue that only the president could solve. That strategy failed to save his presidency, but it had a lasting impact on the way Americans thought about energy. The goal of achieving "energy independence" would dominate the political debate for decades after the embargo, at the expense of other priorities like environmental protection.

The oil crisis empowered other executive officials, too—especially Henry Kissinger. He was at the height of his influence, serving as both national security adviser and secretary of state. While Nixon was preoccupied with Watergate, Kissinger exerted unusual control over U.S. foreign policy. He worked at a frenetic pace, flying between Cairo, Jerusalem, Riyadh, and other cities in the Middle East as part of his "shuttle diplomacy" to tamp down the Arab-Israeli conflict and end the embargo. Kissinger's travels burned colossal quantities of fuel. A single November 1973 Middle East trip by the secretary of state required more than 6,000 gallons of jet fuel per day, equivalent to the transportation petroleum use of 3,600 average Americans.[3] While other Americans scrambled to find a few gallons of gasoline for their cars, Kissinger had no such worries. He seemed indispensable as the one U.S. official who could end the embargo through diplomacy. As Nixon's press secretary Ron Ziegler told Kissinger: "I want you to stand in line in one of these gas stations. It might spur your enthusiasm to work some foreign policy miracles."[4]

The embargo also enhanced the power of the Saudi regime. For the first time, the Saudi government found itself at the center of the world's attention, courted by foreign leaders and the international media. King Faisal became a more influential player in regional and world politics. The oil minister Ahmed Zaki Yamani became a global celebrity, even though he was a commoner whose political status at home was tenuous. And Prince Fahd consolidated his status as the most influential advocate of a close U.S.-Saudi partnership. The kingdom's new wealth and influence convinced the Nixon administration to strengthen U.S. ties with Riyadh, ensuring the U.S.-Saudi alliance would emerge from the embargo even stronger than before.

Saudi Arabia had only reluctantly entered into confrontation with the United States. Not wanting to risk its alliance with Washington, it waited two weeks after the beginning of the October 1973 Arab-Israeli war before finally cutting off exports to the United States. During the following months, the regime secretly violated its own embargo by shipping oil to the U.S. military. Both U.S. and Saudi officials were careful to keep their lines of communication open, ensuring that they would be ready to put the alliance back on track as soon as the crisis passed. In March 1974, Saudi Arabia agreed to end the embargo even though Israel had withdrawn from only tiny portions of the occupied territories, a decision that marked the willingness of the Saudi royal family to collaborate with the United States even over vigorous objections from elsewhere in the Arab world.

THE OCTOBER WAR

On the afternoon of October 6, Egypt and Syria launched a coordinated attack on the Israeli forces occupying the Sinai Peninsula and Golan Heights. The United States and Israel were caught by surprise, missing the Arab preparations for war until just before the fighting began.[5] Even then, the Israeli military was confident that it could easily defeat Egypt and Syria. The Arabs, however, were better prepared than in 1967 and were equipped with more effective Soviet-made weapons. They made significant progress in the first several days of fighting. The Egyptians crossed the Suez Canal and dug in on the other side, while the Syrians advanced into the Golan Heights.

At first, the Nixon administration expected a rapid Israeli victory like the one in 1967 and thought that Israel could win without American help. On October 7, Kissinger told Nixon that Israel would "turn the tide" by the next day.[6] Nixon and Kissinger allowed Israel to pick up small quantities of weapons in the United States, as long as the operation was kept quiet and used only Israeli transport aircraft.

Even so, Arab public opinion blamed the United States for supporting Israel, since the Israeli military used American weapons acquired over the previous several years. U.S. diplomacy also favored Israel. It called for an immediate return to the prewar cease-fire lines, which would have forced Egypt and Syria to give up the territory they had retaken. The U.S. strategy seemed to endorse Israeli occupation of the land seized in 1967, infuriating Faisal.[7] Kissinger asked Faisal to urge Egypt and Syria to pull their forces back, but the king publicly replied that there would be no peace in the region until Israel withdrew from the Arab territories and granted self-determination to the Palestinians.[8]

The Saudi press bitterly criticized the United States for its pro-Zionist stance. The prominent journalist Turki Abdullah al-Sudairi, known for his close ties to the Saudi government, wrote that the United States had given "colonialism a new and cruel character." Turning the Western stereotype of nomadic Arabs on its head, al-Sudairi argued that it was the Americans who were the uncultivated nomads; they were merely "cowboys" who "built their glorious civilization by caring for cattle." Because Americans were rootless people transplanted to the New World, they saw land as nothing but a commodity and could not understand the attachment that the Palestinians felt to their traditional homeland. American foreign policy, al-Sudairi wrote, was like "a real estate office that fixes the boundaries, down to the meter, of who owns this land or that land, without reference to any historical or geographic roots." It was enough, al-Sudairi confided, to give him some sympathy for the Nazis, who had at least understood the importance of ethnic identity tied to the soil.[9]

With anti-American sentiment appearing even in the government-supported Saudi press, U.S. officials worried about the safety of Americans in the kingdom. They prepared to evacuate all 8,400 U.S. citizens in Saudi Arabia, along with Americans elsewhere in the Arab world. The U.S. embassies in Jeddah and Kuwait City even began destroying their sensitive files.[10] In sharp contrast with 1967, however, there were no riots or large demonstrations against the U.S. presence in the kingdom. On October 9, three days into the war, the embassy in Jeddah reported that the situation was calm and no evacuation was necessary.[11]

Also in contrast to 1967, Saudi Arabia did not immediately declare an oil embargo against the United States. The Nixon administration still worried about the threat of a supply disruption, knowing that the world oil market was much tighter than it had been six years earlier. On the first day of the war, Deputy Assistant Secretary of State Alfred Atherton rated the possibility of an embargo as "very high." Deputy Secretary of State Kenneth Rush warned that if the Arabs cut off their oil shipments, "We're all in a helluva fix. We only have 30 days supply and the Europeans have about 60 days. And that is to catastrophe. Within 15 days there would be panic." The task of crisis management fell to the Washington Special Action Group (WSAG), a special interagency body. It asked the CIA, the State and Treasury Departments, and the NSC to prepare contingency plans to cope with an embargo, including fuel rationing.[12]

The oil companies were even more concerned. The chairmen of Aramco's parent companies told Nixon on October 12 that Faisal was furious with the United States. They reported that Saudi Arabia was already planning a cutback in oil production, and that if the United States increased its support of Israel, the Arab producers would trigger "a major petroleum supply crisis." Aramco and other U.S. oil companies might be nationalized. "Much more than our commercial interests in the area is now at hazard," they warned; "the whole position of the United States in the Middle East is on the way to being seriously impaired," with Western Europe, Japan, and the Soviet Union waiting to swoop in and fill the gap.[13]

Senior American policymakers dismissed the warnings as self-interested pleas for the U.S. government to protect the companies' investments. Administration officials already had their hands full with crisis management, including the October War and the Watergate scandal, and were too busy to pay much attention to Exxon and its peers. Some officials were actively hostile to the oil industry's attempts to influence government policy. Kissinger ridiculed the "hysterical calls from oil companies" and dismissed their executives as idiots who had "an unparalleled record of being wrong." He was irritated that the oil executives were trespassing on his diplomatic turf and criticizing U.S. support for Israel. "Vicious, stupid bastards," Kissinger complained; "they shouldn't be playing" with high politics, where they only got in the way.[14]

Nixon and Kissinger's strategy of keeping some distance between the United States and Israel began to collapse after Israel failed to defeat Egypt and Syria within the first two days of the war. Israel had counted on a short conflict and did not have enough weapons or supplies for a long war. On the morning of October 7, Kissinger told White House chief of staff Al Haig that "the Arabs are doing better than anyone thought possible," and that the United States was already "getting frantic appeals" from Israel for more weapons.[15] The United States offered a small quantity of equipment if Israel picked it up secretly in Virginia and transported it on planes from El Al, the Israeli national airline, but El Al did not have enough aircraft for the plan to work. Later, the Nixon administration proposed chartering commercial transport planes, but the private cargo companies were unwilling to fly their planes into a combat zone.

Meanwhile, the administration faced growing political pressure at home to step up its support for Israel. Members of Congress, including Reps. Melvin Price (D-IL), Frank Brasco (D-NY), and Herman Badillo (D-NY) and Sens. Frank Church (D-ID) and Jacob Javits (R-NY), demanded that the United States send more weapons and supplies to the Jewish state. They told the administration to disregard the threat of an embargo, arguing that the only principled course was to ignore Arab blackmail and support Israel.[16] Leading senators also privately lobbied administration officials. Church called Kissinger on October 9 and asked him to replace the military aircraft Israel had lost. Hubert Humphrey (D-MN) did the same, telling Kissinger on October 12 that Israel needed "prompt delivery of the necessary planes." Scoop Jackson also called Kissinger and apparently threatened him with a congressional investigation for holding up the delivery of supplies to Israel. These calls infuriated the secretary of state. Convinced the senators were acting on Israel's behalf, Kissinger demanded that the Israeli ambassador Simcha Dinitz call off the attacks.[17] This domestic pressure was particularly threatening at a time when Nixon was reeling from Watergate and needed all the congressional support he could get.

The most important factor that swung the balance in favor of resupplying Israel was the changing diplomatic and military situation. Kissinger had been counting on the Arabs to accept a cease-fire based on the status quo ante bellum. However, his effort to arrange a UN-sponsored cease-fire collapsed on October 13 when Egypt refused to accept the proposal. At that point it was clear that the war would not end soon. Even more troubling from the American perspective, the Soviet Union began an airlift to resupply Egypt and Syria on October 10.[18] The prospect of the Arab states, assisted by the Soviet Union, defeating Israel on the battlefield was intolerable to Richard Nixon, who was always concerned about American credibility as a critical factor in the Cold War. If the United States allowed Israel to lose, then America's reputation as a reliable ally might be undermined.

THE AIRLIFT

On October 14, Nixon ordered a massive airlift of weapons and supplies to Israel. He overruled both the previous policy of reliance on El Al and civilian charters, and a proposal for a smaller airlift using only a limited number of U.S. military planes. "It's got to be the works," he told Kissinger. "We are going to get blamed just as much for three planes as for 300." The

United States sent C-5 Galaxy transports, the largest aircraft in the world, loaded with American military equipment flying directly into Tel Aviv. Most of America's allies in the North American Treaty Organization (NATO), fearful of provoking an Arab oil embargo, refused to allow the planes to stop and refuel on their territory. Portugal was the lone exception, so the transports refueled in the Azores on their way to Israel. Later that day, Kissinger told Secretary of Defense James Schlesinger that once the administration had committed itself, "we had better win." The United States, Kissinger explained, needed to teach the Soviets that "when they cross us something violent happens."[19]

Nixon and Kissinger feared that since the Soviet Union was helping Egypt and Syria, an Arab victory would be perceived as a Soviet victory—a threat they saw as more serious than an oil embargo. Nixon told his foreign policy team: "We can't allow a Soviet-supported operation to succeed against an American-supported operation. If it does, our credibility everywhere is severely shaken."[20] Kissinger, too, prioritized Cold War considerations over oil concerns. Lord Cromer, the British ambassador, called Kissinger on October 13 to ask about U.S. policy if the oil weapon were used:

> *C:* What will be your posture vis-a-vis when the Arabs start screaming oil at you?
> *K:* Defiance.
> *C:* Just defiance? It is going to be rough, won't it?
> *K:* We have no choice.[21]

Kissinger argued that if the United States bowed to Arab oil pressure, Saudi Arabia and the other producers would just increase their demands. The only solution was to hold firm. "The Arabs," he explained, "have to know that blackmail is a losing game."[22] In any case, Kissinger claimed, U.S. support for Israel was not the real problem. "You put a man in a monopoly position," Kissinger explained, "and he will squeeze you. The Saudis would still squeeze us if Israel disappeared tomorrow." The only solution was to reduce U.S. demand for imported oil.[23]

For Kissinger and other administration officials, the threat of oil blackmail was exacerbated by Watergate and the post-Vietnam reassertion of congressional authority against the executive branch. They had to prove that the White House, even in its weakened state, could still rally the nation to overcome the embargo, even if that involved painful sacrifices. Kissinger recommended an extensive program of domestic energy conservation to "bring maximum pressure on the Arabs." He exclaimed: "The events of this summer have led to a belief all around the world that our authority has been weakened. If we get into a confrontation, we have to show that we are a giant! We have to win!"[24]

The airlift, code-named Nickel Grass, was a colossal demonstration of American oil power. No other nation in the world had the airlift capacity to send thousands of tons of military equipment halfway around the world. Over the next several weeks, Nickel Grass required about thirty-five million gallons of jet fuel.[25] Although the operation initially was intended to be covert, its cover was blown when high winds forced the planes to land in Israel during the day instead of at night. The Nixon administration made a virtue out of necessity, using the now-public airlift to prove that the United States could airlift more tonnage into the Middle East than the Soviet Union. Every day, U.S. officials checked the latest figures on the Soviet airlift to ensure that the United States was always sending more. One U.S. transport even carried a tank across the Atlantic. From a military point of view, it was a meaningless stunt. Even the giant C-5 transports could carry only one tank apiece, and they were far more useful for carrying lighter cargo. The image of a tank rolling off an airplane, however, made a powerful impression on public opinion and demonstrated the unique ability of the U.S. Air Force to move supplies around the world at short notice.[26]

THE THREAT OF THE OIL WEAPON AND THE PRICE INCREASE

Egypt and Syria hoped to win the support of Saudi Arabia and the other Gulf Arab nations, convincing them to use their oil to pressure the United States and force Israel to give up the occupied Arab territories. Anwar Sadat sent his aide Sayed Marei on a tour of the Gulf states, first to Saudi

Arabia and Kuwait, and then Bahrain, Qatar, and the United Arab Emirates. Marei pressed the Gulf Arabs to support Egypt and Syria in the war. His tour was publicized in the local press, adding to the pressure on the Gulf Arabs to take action. One Kuwaiti newspaper reported that Marei had presented a plan for freezing oil production and imposing an embargo on any nation that supported Israel. Marei also suggested adopting even more drastic measures "against the United States such as nationalizing their assets in Arab countries and making direct arrangements between Arab oil producers and consumers in West Europe and Japan (thus cutting out the American role as middle-men)."[27]

Mohamed Hassanein Heikal, a leading Egyptian journalist as well as a close ally and confidant of the Sadat regime, declared on October 13 that "Arab pressure on the United States of America must be brought to bear now, not this hour, but this minute, tangibly, definitely and publicly." It was the oil-producing countries that would be most vital in this effort, Heikal wrote, "because the keys of American interests in this area are in their hands."[28] Since the press in every Arab country was filled with stories of Egyptian and Syrian soldiers risking their lives in the war, Egyptian calls for assistance put great pressure on the other Arab states to contribute to the cause. After the United States began its airlift to Israel, that pressure only increased.

When the October War broke out, critical negotiations were already scheduled between the oil companies and the oil-producing nations. Rising demand was putting upward pressure on prices. The war further undermined the consumers' negotiating position by unsettling the markets, threatening the physical security of oil installations in the Middle East, and increasing the political pressure on the Arab producers to take a hard line against the mostly American-owned oil companies at a time when the United States was backing Israel. As the oil companies' chief legal representative, John J. McCloy, later remarked with considerable understatement: "The October, 1973 Arab/Israeli war did not create an atmosphere conducive to negotiations."[29]

The producers demanded a doubling of posted oil prices from roughly three dollars per barrel to six dollars per barrel. The companies believed that a price increase was inevitable; as the chairmen of Exxon, Mobil, Socal, and Texaco wrote to Nixon on October 12, "The oil industry in the Free World is now operating 'wide open,' with essentially no spare capacity." Market forces had already "pushed crude prices up substantially," and so "a significant increase in posted prices and in the revenues of the producing countries" appeared justified. A doubling of posted prices, however, was so extreme that it could threaten the stability of the world economy and trigger "a serious disruption in the balance of payments position of the Western world."[30] With the companies unwilling to meet the producers' demands, the negotiations broke down.

On October 16, the Gulf oil-producing countries met in Kuwait City and unilaterally announced a 71 percent increase in the posted price, bringing it to $5.11 per barrel. The moment had huge symbolic significance. For the first time, the oil producers had set their own price rather than negotiating it with the oligopoly of Anglo-American companies that had dominated the industry for decades.

Although the price increase would do serious economic damage to the United States and other oil-importing countries, the U.S. government accepted the higher prices. Sisco argued that "we should encourage accommodation," since "the companies have no alternative to go along." The middle of a war, with embargo threats mounting, was no time for "business as usual," he explained. Sisco's colleague William Casey noted that the oil companies were ready to fold no matter what the government did. "This is the most scared bunch of guys you ever saw," Casey responded. Henry Kissinger warned that the producers would keep trying to push the price up, and that a confrontation would be necessary at some point, but he agreed that the time was not yet right. The U.S. government had no coherent strategy for dealing with the producers' demands.[31]

THE PRODUCTION RESTRICTIONS AND EMBARGO

The Saudi government denounced U.S. support for Israel. On October 15, the Saudi ambassador, Ibrahim al-Sowayel, and the minister of the interior, Prince Fahd, protested the airlift. Fahd warned that the United States

should assume "that Saudi Arabia will find itself compelled to support economic sanctions against the United States." The next day, King Faisal
himself wrote "that those responsible in the United States" should "realize
the seriousness of the step" they were taking. The reaction was somewhat
muted, however; Faisal noted that because of the airlift, U.S.-Saudi relations were in danger of becoming "lukewarm."[32]

Some U.S. officials dismissed the Saudi threats. CIA director William
Colby called Faisal's anger over the airlift "only temporary" and explained
that the king "is inclined to blow off emotionally about things, but he usually calms down." Nixon and Kissinger also hoped that their personal diplomacy would keep Saudi Arabia in line despite U.S. support for Israel. They
told Faisal that the airlift was "not intended as anti-Arab" and was meant
only as a response to the Soviet shipment of arms to Egypt and Syria.[33]

Nixon and Kissinger repeated that message in a meeting with the foreign ministers of Saudi Arabia, Kuwait, Algeria, and Morocco on October 17. The Saudi foreign minister Omar Saqqaf, who led the Arab delegation, asked the United States to commit itself to a just peace settlement in
the Middle East, including Israeli withdrawal from the occupied Arab territories and a solution to the Palestinian refugee issue. Nixon declined to
endorse the Arab request, but he did promise "a diplomatic initiative in
which we will use our full weight" to negotiate a peace agreement. Nixon
also promised that he would never allow "domestic politics" to influence
his approach to the Arab-Israeli conflict. He told the visiting foreign ministers that although Kissinger was Jewish, the secretary of state "will not
be moved by domestic pressures in this country." The official notetaker at
the meeting, NSC staffer William Quandt, later recalled that Nixon, in a
misguided attempt to curry favor with his Arab guests, continued in that
vein at some length, telling the foreign ministers that some of his best
friends were Jewish, and that it was possible for Jews to be good Americans, too. Both Kissinger and the Arab foreign ministers shifted uncom-
fortably in their seats until Nixon finished. The moment was so embarrassing that Quandt put his pen down and left Nixon's worst lines out of the
official transcript. The Kuwaiti minister gracefully handled the awkward
moment, saying that he and his colleagues were "not anti-Jewish. We are
all Semites together."[34]

Kissinger had already earned a global reputation for negotiating the U.S. opening to China, the SALT I and Anti-Ballistic Missile agreements with the Soviet Union, and the January 1973 Paris Peace Accords to end the Vietnam War. He and Nixon seemed to believe that Kissinger's reputation as a diplomatic miracle worker would be enough to placate the Arabs. As Kissinger told Brent Scowcroft the next day: "In the nutty Arab world I am sort of a mythical figure. The Arabs think I am a magician." He pointed to Saqqaf's public statement after leaving the White House, when the Saudi foreign minister told the press that his meeting with Nixon had gone well. As Kissinger told the WSAG afterward, "Did you see the Saudi Foreign Minister come out like a good little boy and say they had had very fruitful talks with us?" His dismissive tone implied that Saudi Arabia would behave like a loyal client and overlook American support for Israel. As far as the threat of an embargo went, he declared: "We don't expect an oil cut-off now in the light of the discussions with the Arab Foreign Ministers this morning."[35] He was wrong.

THE OIL WEAPON

Nixon and Kissinger did not know that at the same time they were meeting with the Arab foreign ministers, the Arab oil ministers gathered in Kuwait City were already deciding to deploy the oil weapon. On October 17 the Arab oil-exporting states announced that they had agreed on a plan for production cutbacks. Saudi Arabia, Qatar, Algeria, and Kuwait cut their production by 10 percent and promised to cut another 5 percent each month until Israel withdrew from the occupied territories. The cutbacks were a blunt weapon that could drive up the price of oil but did not distinguish between different consuming countries. Europe and Japan were even more vulnerable than the United States because of their greater dependence on Middle East oil. The inability to target any one country with the cutbacks may have been an advantage in Saudi eyes, since the cutbacks offered a way to use oil as a weapon without directly challenging the United States. Kissinger mistakenly dismissed the cutbacks as "a token thing," but he told

Nixon's press secretary not to say so publicly, since that might embarrass the Arabs into doing something more extreme. He failed to realize that the cutbacks would have severe economic consequences for the United States and other oil consumers. [36]

More militant Arab actors were disappointed with the cutback plan and called for bolder action. On October 18, the PLO urged the Arab oil ministers to shut off all oil shipments to the United States, withdraw their funds from American banks, and implement "a comprehensive boycott on all aspects of the American presence in the Arab world."[37] Iraq nationalized American oil company operations on its territory, and on October 18, Abu Dhabi imposed a complete embargo on the United States. Saudi Arabia initially held back. On October 19, the royal court announced that it was trying to "amend the present position of the government of the United States of America." Only if that effort failed would the kingdom cut off oil shipments.[38]

Riyadh finally acted after Nixon asked Congress for $2.2 billion in aid to Israel on October 19. The package included advanced weapons and equipment, and much of it would come in the form of an outright grant instead of a sale or a loan. Faisal was reportedly furious when he heard the news. The U.S. ambassador James Akins wrote that Faisal was particularly upset by the wide "difference between reassuring tone of various communications he had received from USG, and U.S. announcement of 'incredible' amount of aid" to Israel.[39] One day later, on October 20, Saudi Arabia announced a complete embargo on oil exports to the United States. Most other Arab exporters joined the embargo, which continued even after the war ended with a cease-fire on October 25. The Saudi newspaper *Al-Riyadh* described the embargo as a great sacrifice for the kingdom, which was giving up an important export market, but boasted that the move was a powerful blow against Israel and the American economy.[40] For the most part, though, the Saudi press downplayed the embargo and gave more attention to military operations in the war, including token participation by Saudi forces, both a sign of the greater prestige attached to sacrificing blood instead of profits, and a way of avoiding direct confrontation with the United States.

THE IMPACT OF THE EMBARGO

Although the disruption of the oil market had a dramatic impact on the United States, the embargo itself was mostly ineffective. The oil companies simply shifted non-Arab oil to the American market, while sending Arab oil to other consumer countries.[41] The production cuts had a bigger impact. They, in combination with the failure of U.S. domestic energy policy, caused the gas lines that tormented Joseph Sisco and millions of other Americans. The production cuts reduced the total amount of oil available to the world market, letting OPEC nearly quadruple the posted price to $11.65 by December 1973. Short-term "spot price" contracts rose even higher. The disruptive impact of the price increase was magnified by a cumbersome system of price controls and federal regulations in the domestic U.S. energy market. "Old oil" from wells already in operation was kept under price controls, while "new oil" discovered later was sold at a higher price. Consumers paid the average cost of old and new oil combined. With the price subsidized, there was less incentive to conserve fuel, leaving the inconvenience of waiting in line for gasoline as an extremely inefficient way of reducing demand. The situation was complicated still further by federal allocation rules, which distributed scarce supplies around the country. The system exacerbated shortages in certain regions while other areas enjoyed a surplus.[42]

If the Arab oil producers had followed through on their initial plans and cut production every month until Israel withdrew from the occupied territories, the United States and other oil-consuming nations would have found themselves facing a devastating shortage. On November 1, 1973, the Nixon administration's "energy czar," John Love, predicted that the country would soon face "severe problems," including "factory closings, unavailability of gasoline, and possibly cold homes." Love thought the economic effects might be serious enough "to cause a recession."[43] Five days later, Deputy Secretary of Defense William Clements, a former oil executive, warned that Richard Nixon still did not understand how bad the situation was. "I can't emphasize too strongly the degree of trouble we'll be in," Clements said. "Watergate will be a tea-party compared to this thing by February 1." There was only one way to solve the problem, Clements thought. "The solution is Saudi Arabia."[44]

The embargo was a shocking and disorienting experience for U.S. policymakers. Kissinger's deputy Brent Scowcroft remembered it as a "traumatic" moment when "all of a sudden the oil world turned upside down."[45] Comforting old assumptions were suddenly proved false. U.S. leaders were irritated that a small country in the developing world could impose such costs on the American economy. They sometimes indulged in crude stereotypes and imperialist nostalgia. Kissinger told his staffers: "I know what would have happened in the nineteenth century. But we can't do it. The idea that a Bedouin kingdom could hold up Western Europe and the United States would have been absolutely inconceivable. They would have landed, they would have divided up the oil fields, and they would have solved the problem." To his frustration, though, Kissinger conceded: "That obviously we cannot do."[46]

Secretary of Defense James Schlesinger also mused about seizing the oil fields. On October 24, 1973, just days after the embargo began, Schlesinger told several other Nixon administration officials: "We are moving forces to the Persian Gulf."[47] When White House chief of staff Al Haig mentioned that Schlesinger had raised the idea of "putting troops in to get oil," Kissinger responded: "He is insane." Kissinger also complained: "I do not think we can survive with these fellows in there at Defense—they are crazy."[48] At other times, Kissinger seemed more open to the idea. In November 1973, Schlesinger said: "We have been talking about using the Marines." Kissinger complained: "It is ridiculous that the civilized world is held up by 8 million savages." He also asked: "Can't we overthrow one of the sheikhs just to show that we can do it?"[49]

Such talk was mostly bluster. Plans for invading the Gulf never went far. The CIA studied the feasibility of military action to seize the Saudi oil fields but concluded that the Saudi government could easily sabotage its oil infrastructure, defeating the purpose of the operation.[50] With the Nixon administration winding down U.S. involvement in Vietnam and the American people skeptical of foreign adventures, sending troops to occupy the Arab oil producers would have exposed the White House to a storm of opposition at home. The United States also lacked the military infrastructure to move ground forces into the Persian Gulf. The only permanent U.S. military presence was the "Middle East Force" in Bahrain, a tiny naval detach-

ment that consisted of a single, noncombat transport ship and two destroy-
ers (on loan from other naval commands) that visited the Gulf for about
two weeks each year.[51] Schlesinger complained about the lack of American
bases in the Persian Gulf, griping that the Pentagon's contingency plans
for intervention in the region were "piss-poor."[52] He and other administration officials concluded that the United States needed to build up its military infrastructure in the Gulf to avoid being caught unprepared again, laying the groundwork for the Pentagon's efforts along those lines in the late
1970s.[53]

While the Nixon administration was focused on the embargo, another,
more permanent change was happening in the oil market. On December 22,
1973, the Persian Gulf members of OPEC met in Tehran and raised the
posted price of crude oil from just over five dollars per barrel to nearly twelve
dollars per barrel. Coming after the October increase, it meant that oil
prices had almost quadrupled in just over two months. That shift would
have a much larger economic impact than the embargo, contributing to
stagflation in the United States and fueling a massive economic boom in
Saudi Arabia and the other oil producers.[54]

Although Saudi Arabia profited at the expense of the oil consumers, the
price hike paradoxically gave a boost to the U.S.-Saudi alliance. Now that
the kingdom was much wealthier, it had more to offer the United States as
an investor, an export market, and a source of funds for anticommunist
causes around the world. The Saudi regime also convinced U.S. leaders that
it was a critical voice for moderation in OPEC. After the December 1973
meeting in Tehran, Saqqaf told Akins that Saudi Arabia had held out for
a much lower oil price and had succeeded in moderating the more extreme
demands of the Shah of Iran. The Shah, for his part, rushed to claim the
credit for the price increase. At a news conference he declared: "The industrial world will have to realize that the era of their terrific progress and even
more terrific income and wealth based on cheap oil is finished." The Shah
lectured the oil consumers to "tighten their belts," adding: "If you want to
live as well as now, you'll have to work for it." Such words did little to en-
dear him to Americans. Saudi Arabia exploited the Shah's comments, with
Saqqaf telling Akins a few days later: "You must know from the newspapers and from your reports from Iran that it was the Shah who had insisted

on the increases in prices." While Iran was an important strategic partner of the United States, the Saudi government convinced U.S. leaders that it was a more reliable ally when it came to oil prices. That perception solidified the U.S.-Saudi alliance and helped overcome the strains caused by the embargo.[55]

EMBARGO DIPLOMACY

The oil shortage was not initially a top priority for Henry Kissinger. For one thing, Kissinger knew little about energy policy, telling his staff: "I've never understood the oil business." He later complained: "When people tell me we are consuming six million barrels a day, they might just as well say fifty thousand Coke bottles worth of oil. I don't know what that means."[56] As Joseph Sisco realized when he called in late for work, Kissinger was also personally insulated from the fuel shortages that afflicted millions of other Americans.

As the embargo dragged on, however, Kissinger began to take the energy problem more seriously. One reason was pressure from Richard Nixon, who had to deal with domestic policy and could not afford to ignore the anger of consumers suffering from the gasoline shortage. He told Kissinger that the details of the Middle East peace negotiations did not matter to the American public nearly as much as getting the oil flowing again. "You see," Nixon explained, "my only interest is the embargo. That's the only thing the country is interested in. They don't give a damn what happens to Syria."[57]

Kissinger also came to see the embargo as a threat to American global power. It made America look weak, and it undermined the Western alliance by encouraging Europe and Japan to distance themselves from the United States. Even countries that were not targeted in the embargo were hit hard by the production cuts and price increases of late 1973. European nations like France, Belgium, and Germany were particularly vulnerable because, unlike the United States, they produced almost no oil of their own. Some European countries banned driving on weekends and took other drastic conservation measures. While Kissinger was flying around the world, other U.S. officials serving overseas could not even take a car from their home to their office. Donald Rumsfeld, the U.S. ambassador to NATO headquarters in Brussels, found that he and his staff had to walk or ride bicycles if they wanted to get anywhere over the weekend.[58] To restore their access to oil, American allies in Europe and Japan distanced themselves from the United States and tried to strengthen their relationship with Saudi Arabia and other oil producers.

Kissinger hoped to turn the situation to America's advantage by bringing U.S. allies back into line. The United States could deal with the crisis more easily than Europe and Japan because it was less dependent on Arab oil, and because it had more diplomatic influence in the Middle East. Kissinger told a group of British officials that the only oil producers that really mattered were Iran and Saudi Arabia, and "both of them are completely dependent on American political support." If the United States wanted, it could lock up Iranian and Saudi oil supplies and "drive everyone else to the wall." It was in Europe's best interest to stay in America's good graces and support U.S. initiatives to deal with the oil crisis. Two of Kissinger's staffers reminded him that the United States enjoyed "oil leverage" over the Europeans, since "we have the power to make their oil situation better or worse." Kissinger's strategy revolved around creating an alliance of oil-consuming nations under U.S. leadership. The main obstacle was France, which wanted a more independent European energy policy and a closer relationship with the oil producers. Kissinger organized the Washington Energy Conference in February 1974 to bring the consumers together, laying the groundwork for the International Energy Agency and largely sidelining France's bid for European unity independent of the United States. Kissinger boasted of having "broken" Europe and taught the French a lesson.[59]

For Kissinger's strategy to succeed, he had to demonstrate that only the United States had the diplomatic influence to achieve peace in the Middle East and bring about an end to the oil embargo. He embarked on a round of intense "shuttle diplomacy," flying repeatedly between Israel and its Arab neighbors and serving as a middleman for nations that would not talk to each other directly. Kissinger did not plan to negotiate a comprehensive peace agreement, but rather a series of smaller "disengagement" deals that would involve Israeli withdrawal from small slices of Arab territory. He sought just enough progress to prevent war from breaking out again, to exclude Soviet influence from the region, and to convince Saudi Arabia and the other Arab oil producers to lift the embargo and production restrictions.[60]

At first, the Saudi leadership was adamant that it would not be satisfied with the piecemeal agreements that Kissinger was proposing. Saqqaf told the United States that although negotiations on the Sinai front seemed to be making some progress, a separate Egyptian-Israeli peace would be inadequate. Faisal demanded full Israeli withdrawal from the occupied territories.[61] The Saudi leadership emphasized the need to return Jerusalem to Arab control. In a November 1973 interview with the Lebanese newspaper *Al-Anwar*, King Faisal declared that Jerusalem was "the city of Muslims and Christians," and "the Jews have no holy place in it." When the interviewer pointed out that the Wailing Wall was sacred to Jews, Faisal snapped that they should "build another wall to cry on."[62]

Under American pressure, Faisal gradually backed away from his hardline stance. In November 1973, he suggested that Saudi Arabia could lift the embargo as soon as Israel began its withdrawal from the Arab territories, if the withdrawal schedule was outlined in advance and the United States guaranteed that Israel would keep its promises. In December, the Saudi government relaxed its position further, suggesting that the embargo could end as soon as Israeli-Egyptian disengagement was completed, even though that agreement returned only a tiny sliver of land to Egypt.[63] On December 25, the Arab oil producers boosted their production by 10 percent, greatly easing the world oil shortage. Faisal assured Nixon that as soon as the Middle East peace process started making real progress, U.S.-Saudi relations would be fully restored; in fact, they would be "even stronger" than before the embargo. "I want to forget the past," Faisal wrote, "and look to the future."[64]

By this point, Saudi Arabia was violating its own embargo, just as it had done in 1967. At first, the kingdom denied fuel shipments to the U.S. military. American forces in Vietnam and elsewhere in Asia relied heavily on oil from Saudi Arabia and other Gulf states, and their supplies soon began to run short. In November 1973, Schlesinger complained: "We have no fuel for the B-52s in Southeast Asia."[65] Assistant Secretary of Defense Arthur Mendolia warned that the oil shortage was "very serious" and that the Pentagon "will soon be forced to begin standing down operational forces."[66] Ambassador Akins pleaded with Faisal, arguing that the Saudi embargo was hamstringing the U.S. military in Vietnam and undermining the struggle against communism. In December, Faisal gave tacit approval to Yamani to resume fuel shipments to the U.S. Navy. The issue was so sensitive that Faisal simply remained silent when Yamani outlined the plan, which the oil minister interpreted as consent. The program had to be kept completely secret, even from the rest of the Saudi government. Yamani warned Akins that if any hint of the shipments reached the press, Yamani would immediately stop the deliveries, any chance of ending the embargo would recede, and Yamani himself "would be compromised and could even lose his job." Aramco was supposed to handle the operation with the utmost discretion, but Aramco's chairman, Frank Jungers, promptly contacted the Saudi oil ministry and told them that Yamani had ordered them to supply the U.S. fleet. The ministry staff knew nothing of the secret deal. When they contacted Yamani for clarification, he was furious, and the fuel shipments stopped again. The crisis only passed when Faisal and Yamani decided that "Jungers' stupidity" should not be allowed to undermine the U.S.-Saudi alliance against communism.[67]

The secrecy that surrounded the U.S.-Saudi partnership affected domestic American politics, as well. In spring 1974, Sen. Henry "Scoop" Jackson's committee investigated the oil industry and began issuing subpoenas to Exxon executives about their dealings with Saudi Arabia. Akins was terrified that the investigation would uncover Saudi Arabia's violation of the embargo. He warned Kissinger that "if special oil supply arrangements are disclosed via Jackson hearings, King will be angered, Yamani politically destroyed, and new U.S.-Saudi relationship will be set back." As Akins explained: "Not only would Yamani be ruined but every other Saudi official will see in this a demonstration that dealing with the United States on a confidential basis is personally dangerous." The United States and Saudi Arabia succeeded in keeping the oil shipments secret for years, a reminder that leaders on both sides believed their relationship could only be maintained by shielding it from oversight, even if that meant keeping members of their own governments in the dark.[68]

Yamani saw his influence skyrocket during the embargo. He could order a change in Saudi oil policy practically single-handedly, cutting his own bureaucracy out of the loop. All he needed was the king's approval, along with his personal contacts at the U.S. embassy and Aramco. During the embargo, Yamani became a global celebrity and perhaps the most visible Saudi in the world. Fluent in English and educated in the United States, he epitomized a new kind of globe-trotting Arab elite, seeming to spend almost as many hours in the air as Kissinger.[69]

Yamani's position at home, however, was more ambiguous. As a nonroyal, in some respects he ranked below even the thousands of junior members of the Al Saud. Yamani was reportedly once unable to take his seat on a plane because a minor teenage prince happened to sit there first.[70] Yamani's authority was entirely dependent on the king's support; without royal favor, he had nothing. Yamani's rivals, both royals and commoners, resented his celebrity and his skill at burnishing his image with the Western media.[71] Saqqaf grumbled to Akins that in the rest of the world, "the only Saudi anyone ever listened to was Yamani." He told Akins: "It's your fault; you've built up Yamani."[72] When a Lebanese newspaper asked Prince Fahd about Yamani, he was annoyed. People treat Yamani "as if he were the decisionmaker," Fahd snapped. In fact, others set the policy, and "Minister Yamani carries out the state's decision. That's it."[73]

U.S. officials tried to take advantage of the rivalries within the Saudi government. In January 1974, Akins concluded that Saqqaf and Fahd wanted to lift the embargo, but Yamani favored keeping it in place for the time being. Akins seized the opportunity to meet Saqqaf and Fahd while Yamani was out of the country. He urged them to end the embargo immediately and told Kissinger: "I will also intimate that what is also at stake is the reputation of the King; that is, who makes oil policy, His Majesty and his political advisors or Yamani, whom they frequently characterize as a 'technician'?" There was a danger, Akins explained, "that Yamani will be hurt in any inter-government fight," but he was willing to let that happen.[74] The gambit failed, and the embargo remained in place, but the incident contributed to the simmering animosity between Yamani and other Saudi officials, especially Fahd. Yamani knew his rivals had American support; in a meeting with Akins the previous month, he referred contemptuously to "your lackeys" in the Saudi government.[75]

Even Saqqaf, although he sided with the United States on the embargo, lost out to Fahd in the struggle to direct the new U.S.-Saudi Joint Commission on Economic Cooperation (JECOR) established in the spring of 1974. Fahd took control over the commission, even though he was the minister of the interior and Saqqaf, as foreign minister, arguably had a better claim to oversee the JECOR agreement. Saqqaf was unhappy to be shoved aside.[76] The United States, though, was pleased to work with Fahd, whom U.S. officials thought was the most pro-American of the senior royals, and who had enough power to safeguard U.S. interests in the kingdom. Fahd, for his part, benefited from the prestige and financial resources that came with managing such an important conduit for U.S. economic involvement in the kingdom. Not for the first or last time, U.S. influence boosted the standing of the Saudi royals at the expense of the highly educated, English-speaking technocrats who, at least according to contemporary American theories of modernization and economic development, were better qualified to run the country than princes like Fahd.

THE EMBARGO AND EXECUTIVE POWER

Nixon, too, tried to take advantage of the crisis to reassert his own power in the midst of the Watergate investigation and congressional attempts to curb executive authority. On October 20, 1973, the same day the embargo began, Nixon carried out the so-called Saturday Night Massacre by pushing his attorney general and deputy attorney general to resign after they refused to fire the special Watergate prosecutor, Archibald Cox. Four days later, Nixon vetoed the War Powers Resolution designed to limit the president's power to deploy U.S. military forces without congressional approval. On November 7, Congress overrode Nixon's veto. He slammed the resolution for undermining "this Nation's ability to act decisively and convincingly in times of international crisis." That same day, Nixon announced

"Project Independence," an effort to make the United States self-sufficient in energy by the end of the decade.[77]

Nixon used the crisis to demand an expansion of presidential power. He told Congress that to deal with the "energy emergency," he needed "authority to allocate and ration energy supplies," along with the ability to force power plants to use coal instead of oil, to speed the introduction of nuclear power plants by slashing regulations and letting them operate without holding public hearings, and to exempt all steps taken under the proposed energy emergency legislation from the usual environmental rules.[78] In private, Nixon bluntly dismissed the need for environmental protection. He told an audience of state and local officials that the United States needed to burn more coal regardless of pollution concerns, since "if you are going to freeze to death, it doesn't matter much whether or not the air is clean."[79] Nixon ordered his cabinet: "In all areas, whenever it is a matter of energy or environment, energy comes first."[80]

Nixon's strategy had mixed results. Congress did not pass the Energy Emergency Act until March 1974, and then only after adding new oil price controls that Nixon opposed. He vetoed the bill, mocking Congress for its "delays, confusion, and finally the tangled and ineffective result which is before me today." He succeeded, however, in overcoming environmentalist resistance to several major domestic energy measures. The most notable example was the proposed pipeline to carry oil from northern Alaska to Valdez on the state's southern coast, a project that had been held up for months by environmental concerns. Nixon argued that the pipeline was a vital tool for overcoming the energy crisis, telling Congress "this is no time to hold the Nation's energy future hostage" to environmentalists. His appeal helped break the congressional logjam, and the pipeline bill passed by a large majority.[81] "Energy independence" became a permanent feature of U.S. energy politics, striking a powerful chord with Americans who, in the wake of Vietnam, worried that their nation was losing control over its destiny.[82]

Nixon also hoped the embargo would help him escape from the Watergate scandal. He cast himself as the indispensable leader the country needed to overcome the crisis. He urged Kissinger to negotiate an end to the oil embargo, hoping for a diplomatic achievement that would boost his popularity. Nixon's chief of staff, Al Haig, told Kissinger that if the secretary of state convinced Saudi Arabia to ease the embargo, he should keep it secret until Nixon could announce the breakthrough himself and receive the credit.[83]

Nixon's strategy included direct appeals to the Saudi regime to save his political career. He tried to convince Faisal that he was the only American leader who could stand up to Israel's allies in Congress, and that the Arabs would lose any chance for a favorable peace agreement if he were impeached. Nixon had Kissinger take this message to Saudi Arabia. In December 1973, Kissinger visited the kingdom and met with a group of young Saudis. One of them was Prince Turki al-Faisal, later to become the head of Saudi intelligence. Turki asked what would happen to U.S. involvement in the peace negotiations if Nixon and Kissinger were to leave office. Kissinger told him that it was "imperative for President Nixon to be involved in this process," since there was no guarantee that future presidents would sympathize with the Arabs. In addition, Kissinger said, "If I were to leave, since I have built up a wide network of relationships, it would make a significant difference." He warned Turki: "There is a strong Arab interest in strengthening those of us who are determined to make a major effort to achieve peace" and suggested that when the Saudi government made its oil policies, it should be careful not to hurt "the first administration willing to have a disagreement with Israel."[84]

In a conversation with Faisal, Kissinger suggested that because he was pressuring Israel to withdraw from some of the occupied territories, the Zionist lobby wanted to ruin him. "There are forces in the US," Kissinger explained, "that will undoubtedly try to destroy me because of my effort. That is not so important but they will also try to destroy the President and that is more important." If the embargo continued, Kissinger explained, Nixon's enemies would blame the president and undermine his authority. He urged Faisal to lift the embargo to ensure Nixon's political survival. Kissinger later warned Saqqaf that Nixon faced congressional opposition "from groups in America seeking to defeat his policies." Kissinger urged Saqqaf to end the embargo before Congress could reconvene and spoil Nixon's peacemaking efforts. Kissinger's language was deliberately vague. Nixon was more direct, telling the Saudi ambassador Sowayel that while his administration was not beholden to "the Jewish community," Saudi Arabia might have a harder time dealing with future presidents.[85]

ENDING THE EMBARGO

The Nixon administration was repeatedly frustrated in its efforts to get the embargo lifted. For political reasons, Nixon was desperate to announce an end to the embargo in his January 1974 State of the Union address. Saudi officials, including the intelligence chief Kamal Adham and his deputy Turki al-Faisal, suggested that the embargo might be lifted in time for the speech. In return, they pushed Nixon to insert into his speech a promise to back "a just and durable peace in the Middle East" based on the UN Security Council Resolutions 242 and 338. Shortly before the State of the Union address, however, it became clear that the embargo would continue. Nixon still used his speech to boast about his "personal contacts with friendly leaders in the Middle Eastern area," but he was left with nothing concrete to announce, only the fact that "an urgent meeting will be called in the immediate future to discuss the lifting of the oil embargo." Henry Kissinger privately complained to his deputy Brent Scowcroft that the episode was "revolting," declaring, "If I was the President I would tell the Arabs to shove their oil and tell the Congress we will have rationing rather than submit and you would get the embargo lifted in three days."[86]

The Nixon administration was furious that Saudi Arabia had not lifted the embargo. In early February 1974, Kissinger threatened to publish the secret messages from Saudi Arabia suggesting the embargo might be lifted at the end of January. An incredulous Saqqaf told Ambassador Akins that "he was amazed at the suggestion to publish the exchanges of messages" between their two countries, since in Saudi hands, those messages "constituted an immense power over American politics." Saqqaf continued:

> Every message from Washington, he said, every conversation with the Secretary or with me, was basically a plea to protect Richard Nixon; there was no reference in Washington's messages to the need to help the United

States; there was not even any indication that the oil boycott was hurting the United States. It was just that the Arabs had to take action to protect the Presidency of Richard Nixon.

If the United States wanted to publish those messages, Saqqaf said, he had no objection. Saudi Arabia would also "release any parts of the exchanges which Washington omits." Kissinger, realizing that Saqqaf was right, backed down.[87]

Kissinger had already met some of the Saudi demands in January, when his shuttle diplomacy led to a disengagement agreement that separated Egyptian and Israeli forces in the Sinai. The remaining sticking point was his failure to secure a similar agreement for Israel and Syria on the Golan Heights. By the beginning of March, the Syrian-Israeli negotiations had made enough progress that Saudi Arabia was willing to lift the embargo. The Saudi leaders stressed that they were resuming oil shipments to the United States to help Nixon. Faisal told Kissinger: "We see some people in the United States who are against the President and you, contrary to the interests of the United States. We hope his friends in the United States will rally around the President." Saqqaf agreed, explaining, "We have to lift the embargo, help the Administration in America, and help the people there not be against the Arabs."[88]

On March 18, 1974, the Arab oil ministers met in Kuwait City and voted to end the embargo. The results of Kissinger's diplomacy were far short of the original Arab demands. Israeli had withdrawn from only a tiny sliver of the Sinai Peninsula and would do the same in the Golan. Syria and Libya had wanted the embargo to continue. Even the press in Kuwait, a fellow Gulf monarchy, was highly critical of the decision to resume oil shipments to the United States. The Kuwaiti paper *Al-Ra'i al-Am* asked why the oil producers would lift the embargo before the Syrians, Egyptians, and Palestinians recovered their land. Could it be, *Al-Ra'i al-Am* asked sarcastically, that "America has become a great friend" of the Arabs? The paper ran a political cartoon depicting a bewildered Syrian left empty-handed after the Gulf Arabs dismantled the oil weapon.[89]

The Saudi regime knew that the end of the embargo would be unpopular with many of its own people. In the censored Saudi press, the government deliberately buried the news. Instead, the regime stressed its continued resistance to Israel. King Faisal met with PLO leader Yasser Arafat in Riyadh just before the oil meeting in Kuwait. Afterward, the Saudi defense minister Prince Sultan visited Egypt to see the wreckage of the Israeli defensive fortifications breached by the Egyptian army on October 6, 1973. Sultan praised the heroism of the Egyptian soldiers and announced that Saudi Arabia, too, had sacrificed for the common Arab cause. Faisal "put everything we have in the service of the battle," Sultan declared. Saqqaf reaffirmed the kingdom's hard-line public stance on Israel. He promised that the Arabs would not give up one inch of the land that Israel took in 1967; if Israel tried to hold on to the captured territory, "the Arabs will fight until the end." There would be "no peace," Saqqaf said, "except with withdrawal."[90] Such statements obscured, but did not change, the fact that Saudi Arabia had ended the embargo even though almost all the occupied territories remained in Israeli hands.

* * *

The embargo was a moment of great tension for the U.S.-Saudi alliance, but leaders in both countries were determined to keep their disagreements within bounds. Saudi Arabia maintained its diplomatic contacts with the United States, publicly played down the confrontation, and secretly violated its own embargo by continuing to supply the U.S. military with fuel. Despite occasional talk of sending in the marines, the Nixon administration never seriously considered a military solution. The dispute remained limited because U.S. and Saudi leaders understood that they both had much to gain from their relationship. Nixon even saw the Saudi regime as an ally against his critics in Congress, trying to convince the Saudi leadership to save his political career because he was the only president who could deliver a just peace in the Middle East.

Even before the embargo was officially lifted, the Nixon administration and the Saudi royal family were already looking forward to strengthening their relationship still further. In early March, Kissinger, Akins, and other U.S. officials presented Saudi Arabia with a plan for closer U.S.-Saudi economic and security cooperation. Akins reported: "All the Saudis were enthusiastic; indeed they were as close to euphoria as I could imagine them to be." They "called this initiative the news they had been expecting for 25 years" and "said that the U.S. and Arab economies would be so closely entwined that there could be no turning back." The planning minister Hisham Nazer commented dryly: "It's finally happened. You've come to your senses." Prince Fahd took charge of the effort on the Saudi side. Fahd's brother Sultan frankly admitted to Akins that Fahd wanted to take a key role in managing the U.S.-Saudi alliance for his own benefit, to "strengthen his prestige in Saudi Arabia and in the Arab world." Sultan argued that it was still a good deal for the United States. "I'll let you in on a secret," he told Akins. Fahd was already the "second most important man in the country and he will be our next leader" once Faisal died, so he was someone the United States needed on its side.[91]

The United States was happy to work with Fahd. The kingdom's new wealth made it more appealing as a partner for the United States. The Nixon administration was especially enthusiastic about Saudi Arabia's ability to hold world oil prices down and to serve as a market for American exports and a source of investment for U.S. financial markets.[92] Over the next several years, the United States and Saudi Arabia would build a close economic partnership, and the alliance between Washington and Riyadh would emerge from the embargo even stronger than before.

6

UNMOORED

I n the mid-1970s, the port of Jeddah was in chaos. The new facilities that King Faisal had dedicated in 1973 were already overwhelmed by the sheer volume of imports pouring into the kingdom during the oil boom. The cargoes ranged from American cars and Japanese electronics to sheep and camels, carried in ships followed by sharks waiting to feed on animals that died during the voyage and were thrown overboard. Confronted with such a torrent of goods, the port was hopelessly overburdened. At times, more than one hundred vessels idled offshore, waiting up to nine months for their turn to unload.[1]

Even after the cargo made it to land, it often sat unclaimed. There were not enough cranes, forklifts, trucks, and trained equipment operators to move it all. Some importers could not afford the bribes required to clear customs, up to $15,000 per shipment. Others simply used the public port as an unofficial warehouse so they did not have to pay for facilities of their own. A visiting U.S. diplomat was shocked to see the port was littered with so much material that it spilled out of the warehouses onto the surrounding dirt and concrete, including "ripped open bags of cement, dusty Datsun pick-ups, and machinery and general cargo exposed to the corrosive salt breeze."[2] Perishable food arrived in markets already spoiled because it could not be unloaded in time. One Aramco employee remembered company bar-beques featuring intense discussions about whose marinade recipe could best disguise the taste of meat nearing the end of its shelf life.[3]

The Saudi government took desperate measures to clear the port. It hired a British company to barge thousands of tons of unclaimed goods—every-thing from cars and steel rebar to crates of spoiled food—out to deep water, where it was dumped into the Red Sea. Other contractors transferred cargo from the waiting ships onto surplus U.S. Navy landing craft that could be driven straight onto shore and unloaded without waiting for a turn at the docks. U.S. military veterans flew helicopters out to the ships, filled giant slings with cement, and hauled it back to land. The helicopters shuttled back and forth without a break, keeping their engines running even while they were being refueled. The Saudi construction boom was moving at such a breakneck pace that cement was needed *right away*, even if it meant the co-lossal expense—and vast quantities of fuel—of carrying heavy materials by air.[4]

The oil price increases of late 1973 unleashed a period of spectacular eco-nomic growth in the kingdom. The boom meant real improvement in the lives of many Saudis who received better education, health care, and material comforts, but it also brought new problems. Inequality spiked, with rich Sau-dis becoming even richer and others falling behind. Rapid inflation meant soaring costs for housing, food, and other basic needs. The assassination of King Faisal in 1975 was another source of disorientation. The resulting social tensions threatened Saudi political stability, even as the Al Saud acquired enormous new resources to strengthen their power and buy off dissent.

The economic boom consolidated the U.S.-Saudi alliance. Immediately after the embargo ended, some U.S. policymakers still toyed with the idea of using military force against the oil producers. They also hoped that the pursuit of energy independence would give them more leverage against Saudi Arabia. Even so, U.S. leaders concluded that the kingdom's new wealth and power over the oil market made it an indispensable ally. They sought to bind Saudi Arabia to the United States through a thick web of economic, military, and political connections.

Outside the executive branch and the top levels of the Saudi government, many people in both countries remained skeptical of the alliance. Members of Congress were outraged by the Saudi refusal to grant visas to Jewish Americans, along with the Arab boycott against American companies that did business with Israel. Congressional investigations uncovered extensive corruption and bribery in U.S. exports to Saudi Arabia, especially involving the arms dealer Adnan Khashoggi. Saudi dissidents, who saw their government as far too subservient to the United States, called for the more equitable distribution of oil revenues. Leaders in Washington and Riyadh, however, were determined to strengthen the ties between their two countries even in the face of such resistance.

THE SAUDI BOOM

The Saudi economy was already growing rapidly before 1973, but the huge oil price increases of that fall sent the economic boom into overdrive (figure 6.1). The kingdom's gross domestic product averaged an extraordinary average annual growth rate of nearly 28 percent during the 1970s, making the Saudi economy of 1980 roughly three and a half times larger than in 1970.[5] At the beginning of the decade, Saudi Arabia could barely scrape together enough money to pay its bills. Just a few years later, the kingdom had billions to spare.

The economic boom transformed the kingdom's physical landscape. New roads, houses, hospitals, airports, and factories multiplied across the landscape. In 1980, compared with 1970, Saudi Arabia produced more than 10 times as much electricity, desalinated 9 times as much water, and took in 15 times as much shipborne cargo. There were profound consequences for human development, too. The kingdom employed about three times as many nurses and five times as many doctors as it did ten years earlier.[6] Infant mortality was cut in half between the late 1960s and the early 1980s, while life expectancy rose from fifty to sixty-four.[7]

Saudi economic growth was driven by government spending, consolidating the regime's control over the country. Prince Fahd boasted about the material benefits his government offered its citizens, including "urban beautification," parks, and street lighting. The monarchy created the Real

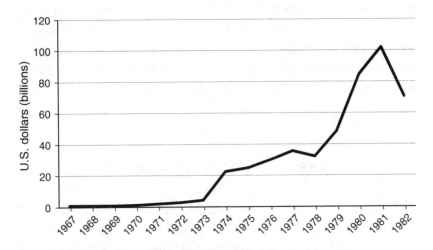

FIGURE 6.1 Saudi oil revenues in billions of U.S. dollars per year, 1967–1982, from Saudi Arabian Monetary Agency (SAMA) annual reports.

Estate Development Fund, which provided subsidies for Saudis unable to afford their own housing. Fahd explained that the fund "connected citizens to the leadership, therefore making the leadership a more important factor in the citizen's life."[8] Housing subsidies were only one example of Saudi welfare spending, which also included cheap water, electricity, and fuel. Even as gasoline prices rose for consumers in the United States and other oil-importing countries, Saudi Arabia cut gasoline prices for its own citizens in 1974.[9] The boom converted millions of Saudis into clients of the state, dependent on government support for jobs, housing, and affordable commodities.

The Saudi regime became more confident in its ability to maintain popular support even as it denied political participation to ordinary citizens. In a newspaper interview, Fahd blithely dismissed the "common misconception that the Western democratic system is like an inevitable model that everyone has to follow." That attitude might have been understandable in the past, Fahd suggested, but not now. Saudi Arabia was blazing a different path. In place of elections, the kingdom offered its citizens *shura* (consultation), the right to take complaints to the leadership. Fahd also bragged that the regime had practically eliminated crime while enriching the nation and preserving Islamic morality. When his interviewer again brought up the question of democracy, Fahd just chuckled and asked: "Didn't the parliamentary system arise in the West on the basis of 'no taxation without representation'?" In Saudi Arabia, he laughed, "we have no taxes at all!"[10]

THE PROBLEMS OF WEALTH

Although the Saudi regime commanded resources that made it the envy of other governments around the world, it also faced new challenges. By staking its political legitimacy on rapid economic growth, the royal family tied its own hands. It raised its people's expectations of the material benefits they should receive from the regime, permanently increasing its budgetary requirements. As the Saudi state increasingly converted itself into a machine for redistributing oil profits, it undermined its freedom of maneuver. It became bloated with tens of thousands of employees in make-work positions who were nearly impossible to fire. Parts of the state that had been devoted to raising taxes, customs fees, and other revenues were abolished or neglected now that the flood of oil money made them irrelevant, which had the side effect of reducing the state's capacity to monitor and regulate the economy.[11]

The government tried to steer economic development through a series of Five Year Plans beginning in 1970, but the growth was so fast that it proved difficult to control. It dislocated whole sectors of the Saudi economy, while shortages of labor and physical infrastructure created severe bottlenecks. Soliman Solaim, the Saudi minister of commerce, later admitted that in the 1970s, "the economy was not ready to absorb all this spending."[12] Bottlenecks in the ports, labor shortages, and the sheer pace of growth all fed rapid inflation, topping 30 percent per year in the mid-1970s.[13] Saudi political cartoons depicted inflation as a hideous beast threatening the people. After King Faisal declared a new campaign against inflation in the summer of 1974, one cartoon in *Al-Riyadh* optimistically showed the "inflation monster" slain by a sword labeled "Faisal's Decisions." Just a month later, though, the same newspaper warned that with prices rising daily, there was "chaos in the marketplace," in the streets, and on the sidewalks, "chaos everywhere." *Al-Riyadh* warned that just going to the grocery store "these days is like going into wars and battles." If you want to survive, "you have to be strong."[14]

Popular discontent with high prices was apparent even in the censored Saudi press. In 1976 *Al-Riyadh* published a letter from a poor young woman who lived with her father. They both worked, but their wages were not enough to pay the rent. She begged the minister of housing to help her. *Al-Madinah* reported that the housing market was plagued by land speculation, with unscrupulous investors bidding up the price of urban property so high that ordinary Saudis could no longer afford a home of their own. Solaim condemned "the greed of some businessmen in taking advantage of the atmosphere of economic freedom" and promised that illegal profiteering would be severely punished.[15]

The proliferation of public benefits during the 1970s, including subsidized gasoline, electricity, drinking water, food, and housing, was intended to shield Saudi consumers from the impact of higher prices. Government support, however, often flowed to Saudis who were already prosperous and well connected. One example was the Real Estate Development Fund that Fahd touted as an example of the regime's munificence. It covered 70 percent of the cost of building a house, with 50 percent to be repaid as an interest-free loan and 20 percent written off altogether. It was a generous scheme, but to qualify, Saudis already had to own the property where they planned to build their house. During the boom, urban land prices were soaring, and the most valuable property was often in the hands of princes and other elites.[16]

Other benefits also went to the privileged. Royals, ministers, and high-ranking bureaucrats distributed government jobs to their friends and family members. Saudis understood that a vital ingredient for economic advancement was *wasta*, meaning "pull" or "connections," in the form of access to an influential patron. The poor, or members of marginalized groups like the Bedouin or the Shia, were typically excluded from those networks.

A few still managed to climb the social ladder. One famous example was Ali Al-Naimi, who rose from a modest Bedouin background to become the first Saudi head of Aramco during the 1980s. Al-Naimi, however, was promoted by American executives who noticed his technical ability and were less sensitive to his humble status in Saudi society. He would have had a much harder time trying to rise through the Saudi government or establishing himself as a major businessman in Riyadh or Jeddah.[17]

Oil wealth flowed unequally to different parts of the kingdom. The biggest winner was Riyadh and the rest of the central province of Najd, the home of the Saudi royal family. Since the beginning of the Saudi kingdom, government functions had been divided between Riyadh and Jeddah on the Red Sea coast. Because Jeddah enjoyed better connections to global trade and transportation networks, it was the nation's diplomatic capital. Hijazi elites, usually based in Jeddah, included many of the kingdom's most important merchant families. Starting in the mid-twentieth century, though, government offices were gradually transferred to Riyadh.[18] The oil boom produced a surge of new public spending, swelling the bureaucracy and rewarding Najdi businesses with government contracts. The process accelerated with Fahd's ascendance. Fahd's associates and clients were mostly Najdi, in contrast with Faisal, who had been the viceroy of the Hijaz and enjoyed close ties to some of its leading families. After 1975, a new class of Najdi entrepreneurs surged ahead of the older Hijazi merchant networks.[19] Even as the city of Riyadh grew rapidly, however, it remained plagued by inequality. Slums inhabited by Bedouin families and immigrants existed alongside huge new developments and soaring real estate prices. The new physical infrastructure built by the Saudi state often reached poorer neighborhoods slowly or not at all, leaving them without electricity and running water.[20]

The richest Saudis accumulated incredible fortunes during the oil boom. The arms dealer Adnan Khashoggi earned huge commissions as an agent for the U.S. defense contractors Northrop and Lockheed and became famous for his jet-setting lifestyle.[21] As prosperous as Khashoggi and other Saudi businessmen became, however, their wealth and influence paled compared with that of princes like Sultan and Fahd. Senior royals could draw on state funds, take a percentage of the government contracts controlled by their ministries, and finance lavish palaces, vacation homes abroad, and other huge expenditures. As the pinnacle of Saudi society, they benefited the most from the oil boom.

THE ASSASSINATION OF KING FAISAL

While Faisal was alive, he restrained the worst excesses of Saudi corruption, or at least gave the appearance of doing so. Faisal had a reputation for piety and asceticism, and he looked the part, with a lean countenance and sunken cheeks caused by a stomach condition that kept him very thin. Faisal also enjoyed the prestige and authority that came from helping his father, Abdulaziz, in the final stages of Saudi unification during the 1920s and 1930s. He stood above the contending factions in the royal family, letting him enforce a degree of fiscal discipline on his relatives.

In March 1975, however, Faisal was assassinated. His nephew Prince Faisal bin Musaid killed the king while he was receiving guests at a *majlis*, a traditional occasion for Saudis to meet their leaders and present petitions. Prince Faisal bin Musaid waited with a group of Kuwaiti delegates until he could approach his uncle, then pulled a pistol from his robes and shot the king twice. King Faisal died soon afterward.

Prince Faisal bin Musaid's motives were unclear. The most popular theory speculated that the assassination was in revenge for the death of his brother Khalid, a religious conservative who was killed while protesting King Faisal's introduction of television broadcasting to Riyadh in 1966. Other rumors swirled around Prince Faisal bin Musaid's time in the United States, where he studied in California and Colorado during the late 1960s and early 1970s. The prince became involved in the American counterculture and was arrested for selling LSD. Soon after the assassination, Fahd asked the FBI to investigate Faisal bin Musaid's activities in America and sent an official from the Saudi Ministry of the Interior to join the inquiry. The Saudi government was especially interested in Faisal bin Musaid's American girlfriend, Christine Surma, but after questioning her and submitting a lengthy report to the Saudis, the FBI found nothing that would explain the assassination. Deputy Secretary of State Robert Ingersoll commented wryly that Faisal bin Musaid's "associations with female company were for purposes other than [to] discuss [the] Saudi political situation." Faisal bin Musaid was convicted and beheaded in June 1975, with many questions still unanswered.[22]

King Faisal's assassination unsettled the Saudi leadership. Crown Prince Fahd was afraid he might be killed, too, and demanded that the United States investigate potential threats against him. Henry Kissinger reassured Fahd that he knew of no plots against the crown prince, promising that he would inform Fahd immediately if anything came to light. The rumors surrounding Prince Faisal bin Musaid's experiences as an American student, including suggestions that Christine Surma was Jewish, also reflected Saudi unease at the increasing number of Saudi students who were exposed to foreign influences while studying abroad.[23]

The throne passed to Faisal's half-brother Khalid. He was a consensus choice acceptable to all leading members of the royal family, but he was not a forceful personality. Khalid was mostly uninterested in the details of government policy, a trait reinforced by his poor health. Day-to-day authority was in the hands of Prince Fahd, the leader of the "Sudairi Seven," a group of full brothers that also included the minister of defense, Prince Sultan; the minister of the interior, Prince Nayef; and the governor of Riyadh, Prince Salman.

Fahd, however, could not command the same respect as Faisal, either from his relatives or from the Saudi public at large. He was a decade and a half younger than Faisal and was not officially king, and during his early life, he had been notorious as a playboy devoted to gambling and high living, in sharp contrast with Faisal's austere image.

Being so closely associated with the Sudairi faction, even though they were the most powerful bloc in the royal family, meant that unlike Faisal, Fahd could not stand above family disputes. Fahd's inability to impose his authority on the rest of the Al Saud meant that other senior princes were free to run their ministries like personal fiefdoms, with less coordination imposed from above. The resulting surge of spending, bureaucratic empire-building, and personal enrichment by some princes and other senior officials exacerbated the challenges of the kingdom's pell-mell economic growth during the 1970s.[24] Within months of Faisal's assassination, the U.S. ambassador James Akins warned that corruption was already growing more blatant.[25] The oil boom was a double-edged sword for the Saudi regime, providing massive new resources for buying off opposition even as it fueled rising inequality that threatened to undermine public support for the monarchy.

JECOR

U.S. experts hoped to guide Saudi development and help the Saudis spend their new wealth more efficiently. The intended mechanism for such cooperation was the U.S.-Saudi Joint Commission for Economic Cooperation (JECOR), negotiated by Kissinger and Fahd in June 1974.[26] Under JECOR, around three hundred U.S. advisers were stationed in the kingdom to train Saudi bureaucrats and manage economic development projects with an annual budget of up to $200 million. The Saudi government deposited funds in a special bank account at the U.S. Federal Reserve under the supervision of the Treasury Department. Because the money came from Saudi Arabia, not the United States, JECOR could avoid some of the congressional oversight that came with other U.S. overseas development programs. JECOR took on a wide variety of infrastructure projects, including water desalination, solar energy, electricity generation, and soil surveys and other natural resource studies. Other projects involved human resource development: teaching Saudi officials how to deal with financial audits, consumer protection, and the training of public administrators. The U.S. Customs Service agreed to station four long-term advisers in the kingdom, while bringing fifteen Saudi customs employees to be trained in the United States every year.[27] At diplomatic gatherings, U.S. government and business leaders mingled with Saudi representatives, pitching a wide array of investment schemes, corporate partnerships, and other deals to trade Saudi money for American expertise (figure 6.2).

Fahd boasted about his success in securing American economic and security assistance. In 1974, he told a Lebanese interviewer that the West had

FIGURE 6.2 Saudi minister of state for foreign affairs Omar Saqqaf chats with U.S. secretary of state Henry Kissinger and Chase Manhattan Bank chairman David Rockefeller at a reception in Washington, DC, August 29, 1974. Bob Daugherty/Associated Press.

often refused to provide Arabs with its most desirable "technology and weapons," so "if we have a chance to get them, without limiting our sovereignty, I don't see how it would be in our interest to miss that opportunity."[28] Three years later, Fahd returned to the same theme, arguing that Saudi Arabia was profiting from American "technical expertise." Fahd welcomed experts from both the U.S. government and private companies that came to the kingdom as part of JECOR, since they had proved their worth "in the huge development projects achieved in American areas naturally similar to our own regions." Perhaps remembering his first visit to the United States with Faisal in 1945, when they stopped in Santa Fe, Fahd was particularly impressed with the U.S. achievement in "turning the deserts of Arizona, Nevada, and New Mexico into prosperous cities" and wanted U.S. aid to help "transfer this experience to our desert areas."[29]

Fahd was not alone in his enthusiasm. JECOR provoked jealousy in other countries that wanted a similar partnership with the United States.

Even Israel envied the developing U.S.-Saudi relationship. Before JECOR was officially signed, the Israeli embassy had already caught wind of the impending deal and asked Nixon to give Israel a similar arrangement.[30] By mid-1975, the United States established joint commissions with Israel, Egypt, Jordan, India, Iran, and Tunisia, but they tended to be on a much smaller scale than JECOR.[31]

JECOR was billed as a way to rationalize Saudi development, ensuring that Saudi revenues were used efficiently to put the kingdom on a sustainable economic path. Some U.S. policymakers, however, had more cynical goals for the project. Kissinger worried that Saudi Arabia's enormous financial reserves were a problem for the United States. Without any immediate fiscal pressures, Riyadh could cut its oil production to support high OPEC prices or to organize another embargo. Surplus wealth also gave Saudi Arabia the ability to shift its investments around the world, threatening the economic stability of the United States and its allies. Kissinger argued that the Saudis "have no concept of how to spend so much money" and wanted JECOR to give them the necessary push.[32] He complained that JECOR's leadership was overly fastidious in picking the development projects it supported. Kissinger mocked the JECOR administrators as "school teachers" who cared too much about ethics and only wanted to sell the Saudi oil minister Ahmad Zaki Yamani "things that are useful. I don't care if they are useless as long as they cost him lots of money."[33]

JECOR's mission of managing Saudi spending was also complicated by a rush of American companies and entrepreneurs to the kingdom, all hoping to make a profit as quickly as possible while the oil boom lasted. So many business leaders descended on Riyadh that every hotel room in the city was booked for months in advance. When Kissinger visited in March 1975, the U.S. embassy could only find quarters for his staff by asking the Saudi government to evict private guests from their rooms.[34] An official from the International Monetary Fund later remembered that on a spring 1974 trip to Riyadh, he and his colleagues stayed three to a room "in a rundown hotel with cockroaches and bedbugs," while private bankers from the United States and Europe slept in the backseats of cabs. In meetings the next day they were unshaven, unwashed, and exhausted, in sharp contrast with the Saudis across the table.[35]

There was so much money to be made during the oil boom that many Americans willingly put up with such indignities. James Larocco, an economic officer at the U.S. embassy in Jeddah during the mid-1970s, spent most of his time dealing with visiting American businesspeople. "It was very easy to sell anything" during those days, he remembered, "because money was falling from the skies." With the Saudis spending so freely, "everyone wanted to be on the gravy train, and the sharp ones left with fat wallets, regardless of the snake oil they were peddling." Larocco's job was to connect American businesses with Saudi buyers even if their products were utterly useless, including light-up plastic fireplaces or unwanted raincoats that were, on the embassy's advice, hastily rebranded as "tarps for Bedouin." On his watch, Larocco admitted, the Saudis bought "a lot of junk that was way overpriced."[36]

JECOR's more conscientious administrators worried that the commission had become simply a machine to generate profits for American companies. JECOR wrote its contracts according to U.S. specifications and technical standards, making it difficult for non-American companies to win Saudi business, and adding to the advantage that the United States already enjoyed because of the decades-long U.S. commercial presence in the kingdom.[37] A 1976 Ford administration report warned that "unofficially, the Commission is widely regarded as a failure." It was not helping the Saudis diversify their economy and become less dependent on oil, which was part of JECOR's official mission. Instead, JECOR had turned into nothing more than "a referral agency, a middle-man between the Saudis and the US private sector." The report's author, Jack Schick, argued that Saudi leaders had lost trust in JECOR and had retreated to dealing only with American firms they already trusted, like Aramco, the Stanford Research Institute (later SRI International), and Bechtel.[38] After retiring from JECOR, the Treasury Department official David Harbinson agreed, lamenting that the commission had become a mere "purchasing and construction operation" focused on short-term projects rather than long-term technical assistance. It funneled Saudi cash to American companies without any coherent plan, tolerating a great deal of inefficiency and "gold-plating" along the way.[39]

The economic turmoil of the boom had real costs for the U.S.-Saudi relationship. As Akins had warned in 1973, every fraudulent U.S.-Saudi business deal was a blow to American prestige in the kingdom.[40] The more the Saudis spent, the faster inflation raged. More imports meant bigger problems with the infrastructure bottlenecks in the ports. Elite Saudis—especially the ones who partnered with foreign companies, skimmed off government contracts, and secured licenses to import products in high demand—all made huge profits during the boom. Others were left behind, suffering from the rising cost of living and watching as the gap between rich and poor grew ever larger. Since the richest Saudis like Fahd and Khashoggi were known for their close ties to the United States, and derived their wealth partly from working with American companies, rising inequality fueled resentment against the alliance between Washington and Riyadh.

CREATING U.S. LEVERAGE OVER SAUDI ARABIA

Compared with Akins and other U.S. officials who focused on long-term cooperation with Saudi Arabia, Secretary of State Henry Kissinger's view of the U.S.-Saudi relationship was more adversarial. He saw Saudi oil power and wealth as assets that might be turned to American advantage with the proper management, but also as threats that could enable another embargo or a crippling series of oil price increases. Kissinger believed that JECOR and other collaborative instruments were important tools, but only in the context of a political strategy to gain American power over the kingdom. In August 1974, Kissinger told his staff: "I want a confrontation, believe me. But I need chips." U.S.-run industrial and military projects in the kingdom fit the bill, providing assets that Saudi Arabia would fear losing if it crossed the United States. In 1975, Kissinger told Republican members of Congress that economic cooperation was a way to "get our hooks into" Saudi Arabia.[41]

Kissinger wanted to drive a wedge between Saudi Arabia and the rest of the developing world. The mid-1970s were the heyday of the New International Economic Order (NIEO), a set of proposals by developing countries at the United Nations for higher commodity prices, more foreign aid, and other changes to the global terms of trade.[42] The oil price increases of 1973–1974 helped inspire the NIEO, as producers of phosphate, copper, and other commodities tried to emulate OPEC's achievement. OPEC endorsed their efforts.[43] Kissinger saw the "unholy alliance" between OPEC and the developing countries as a major threat to the United States. While publicly expressing some sympathy with the NIEO, he privately declared his intention to "pull its teeth and divide these countries up."[44] Other U.S. officials, like Secretary of the Treasury William Simon, were even more hostile, denouncing the NIEO as a scheme to interfere with the free market and take resources from rich countries like the United States. Building a special relationship with Saudi Arabia was one way to drive a wedge between the oil producers and the non-oil developing countries. The United States wanted to convince the Saudi regime that its interests lay with a stable, growing American economy rather than a radically different global economic order.[45]

Kissinger also wanted to divide the OPEC nations from each other. He told Ford in August 1974: "We have to find a way to break the cartel." Kissinger thought that Saudi Arabia could probably accept a reduction in oil prices but would never take any political risks to bring prices down, since "the Saudis belong to the most feckless and gutless of the Arabs." The United States would have to take the initiative to crack OPEC first. In early 1976, Kissinger tried to undermine OPEC's unity by getting Iran to sell discounted oil to the United States. He cared little about the details of oil prices; he simply wanted Iran to break with Saudi Arabia and the rest of OPEC. Kissinger explained: "I want the Saudis to weep."[46]

The counterpart to Kissinger's strategy of dividing OPEC was his attempt to unite the oil-consuming nations. During the October War, Kissinger had been angry at the refusal of most European countries to allow the use of their airfields in resupplying Israel, which he blamed on the Europeans' fear of an Arab oil embargo. He hoped that a consumer alliance would prevent such problems during a future crisis. In the short run, agreements to share the available oil supplies would forestall panic and help the consumers stick together in the face of embargoes and shortages. The appearance of consumer solidarity might also intimidate the producers while restoring the consumers' self-confidence. In the long run, Kissinger hoped

that the oil-importing nations would coordinate their efforts on energy conservation and develop alternatives to imported oil. Kissinger was less concerned about economics than politics. He saw consumer solidarity as a way
of reinvigorating the Western alliance, binding Europe and Japan together
under American leadership in the face of a common threat. In November 1974, he told Ford that the oil crisis was "an opportunity to mobilize
the West like anti-Communism was" in the late 1940s.[47]

Kissinger focused on building leverage against Saudi Arabia and preparing the consumers for another confrontation with the producers
because he doubted that the U.S.-Saudi relationship would hold up over
the long run. The end of the embargo had not resolved the two countries'
differences over Israel. During the mid-1970s, Saudi leaders frequently
reiterated their calls for the return of Jerusalem and other territories taken
by Israel in 1967. In the fall of 1974, Faisal demanded the "liberation" of
the "land and holy places" of Palestine, and the "expulsion of the enemy
from all the occupied territories, including the city of Jerusalem," to end
Israel's "cancerous growth in the region." Shortly after taking the throne
in spring 1975, Faisal's successor Khalid argued that the Middle East conflict would only end when Jerusalem was redeemed "from the clutches of
Zionism."[48]

Kissinger tried to buy time by telling the Saudi leadership what he
thought they wanted to hear. During Nixon's visit to the kingdom in
June 1974, Kissinger told the Saudi foreign minister Omar Saqqaf that he
would push Israel to withdraw from the occupied territories, but he had to
move slowly and not reveal his plan because otherwise "the American Jews
would rise up against it." Kissinger promised: "We know there will be no
peace until the '67 borders, but we can't say it."[49] Kissinger, however, told
the Israelis a very different story, reassuring the Israeli foreign minister
Yigal Allon and Ambassador Simcha Dinitz that in his opinion, a return
to the 1967 frontiers was "impossible."[50] Kissinger pushed Israel to make
limited concessions, but he had no intention of forcing Israel to satisfy the
Arab demands and withdraw from all the occupied territories.[51] When Ford
asked him about the U.S. stance on the 1967 borders, Kissinger told the
president: "You wouldn't be proud of my morals . . . I have bobbed and
weaved all over the place on this. We can't be pinned down."[52]

Kissinger worried that once Saudi Arabia became impatient with his eva-
sions, they could impose another oil embargo. In August 1974 he predicted
that "Saudi Arabia will not be playing political ball with us" unless he could
force major concessions out of Israel, a prospect he found "not very likely."
The result, he warned, could be another oil embargo within months. Kissinger repeated his warnings in September 1974 and March 1975, predicting
that another embargo would cause "a massive anti-U.S. blow-up" and lead
Europe and Japan to abandon the United States.[53]

MILITARY THREATS AND
THE KISSINGER-AKINS SPLIT

American fears of a Saudi-led supply disruption led to renewed speculation about the use of force against the kingdom. If Saudi Arabia and the
other producers cut off their exports, Kissinger told Ford in September 1974,
"we might have to take the oil." He advised Secretary of Defense James
Schlesinger that December that if the Middle East peace negotiations broke
down, "we need contingency plans for seizing the oil fields." And, in January 1975, Kissinger said: "If we face the total oil embargo of the West, we
have to have a plan to use force." He proposed Abu Dhabi or Libya as targets, but Deputy Secretary of Defense William Clements argued that only
Saudi Arabia would provide enough oil to make a military operation
worthwhile.[54]

Any military operation against the Saudi oil fields would have been extremely risky. If it damaged the oil installations, or the Saudi government
sabotaged the production equipment, the fields would be taken offline for
months. A U.S. invasion of the Gulf would inflame public opinion throughout the Arab world and beyond. It was also doubtful whether the American people or Congress would support a war for oil, especially in early 1975,
as the South Vietnamese regime was entering its final collapse and most
Americans were in no mood for another foreign conflict.[55]

Even if he never intended to send U.S. troops into the Gulf, though,
Kissinger and other U.S. leaders hoped that the threat of such action might

help keep Saudi Arabia in line. In a December 1974 interview in *Business Week*, Kissinger publicly raised the possibility of military intervention against the oil producers in the case of "the gravest emergency" involving "actual strangulation of the industrialized world." Secretary of Defense James Schlesinger agreed, declaring that in an emergency the United States would be prepared to use force to secure oil supplies.[56]

Kissinger's and Schlesinger's comments alarmed the Saudi government, especially since they came around the same time as a series of American and Israeli newspaper and magazine articles making the case for invading the Gulf.[57] Yamani told Ambassador Akins that "he had never seen the King so depressed, so worried, and so questioning of his relationship with the United States." Yamani claimed that the Saudi National Guard had been given orders to blow up the oil installations and set the wells on fire, so U.S. soldiers would find nothing but burning ruins if they came to take the oil. Both Akins and Frank Jungers, the chairman of Aramco, believed the threat was credible. The Ford administration tried to defuse the situation, sending conciliatory statements by Ford and Kissinger, without fully disavowing the secretary of state's original comments. Kissinger later claimed that talk of invading the Gulf was not a deliberate policy statement and "resulted from lack of planning and some bureaucratic disputes." Even so, he privately boasted that the threats had intimidated Saudi Arabia and the other oil producers.[58]

The controversy over Kissinger's statement drove a wedge between the secretary of state and James Akins, his ambassador in Saudi Arabia. Akins thought the idea of invading the kingdom was "madness." Once the immediate controversy had passed, Akins gave a press interview in Jeddah calling those who advocated war for oil "criminally insane;" he also submitted a paper to the State Department and the military in which he argued that an invasion of the oilfields would be a disaster. Although Akins was careful not to criticize Kissinger directly, the secretary of state did not take kindly to Akins's outspoken words. In August 1975, Kissinger unceremoniously fired Akins, who only learned about his dismissal from the press.[59]

Their split over the Saudi invasion threats added to tensions between Kissinger and Akins that had been building for years. They were a pair of strong personalities who had a hard time working together. Akins found Kissinger duplicitous and thought he was too favorable to Israel; Kissinger thought Akins was stubborn, arrogant, and disobedient. Their clash also involved a basic difference in their visions for American diplomacy. As a career Foreign Service officer, Akins was deeply knowledgeable about the Arab world. He joined the State Department and learned Arabic in the 1950s. As the ambassador in Jeddah from 1973 to 1975, Akins developed close ties with the Saudi leadership, ties that were too close for Kissinger's liking. In a double-edged compliment, Kissinger told Prince Khalid in June 1974 that Akins was "devoted to your country."[60] By contrast, Kissinger represented a newer style of diplomacy made possible by rapid jet travel, a technology that had still been in its infancy when Akins had joined the Foreign Service. Kissinger flew to other countries for short visits, sometimes only for a matter of hours, meeting with the top leadership and moving on, pursuing a strategy of constant maneuver rather than building the long-term ties and local knowledge valued by experienced ambassadors like Akins. The difference in style was underlined when Kissinger scheduled a meeting with King Faisal and did not invite Akins, who argued that the ambassador always had to be included in such meetings and threatened to resign unless he were invited.[61] Akins's dismissal underlined the rise of a new kind of diplomacy conducted directly between national leaders and high officials, bypassing career diplomats.

THE FAILURE OF ENERGY INDEPENDENCE

Although Akins lost his personal battle with Kissinger, in the long run his cooperative approach toward Saudi Arabia would prevail over Kissinger's more adversarial strategy. A major reason was the U.S. failure to make faster progress in reducing demand for imported oil. Soon after taking office, Ford reaffirmed his commitment to Project Independence, the program that Nixon had announced in November 1973. His energy and economic advisers set targets of "full national self-sufficiency" in oil by 1985 and the establishment of the United States as a net energy exporter by the year 2000.[62]

Those goals were extremely ambitious. Even if they had been achieved, the United States would have remained indirectly vulnerable to oil supply shocks, with American allies in Western Europe and East Asia still reliant on foreign oil. Nevertheless, U.S. officials hoped that even partial progress toward energy independence would give the United States more leverage over other players in the world oil market. Although domestic energy policy was not Kissinger's responsibility, he told the other members of the cabinet in August 1974 that, when it came to energy, "Project Independence is the one thing we can do unilaterally which matters."[63] Kissinger told the president a month later: "What we need is a thriving Project Independence. It is not really my business except we need it."[64]

In January 1975, Ford unveiled his "Energy Independence Act." He called for more domestic production of oil, coal, and nuclear power, along with the formation of a national strategic oil reserve, mandatory fuel economy requirements for automobiles, and a cutback in environmental regulations. The most controversial element of the plan was an increase in oil prices, which was to be accomplished through two mechanisms: lifting domestic price controls and imposing fees on oil imports. Ford argued that higher prices were necessary to protect American national security. He warned that remaining dependent on foreign oil—especially Arab oil—would hurt the U.S. economy and leave the country vulnerable to embargoes. "We will not create more jobs in America," Ford explained, "by paying more money to the Arabs."[65]

In order to enact his plan, however, Ford needed approval from Congress, which was under Democratic control. His proposals attracted ferocious political opposition, especially from consumers who objected to higher oil prices. Congress was also determined to assert its own power in the face of Ford's attempt to bring energy policy under presidential control. The House and Senate voted to block the oil import fee by the enormous margins of 308–114 and 66–28. The import fees and the relaxation of price controls were particularly loathed in the Northeast, which depended on imported oil and stood to lose the most from higher prices. In January 1975, ten northeastern governors met with Ford to denounce his proposals. Pennsylvania governor Milton Shapp called them "a blueprint for economic disaster" that would cause "a shock wave of inflation throughout the country." Massachusetts governor Michael Dukakis said that Ford "was holding the

Northeast hostage for his program," and that he should have developed a plan "that didn't discriminate so outrageously" against New England. Eight of the governors sued to strip Ford of his authority to impose fees on imported oil.[66]

Congress, however, was unable to enact a plan of its own. When several months had passed and no comprehensive energy bill had yet emerged, Ford went on television, theatrically tearing pages off a calendar and asking, "What did the Congress do in February about energy? Congress did nothing," then repeating the accusation for March, April, and May. When Congress did pass a bill, the "Petroleum Price Review Act," in July 1975, Ford promptly vetoed it, denouncing the bill for strengthening price controls and making America more dependent on foreign oil.[67] The whole experience was deeply frustrating for everyone concerned. House majority leader Thomas "Tip" O'Neill (D-MA) called energy perhaps "the most parochial issue that could ever hit the floor," noting that congressional delegations from different regions of the United States had diametrically opposed interests on energy prices. Clarence Brown (R-OH), the senior Republican on the House Subcommittee on Energy and Power, compared his task to that of the tortured Sisyphus of Greek mythology, and Jim Wright (D-TX), in charge of developing the House Democrats' energy plan, admitted that the whole "enterprise has degenerated at times into a farcical comedy of frustrations."[68]

In November 1975, Congress finally passed a compromise bill, the Energy Policy and Conservation Act (EPCA). The act contained several of Ford's original proposals, such as higher fuel economy standards for automobiles and the creation of the Strategic Petroleum Reserve. On the crucial issue of oil prices, though, EPCA tightened price controls in the short term while allowing a gradual increase in prices, at the president's discretion, that would extend through 1979. The bill was anathema to the oil industry and free-market conservatives. House Republicans and the American Petroleum Institute, a leading industry lobbying group, attacked it in the strongest terms.[69] Public mail to Ford was against the bill by a margin of 3,650 to 50, with the angriest letters coming from Texas and other oil-producing states.[70] Sen. John Tower (R-TX) told Ford: "I better call it now. The bill is an absolute and total disaster." Rep. Samuel Devine (R-OH) agreed, contemptuously referring to EPCA as "the OPEC subsidy bill of 1975."[71]

Ford's political and national security advisers argued in favor of EPCA, on the theory that half a loaf was better than none. Ford took their advice and reluctantly signed the bill. One of his aides noted that signing the bill would at least protect Ford politically, since it would "remove the pricing issue and, to a great extent, the petroleum industry from the election debate next year."[72] That prediction proved too optimistic. Ford's decision to sign EPCA damaged his reputation with the conservative wing of the Republican Party, and particularly with voters in oil-producing states.[73] During the summer of 1976, Ford was locked in a close primary battle with his conservative challenger, former California governor Ronald Reagan. The Reagan campaign ran television ads in Texas attacking Ford's energy policies and accusing him of destroying jobs in the oil industry.[74] Ford's compromise on energy policy contributed to Reagan's upset victory in the 1976 Texas presidential primary, enhancing Reagan's electoral viability and pushing the Republican Party to the right.[75]

EPCA represented a major step forward in certain areas, including the Strategic Petroleum Reserve and mandatory fuel economy standards for American automobiles. It did not, however, promise much short-term reduction in U.S. dependence on foreign oil. In fact, even Ford's preferred option of an immediate end to oil price controls would still have left the United States heavily dependent on imported oil at the end of the 1970s.[76] By 1976, it was clear that the United States was making little progress toward energy independence. Robert Hormats, the National Security Council's expert on international economic policy, warned Brent Scowcroft (who had replaced Kissinger as national security advisor) about "the sorry state of US domestic energy policy and its very dubious foundation in Project Independence." He noted that the Federal Energy Agency's import targets under Project Independence *"are simply unreachable,* at any reasonable cost," and so "we are going to remain very vulnerable for the foreseeable future." Hormats concluded that the United States had to build relationships with the key oil-producing countries to "induce moderation" and prevent supply disruptions.[77] The difficulty of securing cooperation with Congress on energy policy, especially the contentious issue of pricing, also motivated the White House to focus instead on foreign policy, where the president's authority was less constrained. Saudi Arabia would be a key partner in that effort.

SECURITY COOPERATION

Saudi Arabia's importance stemmed not only from Saudi control of key oil resources but also from the financial strength that oil exports made possible. The kingdom's new wealth enabled it to become a massive aid donor to other nations in the Middle East and elsewhere in the Islamic world. In 1976, Scowcroft told Ford that Saudi Arabia had accumulated more than \$30 billion in financial reserves, a number that was expected to grow by another \$25 billion each year. Scowcroft forwarded a study from the National Security Council estimating that Saudi Arabia had given other countries more than \$7.7 billion in aid during the previous two years. The largest recipients were Egypt, with \$2.2 billion, and North Yemen, with \$760 million.[78]

Saudi aid went to anticommunist regimes, encouraging Egypt and other Arab nations to move away from the Soviet Union and align themselves more closely with Saudi Arabia and the United States. Prince Abdullah, the commander of the Saudi National Guard, told Ford in 1976 that Saudi Arabia was funding Egypt and Jordan on the condition that they use the money to buy weapons from the United States and other Western countries.[79]

When speaking privately with U.S. officials, some Saudi leaders admitted that antileftism trumped their other foreign policy priorities. In 1975–1976, a brutal civil war began in Lebanon. It pitted the right-wing Christian Phalange movement against mostly Muslim, left-wing forces including the PLO. At that time, Saudi Arabia was funding and publicly supporting the PLO. Nevertheless, the Saudi undersecretary of foreign affairs Abdul Rahman Mansouri told the U.S. ambassador William Porter that the PLO needed to be eliminated as a military force because of its leftist tendencies. When Porter warned that a disarmed PLO would not be able to defend itself and might be "destroyed," Mansouri just shrugged and asked: "What other solution is there?"[80]

The United States was pleased to see Saudi money and influence advancing right-wing causes in the Middle East and beyond. A 1976 CIA report noted that "the Saudi weapon is money" that the Saudi government was using "to constrain the expansion of Soviet influence." As a result, "the growing wealth of the Gulf countries" was "perhaps the most significant . . .

long-term impediment to Soviet progress in the area."[81] The United States even attempted to secure Saudi aid for anticommunist forces in places as far afield as Rhodesia and South Vietnam.[82]

There were limits to what Saudi Arabia could do beyond its borders. The kingdom still had a weak military and no arms industry of its own. As one U.S. official commented: "All they have is money." Because Saudi Arabia had no global intelligence network, at times—such as in mid-1976, when it planned to increase its financial backing for anticommunist forces in Africa—the kingdom simply asked the United States which countries and rebel factions it should support.[83] Saudi wealth also inspired resentment. Aid recipients like Egypt chafed at their dependence on Saudi Arabia, remembering that less than a decade before, Egypt had been the dominant force in Arab politics and Saudi Arabia had been far less powerful. The Egyptian foreign minister Ismail Fahmi complained to Kissinger in 1974 that "the oil people are the biggest political amateurs." Fahmi noted that they failed to back up their financial help with any political support once Egypt began its peace negotiations with Israel.[84] To make up for its limitations as a regional power broker, Saudi Arabia constantly lobbied the United States to support the kingdom's allies in the Middle East with arms, military protection, and political assistance. Those efforts were only partially successful. Riyadh was frustrated, for example, in its efforts to convince the United States to back Somalia against Ethiopia in the mid-1970s. They did, however, lay the groundwork for more extensive cooperation between Washington and Riyadh in later years.

CORRUPTION AND RELIGIOUS DISCRIMINATION

As the U.S. and Saudi governments drew closer, their relationship was still troubled by persistent tensions. One challenge was a series of U.S. investigations into corrupt practices by U.S. defense contractors and the Saudi arms dealer Adnan Khashoggi. A Senate committee chaired by Frank Church (D-ID) began looking into Khashoggi's business dealings with American companies, including Northrop, Lockheed, and Raytheon, in

May 1975. The Senate was joined by the Pentagon and the Securities and Exchange Commission (SEC). Together, they uncovered many examples of bribes to foreign officials and enormous fees paid to Khashoggi.[85] The Saudi government was alarmed at the investigations, which threatened to publicize corrupt dealings within the regime. Foreign Minister Saud al-Faisal warned Ford and Kissinger: "If names get thrown around in these hearings, it would have a very bad influence." Ford and Kissinger promised to tell Frank Church to keep Saudi names out of public view.[86] Even so, the negative publicity was an unwelcome surprise for the Saudi government, which prohibited commissions on arms deals in an attempt to avoid future scandals.[87]

An even more sensitive issue was the long-standing Saudi policy of excluding Jews from the kingdom. In 1976, a U.S. diplomat asked Saud al-Faisal whether the policy applied to members of the U.S. Army Corps of Engineers helping the kingdom with military construction and engineering. Saud answered that "most Jews were Zionists or were very favorably inclined to Israel," and because "Saudi Arabia was virtually at war with Israel," it had to exclude Jews from defense projects.[88] Saudi anti-Semitism drew criticism from Congress, but the Ford administration considered the U.S.-Saudi relationship too important to jeopardize. Kissinger dismissed the issue, telling Ford, "Saudi Arabia has been bigoted forever." If the United States pushed the Saudi regime too hard, it might weaken the government and risk a military coup; the only alternative was to accept Saudi religious discrimination as a necessary price of doing business.[89] Kissinger complained that Congress did not understand the need to look past Saudi Arabia's domestic policies. He called one critic, Sen. Clifford Case (R-NJ), "practically an Israeli agent" because Case proposed "an aid amendment barring aid to the Saudis unless they admit women and Jews." A dismayed Ford responded: "My God. And the Saudis helped us on OPEC, and have billions to invest."[90]

Another problem related to Saudi participation in the Arab boycott against companies that did business with Israel or were controlled by Jewish interests. U.S. corporations working in Saudi Arabia had to show that they abided by the terms of the boycott. Many Americans, including several influential members of Congress, were furious that U.S. companies were willing to work under such a system. At least fourteen bills and two congressional resolutions were introduced to punish the Arab countries or American companies that abided by the boycott. Ford's attorney general Edward Levi, the first Jewish American to occupy that position, filed a lawsuit against Bechtel Corporation for violating antitrust law and discriminating against Jewish employees. Kissinger fought to shield Bechtel, arguing that if U.S. companies were barred from discriminating against Jews, "the Saudis don't care—they will shift all their orders to Europe." The Ford administration reached a negotiated settlement with Bechtel that let the company off with only a light punishment.[91] Nevertheless, the boycott issue was a major irritant. National security adviser Brent Scowcroft called it "the most nettlesome" problem in U.S.-Saudi relations, and other officials in addition to Kissinger feared that it would lead the kingdom to shift large military and infrastructure contracts away from American companies.[92] Fahd warned in May 1977 that it would be much easier for Arab countries to choose other suppliers than it would be for American companies to abandon the lucrative Arab market.[93]

Congressional skepticism about Saudi Arabia limited U.S. arms sales to the kingdom. In 1976, Saudi Arabia asked the United States for a giant shipment of Sidewinder and Maverick air-launched missiles. The sale faced intense congressional opposition. Kissinger told Ford: "We are in a huge mess in Congress. They are coming after us on the Sidewinders and Mavericks for Saudi Arabia."[94] The Democratic presidential nominee Jimmy Carter slammed Ford in a speech to more than two dozen Jewish organizations, accusing the Republicans of "bowing down to foreign blackmail" by tolerating the Arab boycott and offering arms to Saudi Arabia. His running mate, Walter Mondale, made similar accusations, arguing that the Ford administration was disturbing the military balance between Israel and the Arab nations.[95] Kissinger privately complained about Carter's "attacks on Saudi Arabia, which can be a strong force for good," but Ford compromised in the face of congressional opposition and cut the missile sale to a fraction of what the Saudis had originally requested.[96] Ford tried to win credit with the Saudi government anyway, telling King Khalid that he valued the U.S.-Saudi relationship so highly that he had decided to sell the missiles even in the face of "intense political pressure" during an election year.[97]

SAUDI DISSENT

Just as Ford faced criticism for working with Saudi Arabia, the kingdom came under attack from critics elsewhere in the Arab world for its policy of cooperation with the United States. Two Saudi exiles, the former oil minister Abdullah Tariki and the economist and writer Abdelrahman Munif, were among the most prominent critics. In October 1974, Tariki wrote in his journal *Naft al-Arab* (*Arab Oil*) that the oil exporters could never spend all their earnings at home, so they should not hoard their wealth. Investing their reserves in the industrialized nations would also be a mistake. Instead, they should use their money to help the rest of the Arab world and other developing countries in Africa and Asia. Tariki argued that the petrodollar "surplus" was only apparent from a narrow national point of view, one restricted to the oil producers with the smallest populations, like Saudi Arabia and Libya. When the perspective was broadened to include the Arab world or the developing world as a whole, there were more than enough urgent needs to absorb all the new oil revenues.[98]

Munif, later the author of the epic *Cities of Salt* novels, served during the mid-1970s as the editor in chief of *Al-Naft wa al-Tanmiyya* (*Oil and Development*), a new journal published in Iraq that examined the politics of petroleum and economic from a left-wing, Arab nationalist perspective. The first issue launched in October 1975 with the endorsement of the Iraqi government, featuring short pieces by Iraq's president, Ahmed Hassan al-Bakr, and vice president, Saddam Hussein. A year later, the journal denounced the United States for trying to control the Persian Gulf and its oil resources through "the American method of invasion," indirect economic colonialism.[99]

In November 1976, Munif published a sharp critique of U.S. economic and military policy in the Gulf. He argued that the United States tried to keep oil prices low, while ensuring that whatever money it did pay in exchange for oil was immediately recycled by investing in American financial markets or purchasing American products. Arms were the most important of those products. Munif explained that "a leading goal for America is to ignite wars all over the world and to be a major source of weapons used in those wars." If "hot wars" were not possible, the United States would settle for creating "centers of constant tension, thus permitting a wide arena for the arms trade." Unfortunately for his homeland, Munif wrote, the Persian Gulf had become one of those centers of tension, ensuring that the region's prosperity was bled away into the pockets of American defense companies. While Munif never mentioned Saudi Arabia by name, his editorial was a stinging attack on the Saudi regime's support for low oil prices, petrodollar recycling, and arms purchases. The United States controlled the region, Munif explained, through "the special relationship that America enjoys with many Gulf countries." The only source of comfort Munif could offer his readers was that the United States, "which looks like a giant armed from head to toe," had been humiliated in Vietnam. Even a superpower could be defeated, so the Arabs should stand up to the United States and demand independence from American control.[100]

* * *

Tariki's and Munif's writings were a reminder that as the relationship between U.S. and Saudi elites grew closer in the mid-1970s, the alliance still had many critics. The Saudi embrace of the United States angered Saudi dissidents and citizens of other Arab countries, especially as the United States continued to send money and weapons to Israel, and most of the Arab territories occupied in 1967 remained in Israeli hands. Anti-Semitic policies by the Saudi government infuriated members of Congress, who accused the White House of abetting such discrimination. Congressional investigations also uncovered some of the unseemly business practices that greased the wheels of trade between the United States and Saudi Arabia. Many Americans hoped that the United States could achieve energy independence and end its partnership with what they saw as such a distasteful regime. People in both countries could hardly forget that as recently as March 1974, Saudi Arabia had been part of the oil embargo against the United States.

Nevertheless, the U.S.-Saudi alliance emerged from the embargo even stronger than before. From the point of view of the White House, the State Department, the Pentagon, and the corporations that profited from the relationship, Saudi Arabia was now far too rich and influential to ignore. The United States doubled down on its ties with Saudi Arabia. Washington and Riyadh cooperated to support right-wing political forces throughout the Middle East and beyond, while JECOR and an array of lucrative business deals tied the U.S. and Saudi economies together. During the late 1970s, the kingdom's colossal wealth and close relationship with the White House would make it an even more influential actor in world affairs. It began to intervene directly in American politics, trying to shift U.S. foreign policy and economic policy to the right. Saudi Arabia's new influence would start to become clear during a 1978 debate over U.S. arms sales to the kingdom, when, with the help of the new president, Jimmy Carter, and its other American allies, the kingdom overcame fierce resistance and a skeptical Congress to purchase some of the most advanced weapons made in the United States.

7

TURNING RIGHT

During the late spring of 1978, black limousines pulled up nearly every day to the luxurious Madison Hotel in downtown Washington, DC, to pick up a group of Saudi officials. They included the ambassador, Ali Alireza, the ministers of industry and commerce, Ghazi Algosaibi and Soliman Solaim, and two young princes, the intelligence official Turki al-Faisal and the air force pilot Bandar bin Sultan.[1] They were in town to lobby for the sale of the most advanced U.S. jet fighter, the F-15, to Saudi Arabia, as part of a package deal that also included aircraft sales to Egypt and Israel.

The arrangement was intensely controversial. The government of Israel and its American supporters argued that in Saudi hands, the F-15 would pose a direct threat to the Jewish state. Zionist groups were joined by peace activists, including the NAACP's chief lobbyist, Clarence Mitchell, the civil rights leader Bayard Rustin, and Margaret Trexler of the Coalition of American Nuns, who warned that American arms sales only exacerbated the conflict in the Middle East. An overwhelming majority of the American public, 73 percent, opposed the deal.[2] At first, U.S. officials thought they could never win congressional support. They tried to convince Saudi Arabia to give up and ask for a cheaper, less advanced aircraft, but the kingdom insisted on the F-15.[3] President Jimmy Carter decided to ignore the congressional opposition, telling his secretary of state, Cyrus Vance, "We'll fight it out." The administration joined forces with the kingdom to lobby Congress, encouraging Ali Alireza to exploit his personal ties with influential senators. Carter told Vance: "The Saudis & their friends will have to go all out to help us in the Senate."[4]

The kingdom followed through, organizing a massive campaign that included ads in *Time*, *Newsweek*, and other major publications, along with behind-the-scenes lobbying by Washington power brokers like the lawyer and longtime Kennedy family associate Frederick Dutton. Even members of pro-Israel groups admitted that they were impressed with the scale of the effort.[5] In May 1978, Congress approved the deal. The result demonstrated Saudi Arabia's ability to influence U.S. politics and overcome a powerful and well-organized coalition of opponents.

Saudi Arabia had considerable clout in Washington, DC, because by the late 1970s, U.S. policymakers saw the kingdom as the key "swing producer" in the oil market, with more power to shape oil prices than any other nation. Saudi Arabia also emerged as an enormous source of investment capital. The Department of the Treasury and the Federal Reserve worked to attract Saudi funds to the United States, shielding those investments from congressional and public scrutiny at a time when many Americans were suspicious of foreign "petrodollars." The United States began acting like a giant offshore investment haven that offered confidentiality and government protection to its most lucrative clients.

Saudi influence was boosted by the kingdom's alliance with powerful American interests. Corporations like the construction giant Bechtel and Computer Sciences Corporation, the largest software company of its day, lobbied for the F-15 deal. Even if they would not profit directly from the aircraft sale, they looked forward to the business opportunities that would come from closer U.S. ties with Saudi Arabia. The most important ally of all was the White House, which threw its influence into the fight on Capitol Hill. One pro-Israel lobbyist complained about Carter "unleashing the entire Cabinet" to help Saudi Arabia.[6]

The combination of Saudi influence and the U.S. reaction to the energy crisis pushed American politics to the right during the late 1970s. The Carter administration began dismantling the system of price controls that had shielded U.S. consumers from high oil prices, part of a broader wave of deregulation that began even before Ronald Reagan entered the White House. The Carter administration and the Federal Reserve Bank decided to prioritize the fight against inflation at the expense of more traditional Democratic goals like helping workers and limiting unemployment. Saudi Arabia encouraged that shift in U.S. monetary policy, which had profound consequences for the American economy.

Saudi Arabia, too, turned to the right during the late 1970s. The shift was already under way by 1978–1979 and was reinforced by the regime's response to the Iranian Revolution and a pair of internal uprisings in Mecca and al-Hasa in 1979. The royal family stressed its Islamic credentials as a way of deflecting criticism about its close relationship with the United States, its autocratic rule, and its tolerance of corruption.

THE SWING PRODUCER

U.S. policymakers believed that Saudi Arabia had more influence over oil prices than any other country. The key to Saudi oil power was the kingdom's "swing capacity," its ability to increase or decrease production at will. In May 1975, the U.S. ambassador James Akins reported that according to internal Saudi studies, the kingdom could meet its financial obligations with production as low as 2.7 million barrels per day, or even less if the kingdom was willing to draw down its huge financial reserves. Maximum Saudi production capacity was around 11 million barrels per day and was expected to be 16 million by 1977–1978, giving the kingdom a potential swing capacity of more than 13 million barrels. As a result, Akins concluded, "Saudi Arabia's technical domination of OPEC is and will remain even more complete than we had thought. No other country in OPEC will count for two hoots."[7] A 1976 Treasury Department paper agreed, arguing that "the Saudis have become the 'swing producer' in OPEC, playing the leading role in the setting of the cartel's price" because the kingdom "stands alone with its unrivaled combination of huge oil reserves, immense productive capacity and lack of immediate financial need."[8]

Saudi Arabia's ability to convert its swing capacity into political influence rested on something less tangible than the physical size of its oil fields: the widespread belief that the kingdom made its oil price and production decisions based on factors other than narrow economic self-interest. In a March 1975 interview, Fahd claimed that Saudi Arabia favored moderate oil prices because it felt a sense of responsibility for the global economy.[9] In private, Saudi leaders told U.S. officials that the kingdom was the leading voice for moderation in OPEC, waging a lonely battle against more radical states like Iraq and Libya that wanted higher oil prices. The Saudi intelligence chief Kamal Adham reminded Akins that the United States should be grateful for Saudi Arabia's "consistency and responsibility on oil questions." At OPEC meetings, "Saudi Arabia had stood alone" but had won the battle "to keep the lid on prices" and eliminate "anti-American" rhetoric from OPEC's statements.[10]

Some observers, like the MIT economist Morris Adelman, scoffed at such claims.[11] Even so, the Saudi government was quite successful at convincing other countries, especially the United States, that the kingdom was a bulwark against higher oil prices. Kissinger praised Saudi Arabia's "courageous and statesmanlike position" in OPEC and the kingdom's willingness to shoulder "the heavy responsibility it bears for the free world's economic health." Gerald Ford praised Saudi Arabia's "very responsible" approach. The West German chancellor Helmut Schmidt told other Western leaders that "the Saudis are rather sophisticated in their understanding of the mechanisms of the world economy." He explained: "Saudi Arabia is closely linked to the United States. It also has a great deal of funds in the City of London. I believe that they understand our problems."[12] "Sophistication" and "responsibility," in this case, meant following economic policies that served Western interests. The United States often thanked Saudi Arabia for its help on oil prices, but did so privately, so as not to embarrass the Saudi leadership by making them look like American clients.[13]

The most dramatic Saudi intervention in the oil market came in December 1976. Most OPEC members agreed on a 15 percent price increase, but

Saudi Arabia and Abu Dhabi broke ranks with the rest of the organization and held their price increase to only 5 percent. At Fahd's direction, the Saudi government ordered Aramco to go "all-out," maximizing its production "to undermine the OPEC price." Ford thanked King Khalid, expressing "my personal admiration for Saudi Arabia's demonstration of responsible leadership," which was "most commendable and, I am sure, very difficult under the circumstances." The U.S. ambassador in Saudi Arabia, William Porter, wrote that the decision had provoked criticism not only from other OPEC members but also from inside the Saudi government itself. He reported that the ministers of finance, industry, and planning were all "strongly opposed to Fahd's decision to use increased oil production as a weapon in support of what they see as primarily a political objective," winning American approval.[14]

PETRODOLLARS

In addition to control over pricing and production levels, Saudi influence was also bolstered by the kingdom's possession of huge surplus funds to invest. Many Americans feared that with their new wealth, Saudi Arabia and other oil producers could seize economic control over the United States and the rest of the world. Rep. Henry Gonzalez (D-TX), chairman of the House Subcommittee on International Finance, warned in 1974 that "Arab oil producers" could control 70 percent of total world monetary reserves by 1980, predicting that "the approaching petrodollar glut" would destabilize markets worldwide.[15] Sen. Abraham Ribicoff (D-CT) warned that Saudi Arabia could buy General Motors with just one month of oil revenues. "Is it realistic," he asked, "to permit the feudal monarchies of Arabia to buy up the basic industries of the United States while pauperizing the rest of the Western World?" The only solution for the "petrodollar problem," Ribicoff declared, was to reduce American oil consumption and force the producers to cut their prices.[16] Henry Kissinger, too, warned petrodollars could give "the Arabs life and death control over the industrial world—by pulling out the investment they could cause economic chaos." Their money would give them even more power over the developing countries. "If the Arabs take over foreign aid," Kissinger said, "they could buy up the whole Third World."[17]

American fears of Arab oil money played a central role in Sidney Lumet's film *Network* (1976). When the movie's antihero, the crazed newscaster Howard Beale, learns that his employer is about to be bought by an Arab corporation, he takes to the airwaves and denounces the flood of "those Arab petrodollars" into the United States. Echoing Ribicoff's concerns, Beale tells his audience: "Right now, the Arabs have screwed us out of enough American dollars to come right back and, with our own money, buy General Motors, IBM, AT&T, ITT, DuPont, U.S. Steel, and twenty other American companies!" He orders the audience "to get up right now and write a telegram to President Ford saying: 'I'm as mad as hell, and I'm not gonna take this anymore! I don't want the banks selling my country to the Arabs!'"[18] *Network* was fictional, but it captured many Americans' real feelings of anger and uncertainty about Arab investments, which were entangled with larger worries about the decline of U.S. economic primacy, the place of the United States in a rapidly integrating global economy, and racial anxieties about the growing power of the Arab nations and other countries in the Global South.[19]

Most U.S. policymakers, however, decided that Arab investments were not a threat, but an opportunity. In January 1974, while the oil embargo was still under way, a Treasury Department study concluded that OPEC investments would give the oil producers a greater "stake in the continued economic growth and stability" of the consumers, making future embargoes less likely.[20] The White House, the Treasury Department, and the Federal Reserve organized a behind-the-scenes effort to attract Saudi funds to the United States. The Treasury and the Fed were so eager to take the lead that they elbowed each other aside in their rush to attract petrodollars. Richard Debs, the vice president of the Federal Reserve Bank of New York, asked Saudi Arabia to buy U.S. Treasury securities through the Fed, while Gerald Parsky, the assistant secretary of the Treasury, told the Saudis to buy directly from his institution instead. The State Department was confused, not knowing what to tell the Saudi government.[21] In the end, Debs convinced the Saudi Arabian Monetary Agency (SAMA) to open a special account at the New York Fed. By late 1974, SAMA had purchased $840 million in Treasurys and $600 million in FNMA (Fannie Mae) securities through that account. SAMA made other U.S. investments through private New York banks. Anwar Ali, the head of SAMA, told the Secretary of the Treasury William Simon that the 1974 investments were only the beginning. He said the Saudi government had "made a political decision at the highest level" to "make substantial investments in US securities," totaling at least $6 billion per year.[22]

As late as 1973, SAMA's total foreign assets were only about $3 billion. Just three years later, SAMA's foreign exchange reserves reached $45 billion, including $9 billion in its account at the New York Fed. By 1978, SAMA had nearly $15 billion with the New York Fed alone.[23] It deposited billions more with private American banks, although even the U.S. government was unsure where the funds were going. The Treasury Department complained that data on Saudi investment in the United States was "spotty and largely unreliable," while the New York Fed official P. A. Revey told the bank's president, Paul Volcker, in 1977 that "Saudi Arabia's surplus funds continue growing but their actual size and disposition are a matter of some mystery and controversy." The problem was exacerbated by the Treasury Department's reluctance to share any figures about Saudi investments. Revey noted that "the Treasury may be extremely sensitive to these data being made available even to high officials of this Bank."[24]

The Treasury Department was following the wishes of the Saudi regime, which demanded that its investments in the United States be kept secret (figure 7.1). When he met with Simon, Ali "forcefully emphasized" the importance of "complete confidentiality" about both the amount and the types of the investments. After Ali died of a heart attack in November 1974, his replacement, Abdulaziz Quraishi, invited the Department of the Treasury and the Fed to send their representatives to Saudi Arabia so they could negotiate a new sale of Treasury securities. Quraishi stipulated that "the visit must be absolutely secret and that there be no announcements in the United States."[25] The Treasury designed a special mechanism known as "add-ons," which let Saudi debt purchases be hidden from the usual published figures of U.S. debt sales. The Treasury avoided publishing Saudi holdings of U.S. securities by grouping the kingdom with other oil

Bill Cleaver   April 4, 1975

Marshall Burkes

Concession to Certain Dealers on Mid East Oil Money

Bob Cooper of the New York Fed called to discuss a potential procedure for including dealers in orders for agency purchases. Apparently
~~████████~~ would like to consider purchasing $50 million or more on a
fairly regular basis from the agencies. Treasury has shifted the fee
question to the Fed with the impression that fees should not be involved.
However, Cooper asked if we would be agreeable to selecting names from
the following list of eleven dealers: First Boston, White Weld, Morgan
Guaranty, First National City Bank, Continental, Bankers Trust, Chemical,
Merrill Lynch, Discount, Goldman Sachs and Kidder Peabody.

I asked if there was any political discrimination with the Fed's
list of recognized dealers. Bob Cooper said no, but did not elaborate. I
indicated that we would have no objection to selecting from the above list.
We would probably select on the basis of performance during the sale and make
the allocation as broad as practical. Thus, for a $50 million purchase we
would probably involve five dealers.

I don't know whether Farm Credit and FNMA have agreed to this
procedure. We understand that Farm Credit went short on a recent purchase
by ~~the ████~~ and complicated the bookkeeping for a while. It is interesting
to note that such recognized dealers as Chase, First of Chicago and Bank of
America were not included.

[Note: Name of Middle East OPEC Country
deleted by F.H.L.B. Board.]

FIGURE 7.1 Federal Home Loan Bank (FHLB) memorandum, with the
words "Saudi Arabia" and "Saudis" deleted by the FHLB to obscure
Saudi investment in the U.S. mortgage market. The redacted document
was released as part of congressional hearings in 1981.

exporters and publishing the total amount rather than the figures for each
country. The Treasury even chided the CIA, not an organization nor-
mally known for transparency, for disclosing too much information about
foreign investments to Congress and the public.[26]

Keeping the Saudi investments secret served two purposes. At a time
when many Americans were alarmed about the economic impact of petrodollars, secrecy prevented Congress and the American public from inter-
fering with the Treasury Department's campaign to recruit Saudi funds.
Secrecy also helped deflect Arab criticism. The Arab left, including Saudi

dissidents, accused the Saudi government of betraying its fellow Arab countries by investing its funds in the West rather than in the Arab world, at a time when less developed Arab countries like Egypt were badly in need of capital. When a Lebanese journalist asked Prince Fahd about the Saudi commitment to purchase billions of dollars of U.S. Treasurys, the prince denied that any such commitment had been made. He also complained that criticism of Saudi Arabia for sending its money abroad was unfair, since there were few good investment opportunities in the Arab world. Where else was the kingdom supposed to put its investments, Fahd asked, if not the financial markets of the United States and Europe?[27]

American officials believed that Saudi investment in the United States not only strengthened the U.S.-Saudi alliance but also served important economic goals at home. During the mid-1970s, some economists and policymakers worried that Americans were not saving enough, and that by running a budget deficit, the federal government was siphoning badly needed capital away from private borrowers. Investments by Saudi Arabia and other OPEC nations offered a solution. In January 1975, Simon told Ford that he was "deeply troubled" by the potential impact of federal borrowing. The country needed to spend less and save more, but the situation would be eased if "the OPEC nations put a larger amount of their accumulating funds into investments in this country."[28] Simon's comments foreshadowed later shifts in the U.S. economy that would begin in the 1980s, when an enormous flow of foreign capital allowed the United States to finance large budget deficits without crowding out private investment.[29] Saudi purchases of Fannie Mae debt similarly prefigured the flow of foreign investment capital into the U.S. mortgage market in later decades.[30]

Other policymakers hoped that OPEC investments would provide a chance to impose free-market reforms and open the American financial system to global competition. A 1974 Treasury Department paper suggested "the elimination of restrictions on foreign activity in financial markets" as a way to attract OPEC funds, arguing that "the introduction of new competition along with the vast financial wealth of the OPEC states might bring the additional benefit of making capital markets generally more efficient than they currently are."[31] Private corporations and free-market conservatives saw petrodollars as an attractive commercial opportunity and a chance to advocate financial innovations and policy changes that would help investors. In 1974, Chase Manhattan told its shareholders that it was "aggressively" developing "innovative approaches" to petrodollar recycling and that it planned to maintain its "leadership position" in the field during the coming years.[32] The *Wall Street Journal* editorial board argued that the United States should "invite, rather than discourage, all that oil money" by eliminating withholding taxes on interest and dividends for U.S. securities owned by foreigners. The change would mean $200 million in lost revenue per year, but the *Wall Street Journal* argued that it would bolster America's "eminence as an international capital market" and help the United States compete with London, Geneva, and other overseas financial centers.[33] The claim that the United States needed to cut taxes to attract foreign capital and compete in the world market signaled important shifts under way in the American political economy, as financialization and globalization began to accelerate.

CARTER'S DOMESTIC ENERGY POLICY

Not all Americans were as sanguine as the *Wall Street Journal* about the integration of the United States into the global economy. Energy was a prime example, as the Carter administration came to office determined to reduce U.S. reliance on foreign oil. Carter followed the pattern established by Nixon and Ford, framing the energy crisis as a national security problem and a question of American sovereignty. Announcing his proposal for a comprehensive energy policy in April 1977, Carter described the energy crisis as the "moral equivalent of war" and warned: "If we wait, we will constantly live in fear of embargoes. We could endanger our freedom as a sovereign nation to act in foreign affairs." The alternative to energy independence, Carter said, was "national catastrophe."[34]

Carter underlined his militarized approach to energy policy by choosing former secretary of defense James Schlesinger to head the new Department of Energy. The abrasive Schlesinger was controversial even inside the administration. Carter's secretary of the interior, Cecil Andrus, often clashed with Schlesinger after some of the Interior Department's authority over oil and gas drilling was transferred to the Department of Energy. Andrus and other Democrats also distrusted Schlesinger because he had served in the Republican Nixon and Ford administrations.[35]

Nevertheless, Carter was determined to centralize energy policy in the White House and the Department of Energy. He ordered Schlesinger and a small staff to develop their energy policy plan in secret, so it could bypass the usual political horse trading and go directly to Congress for an up-or-down vote. At first, Carter's strategy seemed to work. The plan sailed through the House of Representatives after Speaker Tip O'Neill (D-MA) created a special committee to speed the bill along. The situation was very different in the Senate, which was more fractured than the House and lacked a dominant leader like O'Neill who could corral the necessary votes. Senators from oil-producing states, led by Russell Long (D-LA), attacked Carter's proposals that threatened the economic interests of the oil industry. The bill was weighed down by more than three hundred amendments and stalled by filibusters.

By the time Congress finally passed the National Energy Act in October 1978, it bore little resemblance to Carter's original proposal. Andrus recalled that Congress had acted like "a wrecking crew" and produced something that was "hardly recognizable" compared with the original plan.[36] Its most controversial aspects were all removed, particularly a crude oil "equalization tax" designed to encourage conservation by raising energy prices. Carter did win support for a few important policy measures: ethanol subsidies, taxes on gas-guzzling cars, incentives for the greater use of coal, and the establishment of a new Department of Energy.[37] In the short run, however, the bill did little to reduce U.S. reliance on foreign oil.

Carter was disgusted by the way his energy plan was gutted in the Senate. In September 1977, he wrote in his diary: "Russell Long and others plus the lobbyists are prevailing" and complained: "The influence of the oil and gas industry is unbelievable, and it's impossible to arouse the public to protect themselves."[38] The oil companies were not the plan's only critics. Consumers were asked to pay higher energy prices, and environmentalists were asked to tolerate the expansion of nuclear and coal power to replace oil. Almost every interest group in the country found something to dislike in Carter's plan. He would later write in his memoirs that "the struggle for a national energy policy" was "an exhausting fight," a "bruising fight," and a "bitter four-year struggle"; he lamented, "The energy legislation was just despairing and tedious, like chewing on a rock that lasted the whole four years."[39]

Revisiting the question of energy policy at the end of the 1970s, Carter returned to the same themes of congressional dysfunction and the need for national unity under presidential leadership. In his "Crisis of Confidence" speech of July 1979, Carter told the American people that the effort to re-form national energy policy had run into "a Congress twisted and pulled in every direction by hundreds of well-financed and powerful special in-terests." He asked the public to rediscover "the strength of America" on "the battlefield of energy." Although Carter had pleased environmentalists by installing solar panels on the White House roof just one month earlier, he now made it clear that he would choose energy independence over pro-tecting the environment. Carter demanded more coal and synthetic liq-uid fuels, energy sources that were highly polluting. He also called for a military-style "energy mobilization board" that would "cut through the red tape, the delays, and the endless roadblocks to completing key energy projects." Even in the face of environmental concerns, Carter promised, "when this Nation critically needs a refinery or a pipeline, we will build it."[40] By 1979, although Democrats controlled both Congress and the White House, it was clear that American energy politics were already tilting rightward.

CARTER'S FOREIGN OIL POLICY

Carter's difficulties in working with Congress gave him an incentive to fo-cus on foreign policy, where his executive power was less constrained. The most controversial part of domestic energy policy was the system of oil price controls in place since the early 1970s. The price controls subsidized con-sumption and discouraged production. Oil companies resented the controls, as did other consumer countries like West Germany and France that had to compete with rising U.S. demand for imported oil. The controls, however, were popular with many Americans, especially those who suspected that the entire energy crisis had been manipulated by the oil companies as a pretext for hiking prices. Nixon and Ford both failed to convince Congress to lift the price controls. Congress also blocked Carter's preferred option, a tax that would raise U.S. prices to the world level.

Carter acted unilaterally after he came under intense pressure from other world leaders at an international economic summit in Bonn, West Germany, in July 1978. In response to demands from Helmut Schmidt and other participants in the summit, Carter pledged to raise U.S. oil prices even if Congress refused to cooperate. The Bonn commitment tied Carter's hands and forced him to prioritize international interests over domestic politics. The more conservative, free-market-oriented members of his cabinet like Treasury secretary Michael Blumenthal had hoped for exactly that outcome, seeing foreign pressure as a way to overcome opposition from leftists who still supported price controls. Beginning in 1979, Carter fulfilled his pledge by using his executive authority to order the gradual decontrol of oil prices, even in the face of opposition from the left wing of his own party. Combined with his deregulation of other industries like airlines and trucking, Carter's decontrol of oil prices foreshadowed the shift to market-oriented policies under his successor, Ronald Reagan.[41]

Carter also tried to mitigate the problem of high oil prices by negotiating directly with the oil producers, especially Saudi Arabia. His administration constantly lobbied Saudi Arabia and other OPEC members to boost their protection and keep prices down, knowing that every OPEC price increase meant more inflation and unemployment in the United States. Two months before the December 1977 OPEC meeting in Caracas, Secretary of State Cyrus Vance wrote: "The highest objective of American international economic policy must be to obtain a freeze on oil prices at least through 1978."[42]

The Carter administration was influenced by exaggerated fears that the world was entering an era of permanent energy scarcity. In April 1977, Carter warned that the United States was "now running out of gas and oil." Even when looking beyond America's borders, "each new inventory of world oil reserves has been more disturbing than the last." By the 1980s, Carter predicted, world oil production would stop rising, and demand would overtake the available supplies. The world would have no choice but to cut its oil consumption and develop alternative forms of energy, even if they were more expensive.[43] The CIA shared Carter's concerns.[44] Stansfield Turner, the director of Central Intelligence, told the House of Representatives in 1977 that oil demand would "substantially exceed capacity by 1985," forcing prices up dramatically. The CIA's forecasts only became gloomier with time. Carter's national security advisor Zbigniew Brzezinski wrote in January 1978 that the CIA's new draft study on oil supply vulnerability was "ominous," predicting that "oil *demand* will catch up with production around 1980," producing "a strong upward pressure on prices" that the United States might be powerless to stop.[45] Later that year, the CIA delivered a report that was almost apocalyptic in its predictions of future oil shortages. "The 'crunch' will be massive," the CIA declared, and "will *determine* the economic situation in the world in the 1985–2000 period." The security consequences would be just as serious as the economic consequences. The CIA argued: "The energy factor will have at least as much impact on the role of the United States in the world in the coming decades as nuclear weapons have had in previous decades."[46]

In the face of such grim forecasts, the Carter administration believed that only Saudi Arabia could ensure that enough oil would be available in the near future. The State Department called Saudi Arabia "the strategically pre-eminent source of energy for the West" and "the decisive force within the cartel on both production and pricing policies." Carter was determined to strengthen the U.S.-Saudi alliance to ensure that the oil kept flowing. He visited the kingdom in January 1978 and proclaimed: "The ties which bind us together are strong and unbreakable" (figure 7.2).[47]

Like their predecessors, Carter administration officials concluded that Saudi Arabia was the most responsible and farsighted member of OPEC. The CIA believed that Saudi Arabia kept oil prices down because of its commitment to the U.S.-Saudi alliance and the fear that high energy prices could trigger a recession in the oil-consuming countries, which would undermine the battle against communism. The State Department agreed, explaining: "It is largely because of their concern over the possible political effects of economic stagnation in the Western non-Communist world that

FIGURE 7.2 U.S. president Jimmy Carter and Prince Fahd on Carter's visit to Riyadh, January 1978. Courtesy of the Jimmy Carter Presidential Library and Museum, National Archives and Records Administration.

the Saudis have worked to moderate oil price increases and expand their own production to serve world oil consumer needs."[48]

Some Americans thought that Saudi Arabia had been *too* willing to keep prices down in response to American pleas. Without higher prices, they thought, there would be no reason for consumers to reduce their energy consumption and preserve the world's dwindling supplies of oil. The American economic consultant A. J. Meyer, working for the Saudi government, told the planning minister Hisham Nazer that Riyadh's willingness to keep oil prices low was "a dangerous policy" not only for Saudi Arabia but also for the world economy and the United States itself. He wrote: "I do *not*, in short, agree with the advice given the kingdom by senior US public officials, and the kingdom's apparent acceptance of this viewpoint." The Saudi decision to limit production to 8.5 million barrels per day was perfectly sensible, he suggested, even though U.S. policymakers were constantly pressing for more.[49]

DEFENDING THE DOLLAR

Saudi influence also rested on the kingdom's role in the global financial system.[50] Using that financial power, Saudi Arabia encouraged one of the most important American economic policy shifts of the late 1970s, the decision to prioritize the defense of the dollar and the battle against inflation even at the expense of slower economic growth and higher unemployment. When the Carter administration came to office, the dollar was declining against other world currencies like the German deutsche mark and the Japanese yen. A weak dollar could have both positive and negative effects: it improved the country's competitive position by making exports cheaper, but it could also make imports more expensive and fuel inflation. At first, U.S. officials were largely unconcerned about the dollar's decline, but they grew more alarmed as it accelerated in 1978.[51]

Saudi Arabia was upset with the Carter administration's apparent complacency and lobbied the United States to support the dollar. Oil was priced in dollars, and so were about three-quarters of the kingdom's financial assets, so a cheaper dollar cut into the kingdom's earnings and its overseas investments.[52] Saudi discontent posed three risks to the United States. The first was that in order to compensate for the dollar's decline, Saudi Arabia and the other OPEC nations would raise oil prices. King Khalid warned Carter that the dollar's slide would make it difficult to resist demands for oil price increases by other OPEC members, and Saudi pressure was reportedly a major reason for some of the Carter administration's first attempts to boost the dollar in early 1978.[53] The second danger was that to protect itself from future currency fluctuations, Saudi Arabia might decide to price oil in other currencies, undermining confidence in the dollar and accelerating its decline even further. Finally, Saudi Arabia might decide to pull some of its investments out of the United States.[54]

Global financial markets were anxious. Even unconfirmed rumors that OPEC would consider pricing oil in non-U.S. currencies were enough to cause a "flurry of dollar selling" and put the dollar under heavy pressure in the summer of 1978.[55] The need to maintain Saudi confidence in the dollar gave the kingdom new leverage over American economic policy. In July 1978, Undersecretary of State Richard Cooper flew to the kingdom and met

Abdulaziz Quraishi, the head of SAMA. Quraishi told Cooper that Saudi Arabia was standing by its "policy of sticking to the dollar," but it was under "intense" pressure from the rest of OPEC to consider other pricing arrangements. Quraishi complained that Saudi Arabia was suffering huge financial losses because of currency fluctuations. Although Cooper tried to reassure him, Quraishi demanded more proof that the United States would defend the dollar.[56]

The Saudi oil ministry official Khader Herzallah privately warned that OPEC might start pricing oil in a basket of currencies unless the dollar's slide was reversed by that fall.[57] Later that summer, the Kuwaiti oil minister Ali Khalifa Al Sabah recommended that OPEC consider a change in its pricing arrangements. The U.S. Treasury Department, which feared that even the suggestion of such a move would unsettle currency markets, lobbied Saudi Arabia to issue a statement reaffirming the kingdom's faith in the dollar.[58] Prince Fahd obliged, arguing that the dollar was still the world's most important currency and would rebound by the end of the year. The United States was grateful for Fahd's statement, believing that it had calmed the market.[59] Herzallah and Fahd, however, had effectively given the United States a deadline to reverse the dollar's slide within the next several months if they wanted to prevent OPEC from shifting to a basket of currencies. The U.S. Department of the Treasury was alarmed by that prospect, warning in September 1978: "The exchange markets are nervous and the adoption of the basket would cause a run from the dollar."[60]

On November 1, 1978, the Carter administration made a surprise announcement that it would take a series of forceful steps to defend the dollar. They included a gigantic $28 billion intervention in the market to boost the dollar's value, selling $10 billion worth of securities denominated in foreign currency, and a quadrupling of gold sales to 1.5 million ounces per month. The most controversial step involved a sudden increase in the Federal Reserve's discount rate by a full percentage point, to 9.5 percent. The interest rate hike threatened to slow the economy and put Americans out of work. Several leading liberal economists predicted that it might cause a recession, and the AFL-CIO president, George Meany, called it an "ill-conceived and shocking" move to reward bankers and speculators while hurting ordinary Americans.[61]

Saudi Arabia was far from the only source of pressure on Carter to defend the dollar, even at the expense of American workers. West Germany, corporate leaders, and others had called for the same thing. It is clear, though, that Carter and other members of his administration hoped his decision would boost Saudi confidence in American economic policy. In a letter to Prince Fahd one day after he announced the dollar defense package, Carter handwrote a postscript message: "As was proven yesterday, we will maintain a responsible monetary policy, and I am determined to control inflation in the United States."[62] The next week, Stuart Eizenstat told other members of the administration that "one reason for the painful steps that we took on the dollar was to give ourselves more leverage with regard to oil prices."[63] He later recalled that "Saudi pressure" to defend the dollar influenced the administration's decision, even if many other factors were also involved.[64] David Rockefeller of Chase Manhattan Bank cheered the administration's move, arguing that although it would slow the economy and risk a recession, it would help prevent future OPEC price increases.[65]

The November 1978 dollar defense package, however, was still not enough to satisfy Saudi Arabia. Later that month, Secretary of the Treasury Michael Blumenthal traveled to Jeddah to meet with top Saudi officials. Blumenthal lobbied for an oil price freeze, but the foreign minister Saud al-Faisal and the oil minister Ahmad Zaki Yamani warned that Saudi Arabia did not want to be caught in the embarrassing position of holding oil prices down, only to see the kingdom's earnings cut by another fall in the dollar's value. They stressed that exchange rate stability was a precondition for oil price stability.[66] King Khalid told Carter in December 1978 that to avoid future oil price increases, the administration would need to "continue your efforts towards raising the value of the dollar."[67]

The Saudi warnings continued in early 1979. In January, Prince Fahd claimed that Saudi Arabia had stood alone in stopping OPEC from pricing oil in non-U.S. currencies; he blamed recent oil price increases on inflation and the decline of the dollar.[68] Meeting with the U.S. Treasury official C. Fred Bergsten later that month, Abdulaziz Quraishi demanded that the United States do more to fight inflation. He lectured Bergsten on the need to prioritize monetary stability, saying that "he could not understand how unemployment could ever have become more important than inflation in the US, politically speaking." Quraishi also suggested that the weak dollar was undermining U.S. global leadership, challenging Bergsten to name any nation in history that "had been a world leader and had a weak currency."[69] In February 1979, *Al-Riyadh* complained that the Arabs had lost billions because of the weak dollar and the failure of the United States to control inflation and energy consumption at home.[70] Such warnings carried extra weight in late 1978 and early 1979, as the collapse of the Shah's regime cut off Iranian exports, sent prices soaring, and left Saudi Arabia with even more influence over the global oil market.

THE VOLCKER SHOCK

As president of the New York Federal Reserve Bank, Paul Volcker oversaw the largest single block of Saudi investments in the United States. He visited the kingdom in January 1979 and met with Abdulaziz Quraishi. In a private memo, Volcker noted that Quraishi "went out of his way as I was leaving to urge the importance of a stable dollar in connection with oil pricing decisions." Quraishi warned that Saudi Arabia could not hold the line against oil price increases if the dollar fell. Volcker observed "a good deal of skepticism and nervousness" about the dollar in both Saudi Arabia and Kuwait. "Perhaps some of that can be discounted," Volcker wrote, "but I came away with the feeling that the depreciation of the dollar has provided a more potent economic and political argument for oil price increases than most US commentary has conceded."[71]

In August 1979, Volcker became chairman of the Fed. Soon after he took office, the dollar came under renewed pressure. At a meeting of the International Monetary Fund in Belgrade on October 3, the Saudi finance minister Mohammed Aba al-Khayl said that the kingdom was unhappy about "the renewed instability in exchange markets" and warned that a further decline in the dollar's value would bring more oil price increases.[72] Just three days later, Volcker announced that the Fed would adopt a new and much more hawkish strategy against inflation by restraining the growth of the money supply. Volcker's decision inaugurated a new era in which the Fed prioritized price stability at the expense of jobs.[73] Over the next three years, the Fed would raise interest rates to all-time highs, reducing inflation and boosting the dollar while triggering a recession, reducing the competitiveness of American industry, and throwing millions of Americans out of work.

It is difficult to know how much Saudi concerns about the dollar may have influenced Volcker's decision. At the October 6, 1979, meeting of the Federal Open Market Committee (FOMC) at which the Fed decided to limit the money supply, Volcker noted that he wanted to "just say a few words about the attitudes of foreign countries as I've experienced them first hand," to impress on the other members of the committee "the depth of the feelings" that foreign officials had about U.S. inflation. Although FOMC meetings were recorded, Volcker warned that in this case he wanted his comments "off the record." The tape recorder was deactivated until he finished discussing the subject. It was the only gap in the transcript of the meeting.[74] The context suggests that Volcker was thinking of West Germany, whose leaders had long been pressuring the United States to get inflation under control.[75] Even German worries about the dollar's decline, however, were based partly on the fear that a further slide in the dollar's value would upset Saudi Arabia and trigger more oil price increases. At the Bonn summit in 1978, Helmut Schmidt had warned that according to his conversations with Prince Fahd, Saudi Arabia might be forced to "raise the price of crude earlier and higher than they desire because of the dollar's decline."[76]

Volcker's comments immediately after the October 1979 rate hike also made clear that he believed tackling inflation would help convince the oil producers to limit future price increases. Perhaps remembering what Saudi officials had impressed on him earlier that year, Volcker told a banking conference that "a stronger dollar" would mean that "appeals for moderation in petroleum pricing would have a new force and substance." The more the United States dealt with its economic problems at home and brought inflation under control, Volcker explained, "the more we strengthen our debate with the main suppliers of oil and what prices they will charge."[77]

SOCIAL TENSIONS IN SAUDI ARABIA

Saudi leaders put so much emphasis on the need to control inflation partly because it was such a serious economic challenge for them at home. Just like the boom of the early 1970s, the economic growth that came with the oil price increases of 1978–1979 sent prices skyrocketing and disrupted Saudi society. In September 1978, the newspaper *Al-Riyadh* surveyed fruit and vegetable markets around the Saudi capital and found "insane variation" in grocery prices, up to 100 percent between different parts of the city. The newspaper blamed the problem on middlemen who manipulated the price and cheated both farmers and consumers.[78]

In January 1979, *Al-Riyadh* issued another special report on "the housing crisis," writing that residents were getting pushed out of their homes by chaotic development that left large, unused blocks of land in the city even as new construction pushed ever outward. Some Saudis were evicted from their homes to make room for new building projects. They were often relocated to distant neighborhoods that lacked decent schools and other facilities. Poor planning had been exacerbated by the economic boom, overburdening the city's water supply and other utilities.[79]

In March 1980, the planning minister Hisham Nazer announced that the kingdom had brought inflation down from 45 percent in 1975 to 10 percent in 1979, but only with the help of government-enforced price and rent controls.[80] As the cost of basic commodities grew, the monarchy subsidized them to cushion the impact on Saudi consumers. By the end of the decade, food, water, electricity, and a host of other goods were provided free or at a cost far below their market value. Saudi government subsidies soared from 49 million riyals in 1970 to 11.3 *billion* riyals in 1981.[81] The government's revenue requirements soared in turn. The high oil revenues that had been a luxury in the early 1970s were a necessity by the early 1980s simply to keep the country operating.

Discontent with the monarchy also focused on the royal family's autocratic rule. The Saudi regime repeatedly promised that political reform was on the way, but Saudi officials cautioned that it would take time. In March 1979, Saud al-Faisal promised that the government was working on "the development of political institutions," but it would proceed according to the country's limited "absorptive capacity" for change.[82] In early 1980, after violent uprisings in Mecca and the Eastern Province underlined the extent of popular dissatisfaction, the regime formed a committee headed by Prince Nayef to create a Basic Law (a kind of quasi-constitution), a consultative council, and other reforms. It was clear, though, that no radical changes would take place. *Al-Jazeerah* claimed that the proposed changes only codified ideas that had always been at the heart of the Saudi political system, because "the regime since the time of the late King Abdulaziz" depended on "consultation between the ruler and the ruled, between the king and his people." Saudis were lucky, *Al-Jazeerah* continued, that every citizen has always found "the door of government" open, "to say whatever he pleases" to the leadership.[83] As for a constitution, Nayef denied that one was needed. After all, he explained, Saudi Arabia already had a constitution: the Quran.[84]

Saudi Arabia's lack of political freedoms and legal protections for ordinary citizens was highlighted by a violent incident in 1977. Princess Mishaal, the granddaughter of Prince Mohammed, tried to elope with her lover, Khaled Mulhallal, the nephew of the Saudi ambassador to Lebanon. They tried to leave the country to escape adultery charges but were caught by the police. Although Prince Mohammed had made headlines during his 1945 trip to the United States for his romantic tryst with an Arab American woman, he showed no mercy to his granddaughter for engaging in similar behavior.[85] On Prince Mohammed's orders, Mishaal was shot and Mulhallal was beheaded. In 1980, the story inspired a partly fictionalized British docudrama, *Death of a Princess*. The film embarrassed the Saudi government and caused a major crisis in Saudi relations with Britain.[86] Under pressure from the kingdom, the French and Swedish governments prevented the film from being shown in their countries.[87]

When PBS prepared to show *Death of a Princess* in the United States, the Saudi government accused the film of defaming the kingdom and the Islamic religion. It demanded that PBS include a disclaimer noting the Saudi objections. The episode triggered a debate in the U.S. House of Representatives, with Clement Zablocki (D-WI) and William Broomfield (R-MI) arguing that PBS should pull the film to protect U.S.-Saudi relations, while others led by James Scheuer (D-NY) commended PBS for "standing up to domestic and international pressure."[88] After the film was broadcast, the Saudi newspaper *Al-Bilad* asked Prince Sultan what he thought about the resulting damage to the kingdom's reputation. Sultan tried to look on the bright side, suggesting that the episode had a positive result: it highlighted the kingdom's "application of Islamic law." Even if the criminal is a member of the royal family, Sultan said, "we are proud that we apply the holy law."[89]

American critics also challenged Saudi gender segregation. Jimmy and Rosalynn Carter visited Saudi Arabia at the beginning of January 1978. When Jimmy Carter was invited to a state dinner, the First Lady could not accompany him; in Saudi Arabia, such events were male-only affairs. The feminist activist Gloria Steinem denounced Jimmy Carter for allowing the First Lady to be treated that way. Steinem argued that Carter surely would have protested if Saudi Arabia had barred Jews or African Americans from the dinner, but "there was not one word of comment about the exclusion of women."[90] The Los Angeles chapter of the National Organization for Women (NOW) protested outside the local headquarters of the U.S.-Arab Chamber of Commerce, and NOW coordinator Gloria Allred told the State Department: "The First Lady need not visit any country which forces her, or other women, to sacrifice their dignity or their human rights."[91]

Carter never made human rights a priority in his relations with Saudi Arabia. U.S. policymakers excused Saudi discrimination against women, corporal punishment, and autocratic government as simply the features of a different culture. In 1978, the CIA conceded that Saudi practices, based on "traditional tribal custom and Islamic law," were "frequently at odds with Western human rights concepts" and the Saudi penal code was sometimes "clearly offensive to Westerners." There were "rather severe limitations imposed on participation in the political process," including a complete ban on political parties and independent civil society groups, no free speech, and no elections. Ignoring the long history of dissent in the kingdom, the CIA concluded: "In its own context, however, the Saudi human rights performance rates fairly high marks for consistency, universality of application, and legitimacy in the eyes of most of the people."[92] An NSC report assessing Carter's human rights record at the end of his presidency noted that aid to Saudi Arabia and other important Middle Eastern countries "was never seriously tested against their human rights record." The NSC excused that failure by arguing that "the culture barrier makes the US (and UN) human rights policy largely irrelevant" in every Middle Eastern country except for Israel. The report was more honest when it stated that the U.S. "national interest" in the preservation of the regional status quo had simply trumped any concerns about human rights and democracy.[93]

THE SAUDI TURN TO THE RIGHT

The Saudi regime did not follow through on its promises for political reform. Rather than becoming more democratic, the Saudi political system
became more conservative. The U.S. ambassador James West reported that
Saudi Arabia was undergoing a "return to traditionalism" as early as mid-
1977. He ascribed it to the influence of King Khalid and Khalid's full brother
Prince Mohammed, a noted religious conservative.[94] The rightward turn
gathered speed in 1979, after the Iranian Revolution led the Saudi regime
to stress its Islamic credentials to avoid suffering the same fate as the Shah.
The government announced that some officials had become lax in enforc-
ing the religious laws and promised to crack down.[95] Western expatriates
noticed the shift, including one American who complained in September 1979 about the recent "ultra-conservative swing" in Saudi policing.[96]

The conservative turn was reinforced by a pair of internal challenges to
Saudi rule in late 1979. In November, thousands of Shia in al-Hasa organized mass demonstrations against the Saudi monarchy. The protests were
partly inspired by the Iranian Revolution, with some dissidents adopting
Khomeinist slogans, but they also included secular leftists who focused on
the inequitable distribution of oil wealth and other local issues. The Saudi
regime brutally suppressed the demonstrations. The incident raised concerns
in both the Saudi and U.S. governments about the impact of the Iranian
Revolution on the kingdom. Saudi officials told the United States that, if
necessary, they would deploy troops to "protect foreigners, especially Americans." They also warned the Shia of "heavy military repression" if the protests continued. The Saudi regime tried to mollify the opposition by promising increased investment in al-Hasa, but discrimination against the Shia
continued.[97] The Aramco executive Hassan al-Husseini, who joined the
company in 1979, later recalled that Aramco quietly prohibited Shia employees from working at important refineries and other sensitive facilities.[98]

The other threat came from a dissident Sunni group led by the Saudi
militant Juhayman al-Utaybi. Al-Utaybi and his followers espoused an
apocalyptic vision, claiming that the end of the world was near and that one
of their group was the promised Mahdi, a messianic figure who would lead
the Muslims to victory over their enemies. Al-Utaybi's writings, secretly

published in Kuwait and smuggled into Saudi Arabia, denounced the Saudi monarchy for its "worship of money" and the corrupt, luxurious lifestyles of senior royals. Al-Utaybi was also inspired by the memory of the Ikhwan revolt of the 1920s. His father had been one of the rebels who survived the Battle of Sabila in 1929. Juhayman criticized Abdulaziz for "preventing the continuation of jihad for the sake of God outside the Arabian Peninsula" and argued that the king should have allowed the Ikhwan to invade Iraq.[99]

On November 20, 1979, al-Utaybi and his followers seized control of the Grand Mosque in Mecca, the destination of the hajj and the holiest Islamic site in the world. The militants held out for two weeks, withstanding a siege by regime forces in which 127 soldiers died. Initial U.S. reports on the incident were confused, since the U.S. government had never heard of Juhayman al-Utaybi or his movement. The first American reports blamed Iranians for occupying the mosque. U.S. officials feared that the Mecca attack, in combination with the Eastern Province protests, could be the beginning of a general revolt and breakdown of law and order in the kingdom. They began making plans to evacuate all thirty-five thousand Americans in Saudi Arabia, but after the NSC official William Odom warned that a sudden U.S. evacuation would undermine confidence in the Saudi regime and threaten its stability, Carter ordered that there be "no precipitous withdrawal." In any case, it soon became clear that the attack on the Mecca mosque was the work of a relatively small group—not Iranians, but Saudis. Although government forces recaptured the mosque in early December, the incident badly shook the regime's confidence, since its political legitimacy depended on its status as the guardian of Islam's holy places. The incident also demonstrated that the Saudi monarchy could be politically outflanked by dissident groups arguing that the regime was insufficiently committed to Islamic values.[100]

During the 1970s, the Saudi government had invested heavily in sending Saudi students abroad to study in the United States and other foreign countries. Religious conservatives had always been uncomfortable with the risks that came from mixing with non-Muslim cultures, and such criticism now became more prominent. Mohammed al-Rashdan led the Muslim Students Union of the United States and Canada, an organization funded by donations from Saudi Arabia and other Gulf countries. In an interview with

Al-Riyadh, al-Rashdan warned that once in the United States, Saudi students could be swept away by the "violent current" of American culture. They were exposed to drug abuse, blatant sexuality, moral corruption, and Christian missionary activity. Al-Rashdan complained that when Saudis brought their families to the United States, their children were born in Christian hospitals and went to non-Muslim schools. He stressed that Muslims living abroad needed to build separate institutions to make sure their children grew up to be proper Muslims who spoke Arabic instead of English.[101]

The same fear of cultural contamination was evident in a Saudi crackdown on immigration at home. The surge of foreign workers during the economic boom of the mid-1970s provoked resentment among native Saudis. The new arrivals represented competition for the available jobs, and they also provoked complaints by religious hard-liners because they came from non-Wahhabi Muslim countries or from outside the Islamic world altogether. U.S. advisors, too, worried about the political danger posed by the presence of millions of immigrants. In handwritten notes for a presentation to his client, the planning minister Hisham Nazer, A. J. Meyer noted that perhaps a million foreign workers had moved to Saudi Arabia from Yemen alone. What could be done with these foreigners, Meyer asked? He outlined two options: Saudi Arabia could become an American-style "melting pot" society, which he noted was fraught with "risks," or it could "keep [the immigrants] in ghettos" until it was ready to "export them."[102]

By the end of the 1970s, the Saudi regime hastened to reassure its citizens that it would limit further immigration. Nazer told the Saudi newspaper *Al-Jazeerah* that reliance on foreign workers was "a temporary but necessary process at this stage," but that the government would "reduce the dependence on foreign labor except in cases of extreme necessity."[103] The government formed a working group to examine the issue of foreigners employed in public agencies. It concluded that with any luck, many of the foreign workers could be "replaced by the use of modern office equipment and machinery."[104]

The regime promised that it not only would reduce the economic need for immigrant labor but also would tighten enforcement of the immigration rules. It announced new penalties for unauthorized immigration, warning that "anyone who shelters, conceals, or employs" illegal immigrants would be fined, and anyone who helped them get a residence, visa, or work permit could be thrown in prison.[105] The cabinet also promised pay increases and other bonuses for the border police.[106] The interior minister Prince Nayef warned that some immigrants were sneaking into the country under the pretense of performing pilgrimage to Mecca and Medina and were then "taking advantage of their entry into the kingdom and staying illegally." Despite the tough rhetoric, Saudi Arabia continued to rely on low-paid foreign labor. Nayef argued that foreign, and especially East Asian, immigrants were preferable to Arabs because they had a better work ethic. He declared: "We found that non-Arab workers such as the Koreans, for example, are more reliable than others and work more precisely and quickly. This is rarely available in the Arab labor force."[107]

The government's pledges that it would replace most immigrant workers with Saudis were never fulfilled. The kingdom depended on foreign labor, despite new "Saudization" campaigns announced every few years. The constant promises of action against immigrants still served important political purposes. They bolstered the regime's nationalist and religious credentials and intimidated guest workers, preventing them from demanding better wages and working conditions. A Stanford Research Institute study concluded that immigrant construction workers in Saudi Arabia were routinely denied even the minimal rights they were promised under Saudi law. They worked long hours, were not guaranteed sick leave or vacation pay, and found that part of their wages were held "in reserve" by their employers and could be taken away if they tried to leave or switch jobs. With labor unions outlawed and foreign workers subject to deportation at the whim of the regime, they had little recourse against such abuses.[108]

* * *

In both Saudi Arabia and the United States, politics and economics were intertwined. Nationalism and official Wahhabi Islam reinforced the barriers between Saudis and immigrants, enhancing the power of Saudi employers. They also propped up the Saudi regime. The economic resources provided by oil were not enough; they had to be combined with ideological resources that strengthened the royal family.

In the United States, too, political and economic agendas blended together. Defending his decision to raise interest rates, Paul Volcker argued that a falling dollar would threaten "our ability to lead the Western world." It would undermine "the world system of finance and commerce," a system that bolstered U.S. "political leadership."[109] Restricting the growth of the money supply was a painful step that hurt many American workers and businesses. Volcker argued that high interest rates would still help the country in the long run, and he pointed to international factors that made the fight against inflation even more urgent. A weak dollar unsettled U.S. trading partners like West Germany and even threatened U.S. national security. Saudi Arabia played an important role in this argument, as Volcker claimed that a weak dollar alarmed Saudi Arabia and other oil exporters and gave them an excuse to raise oil prices.

During the 1978 debate over the F-15 sale to Saudi Arabia, the deal's advocates relentlessly stressed Saudi Arabia's importance as a strategic ally. One of the American lobbyists working for the Saudi regime argued that it deserved F-15s because the kingdom was "fundamentally conservative, anticommunist, and tied to the US." King Khalid told Carter that he needed the planes to stop "Communist expansion" in the Middle East. That rhetoric was echoed by many members of Congress. The dismayed journalist Haynes Johnson wrote: "Not for years has Washington rung with such anticommunist fervor." He worried that the United States might eventually decide to send military forces into the Middle East.[110] Johnson was prescient. At the end of the 1970s, the United States consolidated its security relationship with Saudi Arabia and began laying the groundwork for decades of military intervention in the region.

8

ASCENT

Twice a week in early 1980, Saudi C-130 transport aircraft lifted off from the Dhahran air base on the shores of the Persian Gulf. The planes were part of a highly classified global supply chain that would have been the envy of any multinational corporation. It began with the CIA's purchase of weapons on the international arms market. U.S. C-141 transports collected the weapons in Egypt and flew them to Dhahran, where they were transferred to the Saudi C-130s. The Saudi planes flew into Rawalpindi, Pakistan, timing their arrival for dusk to avoid scrutiny. Pakistan's Inter-Services Intelligence agency picked up the weapons in unmarked crates and distributed them to eight separate Afghan insurgent groups, who smuggled them into Afghanistan and used them to fight the Soviet troops occupying their country.

The complicated process helped hide the origin of the arms. The CIA warned that Saudi Arabia was "extremely sensitive" to the risk that its role might become public. In fact, the kingdom was more concerned about secrecy than the CIA itself. U.S. newspapers caught wind of the story as early as mid-1980, and some U.S. officials thought it might be useful for propaganda purposes if the world knew that the United States and its allies had succeeded in pinning down thousands of Soviet troops in Afghanistan. The

Saudi concerns won out, though. For the first half decade of the operation, only Soviet-designed weapons were used, to preserve the fiction that the Afghan rebels might have captured them on the battlefield. Like Saudi investments in the United States, Saudi aid to the Afghan rebels had to be made untraceable.[1]

Just as Saudi pressure had encouraged a rightward shift in U.S. economic policy, it also encouraged a hawkish tilt in U.S. security policy. Saudi leaders thought the United States was too timid in fighting communism, and they deplored the post-Vietnam limits on U.S. covert interventions. American concerns about Saudi security helped draw the United States into confrontations with the Soviet Union and its allies in the Horn of Africa, Yemen, and Afghanistan. They also contributed to the collapse of détente, the return of sharper Cold War tensions, and the dramatic expansion of the U.S. defense budget, a shift that was already under way even before Ronald Reagan became president in 1981.[2]

MIDDLE EAST DIPLOMACY
AND THE ARAB-ISRAELI CONFLICT

Carter's adoption of such a hawkish strategy at the end of the 1970s was in sharp contrast with his initial approach to the Middle East. At first, the administration prioritized diplomacy, especially the search for an Arab-Israeli peace agreement. Carter hoped a peace deal would eliminate a major source of Arab resentment against the United States and make future wars and oil embargoes less likely. U.S. officials believed that Saudi Arabia would be a vital part of the process, since its financial support for Egypt and other Arab states gave it considerable influence in the region. In November 1977, Secretary of State Cyrus Vance announced that Saudi support for "the achievement of a durable Mideast peace" outranked all other goals, even low oil prices, as the top priority for U.S.-Saudi relations.[3]

At first, Saudi leaders were cautiously optimistic about Carter's peace initiative. In May 1977, Fahd told an interviewer: "I'm convinced that Israel doesn't want peace, because it knows perfectly well that peace doesn't serve its racist interests and expansionist goals." Fahd, however, argued that Carter's arrival in the White House was good for the Arabs. He claimed that Carter was "the first president to come to office without being subject to Zionist pressure," because post-Watergate campaign finance reforms had reduced the role of Zionist money in American politics. Fahd offered to increase Saudi oil production to help the United States in exchange for a peace settlement involving Israel's withdrawal from all Arab territories occupied in 1967 and the restoration of Palestinian rights.[4] The foreign minister Saud al-Faisal struck a similar tone in October 1977. He declared that Israel was not interested in peace and warned that if Israel went to war against the Arabs, Saudi Arabia would join the fight, sacrificing "not only its oil and money, but also the blood of its citizens." Saud al-Faisal said he was hopeful, though, that despite Israeli belligerence, Washington would restrain Tel Aviv, since the American public was starting to realize that its interests were not the same as Israel's. He suggested that pressure from the United States and other countries could "force Israel to accept the outlines of a just and lasting solution" to the conflict.[5]

Saudi Arabia pushed the United States to adopt a more pro-Arab line. The United States classified Yasser Arafat's PLO as a terrorist organization and had no official diplomatic contact with it. Fahd argued that the United States should change its policy if the PLO promised to accept UN Security Council Resolutions 242 and 338, which would imply the PLO's recognition of Israeli statehood. The Carter administration was willing to negotiate on that basis. Carter referred to a "Palestinian homeland" and announced that the United States would open direct talks with the PLO if it accepted UN 242. The U.S.-led effort to negotiate a comprehensive Arab-Israeli peace, however, began to stall in mid-1977. It was complicated to manage talks between Israel and a group of Arab countries that had significant disagreements among themselves. Matters became still more difficult in June 1977, after the election of a right-wing Likud Party government in Israel under the hard-line prime minister Menachem Begin. To break the deadlock, in November 1977 Egypt's president Anwar Sadat visited Jerusalem, becoming the first Arab leader to do so. Egypt began negotiating directly with Israel and increasingly left the other Arab states on the sidelines.[6]

Sadat's initiative drove a wedge between Egypt and Saudi Arabia. Sadat did not inform Saudi Arabia or the United States in advance before announcing his decision to go to Jerusalem. The Carter administration lobbied Saudi Arabia to support the Egyptian-Israeli negotiations, and at first, it appeared that the United States might win Saudi endorsement of the deal that Sadat and Begin concluded at Camp David in September 1978.[7] It soon became clear, however, that the Camp David Accords and the Egyptian-Israeli peace treaty of March 1979 fell far short of Saudi expectations. They returned the Sinai Peninsula to Egypt but secured no concrete Israeli commitments to withdraw from the other occupied territories, including Gaza, the West Bank, and the Golan Heights. The status of the Palestinians, along with Jerusalem and its holy sites, was left unresolved. Carter himself was disappointed that he could not secure a more comprehensive agreement, but he was willing to accept a more modest deal that removed the threat to Israel from the most populous Arab nation.[8]

The outcome showed the limits of Saudi influence. Even Egypt, a nation heavily dependent on Saudi financial assistance, ignored Saudi pressure and signed a separate peace agreement with Israel. Sadat hoped that a peace agreement would let him cut Egypt's military budget and redirect funds to domestic priorities, and he knew that he would receive U.S. aid to make up for the lost Saudi funding. Saudi Arabia's inability to convince the United States to force more concessions from Israel put the kingdom back in a familiar position, officially denouncing the U.S. role in the Arab-Israeli conflict while still working closely with the United States on other issues.

In March 1979, Saudi Arabia joined the other Arab states in a conference at Baghdad, where they condemned the Egyptian-Israeli peace deal. Their joint statement declared that Egypt had "left the Arab ranks and chose, in collusion with the United States of America, to stand alongside the Zionist enemy."[9] The Saudi press leveled a barrage of criticism against Sadat as a traitor to the Arab cause. *Al-Riyadh* argued that Sadat had negotiated with Israel "against all the desires and interests" of Egypt's friends, insulted the rest of the Arab world, and ignored the Palestinians.[10] *Al-Riyadh* also accused Egypt of ingratitude, noting that the kingdom had given Egypt $7 billion in financial aid since the 1973 war, while the other Gulf states had given billions more.[11] Egypt responded by encouraging its

own media to attack Saudi Arabia in return, souring the relationship between the two countries. In May 1979, Vance told Carter: "The Egyptian-
Saudi estrangement is increasingly troublesome and is becoming a major
impediment to what we are trying to achieve in the region."[12] Despite U.S.
efforts at mediation, the Saudi-Egyptian feud continued into the early 1980s,
contributing to Egypt's isolation from the rest of the Arab world.[13]

PROTECTING THE COMMERCIAL RELATIONSHIP

Even as the United States and Saudi Arabia were publicly at odds over Israel, the White House and the Saudi government quietly worked together,
ignoring domestic opposition—and even U.S. and Saudi law—to maintain
their alliance. In 1977, Congress prohibited U.S. companies from comply-
ing with the Arab boycott against Israel and required them to report any
boycott requests by Arab governments. The antiboycott legislation passed
the House by the overwhelming margin of 364 to 43.[14] Carter signed the
bill, but the Commerce Department made little attempt to enforce it. Most
American firms operating in the Arab world still followed the boycott, and
few were punished.[15] When Sen. Abraham Ribicoff (D-CT) called for
stricter enforcement, the Treasury official Richard Cooper warned him that
the result could be "serious damage to our export trade to Saudi Arabia."
Forwarding a copy of Cooper's letter to his boss, Secretary of the Treasury
Michael Blumenthal, Undersecretary of the Treasury Anthony Solomon
handwrote a message noting that the subject of the boycott was "politically
sensitive" and should be discussed in person rather than in writing.[16]

For its part, Saudi Arabia tried to limit the impact of the boycott on its
trade with the United States. A 1978 Treasury paper noted that "the Saudi
Government is making every effort" to "reduce harmful effects" on U.S.
companies in the kingdom.[17] Prince Fahd ordered the Saudi Boycott Office to "make things easy for U.S. firms." The head of the Boycott Office,
Badulla Ahrar Khoja, assured the U.S. ambassador James West that he
would protect Ford, Coca-Cola, and RCA, even though they did business
with Israel. Khoja's flexibility not only signaled Saudi Arabia's willingness

to ignore its own laws and regulations. It also suggested the advantages that the largest American corporations enjoyed when doing business with Saudi Arabia. Companies like Ford could count on the U.S. ambassador personally intervening to protect their interests. Their smaller competitors could not rely on the same kind of help.[18]

MILITARIZING THE U.S.-SAUDI ALLIANCE

When Carter took office, the United States had almost no military presence in the Persian Gulf. The navy's "Middle East Force" based in Bahrain did not even include any combat vessels on permanent duty. As James Schlesinger found to his frustration in 1973 when he asked about a military response to the Arab embargo, the Pentagon did not have the bases and transport capability to intervene in the region even if it wanted to bring in units from other parts of the world.[19] The U.S. military had always been reluctant to get involved in the Gulf, seeing it as a distraction from more important missions defending U.S. allies in Europe and East Asia from the Soviet threat. They preferred to leave responsibility for the Gulf in the hands of other countries. Before 1968, that meant Great Britain, the traditional imperial power in the region. After Britain withdrew from its last protectorates in the Gulf, the United States counted on Iran to serve as the dominant military power, eliminating the need for a direct U.S. presence. Most Pentagon annual reports and planning documents barely even mentioned the Middle East.[20]

At first, the Carter administration continued that policy. It tried to head off conflict in the region, negotiating with the Soviet Union to limit both superpowers' military presence in the Indian Ocean.[21] If military intervention did prove necessary, the United States hoped that Iran could take the lead. As a military ally, Saudi Arabia ranked a distant second. From the U.S. perspective, Saudi Arabia did have some advantages over Iran. The large Iranian population and the Shah's ambitious development plans meant that Iran spent its oil revenues as fast as they came in. Saudi Arabia, by contrast, ran a sizable surplus, letting it invest in U.S. financial markets and subsidize other conservative regimes and political movements in the region. Saudi Arabia also had closer ties with many of its fellow Arab countries, especially after Arab-Iranian relations were soured by the Iranian occupation of several disputed islands in the Gulf in 1971. Iran's military forces, however, far outclassed Saudi Arabia's.

Some Carter administration officials were dissatisfied with that strategy. They believed that the 1973–1974 embargo and subsequent price increases had proved that the oil of the Gulf was a vital strategic resource, too important to be left under the unreliable protection of local allies like Iran. One prominent hawk was the Harvard political scientist Samuel Huntington, who served as coordinator of security planning at the NSC in 1977–1978. Huntington helped draft the classified planning document PRM-10 in 1977. It asserted that "the continued flow of Persian Gulf and North African oil is crucial to the war capability of the NATO alliance. Consequently neither the Soviets nor ourselves could ignore the importance of these resources." In the event of conflict with the United States, PRM-10 warned, the Soviet Union could "threaten Persian Gulf oil" by attacking either the oil fields or the transportation routes that brought oil to the United States, Europe, and Japan. U.S. forces needed to be ready to counter Soviet attacks or to "take over the oil fields themselves."[22]

Carter's national security adviser Zbigniew Brzezinski used Huntington's analysis as the basis for PD-18, a secret policy statement in August 1977. Brzezinski told Carter that with Europe so dependent on Gulf oil, there could be "serious strains on Alliance cohesion in the event of a supply emergency." If the Soviet Union or its allies interfered with Gulf oil shipments, U.S. allies in Western Europe might be so desperate that they would abandon NATO and accommodate themselves to the Soviet Union in exchange for continued access to energy.[23] As a result, PD-18 argued that for Cold War reasons, the Gulf was "an area of critical interest to the United States." In order to defend the Gulf as well as the Middle East and Korea, PD-18 recommended that "the United States will maintain a deployment force of light divisions with strategic mobility" that could quickly be deployed overseas in the event of a crisis.[24] This was the basis of the idea for what later became known as the Rapid Deployment Joint Task Force (RDJTF).

At first, however, PD-18 had little impact on U.S. foreign policy. In mid-1977, the Shah's regime in Iran still appeared to be a stable, effective guardian of American interests in the Gulf, and it was easier for the United States to rely on the Iranian alliance to maintain regional stability rather than undertaking that task itself. Building a rapid deployment force and shifting military assets to the Middle East would have been difficult in the post-Vietnam era of shrinking military budgets, and securing military cooperation from states in the region would have been a major diplomatic challenge. As a result, the portions of PRM-10 and PD-18 dealing with the Gulf were largely ignored by much of the U.S. government in 1977 and 1978. They did, however, lay the intellectual groundwork for much of what would come later, after a series of crises affecting Saudi Arabia's neighbors: Somalia, Yemen, Iran, and Afghanistan.

SOMALIA

During the mid-1970s, Somalia was governed by the military dictator Siad Barre. He was a socialist who developed close ties with the Soviet Union and allowed the Soviets to build a large naval base at the Red Sea port of Berbera. In March 1976, Prince Fahd told the United States he was worried about "the unconcealed advance of communism in the African continent" and warned that the Soviet Union was using Somalia to secure naval access to the Red Sea.[25] Fahd thought that Barre might give up his Soviet alliance for the right price, and offered to cover the cost if the United States would send weapons to Somalia. The Ford administration declined. Selling arms to Siad Barre would have threatened U.S. relations with Somalia's neighbor Ethiopia. Congress was also skeptical of U.S. involvement in Africa and might have tried to block any arms sale.[26]

The political situation in the Horn of Africa shifted in early 1977 after a Marxist regime took power in Ethiopia. In response, Siad Barre began to move closer to the West, and Saudi Arabia stepped up its efforts to convince the United States to support Somalia. In April 1977, Saud al-Faisal told U.S. ambassador William Porter that the United States should welcome a rapprochement with Somalia. Saud stressed that he was "quite certain in his own mind that Somalia is ready for a major reorientation of their basic outlook as far as the Soviet Union and the U.S. are concerned."[27] The Carter administration was initially reluctant to take this Saudi advice. Somalia was not a very appealing ally, given its underdevelopment, military weakness, dubious human rights record, and Siad Barre's history of friendship with the USSR.

In July 1977, Somalia invaded Ethiopia. Siad Barre hoped to exploit Ethiopia's postrevolutionary turmoil and seize the Ogaden, a region of eastern Ethiopia inhabited by ethnic Somalis and long claimed by Somali nationalists as part of "Greater Somalia." Saudi Arabia encouraged the invasion as a way of weakening the communist regime in Ethiopia. Riyadh promised $300 million to Siad Barre if he broke with the Soviets, and provided weapons to support the Somali forces in their war with Ethiopia.[28] Saudi aid proved insufficient after the Soviet Union and Cuba intervened on behalf of Ethiopia. Thousands of Cuban troops arrived to repel the Somalian invasion, and by March 1978, the Somali army had been driven back across the border. The Carter administration was split on how to respond, with Vance arguing for restraint and Brzezinski calling for a show of force, including the dispatch of an aircraft carrier task force.[29]

Saudi Arabia was impatient with the American reluctance to help Somalia, seeing it as part of a broader U.S. failure to act aggressively against communism. In May 1978, Fahd told Ambassador West: "If you don't reassert your position as leader of the free world, we here in Saudi Arabia had better be preparing to greet the Russians with rose petals as they cross the Red Sea and the Gulf."[30] Prince Turki al-Faisal, the Saudi intelligence chief, would later recall that "the Communists seemed to be on a roll, expanding everywhere." It appeared, Turki said, as if "everything was working against us." The Saudis were especially concerned about the presence of Soviet advisers and Cuban troops in Ethiopia because of its geographic proximity to the kingdom. The Saudi government feared that "the Cuban troops that reached Ethiopia, which then still had a Red Sea coast, could have easily crossed that seacoast and come across to Saudi shores."[31]

Brzezinski pointed to Saudi concerns to advocate a more hawkish policy in the Horn of Africa. In his memoirs, he noted that he was disturbed by "the foreign implications of perceived U.S. passivity in this strategic area," where "our credibility was under scrutiny by new, relatively skeptical allies in a region strategically important to us." He was particularly influenced by Saudi fears of "the prospect of a Soviet presence across the Red Sea." In December 1977, Brzezinski noted in his diary: "If Ethiopia and South Yemen become Soviet associates, not only will access to Suez be threatened, and this involves the oil pipeline from Saudi Arabia and Iran, but there will be a serious and direct political threat to Saudi Arabia. This is something we simply cannot ignore, no matter how uncomfortable the thought may be."[32] Although Carter decided against deploying an aircraft carrier to the Arabian Sea, by 1980, the United States aligned itself openly with Somalia, providing military aid to Siad Barre's regime and taking over the former Soviet naval base at Berbera. As a result, U.S. concern about a possible threat to Saudi Arabia, and the Saudi desire for a stronger U.S. stance against Soviet and Cuban involvement in Ethiopia, contributed to a major reorientation of U.S. foreign policy in the Horn of Africa.[33]

Saudi Arabia did more than influence U.S. policy. It also provided financial support, arms, and other supplies directly to Somalia. Soviet and Cuban officials recognized Saudi influence in East Africa as one of the major challenges facing the Marxist Ethiopian regime. In 1977, Fidel Castro denounced "the reactionary role of Saudi Arabia" and warned that the Somali right wing was seeking "to deliver Somalia into the arms of Saudi Arabia and Imperialism."[34] A Soviet Foreign Ministry official later complained that "the declaration of Western powers that they would not make weapons available to Somalia is refuted by arms deliveries via third [parties], in particular reactionary Arab countries."[35] At times, the Saudi government even ignored U.S. concerns and supplied Somalia with arms, such as American-made mortars, whose reexport was specifically prohibited by U.S. regulations.[36]

Saudi Arabia also provided ideological backing for the Somali regime by portraying the war as a battle between Islam and atheist Marxism. Transnational Islamic organizations like the Saudi-funded Muslim World League (MWL) played a central role in this campaign. In 1979, the secretary-general of the MWL argued that "it is high time the world of Islam realized the strategic importance of the Horn of Africa region." The non-Muslim Ethiopian regime was threatening key oil trade routes and the Islamic holy places in Mecca and Medina by increasing its influence in the Red Sea, which had been a "Muslim lake."[37] An editorial in the MWL's official journal denounced "Ethiopia, which is openly supported by the Soviet Union," and "the Cuban-Ethiopian marauders" with their "campaigns of destruction and subjugation." The MWL appealed for Muslims around the world to send aid to the Somali refugees.[38] As a result, although Saudi leaders favored a stronger U.S. stance against Ethiopia and in favor of Somalia, they also attempted to reframe the conflict as a struggle on behalf of Islam. Their campaign to rally Muslim opposition to Ethiopia foreshadowed their campaign to mobilize a transnational jihad against the Soviet occupation of Afghanistan after 1979.

YEMEN

An even clearer example of Saudi influence on U.S. foreign policy was the U.S. decision to send weapons to Yemen in 1979. At that time, Yemen was divided between the mutually hostile Yemen Arab Republic (YAR), or North Yemen, which was governed by an Arab nationalist regime, and the People's Democratic Republic of Yemen (PDRY), or South Yemen, which was under a Marxist regime and was closely aligned with the USSR. Initially, Yemen was a low priority for U.S. policymakers. Beginning in the mid-1970s, the United States and Saudi Arabia developed a cooperative program to modernize the YAR's armed forces to help defend against the PDRY, but this program was on a small scale and involved mostly antiquated, 1940s-vintage weaponry.[39]

Saudi Arabia cared much more than the United States about what happened in Yemen. Riyadh was influenced by memories of the 1962–1970 civil war in the YAR and the border clashes with the PDRY during the early 1970s.[40] In February 1978, Fahd asked Ambassador West what the United States would do if the PDRY invaded the YAR. Fahd worried "that such an action would be the first step by the USSR and its surrogates toward their ultimate goal of seizing the Saudi oil fields."[41] Saudi concerns intensified when President Ahmad Hussein al-Ghashmi of North Yemen was assassinated in June 1978, followed just days later by the fall from power and execution of President Salem Rubayi Ali of South Yemen. Rubayi was replaced by Abd al-Fattah Ismail, who strengthened South Yemen's ties with the USSR. Although the developments in the YAR and the PDRY were probably not directed by the Soviet Union, Brzezinski told Carter: "The Saudis, the North Yemenis, the Shah, and others in the region will see this turn of events as further confirmation of their deepest fears, vis. the Soviets, having installed their crew in Kabul, having attempted the same in Baghdad, with Addis in their pocket, have now added another link in the ever-tighter chain encircling the moderate Arabs."[42]

In February 1979, small-scale border clashes broke out between the PDRY and the YAR. The YAR's president Ali Abdullah Saleh asked the United States for aid, telling the U.S. ambassador that his country was being invaded by PDRY forces backed by the Soviet Union. The Carter administration responded by airlifting a massive arms delivery to North Yemen. Carter invoked emergency legislation that allowed him to send $390 million in arms, including advanced weaponry like jet fighters and tanks that had previously been denied to the YAR, without obtaining congressional approval.[43] Carter also approved the dispatch of two AWACS early-warning aircraft and the aircraft carrier USS *Constellation* to the region, as well as three other warships to nearby Djibouti.[44] Carter's order marked a dramatic escalation of U.S. involvement in Yemen, as well as an increased willingness by the White House to act unilaterally, without consulting Congress.

There was, in fact, little evidence that the Soviet Union was behind the incident, or even that the PDRY planned a full-scale invasion of the YAR. The fighting remained confined to border regions and died down by the end of March. The U.S. military attaché in the YAR, John Ruszkiewicz, argued that the YAR leadership had exaggerated the whole incident and that the supposed crisis was largely imaginary. Even so, the U.S. response helped consolidate the U.S.-Saudi partnership. The *New York Times* quoted U.S. officials as explaining that the move was "designed to demonstrate American concern for Yemen and for Saudi Arabia, which is Yemen's main benefactor."[45] American policymakers said the same thing behind closed doors; a classified State Department paper in April 1979 noted that "our effort to accelerate the deployment of an adequate defense force in North Yemen [was] largely at Saudi request."[46] Ambassador West later noted approvingly that "the prompt response of the U.S." to the crisis in Yemen "replenished political capital with the Saudis at a critical time."[47] Maintaining Saudi goodwill had become an end in itself for the United States.

Saudi Arabia subsidized the U.S. arms shipments to the YAR and directly contributed substantial aid to the government in North Yemen. Ruszkiewicz quoted one of his Pentagon colleagues as explaining: "President Carter has to take a stand somewhere in the region, and he can do it cheap in Yemen because Saudi Arabia is paying all the bills."[48] When one former U.S. official was asked why the United States had accepted the Saudi aid, he laughed and said: "Can you imagine getting that kind of money out of Congress for Yemen?"[49]

Relying so heavily on Saudi Arabia might have saved money, but it had other kinds of costs. Saudi Arabia's priorities in Yemen did not always coincide with those of the United States. In 1979, the State Department noted that "the ambivalence in the Saudi attitude toward North Yemen" was causing "snags" in U.S. foreign policy.[50] Saudi Arabia did not trust the regime in Sanaa and hoped to make the YAR strong enough to deter a PDRY attack but not so strong that it would pose a threat to Saudi Arabia itself. In December 1979, the YAR told the United States that Saudi Arabia was using aid "as a tool to manipulate the government of Yemen." The YAR's deputy prime minister Hassan Muhammad Makki "complained that the Saudis retain spare parts and ammunition, and force Yemen to act like a beggar in order to get them." Saudi Arabia also gave some weapons and funding directly to independent-minded tribes in North Yemen, undermining the central authority of the government in Sanaa and contributing to the persistent weakness of the Yemeni state.[51]

THE IRANIAN REVOLUTION

For most of the 1970s, U.S. policy in the Persian Gulf depended on the American alliance with the Shah of Iran. Iran had the most powerful military forces in the region, and the Shah enjoyed close relations with Nixon, Ford, and Carter alike. In 1977–1978, the Shah's regime came under pressure from a diverse coalition of domestic opponents, including liberals, secular leftists, and religious conservatives. Their most influential leader was the Ayatollah Ruhollah Khomeini, a Shia cleric who had been exiled in the 1960s after denouncing the Shah and his relationship with the United States. By late 1978, enormous antigovernment demonstrations filled the streets in Iran. The Shah's regime collapsed in the face of the uprising, with soldiers mutinying and refusing to fire on the protesters. In January 1979, the Shah left the country, and the next month, Khomeini returned to Iran and oversaw the establishment of a Shia theocracy, the Islamic Republic. As Khomeini and his allies consolidated authority over the new regime, U.S.-Iranian relations deteriorated rapidly, especially after a group of Iranian students seized the U.S. embassy in Tehran and took its occupants hostage in November 1979.[52]

The fall of the Shah focused the attention of U.S. policymakers on the Gulf, and particularly on Saudi Arabia. During the revolution, Iranian oil production collapsed because of strikes by oil workers and the general breakdown of law and order in the country. With millions of barrels per day suddenly removed from the market, oil prices soared from less than fifteen dollars per barrel at the beginning of 1978 to nearly forty dollars per barrel by 1980. The economic impact on the United States was dramatic, with gasoline shortages and long lines reappearing across the country in scenes reminiscent of the 1973–1974 embargo. The Carter administration was under enormous political pressure to solve the problem. Stuart Eizenstat, Carter's domestic policy adviser, warned him: "Nothing else has so frustrated, confused, angered the American people—or so targeted their distress at you personally."[53] As the Carter administration sought desperately to alleviate the oil crisis, Saudi Arabia, already seen as the key "swing producer" and supplier of last resort, appeared even more vital after the loss of Iranian production. As Brzezinski told Carter in June 1979: "Our current search for a way out of the oil supply/price bind leads us back to Saudi Arabia." The administration lobbied the kingdom to boost production and limit, even if it could not prevent, the dizzying increase in prices.[54]

The fall of the Shah changed the political, as well as the economic, relationship between the United States and Saudi Arabia. In less than a year, Iran had gone from the most important U.S. military partner in the Gulf to an open adversary of the United States. The loss of such a critical ally made U.S. policymakers increasingly fearful about the security of other Gulf states and gave more ammunition to hawks who wanted to expand U.S. military involvement in the Gulf. In December 1978, Brzezinski told Carter that the entire region from South Asia to the Horn of Africa had become an "arc of crisis," with Saudi Arabia caught in the middle. If American allies in Europe and Japan lost access to Gulf oil, Brzezinski warned, the anticommunist Western alliance might collapse, producing "a fundamental shift in the global structure of power."[55]

The Iranian Revolution alarmed the Saudi monarchy. The sudden collapse of the Shah's regime, even though it enjoyed a close relationship with the United States and was armed with advanced American weapons, raised doubts about whether the United States could save Saudi Arabia from a similar fate. In February 1979, the State Department and the CIA reported that because of the Iranian Revolution, U.S.-Saudi relations were going through their most difficult period in years. U.S. officials repeatedly stressed similar themes over the next several months. Brzezinski, Secretary of Defense Harold Brown, and other Carter administration officials argued that in order to restore Saudi confidence, the United States needed to work more closely with Riyadh and take on a more assertive role in the Gulf.[56]

AFGHANISTAN

In April 1978, a coup brought a Marxist regime to power in Afghanistan. The Afghan communists were soon confronted by a growing insurgency, including hard-line Islamists. The Kabul government began to lose control over the countryside and issued increasingly desperate appeals for Soviet aid. Saudi Arabia, Pakistan, and other anticommunist governments in the region sensed an opportunity to undermine the Soviet Union by supporting the Afghan insurgents. In January 1979, the CIA reported that Saudi funds were flowing to the rebels, although, in a sign of the very limited U.S. intelligence-gathering capabilities in Afghanistan, the CIA could not verify the information or determine if the money was coming from the Saudi government or private Saudi donors. The CIA began exploring options for joint covert operations with Saudi Arabia and Pakistan, and in mid-1979 the United States started to send nonmilitary aid to the Afghan opposition. For the moment, U.S. and Saudi backing for the rebels was limited. Saudi Arabia was reluctant to confront the Soviet Union without clearer assurances of American support. Saudi Arabia also lacked good intelligence in Afghanistan and was uncertain which insurgent groups to support.[57]

In December 1979, Soviet troops invaded Afghanistan, killed the Afghan leader Hafizullah Amin, and installed a new government to prop up communist control over the country in the face of the growing insurgency. Brzezinski immediately told Carter that "if the Soviets succeed in Afghanistan," they could bring Pakistan under their influence, too, and would be in a position to disrupt the vital oil-producing areas and sea lanes of the Persian Gulf and the Indian Ocean. He recommended: "We should concert with Islamic countries both in a propaganda campaign and in a covert action campaign to help the rebels."[58] By the end of January, Saudi Arabia and the United States were jointly funding the shipment of weapons to the Afghan insurgents, purchased in Egypt and sent to Pakistan via the Saudi air base at Dhahran.[59]

The United States and Saudi Arabia worked together to cast the war as a religious struggle against atheist communism. Even before the Soviet invasion of Afghanistan, the Carter administration tried to portray the United States and the Muslim world as natural allies against the Soviet Union. On a visit to Saudi Arabia in March 1979, Brzezinski told Prince Saud al-Faisal that the United States shared "belief in God and religious values" and told King Khalid that "the revival of Islam and Arab institutions was essential; the alternative is communism. It is essential politically and spiritually."[60] Saudi Arabia did its part to mobilize Islamic resistance to the communist government in Afghanistan. At a conference in Mecca, Muhammad Ali al-Harakan, the Saudi religious scholar and head of the MWL, described the civil war in Afghanistan as a jihad in October 1979, when the enemy was still Afghan communists rather than Soviet troops.[61]

After December 1979, the United States and Saudi Arabia stressed that theme even more. Vance told Carter that the administration would "emphasize American willingness to cooperate with all Islamic countries" and "American understanding of Islamic values" as part of an alliance with the Muslim world against the Soviet Union.[62] Saudi Arabia and the transnational organizations that it funded held up their part of the bargain, barraging the Muslim world with propaganda against the Soviet Union. The MWL denounced the Soviet invasion of Afghanistan as "a most frontal challenge to the independence and brotherhood of the entire Muslim world" and warned that it could be a prelude to "Soviet Russia swallowing up the entire Gulf region."[63] The Saudi press ran lurid stories and political cartoons about Soviet atrocities against Islam, and the Saudi-funded Organization of the Islamic Conference met in Islamabad in January 1980 to condemn Soviet actions in Afghanistan.[64]

THE CARTER DOCTRINE

For years, Saudi leaders had been demanding a more aggressive U.S. response to the Soviet Union, especially in the Middle East. They complained that Vietnam had made the United States too reluctant to intervene abroad. In May 1978, Fahd asked Ambassador West: "When is the U.S. going to put aside Vietnam and Watergate and reassert its role as a world leader? Will your Congress ever allow that to happen?" He suggested that Saudi Arabia might need to accommodate itself to Soviet power unless the United States started acting more assertively.[65] After the Soviets invaded Afghanistan, the Saudi information minister Mohammed Yamani said that the United States and its Western allies had been overcome by "laxity" and "irresponsibility," failing to see the threat posed by "this dangerous communist tide."[66] Saudi leaders also scoffed at the willingness of U.S. officials to submit to congressional and public oversight. Prince Turki complained about the U.S. timidity that resulted from "the American defeat in Vietnam through to Watergate and post-Watergate American disengagement from world affairs." He also deplored the "restrictions on American foreign policy action and CIA action" that resulted from and the investigations carried out by Sen. Frank Church (D-ID).[67]

The Saudi critique of U.S. policy in the Cold War overlapped with similar complaints made by hawkish U.S. officials. They worried that Vietnam had dampened Americans' enthusiasm for overseas adventures, and that the Carter administration was too reluctant to act aggressively. They were determined to use the opportunity provided by the perceived Soviet threat to the Gulf to push U.S. foreign policy in a more hawkish direction. In March 1979, Brzezinski told Saud al-Faisal that "the exercise of U.S. power has been hampered in the wake of Vietnam; however, the Vietnam malaise is now coming to an end."[68]

Although Brzezinski and Saud al-Faisal agreed that the United States needed a more forceful response to communism, Brzezinski and other hawks still had to overcome resistance from skeptics in the administration. One month after meeting Saud al-Faisal, Brzezinski warned Carter that he needed "more deliberate emphasis on U.S. strength and resolve in your public statements." Brzezinski recommended: "It might be helpful to stress more often your role as Commander in Chief." He urged, in particular, "an Arabian Gulf security policy" that would announce Carter's willingness to intervene in the region. It would also help Carter's reelection prospects by serving as "a damage limitation initiative for the likely 1980 debate on the consequences of the loss of Iran."[69] In November 1979, the NSC official Robert Hunter proposed that the administration announce "a Carter Doctrine for the Middle East" dealing with "oil-security" issues. It would also give the administration a chance to restore "U.S. resolve," seizing the opportunity provided by the "fading of the 'Vietnam syndrome'" and the return of "public willingness to see us take a leadership position" in the world.[70]

The Soviet invasion of Afghanistan made Carter more receptive to these arguments. He wrote in his memoirs that the Soviet takeover of Afghanistan was "a threat to the rich oil fields of the Persian Gulf area and to the crucial waterways through which so much of the world's energy supplies had to pass."[71] U.S. officials worried that the Soviet presence in Afghanistan either could serve as a base for military aggression against Pakistan and Iran or could so unnerve U.S. allies in the region that they might abandon the United States and seek accommodation with the USSR. This became a powerful argument for rapidly building up U.S. military capabilities in the Middle East. As Brzezinski wrote to Carter in January 1980: "We need to do something to reassure the Egyptians, the Saudis, and others on the Arabian Peninsula that the U.S. is prepared to assert its power, and that requires a visible military presence in the area now."[72]

The new policy was announced in Carter's January 1980 State of the Union address. He declared: "Let our position be absolutely clear: An attempt by any outside force to gain control of the Persian Gulf region will be regarded as an assault on the vital interests of the United States of America, and such an assault will be repelled by any means necessary, including military force."[73] As Robert Hunter had proposed, the policy became known as the "Carter Doctrine." It was intended both to deter any Soviet designs on the Gulf and to reassure local allies, especially Saudi Arabia, that the United States was fully committed to their defense. Shortly after the speech, Vance told Carter that it had restored American allies' confidence in the United States.[74] Brzezinski was especially pleased with the Saudi reaction. After meeting with Saudi leaders, he told Carter that their attitude toward the United States had improved dramatically: "There is no doubt that your State of the Union message has had a fundamental impact. *They now take us seriously.*"[75]

EXPANDING THE U.S. MILITARY AND PIVOTING TO THE GULF

The problem with the Carter Doctrine was that the United States did not have the troops, the bases, or the transport capability to match Soviet power in the Gulf. U.S. officials feared a Soviet invasion of Iran, one that might be a prelude to an attack on Saudi Arabia. The Soviet Union was much closer to the region and could march its army directly over the Iranian border, while the United States would have to send its forces thousands of miles by air or sea. On short notice the United States could send no more than two divisions to Iran, where they might have to face sixteen to twenty Soviet divisions. In September 1980, the NSC warned: "We cannot defend

Iran on any line today against a determined Soviet attack. We simply do not have the forces."[76]

U.S. officials saw Saudi Arabia not only as an ally that needed protection from the Soviet threat but also as a vital base for U.S. forces operating elsewhere in the region. The NSC staffer Fritz Ermarth argued that "for the Soviets to believe that they would run into a credible U.S. showing in the event of a major thrust toward the Gulf," the United States would need "both air and ground forces in Saudi Arabia."[77] The chairman of the Joint Chiefs of Staff, General David Jones, noted that even a small, two-division U.S. expeditionary force in Iran would need Saudi logistical support.[78]

The United States, however, did not have access to Saudi bases. The State Department noted that "the Saudis are quite opposed to a direct U.S. military presence" in the Gulf.[79] Knowing that open collaboration with the United States would be unpopular, Saudi leaders stressed that they would never permit foreign bases on their soil. In March 1979, Prince Saud al-Faisal told an interviewer that the kingdom was satisfied with its own defense capabilities and had no plans to ask for protection from American troops. That fall, Crown Prince Fahd and the defense minister Prince Sultan announced that they did not need foreign help to defend the kingdom. Even after the Soviet Union invaded Afghanistan in December 1979, the Saudi government refused to alter its public stance. Saud al-Faisal reiterated that the kingdom "will not make an agreement on any kind of facilities, with the Americans or anyone else," and Sultan declared that "no country has ever thought of asking U.S. to put foreign feet" in the kingdom, since everyone knew that Saudi Arabia would never agree to host foreign troops.[80]

One way to compensate for U.S. weakness in the Gulf was what Brzezinski and Brown called "horizontal escalation," retaliating against a Soviet invasion of Iran by attacking Soviet interests elsewhere. Secretary of State Edmund Muskie was appalled by the suggestion, calling it "a formula for moving toward World War III." He told his colleagues that they could not count on domestic support, since "Congress would ask whether or not a nuclear war would be worth it for 11 percent of our oil." Brzezinski and Brown, however, argued that because Gulf oil was vital for America's allies, Soviet control over the Gulf could mean a Soviet victory in the Cold

War. When they pressed him, even Muskie conceded that "the loss of the Persian Gulf would lead to the loss of Europe." The administration agreed to warn the Soviets to stay away from the Gulf, and to share U.S. intelligence with both Iraq and Iran. Neither of those countries was friendly to the United States, but the Carter administration was determined to preserve their independence so they could serve as buffer states between Saudi Arabia and the USSR.[81]

Over the longer term, the Carter administration was determined to expand the U.S. military capability to intervene in the Gulf. It dusted off the idea of a rapid deployment force that PD-18 had suggested in 1977. The result was the RDJTF, a collection of military units that could be sent to the Middle East on short notice. The Defense Department made plans to purchase a series of fast transport ships that could move large quantities of military equipment to the Gulf, while other stocks of equipment were prepositioned in the region on fleets of stationary ships. The United States began negotiations with Egypt, Oman, Somalia, and Kenya to construct military bases and facilities for the use of U.S. forces. Because of Saudi opposition, the United States could not establish permanent bases in Saudi Arabia itself, but the kingdom was soon ringed with American naval forces, facilities, and security agreements that were designed to safeguard the oil supplies of the Gulf (figure 8.1). To oversee this network of military forces, administration officials began planning for an independent military command dedicated to the Middle East, which eventually became U.S. Central Command (CENTCOM).[82]

Building a new military infrastructure in the Gulf was expensive and required the deployment of troops that were also needed in Europe, Korea, and other potential Cold War battlefields. As a result, Carter's pivot to the Gulf encouraged a broader expansion of the U.S. military. In 1980, the administration asked for a large increase in the defense budget, even as it cut domestic spending and stressed the need for fiscal restraint. Much of the new spending was intended to enhance U.S. capabilities in the Gulf. It included funding for more air and naval patrols in the region, $9 billion to boost the military's rapid deployment capabilities with fast transport ships, cargo aircraft, and tankers. Also included was a fleet of "maritime prepositioning ships" full of heavy equipment and weapons that could wait

FIGURE 8.1 Active and proposed U.S. military installations surrounding Saudi Arabia, early 1980s.

offshore. In an emergency, planeloads of U.S. Marines could fly in and use the equipment, dramatically shortening the amount of time it would take to send fully equipped units to the Gulf.[83]

The hawkish mood extended beyond the White House. For most of the 1970s, Congress had demanded cuts in the defense budgets proposed by Nixon, Ford, and Carter. Now, the opposite was true, and Congress approved even more funding for the Pentagon than Carter had requested, more than doubling the proposed increase in weapons research and procurement. The liberal Rep. Paul Simon (D-IL) recognized that it was hopeless to resist the pressure for more arms purchases, noting that congressional support for defense spending was "overwhelming."[84]

American fears about losing access to Gulf oil created a hawkish new mood in the United States. A poll taken two weeks after Carter's speech showed that 64 percent of Americans favored sending U.S. troops to the Persian Gulf if the Soviets invaded. That figure was almost as high as the number of Americans (67 percent) who favored defending Western Europe.[85] The retired diplomat George F. Kennan wrote with dismay: "Never since World War II has there been so far-reaching a militarization of thought and discourse in the capital. An unsuspecting stranger, plunged into its midst, could only conclude that the last hope of peaceful, nonmilitary solutions had been exhausted—that from now on only weapons, however used, could count."[86]

Even some of the most prominent leaders of the Democratic left proclaimed their support for an expanded military presence in the Gulf. Sen. Ted Kennedy (D-MA), running against Carter for the Democratic presidential nomination, criticized the Carter Doctrine and suggested that the United States should ration gasoline at home to eliminate the need for oil imports. Kennedy, however, also declared: "The United States should not tolerate the interruption of oil supply in the Middle East by the Soviet Union. That would be completely unacceptable, and the United States would have to take whatever steps necessary including military steps to ensure continuation of oil supply from that region of the world." Kennedy called for the buildup of "American naval and air forces" in the Gulf and expressed his support for a larger defense budget.[87] Remarkably, even Sen. George McGovern (D-SD) argued in favor of sending U.S. troops to defend "Saudi Arabia and the oil-producing emirates of the Arabian peninsula" not only from external attack but from internal threats as well. The fact that such a famous critic of the Vietnam War was now willing to use American troops to put down domestic Saudi opposition indicated how far the political center of gravity had shifted to the right.[88]

TARGETING IRAN

The Carter Doctrine announced the U.S. determination to defend the Gulf against an "outside force" assumed to be the Soviet Union and its allies.

Soon, however, the U.S. security umbrella was also extended to cover threats to Saudi Arabia from a new adversary: the Islamic Republic of Iran.

At first, Saudi leaders expressed cautious optimism about the Iranian Revolution. In February 1979, Saud al-Faisal announced that Saudi Arabia hoped to promote Islamic unity alongside the Ayatollah Khomeini. He dismissed the division between Sunni and Shia Muslims as "a political dispute, not a religious one," and said it was no barrier to Saudi-Iranian cooperation. In June, Prince Nayef said that while it was too soon to say what the outcome of the Iranian Revolution would be, since "things have not yet crystallized," he was pleased to see the new regime's emphasis on Islamic values. "What happened in Iran is what we have always called for," Nayef said. "In the past, we told Iranian officials that they were Muslims," but they had always been reluctant to follow Saudi advice and embrace their Islamic identity—until now. As late as June 1980, Mohammed Yamani approvingly described Iran as "an Islamic state," and said "we have very close relations with it."[89]

By that point, though, Iranian relations with both Saudi Arabia and the United States were already deteriorating. The November 1979 protests in al-Hasa convinced the Saudi regime that the Iranian Revolution was inciting opposition by Shia dissidents in the kingdom. After the demonstrations began, a senior Saudi official speculated about the idea of war with Iran and noted that if fighting broke out, the Saudi government would need to use "troops to control the Shia population."[90] November 1979 marked a sharp increase in U.S.-Iranian hostility, too, as more than fifty U.S. embassy personnel in Tehran were taken hostage by a group of Iranian protesters and held captive for more than a year.

Iran's emergence as the primary regional adversary of the United States and Saudi Arabia was underlined by the outbreak of the Iran-Iraq War. Hoping to capitalize on Iran's postrevolutionary turmoil and eliminate the political threat posed by Khomeini's ideology, the Iraqi leader Saddam Hussein ordered an invasion of Iran on September 22, 1980. The United States was caught by surprise and announced that it was neutral in the conflict, but over time it tilted toward Iraq. At the beginning of the war the Iraqi air force sent some of its planes to other Arab countries, including Saudi Arabia. The official rationale was to keep the aircraft out of range of

Iranian attacks, but Iraq probably also hoped to use foreign air bases to launch raids on Iran. Just four days into the war, the United States learned that Iraq was planning to attack Iran from Omani territory. A U.S. report warned: "There is a high likelihood that Iran would decide to retaliate against the Arab states of the Gulf if Iraq attacks Iranian territory and forces in the lower Gulf." The United States especially worried that "the next target may be Saudi Arabia if the West fails to get Iraq to stop the fighting."[91]

Having invited Iranian attack by hosting Iraqi aircraft, Saudi Arabia urgently asked the United States for the deployment of AWACS early-warning aircraft, ground radars, and surface-to-air missiles. Some members of the Carter administration objected, including Secretary of State Edmund Muskie, who feared that helping Saudi Arabia would mean abandoning U.S. neutrality and becoming directly embroiled in the conflict.[92] Brzezinski retorted that "we should not make a fetish out of 'neutrality' when our most vital assets are at risk," since the United States had to be ready to defend "the Saudi oil installations." As he had before, Brzezinski argued that failing to protect Saudi Arabia would make the United States, and Jimmy Carter, look weak. "The whole world," he wrote, "knows that we have a vital stake in Saudi oil, and our passivity in the face of a Saudi request would become known, and be extraordinarily destructive both in terms of our international standing abroad and our political position at home."[93] Carter approved the deployment of the AWACS, radars, and missiles, showing that the United States would defend Saudi Arabia not only from the Soviet Union and its allies but also from regional rivals—even when Saudi Arabia had helped instigate the confrontation in the first place.

* * *

U.S. foreign policy in the Persian Gulf changed dramatically between 1977 and 1981. Carter came into office prioritizing diplomacy, hoping for an Arab-Israeli peace agreement and a deal with the Soviet Union to limit both U.S. and Soviet forces in the Indian Ocean. He left office proclaiming the Gulf to be part of the U.S. sphere of influence, promising to protect it with military force, and demanding a massive increase in defense spending.

Saudi Arabia played a critical role in that shift. Saudi leaders demanded that the United States do more to stop the spread of Soviet influence and urged the Carter administration to support anticommunist forces in Somalia, Yemen, and Afghanistan. U.S. officials listened to Riyadh because they wanted Saudi cooperation on economic and security questions, but also because the Saudi pleas coincided with what hawks in the Carter administration wanted to see in any case: a more aggressive approach to the Cold War. By the end of the 1970s, U.S. foreign policy had tilted far to the right. Although that development would later be associated with Ronald Reagan's presidency, Reagan's election only reinforced developments that were already under way.

The hawkish shift in U.S. foreign policy helped end détente and cause a revival of Cold War tensions during the 1980s. The U.S. commitment to defend Saudi Arabia, however, ensured that the U.S. pivot to the Gulf would outlast the Cold War itself. As the Soviet Union weakened and finally collapsed in 1991, the United States and Saudi Arabia would redirect their attention toward Iraq and Iran, laying the groundwork for decades of conflict to come.

CONCLUSION

On November 29, 1973, the oil tanker *Iddi* sailed into New York Harbor. It was a cool fall day, partly cloudy with a brisk wind. From their dock in Queens, the crew had a clear view of the World Trade Center in lower Manhattan, where construction had finished that spring (figure 9.1).

Like the twin towers of the World Trade Center, the *Iddi* was a symbol of global commerce. The ship was built in Sweden and crewed by Norwegians, including its captain, Harry Olaf Thyberg. During the previous year, it had sailed to Saudi Arabia, Iran, the United Arab Emirates, Singapore, Hawaii, and South Africa. When it reached New York, the *Iddi* was hauling a cargo of oil from Freeport in the Bahamas, where oil from many different countries was delivered by giant supertankers, pumped into storage tanks, and loaded onto ships like the *Iddi* that were small enough to enter American harbors. As for the source of the oil, Thyberg shrugged: "There's no telling where the crude originally came from."[1]

In 1973, New York City increasingly depended on global trade and finance. Many observers credited the shift to economic and technological forces that were bringing the world closer together. Oil was vital to that

FIGURE 9.1 New York from the *Iddi*, November 1973. The newly completed World Trade Center is visible on the horizon to the left. Eddie Hausner/*New York Times*/Redux.

process, as the preeminent fuel of global mobility and the only energy source that could be profitably transported between places as far apart as the Persian Gulf and the United States. Politics, however, determined how those economic and technological changes played out. The Saudi-led embargo and production restrictions of October 1973 made the *Iddi*'s cargo far more valuable. Thyberg noted that "tankers from every oil-importing nation in the world were in the harbor at Freeport," competing for supplies that would dwindle as the embargo took hold.

A half-dozen miles southwest of the *Iddi* lay the Brooklyn Navy Yard, where Seatrain Shipbuilding was constructing a series of supertankers, the largest ever assembled in the United States: the *Brooklyn*, the *Williamsburg*, the *Stuyvesant*, and the *Bay Ridge*. As their names suggested, the shipyard was a point of civic pride. The Navy Yard had employed twenty thousand workers during World War II, but the Pentagon later downsized it and eventually closed it altogether in 1967. Two years later, Richard Nixon proposed a $3.8 billion program to reinvigorate the American shipbuilding industry. That federal money convinced Seatrain, a container shipping company, to expand into the shipbuilding business, hire thousands of workers, and resurrect the Navy Yard.[2]

The oil shock threw a wrench in those plans. High oil prices reduced demand and created a surplus of shipping capacity. By early 1975, dozens of American tankers lay unused in port, orders for new tankers had dried up, and Seatrain was headed toward bankruptcy. The shipping industry pinned its hopes on the Energy Transportation Security Act of 1974, which would have required 20 percent of the oil imported into the United States to be carried on American tankers.

The oil crisis again proved an obstacle. Gerald Ford pocket-vetoed the bill, arguing it would boost shipping costs and increase oil prices that were already too high, as well as damage relations with America's trading partners. Seatrain promptly laid off 1,800 workers. Most were people of color who faced grim employment prospects now that the shipbuilding jobs were gone. The workers had been promised a future of stable, unionized employment at the shipyard, but as the laid-off electrician Andres Nieves bitterly remarked: "It wasn't a long future." In the spring of 1979, during the second oil price shock, Seatrain Shipbuilding closed completely and fired its last 1,300 workers. No company ever built supertankers in the United States again.[3]

* * *

Sitting on opposite sides of the East River, Seatrain and the World Trade Center symbolized the changing fortunes of American manufacturing and finance in the 1970s. Seatrain was only one of many manufacturing businesses to close as a wave of deindustrialization washed over the country. Soaring oil prices made the American economy more volatile, upsetting the economic calculations that companies used to make investment decisions. Some firms, like Seatrain, simply collapsed. The ones that survived became less willing to pay their workers high wages and guarantee them long-term employment.

Government leaders accepted, and even encouraged, that economic shift. The Ford administration tolerated the decline of the U.S. shipbuilding industry. Jimmy Carter and Paul Volcker—with encouragement from Saudi Arabia—risked higher unemployment to cut inflation and defend the dollar. As the economy deteriorated in the early 1980s, Volcker's successor at the New York Fed, Anthony Solomon, cheered the effects of the recession on the labor market. Solomon praised employers for taking "a tougher attitude toward labor negotiations." He told a group of visiting foreign central bankers: "A growing number of unionized workers have been making wage and benefits concessions to protect their jobs," delivering "the first major change for the better on the wage front."[4] Solomon and Volcker believed that austerity was necessary to deal with the economic effects of the oil crisis and the inflation it had spawned.

The industries that suffered the most were the ones most directly exposed to changes in oil prices.[5] From the late 1940s to the early 1970s, firms had assumed that oil prices would remain stable. The oil crisis made that assumption obsolete, turning business planning into a gamble. The American automobile industry was the most prominent victim, as consumers turned to smaller European and Japanese cars. Chrysler nearly went bankrupt, surviving only after the federal government bailed it out in 1979. The terms of the bailout included lower wages and benefits for Chrysler's unionized employees, adding to the pressure on U.S. manufacturing workers as factories shuttered across the nation.[6]

Many smaller manufacturers could not count on government support and went bust during the late 1970s and early 1980s. There were fatal consequences for some companies in other industries, too. The airline Braniff International expanded rapidly during the 1970s, starting new overseas routes and operating Concorde flights to Texas. The oil price increases of 1978–1979, combined with Volcker's punishingly high interest rates, destroyed Braniff's profitability. When oil prices began to ease in the early 1980s, it was too late for the airline. It abruptly ceased operations in May 1982, throwing thousands of employees out of work and stranding travelers. Murray Weidenbaum, chairman of Reagan's Council of Economic Advisers, told reporters that the administration had no problem letting Braniff go bankrupt. It was "an opportunity to show that we really believe in a free enterprise system of profit and loss."[7]

The financial sector also suffered from oil price volatility, but the government treated it very differently. The bank Continental Illinois began to fail at the same time as Braniff. It made bad loans to oil and gas companies that went bust as energy prices fell. In May 1982, the failure of the oil refiner Charter Company left Continental with huge losses. The bank's position steadily eroded, until by mid-1984 it was on the verge of collapse. Executives from other banks, however, warned that Continental was so large, and so intertwined with the rest of the industry, that its bankruptcy would put the entire financial system in danger. The Fed stepped in with a $4.5 billion rescue package, an episode that first popularized the term "too big to fail." The largest banks would be protected from the consequences of their bad bets.[8]

The U.S. effort to attract petrodollars during the 1970s was another example of the growing financialization of the American economy. The government created special arrangements to attract billions of dollars of Saudi money into U.S. Treasurys and Fannie Mae securities, adopting techniques long used by offshore investment hubs to lure foreign capital—including the promise of secrecy.

Saudi investors had no experience with congressional inquiries or investigatory journalism at home, and no desire to deal with such problems abroad. They wanted their investments anonymous at a time when "petro-dollars" had become something of a dirty word in the industrialized countries. The Pakistani American entrepreneur Munawar Hidayatallah noted those concerns when a U.S. congressional subcommittee asked him about his role channeling Gulf investment abroad. Hidayatallah's company was based in the tax haven of Luxembourg and put some of its money in Freeport, where the *Iddi* had loaded its oil. Hidayatallah explained: "I find that most of our investors from the Middle East are very private people, very shy about this new wealth that they have discovered." He nonchalantly admitted that his reasons for basing his company in a tax haven were: "One, to give us the flexibility to invest through an offshore corporation; and, two, to create a veil as far as traceability of individuals is concerned."[9]

After the 1970s, the idea that money should move around the world as freely as possible, unconstrained by political oversight or limits, gained traction in the United States as well. Those intangible flows of capital depended, though, on the material power of oil: the airplanes, tankers, and other machines that knit the global economy together and allowed elites to travel, make deals, coordinate their investments in distant countries, and even evade prosecution by leaving the country. When U.S. investigators targeted the Saudi businessmen Adnan Khashoggi and Ghaith Pharaon, suspected of corrupt business practices, Khashoggi and Pharaon simply stayed out of the United States and ignored the subpoenas and fines.[10]

* * *

During the 1980s, the economic limits of Saudi oil power became clear. The global oil market went into surplus, and prices fell. The United States and other consumer countries imported less oil as conservation measures from the 1970s finally took hold. Smaller cars became popular, coal displaced oil in electric power generation, and companies bought more efficient machinery. Production in new areas like Alaska, Mexico, and the North Sea came online, threatening OPEC's dominance. During the first half of the 1980s, Saudi Arabia steadily cut production to support the OPEC price. By 1985, Saudi exports had dropped so far that the kingdom was running an annual budget deficit of $20 billion and had used up one-third of the enormous financial assets it had accumulated during the boom.[11] Fed up with absorbing the brunt of OPEC production cuts, Saudi Arabia reversed course in late 1985 and dramatically expanded its exports. Prices plunged from almost thirty dollars per barrel to less than fifteen dollars per barrel.

The U.S.-Saudi alliance endured through the era of low oil prices. Although Saudi Arabia was not as wealthy as before, and its oil seemed less important now that the world market was in surplus, U.S. policymakers concluded that the kingdom's ability to open the tap and send prices plummeting only proved its importance as OPEC's "swing producer." They also feared that over the long run, low oil prices would devastate the domestic American oil industry and renew U.S. dependence on cheap oil from the Persian Gulf.[12]

The alliance also survived because it was based on more than Saudi control over crude oil production. Saudi funding let the White House order covert interventions abroad without securing congressional authorization. The Reagan administration, determined to roll back communism around the world and frustrated in its dealings with a Democratic Congress, was even more enthusiastic than its predecessors about using Saudi aid. The joint U.S.-Saudi program to fund the mujahideen in Afghanistan expanded dramatically after Reagan came to office. Saudi, Pakistani, and U.S. support for the insurgents helped force the Soviet Union to withdraw its forces from Afghanistan in 1989, a defeat that weakened the USSR and contributed to its collapse just two years later. Foreign support for the insurgency also empowered some of the most violent, reactionary groups in Afghan politics and influenced the rise of global jihadism. Thousands of Arab volunteers traveled to Afghanistan to fight alongside the mujahideen, including the Saudi citizen Osama bin Laden.

The Saudi regime collaborated with the United States to fund other political causes. That support included millions of dollars for the anticommunist "Contra" rebels in Nicaragua, facilitated by the Saudi ambassador to the United States Bandar bin Sultan and the private Saudi businessman Adnan Khashoggi. The Saudi connection was uncovered during the Iran-Contra scandal, when Congress and the press revealed that the Reagan administration had sold arms to Iran in exchange for the release of American hostages, using the proceeds to fund the Contras. The operation let the

Reagan administration circumvent the U.S. arms embargo against Iran and the congressional prohibition against intervention in Nicaragua.[13]

In 1981, Reagan underlined his commitment to the U.S.-Saudi alliance by approving a sale of AWACS aircraft to Saudi Arabia, along with bomb racks and fuel tanks to upgrade the F-15s already in the kingdom's air force. The sale was intensely controversial in Congress, as critics objected that the new equipment would threaten Israel. The administration pushed ahead anyway, with Reagan individually meeting forty-four senators to lobby for their votes. The sale barely passed with a vote of 52 to 48.[14]

The administration also expanded direct military involvement in the Persian Gulf to protect Saudi Arabia. As the Iran-Iraq War dragged on, Saudi Arabia and the other Arab Gulf states gave extensive financial aid and other assistance to Iraq, which they saw as a buffer against the revolutionary Iranian regime. The Reagan administration backed the kingdom against Iran. In June 1984, two Saudi F-15s shot down a pair of Iranian aircraft that strayed too close to Saudi Arabia. The Saudi planes were directed by a U.S. Air Force AWACS plane and refueled by a U.S. tanker.[15] The U.S. tilt in favor of Iraq and the other Arab states became increasingly overt. By the late 1980s, U.S. forces were in an undeclared war with Iran. The fighting culminated in the destruction of an Iranian airliner by the cruiser USS *Vincennes* in 1988, killing almost three hundred civilians.[16] Over the course of the decade, Iran began to replace the Soviet Union as the target of both U.S. and Saudi military planning in the Gulf.

The United States was committed to defending Saudi Arabia against regional threats. It demonstrated this commitment during the Gulf War of 1990–1991. In August 1990, Iraq invaded Kuwait. The United States feared that Saddam Hussein's next move could be an attack on Saudi Arabia. The George H. W. Bush administration immediately ordered Operation Desert Shield, a rapid buildup of U.S. troops and equipment to defend Saudi Arabia.

The military infrastructure prepared since the late 1970s sprang into action. U.S. troops found the kingdom equipped with bases and airfields built to American standards, and U.S.-made weapons that could be used with no additional training. Thousands of tanks, vehicles, and heavy supplies were loaded onto the SL-7 cargo ships and moved at high speed across the

FIGURE 9.2 The aircraft carrier USS *Saratoga* at Jeddah during the Gulf War, February 14, 1991.

Atlantic. They arrived at the same ports, including the port at Jeddah dedicated by King Faisal in 1973, that had been receiving American cars and other civilian goods for decades (figure 9.2). Lighter equipment, and the soldiers themselves, came by air. The same C-5 and C-141 transport aircraft that had carried weapons to Israel in 1973 now brought U.S. forces to Saudi Arabia. The Pentagon's own airlift capacity was insufficient, however, and for the first time the Pentagon activated the Civil Reserve Air Fleet (CRAF) program, which let it requisition civilian airliners for military use. Under CRAF, domestic American airlines hauled 65 percent of the troops and 22 percent of the air cargo during the buildup in Saudi Arabia. Economic and military globalization intertwined with each other, using the same oil-burning machines to move people, goods, and weapons around the world.[17]

Americans remained deeply split on extending military protection to Saudi Arabia. In November 1990, as U.S. troops arrived in the kingdom, dozens of Saudi women challenged the rules by publicly driving in Riyadh. The protest drew international attention to Saudi gender segregation. The

FIGURE 9.3 Former National Organization for Women (NOW) president Eleanor Smeal and other NOW members picket the Saudi embassy in Washington, DC, demanding civil rights for Saudi women as a precondition for U.S. intervention in the Gulf War. November 27, 1990. Mark Reinstein/Alamy.

National Organization for Women (NOW) marched on the Saudi embassy in Washington, denouncing Saudi "gender apartheid" and arguing that the United States should not protect such an undemocratic regime (figure 9.3). NOW's president Molly Yard called Saudi Arabia and Kuwait "despotic, clan-run monarchies" unworthy of U.S. support. A *Los Angeles Times* poll showed a huge gender gap in American opinion about war with Iraq: men narrowly supported war, while women rejected it by a ratio of two to one. Other groups denounced the idea of war for oil. The National Campaign for Peace in the Middle East wrote, "We are not willing to die, or have our family members or friends die for big oil company profits."[18] In January 1991, the Senate passed a resolution authorizing the use of military force with a narrow margin of 52 to 47. Most Democrats in Congress continued to oppose the war.

Less than a week later, the United States and its allies launched Operation Desert Storm. It began with more than a month of bombing against the Iraqi forces dug in along the border with Saudi Arabia. On February 24, U.S. and allied forces crossed the border and defeated the Iraqi army in just four days. The kingdom provided vital bases for coalition troops and helped cover the cost of the war, but its own forces played only a small role in the fighting. Despite spending vast sums on its military, Saudi Arabia was still incapable of defending itself without foreign help.

Even after Iraq agreed to a cease-fire and withdrew from Kuwait, thousands of U.S. troops stayed in the kingdom for the next twelve years. The United States had been planning for that moment since the 1970s, but the Saudi regime had always publicly denied its willingness to host foreign troops and bases. Many Saudis were unprepared for the sudden appearance of American troops. The continued presence of U.S. forces after the war became the source of deep political tension in Saudi Arabia, revealing the failure of the United States to secure support for its role in the Gulf from the Saudi people as well as the regime.

* * *

For decades, critics of the Saudi regime had condemned its reliance on the United States. While the most influential of those critiques had once come from Arab nationalists and leftists, conservative Islamist voices became more prominent after the kingdom's turn to the right in the 1970s and 1980s.

In 1989, Abu Muhammad al-Maqdisi, an activist born in Palestine but influential in Saudi Islamist circles, wrote an attack on the Saudi royal family and the U.S.-Saudi relationship that had solidified during the 1970s. Al-Maqdisi denounced the JECOR agreement that Kissinger and Fahd had negotiated, Saudi purchases of U.S. Treasurys, the Saudi commitment to low oil prices as a way of winning American favor, and the royal family's wasteful purchases of American weapons that, according to al-Maqdisi, only lined the pockets of corrupt arms dealers and U.S. defense contractors. Some of al-Maqdisi's sharpest attacks were on "the crime of bringing Christians into the Arabian Peninsula," including the Americans required to maintain the expensive weapons systems purchased by the regime. He concluded scornfully: "Saudi Arabia now looks like an American base."[19]

Al-Maqdisi's themes found a receptive audience as U.S. troops arrived on Saudi shores and stayed there long after the Gulf War ended. Critics were outraged at the presence of non-Muslims in the kingdom and the colonial relationship between Saudi Arabia and the United States implied by the existence of large U.S. military bases on Saudi soil.

One of those critics, Osama bin Laden, attained worldwide notoriety by founding the Al-Qaeda terrorist network. Bin Laden had first taken up arms against the Soviets in Afghanistan, part of the jihad encouraged by the Saudi and U.S. governments. After the Gulf War, Bin Laden concluded that the Saudi regime had become an American puppet and dedicated himself to bringing down the corrupt alliance between Washington and Riyadh. Bin Laden charged the Al Saud with betraying Islam and monopolizing the kingdom's wealth, mismanaging oil production while ordinary Saudis were trapped in poverty.[20]

On September 11, 2001, a group of nineteen members of Al-Qaeda, including fifteen Saudis, hijacked four American airliners. They flew one plane into the Pentagon and two into the twin towers of the World Trade Center, symbols of American power and critical nodes in the military and economic networks that bound the two countries together.

In the aftermath of the 9/11 attacks, the Saudi regime became deeply unpopular in the United States. Polls consistently found that a majority of Americans held negative views of the kingdom, with only 3 to 4 percent holding a "very favorable" opinion.[21] Many Americans accused the Saudi government of supporting the 9/11 attacks. Conspiracy theories proliferated about the ties between the Bush family and the Saudi royals, the hurried evacuation of Saudis from the United States after 9/11, and the "missing pages" of the 9/11 Commission Report (a twenty-eight-page section concerning allegations of Saudi government involvement in the attacks was withheld from the public between 2003 and 2016).

For their part, most Saudis opposed the 2003 U.S. invasion of Iraq, American support for Israel, and U.S. foreign policy in general. In 2007, only 9 percent of Saudis approved of the U.S. government leadership.[22] Nevertheless, cooperation between the U.S. and Saudi governments only intensified after 9/11. Especially after Al-Qaeda carried out a wave of attacks in Saudi Arabia itself in 2003, the Saudi regime expanded its security collaboration and intelligence-sharing with the CIA and other U.S. agencies. The kingdom also continued to purchase billions of dollars of American arms.

Today, the American public remains deeply skeptical of the alliance with Saudi Arabia. A recent poll found that only 4 percent of Americans consider the kingdom an "ally," while 42 percent see it as either "unfriendly" or an "enemy."[23] The Saudi regime's assassination of the journalist Jamal Khashoggi and the human toll of the Saudi-led war in Yemen have intensified American criticism of Riyadh and provoked congressional protests. Even so, U.S. president Donald Trump has made the strengthening of the U.S.-Saudi relationship a top priority of his administration's foreign policy. He chose Saudi Arabia as the destination of his first trip abroad after becoming president and regularly points to what he sees as the benefits of the U.S. partnership with Riyadh, including lucrative arms deals and Saudi cooperation on oil prices. The U.S.-Saudi relationship continues to be an alliance between elites, even in the face of popular opposition.

* * *

U.S. and Saudi leaders benefit from the wealth and power that comes from controlling oil. Their alliance, however, has imposed enormous costs on both countries. Saudi Arabia is the world's largest arms importer, with its purchases nearly tripling over the last decade. The vast bulk of those imports have come from the United States, making the kingdom the leading foreign customer for American weapons.[24] The surge in Saudi military spending has come even though oil prices have collapsed as a result of the boom in oil and gas produced through hydraulic fracturing, or "fracking."[25] At a time when the kingdom faces increasing budgetary challenges, it continues to pour a huge portion of its national wealth into weapons that, for all their sophistication, have been unable to deliver victory even over the lightly armed Houthi fighters in Yemen.

The United States, too, has sacrificed a great deal to expand its defense budget. Although the fracking boom has made the United States less reliant on imported oil than at any other time in the last half-century, it has not severed the military ties between Washington and Riyadh—which were never primarily about securing oil for American consumption. The post-9/11 wars in Afghanistan, Pakistan, and Iraq are the culmination of an interventionist strategy deeply shaped by the U.S.-Saudi alliance and the pivot to the Gulf that began under Carter. Experts have estimated the cost of those wars at more than $6 trillion and counting.[26] The diversion of such enormous resources to defense has constrained what the country can spend on health, education, and all other priorities.

Other consequences of the U.S.-Saudi alliance have affected the entire planet. U.S. and Saudi leaders have worked to maintain a global economy based on oil. Over the last several decades, however, the cost of fossil fuel dependence has become increasingly apparent. In May 1990, three months before George H. W. Bush ordered American troops into the Persian Gulf, the UN Intergovernmental Panel on Climate Change (IPCC) released its first report. It described the scientific consensus on global warming, the likely effects of climate change, and the necessary steps for reducing greenhouse gas emissions. Government and corporate leaders in the United States and Saudi Arabia have often blocked action against greenhouse gas emissions. The George W. Bush and Donald Trump administrations pulled out of the Kyoto and Paris climate agreements, and American energy companies and lobbying groups have sown doubt about climate science. The Saudi regime has cooperated with the U.S. government and American industry groups in those efforts. In 1992, a leading climate activist singled out the United States and Saudi Arabia as two of the leading "foot-dragging" governments on climate change.[27] The Saudi diplomat Mohammad Salim Al Sabban made headlines for his 1995 confrontation with Benjamin Santer, an American climate scientist and IPCC author. Al Sabban was so proud of the moment that, more than two decades later, he pinned a *Riyadh Post* article about it to the top of his Twitter feed, suggesting that he had given a master class in the "game of negotiations" and stood up to the global "climate conspiracy."[28]

The United States and Saudi Arabia are also home to other views about climate change. The United States has often supported global efforts to reduce carbon emissions, even if its commitment to those efforts has been inconsistent. Many Saudis have also become more conscious about the urgency of protecting the environment. The Saudi oil minister Ali al-Naimi has acknowledged the need to manage greenhouse gas emissions, and the Saudi government has called for more sustainable development and water conservation in the kingdom. Even Muhammad Al Sabban has predicted that oil demand will peak and begin to fall by 2028, due to concerns about climate change and the spread of new technologies like electric cars.[29]

A world dependent on fossil fuels has come to seem inevitable. U.S. and Saudi elites have worked hard to cultivate that sense of inevitability—to make their choices seem, as Fahd would say, *min al-tabi'i*: only natural. But the U.S.-Saudi alliance, and the kind of oil-fueled politics that it supports, are the product of decades of deliberate work in the face of considerable resistance. When Nixon and Faisal shook hands in 1974, they upheld a political and economic order whose consequences we still live with today. That order is deeply entrenched, but it is not natural or inevitable. Understanding how it came to be can help us build a different future.

NOTES

ABBREVIATIONS

AAD — Access to Archival Databases, National Archives and Records Administration

ADST — Association for Diplomatic Studies and Training

AJMP — Albert J. Meyer Papers, Harvard University Archives

APP — American Presidency Project, University of California at Santa Barbara

ASP — Anthony Solomon Papers, Federal Reserve Bank of New York

CFB — Records of Assistant Secretary for International Affairs C. Fred Bergsten, National Archives and Records Administration

DNSAMC — Digitized National Security Adviser Memoranda of Conversations, Gerald R. Ford Presidential Library

FRBNY — Federal Reserve Bank of New York

FRUS — *Foreign Relations of the United States* (Washington, DC: United States Government Publishing Office)

GFL — Gerald R. Ford Presidential Library

JCL — Jimmy Carter Presidential Library

JFKL — John F. Kennedy Presidential Library

KTCT — Henry A. Kissinger Telephone Conversation Transcripts

NARA — National Archives and Records Administration

NIE — National Intelligence Estimate

NSAMC — National Security Adviser Memoranda of Conversations, Gerald R. Ford Presidential Library

NSC — National Security Council

NSF   National Security Files
OASIA   Office of the Assistant Secretary of International Affairs, Record Group 56,
           National Archives and Records Administration
PVP   Paul Volcker Papers, Federal Reserve Bank of New York
RAC   Remote Archives Capture, Jimmy Carter Presidential Library
RNL   Richard Nixon Presidential Library
RRL   Ronald Reagan Presidential Library
W'A   *Al-Wathā'iq al-'Arabiyya* (Arab Political Documents) (Beirut: American
           University of Beirut)
WMP   William E. Mulligan Papers, Georgetown University
WSAG   Washington Special Action Group
WSP   William Simon Papers, Lafayette College Special Collections
ZBM   Zbigniew Brzezinski Materials, Jimmy Carter Presidential Library

INTRODUCTION

1. "122 of Media, 14,775 Miles," *Baltimore Sun*, June 11, 1974; interview with Hume Horan, November 3, 2000, the Association for Diplomatic Studies and Training (ADST) Foreign Affairs Oral History Project, https://adst.org/oral-history.

2. Richard Nixon Daily Diary, June 1–15, 1974, Richard Nixon Presidential Library and Museum, (RNL), Yorba Linda, CA, https://www.nixonlibrary.gov/sites/default/files/virtuallibrary/documents/PDD/1974/125%20June%201-15%201974.pdf; Nixon and Faisal remarks, June 14, 1974, American Presidency Project (APP), University of California at Santa Barbara, https://www.presidency.ucsb.edu.

3. Much of the existing literature has adopted this language of a "partnership" or "special relationship." See, for example, Rachel Bronson, *Thicker Than Oil: America's Uneasy Partnership with Saudi Arabia* (Oxford: Oxford University Press, 2006); Thomas Lippman, *Inside the Mirage: America's Fragile Partnership with Saudi Arabia* (New York: Basic Books, 2004); Parker T. Hart, *Saudi Arabia and the United States: Birth of a Security Partnership* (Bloomington: Indiana University Press, 1998); David Ottaway, "The King and Us: U.S.-Saudi Relations in the Wake of 9/11," *Foreign Affairs* 88, no. 3 (2009): 121–31. One exception is the former CIA official Bruce Riedel, who uses the term "alliance" to describe the U.S.-Saudi relationship in *Kings and Presidents: Saudi Arabia and the United States since FDR* (Washington, DC: Brookings Institution Press, 2017).

4. The existing literature draws primarily on perspectives from the leading supporters of the U.S.-Saudi relationship—the White House, the State Department, and the oil company Aramco. As a result, it understates the extent of opposition to the alliance. To understand the relationship, we must take account of domestic politics and congressional debates. On reincorporating domestic politics into the study of U.S. foreign relations, see Fredrik Logevall, "Politics and Foreign Relations," *Journal of American History* 95, no. 4 (2009): 1074–78; Mitchell B. Lerner and Andrew L. Johns, *The Cold War at Home and Abroad: Domestic Politics and US Foreign Policy Since 1945* (Lexington: University Press of Kentucky, 2018).

5. Saud al-Faisal interview with *Hawadith*, February 3, 1979, *Al-Wathā'iq al-'Arabīyya* (Arab political documents; *W'A*) 1979, Doc. 56. He declared: "Naḥnu lā nadkhul fī āḥlāf khārij al-āṭārayn al-'Arabī wa al-Islāmī (we do not enter into alliances outside the Arab and Islamic frameworks)."

6. "Kalima *Al-Riyāḍ*," *Al-Riyadh*, June 15 and 16, 1974.

7. The extra security came after a rumored assassination attempt on Faisal. "Threat on King's Life Tightens Security for Nixon," *Baltimore Sun*, June 16, 1974.

8. David Parker to "All Personnel Going on the Middle East Trip," June 5, 1974, Folder 3, National Security Council (NSC) Files, Saunders Middle East Negotiations, Box 1189, RNL.

9. Senator Henry "Scoop" Jackson (D-WA), for example, slammed the Nixon administration's agreements with Saudi Arabia signed in early June. Neil Mehler, "Sen. Jackson Rips U.S., Saudi Arabia Trade Pact," *Chicago Tribune*, June 9, 1974.

10. Fahd interview with *Al-Anwar*, October 25, 1974, *W'A* 1974, Doc. 305. Fahd was exaggerating; in 1974, Saudi Arabia was only the world's third-largest oil producer, after the Soviet Union and the United States. Saudi Arabia, was, however, the world's largest oil *exporter*, since the United States and the USSR consumed most of their oil at home.

11. Bundy to Taylor, January 11, 1963, *Foreign Relations of the United States* (*FRUS*) 1961–63, Vol. 18, Doc. 132.

12. On the bitter political disputes unleashed by the energy crisis in the United States, see Meg Jacobs, *Panic at the Pump: The Energy Crisis and the Transformation of American Politics in the 1970s* (New York: Hill and Wang, 2016); Rüdiger Graf, *Oil and Sovereignty: Petro-Knowledge and Energy Policy in the United States and Western Europe in the 1970s*, trans. Alex Skinner (New York : Berghahn, 2018); Richard H. K. Vietor, *Energy Policy in America Since 1945: A Study of Business-Government Relations* (Cambridge: Cambridge University Press, 1984), 193–344. On Americans' difficult cultural adjustment to greater dependence on imported oil, see Sebastian Herbstreuth, *Oil and American Identity: A Culture of Dependency and US Foreign Policy* (London: I.B. Tauris, 2016); Melani McAlister, *Epic Encounters: Culture, Media, and U.S. Interests in the Middle East Since 1945* (Berkeley: University of California Press, 2005), 125–54; Natasha Zaretsky, *No Direction Home: The American Family and the Fear of National Decline, 1968–1980* (Chapel Hill: University of North Carolina Press, 2007), 71–104.

13. Nixon and Faisal remarks, June 14, 1974, APP. Nixon also privately asked Faisal for "the favor of influencing the oil producing countries to reduce the price of oil." Memorandum of conversation (hereafter memcon), June 15, 1974, *FRUS* 1969–76, Vol. E-9, Part 2, Doc. 113. Although the 1970s were a transformative decade for the alliance, some of the best work on U.S.-Saudi relations stops in the early 1960s. See Nathan J. Citino, *From Arab Nationalism to OPEC: Eisenhower, King Sa'ūd, and the Making of U.S.-Saudi Relations* (Bloomington: Indiana University Press, 2002); Robert Vitalis, *America's Kingdom: Mythmaking on the Saudi Oil Frontier* (Stanford, CA: Stanford University Press, 2007). The recent declassification of U.S. documents through the late 1970s has made it possible to take the story further, an important task as historians have identified that decade as a

pivotal moment for international relations, globalization, and the rise of the post-Cold War order. See, for example, Thomas Borstelmann, *The 1970s: A New Global History from Civil Rights to Economic Inequality* (Princeton, NJ: Princeton University Press, 2011); Niall Ferguson et al., eds., *The Shock of the Global: The 1970s in Perspective* (Cambridge, MA: Harvard University Press, 2010); Daniel J. Sargent, *A Superpower Transformed: The Remaking of American Foreign Relations in the 1970s* (Oxford: Oxford University Press, 2014).

14. On exaggerated "peak oil" fears, especially during the 1970s, see Roger J. Stern, "Oil Scarcity Ideology in US Foreign Policy, 1908–97," *Security Studies* 25, no. 2 (April 2016): 214–57. For critiques of the belief that the United States needs to secure access to oil through military force or a special relationship with Saudi Arabia, see Vitalis, "The Twentieth-Century Origins of a Twenty-First-Century Pseudo-science," *Montreal Review*, February 2013, http://www.themontrealreview.com/2009/America-s-Kingdom .php; "Oil: The Stuff of Mass Delusion," *Jadaliyya*, March 9, 2016, https://www.jadaliyya .com/Details/33053. Both Stern and Vitalis draw on the work of the Massachusetts Institute of Technology (MIT) economist M. A. Adelman, a leading critic of U.S. oil policy during the 1970s. For an introduction to Adelman's views, see Adelman, *The Genie Out of the Bottle: World Oil Since 1970* (Cambridge, MA: MIT Press, 1995).

15. The main counterexample, the 1973–74 embargo, had a major psychological impact but was less effective in targeting the United States than generally assumed. The gasoline lines that plagued U.S. consumers were caused less by the embargo than by the oil production cuts and huge price increases of late 1973, combined with a flawed domestic energy policy system that created uneven fuel shortages around the country. Saudi Arabia also softened the impact of the embargo by secretly continuing to supply fuel to the U.S. military. See chapter 5 for more details.

16. Skeptics like Adelman argued that Saudi Arabia only pretended to fight for lower oil prices, and was, in fact, perfectly happy to profit from the price hikes for which other OPEC members took credit. However, using newly available OPEC records, Giuliano Garavini's *The Rise and Fall of OPEC in the Twentieth Century* (Oxford: Oxford University Press, 2019) has shown that closed-door OPEC meetings during the 1970s often featured contentious debates between Saudi Arabia and price hawks like Iraq, appearing to confirm what Saudi leaders told the United States.

17. Henry Mitchell, "Henry and the Prince and 1,400 Guests," *Washington Post*, June 8, 1974.

18. Memcon, June 15, 1974, digitized National Security Adviser Memoranda of Conversations (DSNAMC), Gerald Ford Library (GFL), Ann Arbor, MI, https://www.fordlibrarymu seum.gov/library/guides/findingaid/Memoranda_of_Conversations.asp.

19. Bronson, *Thicker than Oil*, takes a favorable view of U.S.-Saudi cooperation against communism. For more critical perspectives, see Mahmood Mandani, *Good Muslim, Bad Muslim: America, the Cold War, and the Roots of Terror* (New York: Doubleday: 2005), 119–77; Vijay Prashad, *The Darker Nations: A People's History of the Third World* (New York: New Press, 2007), 260–75.

20. For U.S. government and corporate development assistance in the kingdom, see Thomas Lippman, *Inside The Mirage: America's Fragile Partnership With Saudi Arabia* (New York:

Basic Books, 2004); Chad H. Parker, *Making the Desert Modern: Americans, Arabs, and Oil on the Saudi Frontier, 1933–1973* (Amherst: University of Massachusetts Press, 2015); Sarah Yizraeli, *Politics and Society in Saudi Arabia: The Crucial Years of Development, 1960–1982* (New York: Columbia University Press, 2012). For challenges to the claims by Aramco and the U.S. government that they modernized Saudi Arabia and improved the lives of the Saudi people, see Vitalis, *America's Kingdom*, on Aramco's racial segregation and labor repression; Toby Craig Jones, *Desert Kingdom: How Oil and Water Forged Modern Saudi Arabia* (Cambridge, MA: Harvard University Press, 2010) on the destructive ecological consequences of oil development; and Citino, *Envisioning the Arab Future: Modernization in U.S.-Arab Relations, 1945–1967* (Cambridge: Cambridge University Press, 2017), 112–22; Pascal Menoret, "The Suburbanization of Islamic Activism in Saudi Arabia," *City and Society* 29, no. 1 (2017): 162–86, on the U.S. role in shaping Saudi urban policy. On social change in Saudi Arabia during the oil boom, see Soraya Altorki and Donald P. Cole, *Arabian Oasis City: The Transformation of 'Unayzah* (Austin: University of Texas Press, 1989).

21. Scholars have taken an increasing interest in Saudi opposition politics. The Sunni Islamist opposition has usually been the main focus, especially after the 9/11 attacks. See Mamoun Fandy, *Saudi Arabia and the Politics of Dissent* (Basingstoke, Hampshire: Macmillan, 1999); Thomas Hegghammer, *Jihad in Saudi Arabia: Violence and Pan-Islamism Since 1979* (Cambridge: Cambridge University Press, 2010); Stéphane Lacroix, *Awakening Islam: The Politics of Religious Dissent in Contemporary Saudi Arabia*, trans. George Holoch (Cambridge, MA: Harvard University Press, 2011). Recently, more scholars have begun to explore the history of political opposition from the Shia minority and the secular left. See Rosie Bsheer, "A Counter-revolutionary State: Popular Movements and the Making of Saudi Arabia," *Past and Present* 238, no. 1 (February 2018): 233–77; Toby Matthiesen, "Migration, Minorities, and Radical Networks: Labour Movements and Opposition Groups in Saudi Arabia, 1950–1975," *International Review of Social History* 59, no. 3 (2014): 473–504; Toby Matthiesen, *The Other Saudis: Shiism, Dissent and Sectarianism* (Cambridge: Cambridge University Press, 2014); Toby Craig Jones, "Rebellion on the Saudi Periphery: Modernity, Marginalization, and the Shi'a Uprising of 1979," *International Journal of Middle East Studies* 38, no. 2 (2006): 213–33. For more historical scholarship that takes a critical perspective on the Saudi regime, see the work of Madawi Al-Rasheed, including the overview *A History of Saudi Arabia*, 2nd ed. (New York: Cambridge University Press, 2010).

22. The idea that the Saudi people could not govern themselves and needed guidance, both from the royal family and from the United States, was reinforced by long-standing U.S. and European stereotypes about the incompatibility of Islamic and Arab culture with democracy. The critique of those assumptions by Edward W. Said in *Orientalism* (New York: Pantheon Books, 1978) has influenced much of the subsequent literature about American views of the Middle East, including Matthew F. Jacobs, *Imagining the Middle East: The Building of an American Foreign Policy, 1918–1967* (Chapel Hill: University of North Carolina Press, 2011); Osamah F. Khalil, *America's Dream Palace: Middle East Expertise and the Rise of the National Security State* (Cambridge, MA: Harvard University

Press, 2016); Douglas Little, *American Orientalism: The United States and the Middle East Since 1945*, 3rd ed. (Chapel Hill: University of North Carolina Press, 2008); McAlister, *Epic Encounters*; Karine V. Walther, *Sacred Interests: The United States and the Islamic World, 1821–1921* (Chapel Hill: University of North Carolina Press, 2015). The U.S. willingness to disregard purported commitments to democracy, however, was hardly unique to the Middle East. During the Cold War, American policy makers promoted right-wing autocrats over democrats around the world, justifying their stance with the same appeals to vaguely defined "reform" and "modernization" used to defend U.S. support for the Saudi regime. See, for example, Michael E. Latham, *The Right Kind of Revolution: Modernization, Development, and U.S. Foreign Policy from the Cold War to the Present* (Ithaca, NY: Cornell University Press, 2011), esp. 123–56.

23. Memcons, June 6, 1974; June 15, 1974, DSNAMC, GFL. Officially, Saqqaf was the Saudi minister of state for foreign affairs, with King Faisal serving as his own foreign minister. In practice, Saqqaf acted as the Saudi foreign minister in all but name. This book refers to him informally by that title, just as many diplomats did at the time.

24. A recent wave of scholarship has emphasized other ways in which practices developed overseas during the Cold War came back to influence political and economic institutions in the United States and other industrialized nations. See, for example, Amy Offner, *Sorting Out the Mixed Economy: The Rise and Fall of Welfare and Developmental States in the Americas* (Princeton, NJ: Princeton University Press, 2019); Vanessa Ogle, "Archipelago Capitalism: Tax Havens, Offshore Money, and the State, 1950s–1970s," *American Historical Review* 122, no. 5 (December 2017): 1431–58; Stuart Schrader, *Badges without Borders How Global Counterinsurgency Transformed American Policing* (Berkeley: University of California Press, 2019).

25. On petrodollars, see David E. Spiro, *The Hidden Hand of American Hegemony: Petrodollar Recycling and International Markets* (Ithaca, NY: Cornell University Press, 1999); David Wight, "The Petrodollar Era and Relations Between the United States and the Middle East and North Africa, 1969–1980" (PhD diss., University of California at Irvine, 2014).

26. Ogle, "Archipelago Capitalism."

27. U.S. historians and other scholars have recently focused on the 1970s as a period when the U.S. economy shifted from a New Deal model based on manufacturing, a unionized workforce, wage equality, and the welfare state, to a market-oriented model characterized by rising inequality, government austerity, and the growth of the financial industry. The most important works include Jefferson Cowie, *Stayin' Alive: The 1970s and the Last Days of the Working Class* (New York: New Press, 2010); Jacobs, *Panic at the Pump*; Greta R. Krippner, *Capitalizing on Crisis: The Political Origins of the Rise of Finance* (Cambridge, MA: Harvard University Press, 2011); Kim Phillips-Fein, *Fear City: New York's Fiscal Crisis and the Rise of Austerity Politics* (New York: Metropolitan Books, 2017); Judith Stein, *Pivotal Decade: How the United States Traded Factories for Finance in the Seventies* (New Haven, CT: Yale University Press, 2010). For the case that oil has pushed U.S. politics rightward, see Matthew Huber, *Lifeblood: Oil, Freedom, and the Forces of Capital* (Minneapolis: University of Minnesota Press, 2013);

Timothy Mitchell, *Carbon Democracy: Political Power in the Age of Oil* (London: Verso, 2011).

28. Memcon, June 15, 1974, DSNAMC, GFL. Kissinger's own Jewish identity did not prevent him from occasionally echoing Nixon's crude anti-Semitism.

29. Memcon, June 15, 1974, *FRUS 1969–76*; Nixon and Faisal remarks, June 15, 1974, APP.

30. Memcon, June 15, 1974, *FRUS 1969–76*.

1. WHEELS OF EMPIRE

1. Brief descriptions of Faisal's 1943 tour are in Alexei Vassiliev, *King Faisal of Saudi Arabia: Personality, Faith and Times* (London: Saqi Books, 2013), 156–58; Bruce Riedel, *Kings and Presidents: Saudi Arabia and the United States Since FDR* (Washington, DC: Brookings Institution Press, 2017), 5; Mark Weston, *Prophets and Princes: Saudi Arabia from Muhammad to the Present* (Hoboken, NJ: Wiley, 2008), 170. However, they are unreliable on the details of Faisal's itinerary, confusing it with his second trip to the United States in 1945. The best description of Faisal's 1943 arrival is from the memoirs of his translator Abdullah Balkhair, *'Abd Allāh Balkhayr Yatadhakkar* (Abdullah Balkhair remembers) (Jeddah: 'Abd al-Maqṣūd Muḥammad Sa'īd Khawjah, 1998), 329–37. The later stages of Faisal's trip can be reconstructed through contemporary press coverage. For his arrival in the United States, see "Saudi Arabia King's Two Sons Reach U.S.," *Baltimore Sun*, September 29, 1943; "Saudi Arabia's Minister Entertained in Capital," *Christian Science Monitor*, October 1, 1943.

2. Stuart Asher, "Bursting Arabian Knights' Oil Bubble," *Philadelphia Inquirer*, November 28, 1943.

3. "Prince Faisal Is Here: Foreign Minister of Saudi Arabia Arrives from Capital," *New York Times*, October 5, 1943; "Arab Princes Fly a la Sinbad in Visit to Grumman," *Brooklyn Daily Eagle*, October 9, 1943; "Bursting Arabian Knights' Oil Bubble," *Philadelphia Inquirer*, November 28, 1943; "2 Arab Princes, Guests of U.S., Ride De Lux," *Chicago Daily Tribune*, October 11, 1943; "Royalty Visits Arizona Forest," *Arizona Republic*, October 14, 1943; "Arabian King's Sons and Party Here on Tour," *Los Angeles Times*, October 16, 1943; "Arabian Prince, Nubian Guard, Retinue on S.F. Goodwill Visit," *San Francisco Examiner*, October 19, 1943; "Arabian Princes Tour Marinship!," *San Anselmo Herald*, October 28, 1943. Faisal's visit to the Grand Canyon on October 14 was recorded by a park official and later remembered by local residents; Traci Wyrick, "Park Naturalist Louis Schellbach's Log Books," *The Ol' Pioneer: The Magazine of the Grand Canyon Historical Society* 22, no. 2 (Spring 2011): 11; Traci Wyrick, "Louis Schellbach's Log Books: Part IV," *The Ol' Pioneer* 22, no. 4 (Fall 2011): 15. For the visit to Chicago, see Amhed Al-Dajani, *Khālid ibn 'Abd al-'Azīz: Sīra Mālik wa Nahḍa al-Mamlaka* (Khalid Bin Abdulaziz: A king's biography and a kingdom's renaissance) (Riyadh: Maktaba al-Malik Fahd al-Watanīa, 2002), excerpted on the website of the King Khalid Foundation, http://www.kingkhalid.org.sa. Faisal's visit to New York is described in "Al-Ḥifāwa al-Bālīgha fī Amrīkā" (Great hospitality in America), *Umm al-Qura*, October 15, 1943.

4. Memoranda of conversation, November 1, 1943, *FRUS* 1943, Vol. 4, Docs. 879–83; "Prince Faisal Favors an Arab Legation in U.S.," *New York Herald Tribune*, November 10, 1943.

5. This book refers to the first Saudi king by his given name, Abdulaziz. In the United States, he was, and is, often known as Ibn Saud, derived from the name of the Saudi dynasty.

6. Abdulaziz H. Al Fahad, "The `Imama vs. the `Iqal: Hadari-Bedouin Conflict and the Formation of the Saudi State," in *Counter-narratives: History, Contemporary Society, and Politics in Saudi Arabia and Yemen*, ed. Madawi Al-Rasheed and Robert Vitalis (New York: Palgrave Macmillan, 2004), 35–75; Nadav Samin, *Of Sand or Soil: Genealogy and Tribal Belonging in Saudi Arabia* (Princeton, NJ: Princeton University Press, 2015), 39–40.

7. The names of the men who founded the Al Saud and Al al-Sheikh, along with many other characters in this book, include the element "Ibn" or "Bin," which means "son of." In Arabic, it can appear in different forms depending on its placement in a name or a sentence. This book generally uses "Ibn" except in cases when "Bin" is standard in English (for example, with the Bin Laden construction family).

8. The name "Wahhabi" is controversial. Its adherents often prefer other terms, including *salafiyyūn* (Salafis), followers of Islam as practiced by Muhammad and his immediate successors; *ahl al-ḥadīth* or *ahl al-sunna*, the people of the hadith or the sunna (canonical Muslim teachings); *muwaḥḥidūn*, lit. "Unitarians" (a translation that gives a comical impression in English when one reads about intolerant Unitarians imposing their beliefs on others); or simply "Muslims." Those terms, though, are less specific than "Wahhabi" and can create ambiguity. Because "Wahhabism" (*wahhābiyya*) is the most specific and widely recognized name for the movement in both English and Arabic, I use it here. The best introduction to Wahhabism is David Commins, *The Mission and the Kingdom: Wahhabi Power Behind the Saudi Throne*, rev. ed. (New York: I. B. Tauris, 2016). Thanks in part to Saudi funding, the writings of Ibn Abd al-Wahhab are available in multiple languages. For an English edition of his most important book, see Muḥammad ibn 'Abd al-Wahhab, *Kitab At-Tauhid: The Book of Monotheism* (Riyadh: Darussalam, 2011).

9. On the origins of the first Saudi state, see Madawi Al-Rasheed, *A History of Saudi Arabia*, 2nd ed. (Cambridge: Cambridge University Press, 2010), 13–21; Alexei Vassiliev, *The History of Saudi Arabia* (New York: New York University Press, 1998), 29–139.

10. Khalifa Fahad, *Jaḥīm al-Ḥukm al-Saʿūdī wa Nīrān al-Wahhābiyya* (The hell of Saudi rule and the flames of Wahhabism) (London: Al-Sīfa li al-Nashr wa al-Tawzʿīa, 1989), 5, 20, 54. Fahad writes that Muhammad ibn Saud made his alliance with Ibn Abd al-Wahhab for the sake of *al-dunyā wa al-mulk*, lit. "the world and kingship."

11. Abdullah bin Abd al-Mohsen al-Turki, *Al-Malik ʿAbd al-ʿAzīz Āl Saʿūd: Umma fī Rajul* (King Abdulaziz: A nation in a man) (Riyadh: Wizāra al-Shuʿūn al-Islāmiyya wa al-Awqāf wa al-Dʿawa wa al-Irshād, 2000), 87, 90.

12. Fahad, *Jaḥīm al-Ḥukm al-Saʿūdī*, 3.

13. On the British role in the negotiations over the Kuwaiti-Iraqi-Najdi border, see John Craven Wilkinson, *Arabia's Frontiers: The Story of Britain's Boundary Drawing in the Desert* (London: I. B. Tauris, 1991); E. Lauterpacht et. al., *The Kuwait Crisis: Basic Documents* (Cambridge: Cambridge University Press, 1991), 45–49.

14. For British airpower in this episode, see Priya Satia, "The Defense of Inhumanity: Air Control and the British Idea of Arabia," *American Historical Review* 111, no. 1 (2006): 16–51. For the war against the Ikhwan from the perspective of the British commander, see John Bagot Glubb, *War in the Desert: An R.A.F. Frontier Campaign* (London: Hodder and Stoughton, 1960); Tancred Bradshaw, *The Glubb Reports: Glubb Pasha and Britain's Empire Project in the Middle East, 1920–1956* (Basingstoke, Hampshire: Palgrave Macmillan, 2016), 14–29.

15. "Kalām Rijāl al-Muṭāyir" (Speech by the men of the Mutayr tribe), *Umm al-Qura*, December 12, 1928. This open criticism of Abdulaziz quoted in *Umm al-Qura*, the official Saudi government newspaper, surprised me when I first read it; I was accustomed to the heavily censored Saudi press of later decades. For the Ikhwan's opposition to automobiles, see Christine Moss Helms, *The Cohesion of Saudi Arabia: Evolution of Political Identity* (Baltimore: Johns Hopkins University Press, 1981), 253.

16. For a first-hand account of the battle, see Mohammed Almana, *Arabia Unified: A Portrait of Ibn Saud* (London: Hutchinson Benham, 1980), 95–107.

17. John S. Habib, *Ibn Sa'ud's Warriors of Islam: The Ikhwan of Najd and Their Role in the Creation of the Sa'udi Kingdom, 1910–1930* (Leiden: Brill, 1978), 136–55; Helms, *The Cohesion of Saudi Arabia*, 250–74; Al-Rasheed, *History of Saudi Arabia*, 66–68.

18. Rosie Bsheer, "A Counter-revolutionary State: Popular Movements and the Making of Saudi Arabia," *Past and Present* 238, no. 1 (February 1, 2018): 243–44; Vassiliev, *History of Saudi Arabia*, 282–83.

19. "Bayna al-Ruqī wa al-Tafranj" (Between progress and Frankification), *Umm al-Qura*, July 19, 1929.

20. For Rihani's admiring portrait of Abdulaziz, see Ameen Fares Rihani, *Maker of Modern Arabia* (Boston: Houghton Mifflin, 1928). For similarly positive depictions of the Saudi kingdom by Hafiz Wahba, see Wahbah, *Jazīra al-'Arab fī al-Qarn al-'Ishrīn* (The Arabian Peninsula in the twentieth century, 3rd ed. (Cairo: Maṭba'a Lajna al-Ta'līf wa al-Tarjamah wa al-Nashr, 1956); Wahba, *Arabian Days* (London: A. Barker, 1964). On the role of Lebanese advisers in the early history of the kingdom, see Fawwaz Traboulsi, "Saudi Expansion: The Lebanese Connection, 1924–1952," in *Kingdom Without Borders: Saudi Arabia's Political, Religious and Media Frontiers*, ed. Madawi Al Rasheed (Oxford: Oxford University Press, 2008), 65–78.

21. Michael Christopher Low, "Ottoman Infrastructures of the Saudi Hydro-State: The Technopolitics of Pilgrimage and Potable Water in the Hijaz," *Comparative Studies in Society and History* 57, no. 4 (2015): 969–71; Karl Twitchell, *Saudi Arabia: With an Account of the Development of Its Natural Resources* (Princeton, NJ: Princeton University Press, 1947).

22. On the incorporation of the Hijaz into the Saudi kingdom, see William Ochsenwald, "Islam and Loyalty in the Saudi Hijaz, 1926–1939," *Die Welt Des Islams* 47, no. 1 (2007): 7–32. For the later commemoration of the kingdom's founding, see, for example, the semi-official Saudi newspaper *Al Riyadh*'s 1980 National Day special issue, celebrating Abdulaziz for uniting the nation and ending Bedouin raids: "Al-Amn fī al-Ahd al-Malik al-Mu'asis" (Security in the era of the founding king), *Al-Riyadh*, September 23, 1980.

23. The only other case of a country's common name being derived from its ruling family is Liechtenstein.

24. Ibn Batla Poem 10, P. Marcel Kurpershoek, *Bedouin Poets of the Dawasir Tribe: Between Nomadism and Settlement in Southern Najd* (Leiden: Brill, 1999), 198–99.

25. Ibn Batla Poem 9, Kurpershoek, *Bedouin Poets of the Dawasir Tribe*, 27–28.

26. Abdulaziz H. Al Fahad, "Raiders and Traders: A Poet's Lament on the End of the Bedouin Heroic Age," in *Saudi Arabia in Transition: Insights on Social, Political, Economic and Religious Change*, ed. Bernard Haykel, Thomas Hegghammer, and Stéphane Lacroix (Cambridge: Cambridge University Press, 2015), 231–33.

27. St. John Philby, "Pax Wahhabica," *English Review, 1908–1937* 62, no. 3 (1936): 311, 313.

28. Habib, *Ibn Sa'ud's Warriors of Islam*, 146.

29. *Oriento Moderno*, May 1935, from Ibrahim al-Rashid, ed., *Documents on the History of Saudi Arabia*, vol. 3 (Salisbury, NC: Documentary Publications, 1976), 211–12.

30. Anthony Cave Brown, *Oil, God, and Gold: The Story of Aramco and the Saudi Kings* (Boston: Houghton Mifflin, 1999), 55.

31. George Antonius, *The Arab Awakening: The Story of the Arab National Movement* (London: H. Hamilton, 1938), 347–49.

32. Antonius, *The Arab Awakening*, 349.

33. Ochsenwald, "Islam and Loyalty in the Saudi Hijaz," 13; John M. Willis, "Governing the Living and the Dead: Mecca and the Emergence of the Saudi Biopolitical State," *American Historical Review* 122, no. 2 (2017): 353.

34. Division of Near Eastern Affairs, U.S. State Department, "Economic Situation in the Hejaz and Nejd and Its Dependencies," January 27, 1931, from al-Rashid, *Documents on the History of Saudi Arabia*, vol. 3, 112.

35. "Wasā'il al-Iṣlāḥ wa al-'Umrān " (Means of repair and construction), *Umm al-Qura*, February 27, 1927.

36. "Mashārī' 'Umrāniyya" (Construction projects), *Umm al-Qura*, August 12, 1929.

37. The urban redevelopment hailed by *Umm al-Qura* was a typical high modernist project, one that made the city more "legible" to the government by opening the streets to surveillance and control. The classic work on this subject is James C. Scott, *Seeing Like a State: How Certain Schemes to Improve the Human Condition Have Failed* (New Haven, CT: Yale University Press, 1998).

38. "Niẓām Tasyīr al-Sayārāt bayna Jidda wa Makka" (A system for the management of cars between Jeddah and Mecca), pts. I and II, *Umm al-Qura*, September 10 and 17, 1926.

39. "Ibn Saud Helps Pilgrims," *New York Times*, March 11, 1926.

40. Joseph Levy, "King Ibn Saud Would Make Arabia Great," *New York Times*, April 15, 1928.

41. Abdullah Al-Arian collected a long list of articles from the *New York Times* hailing Saudi reform efforts beginning in 1953, but the genre is even older than that. Al-Arian, "Seventy Years of the New York Times Describing Saudi Royals as Reformers," *Jadaliyya*, November 27, 2017, http://www.jadaliyya.com/Details/34727/Seventy-Years-of-the-New -York-Times-Describing-Saudi-Royals-as-Leading-Reform.

42. Philby to Wadsworth, December 29, 1929; Murray to State, January 14, 1931; Rihani to Murray, June 22, 1931, from al-Rashid, ed., *Documents on the History of Saudi Arabia*, vol. 3,

67–68, 105, 117. American admiration for Saudi Arabia as a modernizing and motorizing society has a long history; see Paul Baltimore, "From the Camel to the Cadillac: Automobility, Consumption, and the U.S.-Saudi Special Relationship" (PhD diss., University of California at Santa Barbara, 2014).

43. Provisional Agreement Between the United States of America and the Kingdom of Saudi Arabia, November 7, 1933, *FRUS* 1933, Vol. 2, Doc. 758.

44. Ochsenwald, "Islam and Loyalty in the Saudi Hijaz," 12.

45. Brown, *Oil, God, and Gold.*

46. Thomas Barger letter to parents, February 26, 1938, from Wallace Stegner papers. Box 84, Folder 2, J. Willard Marriott Library, Special Collections, University of Utah. Thanks to Julia Huddleston for making this document available. See also Thomas C. Barger, *Out in the Blue: Letters from Arabia 1937–1940* (Vista, CA: Selwa Press, 2000); Robert Vitalis, *America's Kingdom: Mythmaking on the Saudi Oil Frontier* (Stanford, CA: Stanford University Press, 2007), 58–59.

47. For the redistribution of royal land grants as a central feature of the Saudi political economy, see Bernard Haykel, "Oil in Saudi Arabian Culture and Politics: From Tribal Poets to Al-Qaeda's Ideologues," in *Saudi Arabia in Transition*, ed. Bernard Haykel, Thomas Hegghammer, and Stéphane Lacroix (Cambridge: Cambridge University Press, 2015), 135; Kiren Aziz Chaudhry, *The Price of Wealth: Economies and Institutions in the Middle East* (Ithaca, NY: Cornell University Press, 1997), 172–84. For the name Al-Shubook, see Pascal Menoret, *Joyriding in Riyadh: Oil, Urbanism, and Road Revolt* (Cambridge: Cambridge University Press, 2014), 62. To see its contemporary use as a critique against the Al Saud, search Twitter for [#الشبوك].

48. U.S. House of Representatives, *Report of the United States Revenue Commission on Petroleum as a Source of National Revenue*, 39th Cong., 1st Sess., Ex. Doc. 51, 3.

49. John D. Rockefeller, *Random Reminiscences of Men and Events* (Garden City, NY: Doubleday, Page, 1913), 63. On the limits of the State Department's ability to protect Standard Oil's overseas operations, see Alison Frank, "The Petroleum War of 1910: Standard Oil, Austria, and the Limits of the Multinational Corporation," *The American Historical Review* 114, no. 1 (2009): 16–41.

50. Report by Consul-General G. H. Heap, December 20, 1879, United States Bureau of Foreign and Domestic Commerce, *Commercial Relations of the United States with Foreign Countries* (Washington, DC: U.S. Government Printing Office, 1880), 584.

51. Adam Tooze, *The Deluge: The Great War, America, and the Remaking of the Global Order, 1916–1931* (New York: Viking, 2014), 39; Anand Toprani, "Oil and Grand Strategy: Great Britain and Germany, 1918–1941" (PhD diss., Georgetown University, 2012), 46–66.

52. Alison Frank, *Oil Empire: Visions of Prosperity in Austrian Galicia* (Cambridge, MA: Harvard University Press, 2005), 173–204.

53. Joseph Pennell, *That Liberty Shall Not Perish from the Earth*, 1918, Library of Congress, https://www.loc.gov/resource/ppmsca.18343/. For other exaggerated warnings of American vulnerability to invasion, see the film *Battle Cry of Peace* (1915) and Hudson Maxim, *Defenseless America* (New York: Hearst's International Library Co., 1915).

54. For a firsthand account of the difficulty of cross-country auto travel at the beginning of the twentieth century (along with racialized descriptions of the Native Americans and Hispanic Americans met along the way), see A. L. Westgard, *Tales of a Pathfinder* (Washington, DC: Andrew B. Graham, 1920). Westgard was an officer of the NHA.

55. National Highways Association, "United States Highways," 1915, https://collections.lib.uwm.edu/digital/collection/agdm/id/1476. From the collections of the University of Wisconsin at Milwaukee.

56. Dwight D. Eisenhower, "Through Darkest America," in *At Ease: Stories I Tell to Friends* (Garden City, NY: Doubleday, 1967), 155–68.

57. *Report of the Chief of the Motor Transport Corps to the Secretary of War* (Washington, DC: US Government Printing Office, 1920), 11.

58. For the history of the U.S.-Mexico border and the Border Patrol, see Rachel St. John, *Line in the Sand: A History of the Western U.S.-Mexico Border* (Princeton, NJ: Princeton University Press, 2011); Kelly Lytle Hernandez, *Migra! A History of the U.S. Border Patrol* (Berkeley: University of California Press, 2010).

59. For the U.S. auto companies' dominance of the world export market, see Frank Costigliola, *Awkward Dominion: American Political, Economic, and Cultural Relations with Europe, 1919–1933* (Ithaca, NY: Cornell University Press, 1988), 154–55.

60. Aldous Huxley, *Brave New World* (London: Chatto and Windus, 1932); Stefan Johannes Link, "Transnational Fordism: Ford Motor Company, Nazi Germany, and the Soviet Union in the Interwar Years" (PhD diss., Harvard University, 2012).

61. Franklin D. Roosevelt, press conference, November 15, 1938; Franklin D. Roosevelt, message to Congress on appropriations for national defense, May 16, 1940.

62. On American interventionists and their fears of Axis victory, especially after the German conquest of France in 1940, see Stephen Wertheim, "Tomorrow, the World: The Birth of US Global Supremacy in World War II" (PhD diss., Columbia University, 2015).

63. Henry Luce, "The American Century," *Life*, February 17, 1941. For the emphasis on air travel in discourses of American power and world order, see Jenifer Van Vleck, *Empire of the Air: Aviation and the American Ascendancy* (Cambridge, MA: Harvard University Press, 2013), including 10–11 for the role of the airplane in Luce's essay.

64. For overviews of oil in World War II, see Daniel Yergin, *The Prize: The Epic Quest for Oil, Money, and Power* (New York: Free Press, 2008), 287–370; Robert Goralski and Russell W. Freeburg, *Oil and War: How the Deadly Struggle for Fuel in WWII Meant Victory or Defeat* (New York: Morrow, 1987). For Germany's resource constraints, see Adam Tooze, *The Wages of Destruction: The Making and Breaking of the Nazi Economy* (New York: Viking, 2007). For the Wehrmacht's dependence on horses, see U.S. War Department, "German Horse Cavalry and Transport," *Intelligence Bulletin*, March 1946, 53–66.

65. U.S. Senate, Special Committee to Investigate Petroleum Resources, *Petroleum in War and Peace: Papers Presented by the Petroleum Administration for War Before the Senate Special Committee to Investigate Petroleum Resources* (Washington, DC: U.S. Government Printing Office, 1945).

66. For the expansion of U.S. ties with Saudi Arabia during World War II, see Aaron David Miller, *Search for Security: Saudi Arabian Oil and American Foreign Policy, 1939–1949*

1. WHEELS OF EMPIRE

(Chapel Hill: University of North Carolina Press, 1980); Irvine H. Anderson, *Aramco, the United States, and Saudi Arabia: A Study of the Dynamics of Foreign Oil Policy, 1933–1950* (Princeton, NJ: Princeton University Press, 1981).

67. No serious attack on Saudi Arabia ever materialized; Dhahran suffered only an isolated air raid by a single Italian bomber.

68. Moffett to Roosevelt, April 16, 1941; Roosevelt to Jones, July 18, 1941, *FRUS* 1941, Vol. 3, Docs. 624, 643.

69. State to Kirk, February 6, 1942; Wells to Roosevelt, February 12, 1942, *FRUS* 1942, Vol. 4, Docs. 669–70.

70. Everett DeGolyer, "Preliminary Report of the Technical Oil Mission to the Middle East," *Bulletin of the American Association of Petroleum Geologists* 28, no. 7 (July 1944): 919–23.

71. Charles Rayner testimony, *American Petroleum Interests in Foreign Countries*, U.S. Senate hearings, June 27–28, 1945 (Washington, DC: Government Printing Office, 1946), 6.

72. David S. Painter, *Oil and the American Century: The Political Economy of U.S. Foreign Oil Policy, 1941–1954* (Baltimore: Johns Hopkins University Press, 1986), 32–51.

73. State to Kirk, March 11, 1943; State to Kirk, March 26, 1943, *FRUS* 1943, Vol. 4, Docs. 898, 900.

74. Kirk to State, February 26, 1943; Kirk to State, April 13, 1943, *FRUS* 1943, Vol. 4, Docs. 896, 903.

75. *FRUS* 1943, Vol. 4, Doc. 879; Miller, *Search for Security*.

76. A model of the *Quincy* is displayed prominently in the Saudi embassy in Washington, DC. Author's visit to Saudi embassy, October 15, 2009. The U.S. embassy in Riyadh displays a similar model during special events. Rachel Bronson, *Thicker Than Oil: America's Uneasy Partnership with Saudi Arabia* (Oxford: Oxford University Press, 2006), 42. For a Saudi museum exhibit celebrating the meeting, see John Coppola, "A Pride of Museums in the Desert: Saudi Arabia and the 'Gift of Friendship' Exhibition," *Curator: The Museum Journal* 48, no. 1 (2005): 90–100.

77. Roosevelt and Abdulaziz's exchange was recorded in memcon, February 14, 1945, *FRUS* 1945, Vol. 8, Doc. 2. Eddy's memoir of the meeting is William Alfred Eddy, *F.D.R. Meets Ibn Saud* (New York: American Friends of the Middle East, 1954). See also Ross Gregory, "America and Saudi Arabia, Act I: The Conference of Franklin D. Roosevelt and King Ibn Saud in February 1945," in *Presidents, Diplomats, and Other Mortals: Essays Honoring Robert H. Ferrell*, ed. J. Garry Clifford and Theodore A. Wilson (Columbia: University of Missouri Press, 2007), 116–33.

78. Michael Saba, *King Abdulaziz: His Plane and His Pilot* (Sioux Falls, SD: Gulf America Press, 2009).

79. "Visiting Firemen," *Pittsburgh Press*, April 10, 1945; "Arabian Princes to Visit Port Arthur," *Austin American-Statesman*, April 19, 1945; "Santa Fe Turns Out en Masse to Meet Princes," *Santa Fe New Mexican*, April 23, 1945; "Arab Royalty Is Colorful Group," *Oakland Tribune*, April 24, 1945; "Arab Prince to Be Guest of Detroit," *Detroit Free Press*, July 1, 1945; "Arabian Royal Visitors Enjoy Ride in Tanks," *Detroit Free Press*, July 6, 1945.

263

80. "Saudi Arabia Princes Give Party in American Fashion," *Bakersfield Californian*, May 25, 1945.

81. "Saudi Arabian Princes Make Inspection Tour," *Princeton Bulletin* 1, no. 105 (November 8, 1943); "Princeton Host to Arab Royal Princes," *Princeton Herald* 21, no. 2 (November 12, 1943); "Royal Guests," *Princeton Alumni Weekly*, November 19, 1943. On Philip Hitti and Princeton's Arabic training program during World War II, see Osamah F. Khalil, *America's Dream Palace: Middle East Expertise and the Rise of the National Security State* (Cambridge, MA: Harvard University Press, 2016), 44–46.

82. "Prince Faisal Favors an Arab Legation in U.S.," *New York Herald Tribune*, November 10, 1943. The Saudi official gazette *Umm al-Qura* emphasized the princes' meetings with "senior members of the Arab communities in New York." "Al-Ḥifāwa al-Bālīgha fī Amrīkā," *Umm al-Qura*, October 15, 1943.

83. Author's telephone interview with JoAnn Shaya Fidel, June 10, 2019; "Shaya May Act as Interpreter for Arabs," *Santa Fe New Mexican*, April 19, 1945; "Named to Greet Arab Princes," *Santa Fe New Mexican*, April 20, 1945; "Santa Fe Girl Gets Autograph of 5 Princes of Arabia," *Santa Fe New Mexican*, April 23, 1945. For Shaya's biography, see "Raymond Shaya Flies Friday for First Visit to Homeland," *Santa Fe New Mexican*, July 10, 1969; Monika Ghattas, *Los Arabes of New Mexico: Compadres from a Distant Land* (Santa Fe, NM: Sunstone Press, 2016), 66, 124, 127, 144–45.

84. "Al-Amīrān al-Saʿūdiyān Tʾūdīhumā fī Nū Yūrk" (Two Saudi princes take their leave from New York), *Al-Basīr*, November 8, 1945, King Khalid Foundation, kingkhalid.org.sa.

85. "Flying Visit to Detroit Is Made by Arab Royalty," *Detroit Free Press*, July 5, 1945; "5 Princes at Detroit," *Windsor Star*, July 5, 1945; "News from Around Michigan," *Lansing State Journal*, July 6, 1945.

86. The most detailed account of the episode is "Denying a Mysterious Interlude," *Philadelphia Inquirer*, September 2, 1945. See also "Prince Is Friend of Detroit Girl," *Detroit Free Press*, August 5, 1945; "Detroit Girl Flying to Meet Arabian Prince, Says Boss," *Los Angeles Times*, August 5, 1945.

87. "Student at U.C., 23, to Be S.F. Delegate," *Oakland Tribune*, April 3, 1945; "Arab Royalty Is Colorful Group"; "U.C. Student Made Delegate to S.F. Meet," *San Mateo Times*, April 3, 1945. Marianne Alireza recounted her meeting with Ali in her memoir *At the Drop of a Veil* (Boston: Houghton Mifflin, 1971), 12–25.

88. On Saud al-Faisal's time at Princeton, see biographical sketch, Box 1, Folder 70, William E. Mulligan Papers (hereafter WMP), Georgetown University.

89. "Campaign to Open Doors of Palestine to Jewish Immigration After 1944," *Arizona Republic*, October 24, 1943.

90. 90 Cong. Rec. A1099–A1100 (1944); 90 Cong. Rec. A1648–A1651 (1944).

91. 90 Cong. Rec. 2598 (1944).

92. "Arabians' Visit Linked to Oil and F.D.R. Trip," *Chicago Tribune*, December 15, 1943.

93. Comments by Rep. Charles Vursell and Rep. Karl Mundt, 91 Cong. Rec. A4475, A4559–A4560 (1945).

94. Albert Leman, "News Behind the News: Winning the War," *San Mateo Times*, October 12, 1943.

2. ROADS TO PROFIT

1. Henry Raymont, "Faisal Is Guest of David Rockefeller at Luncheon," *New York Times*, June 27, 1966.
2. Memcon, June 21,1966, *FRUS* 1964–68, Vol. 21, Doc. 275.
3. "Mayor Says Capital Ordered Fatted Calf," *New York Daily News*, June 23, 1966; "Faisal Given the Silent Snub Here," *New York Daily News*, June 24, 1966; "King Faisal Shuns Snub," *The Record* (Rockland County), June 24, 1966.
4. "Lindsay and Rockefeller Snub Faisal," *Washington Post*, June 24, 1966.
5. Interview with Izzidine Shawa, Los Angeles, August 29, 1946, Folder 1, Collection 46032, Hoover Institution Archives, Stanford, CA.
6. Abdulaziz to Truman, October 26, 1947, *FRUS* 1947, Vol. 5, Doc. 837; *FRUS* 1948, Vol. 5, Part 1, Doc. 160. For more on Saudi protests against U.S. support for Israel, see *FRUS* 1947, Vol. 5, Docs. 803, 806, 882; *FRUS* 1948, Vol. 5, Part 2, Docs. 3, 10, 174, 205, 425, 611.
7. Faisal speech, January 7, 1949, Faisal Doc. 7, from the online Saudi document collection Muqatel, http://muqatel.com/openshare/Wthaek/index.htm.
8. Steven L. Spiegel, *The Other Arab-Israeli Conflict: Making America's Middle East Policy, from Truman to Reagan* (Chicago: University of Chicago Press, 1985), 26. For more on oil and the U.S. debate on supporting Israeli independence, see Spiegel, 16–49; Irene L. Gendzier, *Dying to Forget: Oil, Power, Palestine, and the Foundations of U.S. Policy in the Middle East* (New York: Columbia University Press, 2015).
9. Henderson to Marshall, May 26, 1948, *FRUS* 1948, Vol. 5, Part 1, Doc. 13.
10. Childs to State, *FRUS* 1947, Vol. 5, Doc. 934.
11. Al-Rasheed, "Saudi Arabia and the 1948 Palestine War: Beyond Official History," in *The War for Palestine: Rewriting the History of 1948*, Eugene Rogan and Avi Shlaim (Cambridge: Cambridge University Press, 2007), 228–247.
12. Jafar al-Baqali, "Būrtrīh: Nāṣir al-Saʿīd, Nihāya Rajul Shujāʿ" (Portrait: Nasir al-Said, the end of a brave man), *Al-Akhbar*, May 19, 2015; Nasir al-Said, *Tarīkh Āl Saud* (History of the Al Saud) (Beirut: Ittiḥād Shaʿb al-Jazīra al-ʿArabiyya, 1985).
13. On U.S.-Saudi disagreement over Palestine, tempered by the Saudi desire to secure U.S. help against the Hashemites, see Maurice Jr. Labelle, "'The Only Thorn': Early Saudi-American Relations and the Question of Palestine, 1945–1949," *Diplomatic History* 35, no. 2 (2011): 257–81. For Saudi complaints about the Hashemites, see memcon, November 1, 1943, *FRUS* 1943, Vol. 4, Doc. 880.
14. Memcon, April 24, 1948, *FRUS* 1948, Vol. 5, Part 1, Doc. 182.
15. Memcon, December 9, 1949, *FRUS* 1949, Vol. 6, Doc. 1129.
16. Truman to Ibn Saud, *FRUS* 1950, Vol. 5, Doc. 658.
17. Grew to Truman, June 26, 1945, *FRUS* 1945, Vol. 8, Doc. 895; Robert Vitalis, *America's Kingdom: Mythmaking on the Saudi Oil Frontier* (Stanford, CA: Stanford University Press, 2007), 80–83.
18. Anand Toprani, "The French Connection: A New Perspective on the End of the Red Line Agreement, 1945–1948," *Diplomatic History* 36, no. 2 (2012): 261–99.

19. Anthony Sampson, *The Seven Sisters: The Great Oil Companies and the World They Shaped* (New York: Viking, 1975); John Blair, *The Control of Oil* (New York: Pantheon Books, 1976); Theodore Moran, "Managing an Oligopoly of Would-Be Sovereigns: The Dynamics of Joint Control and Self-Control in the International Oil Industry Past, Present, and Future," *International Organization* 41, no. 4 (Autumn 1987): 575–607.

20. The Department of the Interior might seem like a curious inclusion on this list, but it had a close working relationship with many of the oil companies that had operations on federal land. It was also more involved in U.S. foreign relations than its name would suggest; see Megan Black, *The Global Interior: Mineral Frontiers and American Power* (Cambridge, MA: Harvard University Press, 2018).

21. Report by the Department of Justice, January 6, 1953; report by the Departments of State, Defense, and the Interior, January 6, 1953, *FRUS 1952–1954*, Vol. 9, Part 1, Docs. 279, 281; memorandum of discussion, January 9, 1953, *FRUS 1952–54*, Vol. 1, Part 2, Doc. 161; U.S. Senate, Subcommittee on Multinational Corporations, *Multinational Oil Corporations and U.S. Foreign Policy: Report to the Committee on Foreign Relations by the Subcommittee on Multinational Corporations* (hereafter *MNC Report*), 93rd Cong. (Washington: U.S. Government Printing Office, 1975), 107.

22. Kai Bird, *The Chairman: John J. McCloy and the Making of the American Establishment* (New York: Simon and Schuster, 1992), 441–45.

23. Sarah Yizraeli, *The Remaking of Saudi Arabia: The Struggle Between King Sa'ud and Crown Prince Faysal, 1953–1962* (Tel Aviv: Moshe Dayan Center, Tel Aviv University, 1997), 136; Vitalis, *America's Kingdom*, 74–76; John Henry, "American Railroad on the Arabian Desert," *Popular Mechanics*, April 1952; Harry Ellis, "Diesel Whisks Arab Prince over Sands," *Christian Science Monitor*, March 17, 1953; "The Railroad Project," Folder 25, Box 5, William E. Mulligan Papers (WMP), Georgetown University.

24. "Arabia Steeds en Route Here," *Oakland Tribune*, March 9, 1947; "King's Gifts to Oakland Girl, 2 Arabian Horses, Reach Here," *Oakland Tribune*, March 26, 1947; "King of Arabia Sends U.C. Coed 2 Fine Horses," *San Francisco Examiner*, March 9, 1947.

25. Faisal speech at opening of Shura Council, July 19, 1950, Faisal doc. 8, Muqatel.

26. Saud speeches at opening of Shura Council, November 21, 1947, and to pilgrims in Mecca, August 29, 1952, Saud docs. 5, 11; Faisal speech at opening of Shura Council, July 19, 1950, Faisal Doc. 8, Muqatel.

27. Steve Coll, *The Bin Ladens: An Arabian Family in the American Century* (New York: Penguin, 2008), 19–121.

28. Michael Field, *The Merchants: The Big Business Families of Saudi Arabia and the Gulf States* (Woodstock, NY: Overlook Press, 1985).

29. Rosie Bsheer, "A Counter-revolutionary State: Popular Movements and the Making of Saudi Arabia," *Past and Present* 238, no. 1 (February 2018): 233–77; Toby Matthiesen, "Migration, Minorities, and Radical Networks: Labour Movements and Opposition Groups in Saudi Arabia, 1950–1975," *International Review of Social History* 59, no. 3 (2014): 473–504.

30. "Navy Purchases of Middle East Oil," *Investigation of the National Defense Program: Additional Report* (Washington, DC: U.S. Government Printing Office, 1948), 1–33.

31. "Development of Aramco Relations with the Saudi Arab Government," October 1948; "Scandal—Jews and Oil," *Al Misri*, June 6, 1948, from "Public Relations in the Middle East," Folder 25, Box 5, WMP.

32. On the strikes, see Vitalis, *America's Kingdom*, 92–95, 145–53, 159–60, 171–83; Matthiesen, "Migration, Minorities, and Radical Networks," 487–91; Nathan J. Citino, *From Arab Nationalism to OPEC: Eisenhower, King Sa'ūd, and the Making of U.S.-Saudi Relations* (Bloomington: Indiana University Press, 2002), 57–60, 100–101. For an American worker's recollection of the 1953 strike, see Michael Sheldon Cheney, *Big Oil Man from Arabia* (New York: Ballantine Books, 1958), 226–39.

33. Interview with Baldo Marinovic, May 3, 1993, in *American Perspectives of Aramco, the Saudi-Arabian Oil-Producing Company, 1930s to 1980s*, ed. Carol Hicke (Bancroft Library, University of California, Berkeley, 1995), 229–30, https://archive.org/details/aramcooilproducoohickrich. For a similar assessment of Ibn Jiluwi's harsh methods, see Cheney, *Big Oil Man from Arabia*, 67–70.

34. "Background and Implications of the Conflict Within the Saudi Ruling Family," State Department Office of Intelligence Research and Analysis, April 1, 1958.

35. Khalifa Fahad, *Jaḥīm al-Ḥukm al-Sa'ūdī wa Nīrān al-Wahhābiyya* (The hell of Saudi rule and the flames of Wahhabism) (London: Al-Sīfa li al-Nashr wa al-Tawz'ia, 1989), 201.

36. Abdelrahman Munif, *Cities of Salt*, trans. Peter Theroux (New York: Random House, 1987).

37. Abdelrahman Munif, *The Trench*, trans. Peter Theroux (New York: Vintage, 1993), 406–7.

38. Rachel Bronson, *Thicker Than Oil: America's Uneasy Partnership with Saudi Arabia* (Oxford: Oxford University Press, 2006), 46.

39. William Mulligan, Report on the Visit of King 'Abdul 'Aziz ibn Sa'ud to the Arabian American Oil Company, January 1947, 59, Folder 6, Box 6, WMP.

40. David S. Painter, "The Marshall Plan and Oil," *Cold War History* 9, no. 2 (2009): 159–75. For oil as an alternative to the unionized coal industry, see Painter, "Oil and the Marshall Plan," *The Business History Review* 58, no. 3 (1984), 361; Timothy Mitchell, *Carbon Democracy: Political Power in the Age of Oil* (London: Verso, 2011), 12–42. For Wallace's critique of the plan, see Benn Steil, *The Marshall Plan: Dawn of the Cold War* (New York: Simon and Schuster, 2018), 214–15.

41. *MNC Report*, 83; Caltex memorandum, June 13, 1947, from U.S. Senate, Subcommittee on Multinational Corporations, 93rd Cong., *Multinational Oil Corporations and U.S. Foreign Policy: Hearings before the Subcommittee on Multinational Corporations* (hereafter *MNC Hearings*), (Washington, DC: U.S. Government Printing Office, 1975), Part 8, 191–92.

42. David S. Painter, *Oil and the American Century: The Political Economy of U.S. Foreign Oil Policy, 1941–1954* (Baltimore: Johns Hopkins University Press, 1986), 113–14.

43. Steve Everly and Charles Crumpley, "Truman OK'd Sabotage Plot," *Kansas City Star*, February 25, 1996; Steve Everly, "U.S., Britain Developed Plans to Disable or Destroy Middle Eastern Oil Facilities from Late 1940s to Early 1960s in Event of a Soviet Invasion (National Security Archive Briefing Book 552)," https://nsarchive.gwu.edu/briefing

-book/iran-nuclear-vault/2016-06-23/US-britain-developed-plans-disable-or-destroy -middle; Bronson, *Thicker Than Oil*, 58–59.

44. Kenneth T. Jackson, *Crabgrass Frontier: The Suburbanization of the United States* (Oxford: Oxford University Press, 1985), 190–218; Kathleen J. Frydl, *The G.I. Bill* (Cambridge: Cambridge University Press, 2009), 263–302.

45. Dwight D. Eisenhower, *At Ease: Stories I Tell to Friends* (Garden City, NY: Doubleday, 1967), 155–68; Owen D. Gutfreund, *Twentieth-Century Sprawl: Highways and the Reshaping of the American Landscape* (Oxford: Oxford University Press, 2004); Richard F. Weingroff, "Federal-Aid Highway Act of 1956: Creating the Interstate System," *Public Roads* 60, no. 1 (1996), 10–17, 45–51.

46. Isabel Wilkerson, *The Warmth of Other Suns: The Epic Story of America's Great Migration* (New York: Random House, 2010).

47. For an overview of federal policy support for residential segregation, see Richard Rothstein, *The Color of Law: A Forgotten History of How Our Government Segregated America* (New York: Liveright, 2017). For discriminatory HOLC practices and redlining in the case of Detroit, see Thomas J. Sugrue, *The Origins of the Urban Crisis: Race and Inequality in Postwar Detroit*, rev. ed. (Princeton, NJ: Princeton University Press, 2014).

48. Kevin M. Kruse, *White Flight: Atlanta and the Making of Modern Conservatism* (Princeton, NJ: Princeton University Press, 2005), 107–16.

49. Report to the National Security Council, March 20, 1953, *FRUS* 1952–54, Iran 1951–54, Second Edition, Doc. 180; CIA report, October 20, 1953, *FRUS* 1952–54, Iran 1951–54, Second Edition, Doc. 336.

50. On the 1953 coup, see Ervand Abrahamian, *The Coup: 1953, the CIA, and the Roots of Modern U.S.-Iranian Relations* (New York: New Press, 2013); Ali Rahnema, *Behind the 1953 Coup in Iran: Thugs, Turncoats, Soldiers, Spooks* (Cambridge: Cambridge University Press, 2014).

51. Salim Yaqub, *Containing Arab Nationalism: The Eisenhower Doctrine and the Middle East* (Chapel Hill: University of North Carolina Press, 2004).

52. Gamal Abdel Nasser, *The Philosophy of the Revolution* (Washington, DC: Public Affairs Press, 1955), 106.

53. Yaqub, *Containing Arab Nationalism*, 228.

54. The best guide to U.S.-Saudi relations in the 1950s is Citino, *From Arab Nationalism to OPEC*. For the tanker dispute, see Nathan J. Citino, "Defending the 'Postwar Petroleum Order': The US, Britain and the 1954 Saudi-Onassis Tanker Deal," *Diplomacy and Statecraft* 11, no. 2 (July 2000): 137–60. For Saud's remarks on Buraimi, see his statement of December 30, 1960, Saud Doc. 85, Muqatel.

55. U.S. Senate, Committee on Foreign Relations, *The President's Proposal on the Middle East* (Washington, DC: U.S. Government Printing Office, 1957), 528–29; 85 Cong. Rec. 1368 (1957). Charles Bennett, "Mayor Bars Fete for Saud," *New York Times*, January 29, 1957.

56. "Navy Drops Proviso Aiding Arab Boycott," *Washington Post*, February 20. 1960.

57. "Jewish Veterans Protest Saudi Ban," *New York Times*, February 26, 1956; "Aramco's Ban Here on Jews Overruled," *New York Times*, July 16, 1959; "Aramco Denies Job Bias," *Christian Science Monitor*, December 27, 1962.

58. 1960 Democratic Party Platform, APP.

59. 85 Cong. Rec. A622–23 (1957).

60. "Report Slave Sales of African Natives," *Chicago Defender,* February 7, 1953; Mario Rossi, "Vestiges of Slavery Probed by UN: Slaves Marketed," *Christian Science Monitor,* June 22, 1953; Kennett Love, "Rise in Slavery Linked to Arabs," *New York Times,* February 21, 1956; Kenneth Miller, "The Slave Trade: Grim Africa-to-Arabia Traffic Is Reported Reviving," *Wall Street Journal,* April 10, 1956.

61. "King Saud's Visit to U.S. Draws Fire," *Baltimore Afro-American,* February 2, 1957; "Powell Lauds Saud; Gets Blast from Jewish Body," *Philadelphia Tribune,* November 20, 1956; C. Y. Adnata, "Paging the NAACP!," *New York Amsterdam News,* March 30, 1957.

62. "U.S. Won't Sign Slavery Pact," *Washington Post,* August 16, 1956.

63. Hare testimony from Senate Foreign Relations Committee hearings, January 23, 1957, *Executive Sessions of the Senate Foreign Relations Committee,* vol. 9 (Washington, DC: U.S. Government Printing Office, 1979), 72–73; Wadsworth testimony from Senate Foreign Relations Committee and Armed Services Committee hearings, February 1957, *The President's Proposal on the Middle East* (Washington, DC: U.S. Government Printing Office, 1957), 670–71.

64. On Tariki, see Stephen Duguid, "A Biographical Approach to the Study of Social Change in the Middle East: Abdullah Tariki as a New Man," *International Journal of Middle East Studies* 1, no. 3 (1970): 195–220; Muhammad ibn 'Abd Allah Sayf, *'Abd Allāh Al-Ṭurayqī: Ṣukhūr al-Nafṭ Wa-Rimāl al-Siyāsah* (Abdullah Tariki: The rocks of oil and the sands of politics) (Beirut: Al-Mu'assasa al-'Arabīyya li al-Dirāsāt wa al-Nashr, 2007).

65. On the Saud-Faisal rivalry, see Yizraeli, *The Remaking of Saudi Arabia.* On the Saudi plot against Nasser, see Rountree to Dulles, March 14, 1958, *FRUS* 1958–1960, Vol. 12, Doc. 311. For Dulles's comments on Faisal, see editorial note, *FRUS* 1958–1960, Vol. 12, Doc. 313.

66. Vitalis, *America's Kingdom,* 220–23; Bsheer, "A Counter-revolutionary State," 233–36. Tariki told a U.S. correspondent in 1958 that Saudi Arabia would become a constitutional monarchy. William L. Ryan, "Saudi Rule Seen in Drastic Shift," *New York Times,* June 4, 1958.

67. On OPEC's founding, see Giuliano Garavini, *The Rise and Fall of OPEC in the Twentieth Century* (Oxford: Oxford University Press, 2019), 88–134; Christopher R. W. Dietrich, *Oil Revolution: Anticolonial Elites, Sovereign Rights, and the Economic Culture of Decolonization* (Cambridge: Cambridge University Press, 2017), 61–88. On the relative moderation of OPEC's agenda compared with more radical proposals like full nationalization or the sharing of oil wealth with the entire Arab world, see Citino, *From Arab Nationalism to OPEC.* On American reactions to OPEC and the oil companies' fears of the new organization, see Victor McFarland, "The US Response to OPEC," in *Handbook of OPEC and the Global Energy Order: Past, Present and Future Challenges,* ed. Dag Harald Claes and Giuliano Garavini (Abingdon: Routledge, 2020), 121–132. For Tariki's early contacts with Venezuela, see Abdullah Tariki, "Arab–Latin American Cooperation in the Energy Field," in *Arab–Latin American Relations: Energy, Trade, and Investment,* ed. Fehmy Saddy (New Brunswick, NJ: Transaction Books, 1983), 25–38. Eisenhower's comment is from memcon, September 21, 1960, *FRUS* 1958–60, Vol. 12, Doc. 91.

68. Immediately after Saud reclaimed power in 1960, the State Department noted that while he had "a certain shrewdness in dealing with internal problems of a traditional nature," he was "ignorant of sound fiscal management" and was ill-prepared to deal with "the forces of modern reformist Arab nationalism." Cumming to Herter, December 22, 1960, *FRUS* 1958–1960, Vol. 12, Doc. 345.
69. Robert Komer Oral History Interview by Elizabeth Farmer, July 16, 1964, 14, John F. Kennedy Presidential Library (JFKL), Boston, MA.
70. National Intelligence Estimate 36–61, June 27, 1961, *FRUS* 1961–1963, Vol. 18, Doc. 68.
71. Jidda to State, April 30, 1962, 3/17/62–4/30/62, Box 156A, National Security Files (NSF), JFKL.
72. Bronson, *Thicker Than Oil*, 78–79; *FRUS* 1961–1963, Vol. 17, Doc. 81, footnote 2.
73. Battle to Dungan, March 21, 1961, 1/1/61–8/18/61, Box 156A, NSF, JFKL.
74. DEPTAR WASHDC to State, November 16, 1961, 8/19/61–11/19/61, Box 156A, NSF, JFKL.
75. Komer to Kennedy, February 12, 1962, 2/1/62–2/19/62, Box 156A, NSF, JFKL.
76. Jidda to State, April 30, 1962, 3/17/62–4/30/62, Box 156A, NSF, JFKL; Jidda to State, September 7, 1962, Box 5, White House Central Subject–Classified File (WHCF), JFKL.
77. Komer to Bundy, July 13, 1962, 7/62–9/62, Box 157, NSF, JFKL.
78. "Saud Ousts Brother from Cabinet Post," *Washington Post*, September 13, 1961; "Kinsman of Saud Asks for Reform," *New York Times*, August 16, 1962.
79. Dhahran to State, March 19, 1962, 3/17/62–4/30/62, Box 156A, NSF, JFKL; Dhahran to State, March 28, 1962, 3/17/62–4/30/62, Box 156A, NSF, JFKL.
80. Report of the Special U.S. Economic Mission to Saudi Arabia, Reports Box 1, Albert J. Meyer Papers (AJMP), Harvard University Archives, Cambridge, MA; Jidda to State, July 2, 1962, 7/62–9/62, Box 157, NSF, JFKL; scope paper, Faisal Briefing Book 10/62, Box 158, NSF, JFKL.
81. Meyer, handwritten notes after meeting with Saudi leaders, Saudi Arabia Mission—June 1962, Box 11, Correspondence, Speeches, and Other Papers (CSOP), AJMP.
82. Addendum to the Report of the Special U.S. Economic Mission to Saudi Arabia, Saudi Arabia Mission—June 1962, Box 11, CSOP, AJMP.
83. Addendum to the Report, AJMP; Report of the Special U.S. Economic Mission, AJMP; Meyer notes after meeting Saudi leaders, AJMP; Background and Briefing for the Saudi Arabia Economic Team, Saudi Arabia Mission—June 1962, Box 11, CSOP, AJMP.
84. State to Jidda, November 7, 1962, 11/62–12/62, Box 157, NSF, JFKL; Komer to Kennedy, Faisal Briefing Book 10/62, Box 158, NSF, JFKL.
85. Jidda to State, March 13, 1962, 2/2–/62-3/16/62, Box 156A, NSF, JFKL.
86. Asher Orkaby, *Beyond the Arab Cold War: The International History of the Yemen Civil War, 1962–68* (Oxford: Oxford University Press, 2017); Jesse Ferris, *Nasser's Gamble: How Intervention in Yemen Caused the Six-Day War and the Decline of Egyptian Power* (Princeton, NJ: Princeton University Press, 2013).
87. Jidda to State, October 13, 1962, 10/62, Box 157, NSF, JFKL; Jidda to State, October 4, 1962, 10/62, Box 157, NSF, JFKL.
88. Situation in Saudi Arabia, CIA memorandum, October 15, 1962, Box 157, NSF, JFKL.

89. Dhahran to State, October 17, 1962, Box 157, NSF, JFKL.
90. Beirut to State, October 16, 1962, NSF Box 157, JFKL; Dhahran to State, October 18, 1962, Box 157, NSF, JFKL.
91. Possible Forced Abdication of King Saud, CIA memorandum, October 15, 1962, Box 157, NSF, JFKL; Dhahran to State, October 17, 1962, Box 157, NSF, JFKL.
92. Memcon, October 5, 1962, *FRUS* 1961–1963, Vol. 18, Doc. 71. Briefing Kennedy in advance of his meeting with Faisal, Komer told the president that the crown prince "may want to say a few things about his own future." Komer to Kennedy, Faisal Briefing Book 10/62, Box 158, NSF, JFKL. If Kennedy and Faisal did talk about the Saudi succession, that conversation was not included in the declassified records. Sabbagh later claimed that while the United States expected Saud to fall from power, Sabbagh and his colleagues were "passive bystanders" to the coup. Sabbagh interview, November 9, 1989, ADST. Saud was in such poor health in late 1962 that most U.S. officials did not expect him to live much longer. It is possible, though, that Saud's illness provided an additional incentive to make sure Faisal was installed as prime minister, preventing a dangerous interregnum if Saud died before Faisal could consolidate power. A similar situation led to the fall of the Yemeni monarchy in September 1962, when the old ruler, Imam Ahmad bin Yahya, died and antiroyalist officers in the military launched a coup shortly afterward.
93. The retired Aramco executive Michael Ameen reported that Aramco and the CIA helped install Faisal in power. Author's interview with Michael Ameen, Kingwood, TX, May 28, 2011.
94. For decades, Faisal's defenders have held up his "Ten Point Program" as proof of his status as a great reformer. An English translation is available from the King Faisal Foundation run by his sons at https://kff.com/en/King-Faisal.
95. Jidda to State, December 19, 1962, 11/62–12/62, Box 157, NSF, JFKL; memcon, March 3, 1963, 1/63–3/63, Box 157, NSF, JFKL.
96. Memcon, March 3, 1963, 1/63–3/63, Box 157, NSF, JFKL.
97. Jidda to State, January 10, 1963, 1/63–3/63, Box 157, NSF, JFKL; Jidda to State, March 3, 1963, Box 157, NSF, JFKL; Jidda to State, March 4, 1963, Box 157, NSF, JFKL.
98. Joint Chiefs to McNamara, March 6, 1963, *FRUS* 1961–63, Vol. 18, Doc. 177; Komer to Kennedy, March 6, 1963, *FRUS* 1961–63, Vol. 18, Doc. 178.
99. Memorandum for the record, January 28, 1963; memorandum for the record, February 25, 1963, *FRUS* 1961–63, Vol. 18, Docs. 145, 164. On Kermit Roosevelt, see Hugh Wilford, *America's Great Game: The CIA's Secret Arabists and the Shaping of the Modern Middle East* (New York: Basic Books, 2013); Douglas Little, "Mission Impossible: The CIA and the Cult of Covert Action in the Middle East," *Diplomatic History* 28, no. 5 (2004): 663–701.
100. Bundy to Taylor, January 11, 1963, *FRUS* 1961–63, Vol. 18, Doc. 132.
101. Jidda to State, June 27, 1963, 6/15/63–6/30/63, Box 157, NSF, JFKL.
102. Strong to Grant, May 20, 1963; Jidda to State, June 25, 1963, 6/15/63–6/30/63, Box 157, NSF, JFKL.
103. Parker Hart interview, January 27, 1989, ADST.
104. Bronson, *Thicker Than Oil*, 94–96; Nadav Safran, *Saudi Arabia: The Ceaseless Quest for Security* (Ithaca, NY: Cornell University Press, 1988), 200–202; Nikolas Gardner, "The

Harold Wilson Government, Airwork Services Limited, and the Saudi Arabian Air Defence Scheme, 1965–73," *Journal of Contemporary History* 42, no. 2 (2007): 345–63.

105. Khashoggi biography, October 31, 1971, Folder 70, Box 1, WMP. There is no scholarly treatment of Khashoggi's career, only the rather sensationalized biography by Ronald Kessler, *Khashoggi: The Story of the World's Richest Man* (London: Bantam Press, 1986).

106. Gamal Abdel Nasser speech in Port Said, December 12, 1966, http://nasser.bibalex.org /Speeches/browser.aspx?SID=1197.

107. Faisal speech in Mecca, February 1, 1963, Faisal Doc. 22, Muqatel.

108. Memorandum for the record, December 3, 1964, *FRUS* 1964–68, Vol. 21, Doc. 234.

109. Dhahran to State, March 7, 1963, 63/1–63/3, Box 157, NSF, JFKL.

110. On the major philanthropic organizations and U.S. foreign policy, see Volker R. Berghahn, "Philanthropy and Diplomacy in the 'American Century,'" *Diplomatic History* 23, no. 3 (July 1999): 393–419; Edward H. Berman, *The Influence of the Carnegie, Ford, and Rockefeller Foundations on American Foreign Policy: The Ideology of Philanthropy* (Albany: State University of New York Press, 1983); Inderjeet Parmar, *Foundations of the American Century: The Ford, Carnegie, and Rockefeller Foundations in the Rise of American Power* (New York: Columbia University Press, 2012).

111. Ford Foundation, "Annual Project Report for Saudi Arabia, November 1963– November 1964," Ford Foundation Archives Virtual Vault (FFAVV), Rockefeller Archive Center, Sleepy Hollow, NY; "Status of Work: The Saudi Arabian Economic Plan," 1966, FFAVV; Conrad C. Stucky, "The Saudi Arabian Experience: A Cooperative Effort for Achieving Development," 1972, FFAVV.

112. Talbot to Special Group, May 18, 1964; Paper Prepared in the Department of State, April 6, 1967, *FRUS* 1964–68, Vol. 21, Docs. 227, 287.

113. Russi Karanjia interview with Nasser, *Blitz*, August 5, 1966, http://nasser.bibalex.org /Speeches/html.aspx?SID=1166; Faisal speech, February 1, 1963, Faisal Doc. 22, Muqatel.

3. IGNITION

1. On the history of the al-Malaz racetrack and the surrounding area, see Hammoud Al-Duwaihi, "Tʿalliq bi al-Khayl'" (Concerning "the horses"), *Al-Riyadh*, September 28, 2012, http://www.alriyadh.com/771870; Suleiman Al-Hadithi, "Al-Malaz . . . Qiṣa al-Ḥay al-Khālid fī al-dhākira al-Saʿudīa" (Al-Malaz . . . The story of a neighborhood forever in Saudi memory), *Al-Iqtisadiyya*, December 21, 2018, http://www.aleqt.com/2018 /12/21/article_1510571.html; Pascal Menoret, "The Suburbanization of Islamic Activism in Saudi Arabia," *City and Society* 29, no. 1 (2017): 168–69.

2. "Jalāla al-Malik al-Muaʿẓam Yaltaqī bi-Ibnāʾ al-Shʿab as-Saʿudī" (His great majesty the king meets the Saudi people), *Umm al-Qura*, June 9, 1967.

3. Nasir Al-Said, *Tarīkh Āl Saud* (History of the Al Saud) (Beirut: Ittiḥād Shaʿb al-Jazīra al-ʿArabiyya, 1985), 609–10. Aramco corroborated al-Said's account of the chaos at Faisal's speech, even though it went unmentioned in the official press. For the company's

report on the incident, see Aramco Local Government Relations, "The June 1967 Riots," Folder 8, Box 16, WMP.

4. On the Yemeni civil war, see Asher Orkaby, *Beyond the Arab Cold War: The International History of the Yemen Civil War, 1962–68* (Oxford: Oxford University Press, 2017); Jesse Ferris, *Nasser's Gamble: How Intervention in Yemen Caused the Six-Day War and the Decline of Egyptian Power* (Princeton, NJ: Princeton University Press, 2013). The classic study of the Saudi-Egyptian rivalry is Malcolm H. Kerr, *The Arab Cold War: Gamal 'Abd Al-Nasir and His Rivals, 1958–1970*, 3rd ed. (Oxford: Oxford University Press, 1971).

5. Memorandum for the record, May 24, 1967, *FRUS 1964–68*, Vol. 34, Doc. 229.

6. "Mu'tamar al-Bitrūl Yaftatah al-Yawm" (Oil conference opens today), *Al-Bilad*, June 4, 1967.

7. For the prewar mobilization of the Saudi armed forces, see *Al-Bilad*, June 4, 1967. For the cables to Faisal, see "Al-Sh'ab al-Sa'ūdī bi-Kāfa Qiṭā'āṭihi al-'Askariyya wa al-Madaniyya Yustajīb li-I'lān Qā'idihi" (The Saudi people in all their military and civilian sectors respond to the declaration of their leader), *Umm al-Qura*, June 9, 1967.

8. National Intelligence Estimate (NIE) 36-6-70, April 7, 1970; CIA memorandum, July 15, 1971, *FRUS 1969–76*, Vol. 36, Docs. 140, 153.

9. For Aramco's reporting on the demonstrations, see "The June 1967 Riots,", WMP. For recollections by the company's American employees, see interviews with Elizabeth and Paul Arnot, R. W. "Brock" Powers, and Peter Speers in *American Perspectives of Aramco, the Saudi-Arabian Oil-Producing Company, 1930s to 1980s*, ed. Carol Hicke (Bancroft Library, University of California, Berkeley, 1995), 177–78, 424–29, 501–3. For an approving reference to the destruction of American cars, see al-Said, *Tarikh Āl Saud*, 610.

10. Anthony Cave Brown, *Oil, God, and Gold: The Story of Aramco and the Saudi Kings* (Boston: Houghton Mifflin, 1999), 276.

11. Aramco cable, June 8, 1967, from editorial note, *FRUS 1964–68*, Vol. 34, Doc. 233.

12. State to Jidda, June 8, 1967, *FRUS 1964–68*, Vol. 21, Doc. 290; Brown, *Oil, God, and Gold*, 272–78; Hicke, *American Perspectives of Aramco*.

13. "Majlis al-Wuzarā' bi-Ri'āsa Fayṣal al-Mu'aẓam Yuqarar Awqaf al-Bitrūl" (The Council of Ministers headed by the great Faisal decides to stop oil), *Umm Al-Qura*, June 9, 1967.

14. Hermann Eilts interview, August 12, 1988, ADST.

15. Memcon, July 18, 1967, *FRUS 1964–68*, Vol. 34, Doc. 258.

16. Aramco cables, June 10 and 11, from editorial note, *FRUS 1964–68*, Vol. 34, Doc. 258.

17. The best overview of the 1967 embargo is Christopher R. W. Dietrich, *Oil Revolution: Anticolonial Elites, Sovereign Rights, and the Economic Culture of Decolonization* (Cambridge: Cambridge University Press, 2017), 124–27, 142–48. See also M. S. Daoudi and M. S. Dajani, "The 1967 Oil Embargo Revisited," *Journal of Palestine Studies* 13, no. 2 (1984): 65–90; Joseph Mann, "A Reassessment of the 1967 Arab Oil Embargo," *Israel Affairs* 19, no. 4 (October 2013): 693–703; Rachel Bronson, *Thicker Than Oil: America's Uneasy Partnership with Saudi Arabia* (Oxford: Oxford University Press, 2006), 98–102.

18. Department of Defense paper, c. October 1969, *FRUS 1969–76*, Vol. 36, Doc. 10; report of Working Group on Economic Vulnerabilities, May 31, 1967, *FRUS 1964–68*, Vol. 19,

Doc. 115; teleconference (hereafter telcon), Rusk and Solomon, June 8, 1967, *FRUS* 1964–68, Vol. 29, Doc. 214; briefing by CIA director John McCone, *FRUS* 1964–68, Vol. 34, Doc. 252; Bronson, *Thicker Than Oil*, 101; Eilts interview, ADST, 23.

19. "Istiʾnāf Ḍakh al-Bitrūl al-Saʿūdī" (Resumption of the pumping of Saudi oil), *Umm al-Qura*, June 16, 1967.

20. "Saudi Minister Urges Arabs to Reconsider Oil Boycott," *Financial Times*, July 1, 1967; Thomas F. Brady, "Saudis Question Embargo on Oil," *New York Times*, July 1, 1967.

21. For Saudi coverage of the summit, see "Inʿiqād Muʾtamar al-Qimma al-ʿArabī al-Rābiʿ fī al-Sūdān al-Shaqīq" (The fourth Arab summit conference in the brotherly Sudan), *Umm al-Qura*, September 1, 1967; "al-Shʿab al-Saʿūdī Yakhraj li-Istiqbāl al-Fayṣal Qādiman min al-Kharṭūm" (The Saudi people come out to receive Faisal arriving from Khartoum), *Umm al-Qura*, September 8, 1967.

22. Irwin to State, January 19, 1971, *FRUS* 1969–76, Vol. 36, Doc. 75. On the end of the embargo and the Syrian response, see "Arabs Agree to Resume Flow of Oil," *The Guardian*, September 1, 1967, and "Syrians Choose the Extreme Course," *The Guardian*, September 18, 1967.

23. Jidda to State, June 9, 1967, *FRUS* 1964–68, Vol. 21, Doc. 291.

24. Ferris, *Nasser's Gamble*, 290–94; Orkaby, *Beyond the Arab Cold War*, 197–98.

25. Interview with Abdullah Tariki, "Al-Nafṭ wa Hazīma al-Khāmis min Haziran" (Oil and the defeat of June 5), *Dirāsāt ʿArabiyya* 4, no. 9 (July 1968), from Abdullah Tariki, *ʿAbd Allāh Al-Ṭurayqī: Al-Aʿmāl al-Kāmila* (Abdullah Tariki: Complete works) (Beirut: Markaz Dirāsāt al-Waḥda al-ʿArabīyya, 1999), 516–18. For more on Tariki, see Muhammad ibn ʿAbd Allah Sayf, *ʿAbd Allāh Al-Ṭurayqī: Ṣukhūr al-Nafṭ Wa-Rimāl al-Siyāsah* (Abdullah Tariki: The rocks of oil and the sands of politics); Stephen Duguid, "A Biographical Approach to the Study of Social Change in the Middle East: Abdullah Tariki as a New Man," *International Journal of Middle East Studies* 1, no. 3 (1970): 195–220.

26. Al-Said, *Tarikh Āl Saud* (History of the Al Saud) (Beirut: Ittiḥād Shaʿb al-Jazīra al-ʿArabiyya, 1985), 611–12.

27. CIA memorandum, August 28, 1969; National Security Council (NSC) staff paper, c. October 1969; NIE 20/30-70, November 14, 1970, *FRUS* 1969–76, Vol. 36, Docs. 8, 14, 61.

28. Townsend to Hoopes, June 2, 1967, *FRUS* 1964–68, Vol. 19, Doc. 137; State to Paris, June 17, 1967; State to Bonn, June 19, 1967, *FRUS* 1964–68, Vol. 34, Docs. 245, 246.

29. Alsop's column was widely reprinted in U.S. and Canadian newspapers between June 19 and 23, 1967; for example, "French Attempting to Use Arab Emotions to Get Oil Interests," *Los Angeles Times*, June 20, 1967. See Paris to State, June 27, 1967; McCone briefing memorandum, June 29, 1967, *FRUS* 1964–68, Vol. 34, Docs. 250, 252.

30. State to Jidda, June 11, 1967, *FRUS* 1964–68, Vol. 34, Doc. 257.

31. Rostow to Johnson, June 13, 1967; Jidda to State, July 20, 1968, *FRUS* 1964–68, Vol. 21, Docs. 294, 313; Dhahran to State, February 5, 1969, *FRUS* 1969–76, Vol. 24, Doc. 127.

32. Amy Kaplan, *Our American Israel: The Story of an Entangled Alliance* (Cambridge, MA: Harvard University Press, 2018), 94–135; Melani McAlister, *Epic Encounters: Culture,*

Media, and U.S. Interests in the Middle East Since 1945 (Berkeley: University of California Press, 2005), 155–97; Salim Yaqub, *Containing Arab Nationalism: The Eisenhower Doctrine and the Middle East* (Chapel Hill: University of North Carolina Press, 2004), 61–62.

33. Kenneth Kolander, "Phantom Peace: Henry 'Scoop' Jackson, J. William Fulbright, and Military Sales to Israel," *Diplomatic History* 41, no. 3 (June 2017): 567–93; David Rodman, "Phantom Fracas: The 1968 American Sale of F-4 Aircraft to Israel," *Middle Eastern Studies* 40, no. 6 (November 2004): 130–44; Craig Daigle, *The Limits of Détente: The United States, the Soviet Union, and the Arab-Israeli Conflict, 1969–1973* (New Haven, CT: Yale University Press, 2012), 61.

34. Dhahran to State, June 13, 1970, POL 15-1 SAUD 1/1/70, Box 2586, Subject Numeric Files, 1970-73 (SNF), Record Group 59 (RG 59), National Archives and Records Administration (NARA), College Park, MD.

35. Jidda to State, June 13, 1967, *FRUS* 1964–68, Vol. 21, Doc. 295.

36. NSC policy statement on Saudi Arabia, November 21, 1969, *FRUS* 1969–76, Vol. 24, Doc. 133.

37. Jidda to State, July 13, 1970, POL 23 SAUD 1/1/70, Box 2586, SNF, RG 59, NARA.

38. Dhahran to State Department, February 5, 1969, *FRUS* 1969–76, Vol. 24, Doc. 127.

39. Interview with Hume Horan, November 3, 2000, ADST. Several years earlier, the U.S. Senate had denounced the continued circulation of the *Protocols*. See U.S. Senate, Committee on the Judiciary, *Protocols of the Elders of Zion: A Fabricated "Historic" Document* (Washington. DC: U.S. Government Printing Office, 1964).

40. Muslim World League (MWL) statement, June 18, 1967, *Al-Wathā'iq al-'Arabiyya* (*W'A*) 1967, Doc. 300.

41. MWL resolutions, October 20, 1968, *W'A* 1968, Doc. 234; MWL resolutions, October 20, 1969, and Mohammed Sorour al-Sabban to Lyndon Johnson, October 25, 1969, *W'A* 1969, Docs. 324 and 330. For a biographical sketch of Al-Sabban, see "Al-Ṣabbān: Wazīr Al-Mālīa Aladhī Ghanā Lahu Muḥammad 'Abd al-Wahhāb" (Al-Sabban: A minister of finance to whom Muhammad Abdel Wahhab sang), *Okaz*, June 6, 2012, https://www.okaz.com.sa/article/483982.

42. Address by King Faisal in Riyadh, August 22, 1969, *W'A* 1969, Doc. 349.

43. Jidda to State, July 6, 1970, POL 15-1 SAUD 1/1/70, Box 2586, SNF, RG 59, NARA.

44. Jidda to State, January 4, 1970, DEF 12-5 SAUD 1/1/70, Box 1793, SNF, RG 59, NARA; Jidda to State, October 20, 1970, FN Saud 1/1/70, Box 945, SNF, RG 59, NARA.

45. Jidda to State, January 29, 1970, DEF 12-5 SAUD 1/1/70, Box 1793, SNF, RG 59, NARA; Jidda to State and Defense, January 27, 1970, *FRUS* 1969–76, Vol. 24, Doc. 137; Stans to Nixon, May 26, 1971, *FRUS* 1969–76, Vol. 24, Doc. 150, footnote 3.

46. After the fighting at Wadiah, the U.S. State Department reported: "This Saudi military success appears to have enhanced the regime's prestige and given a badly needed morale boost to the regime and to the Saudi military." Assessment of Saudi Internal Security Situation, January 23, 1970, POL 23 SAUD 1/1/70, Box 2586, SNF, RG 59, NARA.

47. Saunders to Kissinger, February 5, 1971, CIA Electronic Reading Room (ERR), https://www.cia.gov/library/readingroom/docs/LOC-HAK-11-5-40-9.pdf; CIA memorandum

for Kissinger, March 13, 1973, CIA ERR, https://www.cia.gov/library/readingroom/docs/CIA-RDP80M01048A000300330005-0.pdf.

48. Abu Dhabi to State, October 15, 1972, POL SAUD—S Yemen 1/1/70, Box 2587, SNF, RG 59, NARA.

49. CIA memorandum, "The Persian Gulf: The End of Pax Britannica," September 21, 1972, *FRUS* 1969–76, Vol. 24, Doc. 122.

50. Abu Dhabi to State, May 12, 1973, Trucial States 1969–74, Box 632, NSC Files, Country Files—Middle East, RNL.

51. Kuwait to State, February 10, 1970, POL 23 SAUD 1/1/70, Box 2586, SNF, RG 59, NARA.

52. Memcon, October 13, 1969, *FRUS* 1969–76, Vol. 24, Doc. 131, footnote 3.

53. NIE 36-6-70, April 7, 1970; CIA memorandum, July 15, 1971, *FRUS* 1969–76, Vol. 24, Docs. 140, 153; State to Jidda, April 1, 1971, POL 1 SAUD-US 3/30/70, Box 2587, SNF, RG 59, NARA. The royal family's restrictions on its own army were an extreme example of coup-proofing, a strategy often employed by authoritarian regimes to minimize the chances of an uprising by their own armed forces. See Caitlin Talmadge, *The Dictator's Army: Battlefield Effectiveness in Authoritarian Regimes* (Ithaca, NY: Cornell University Press, 2015).

54. On the "flying princes," see Jidda to State, July 20, 1970, *FRUS* 1969–76, Vol. 24, Doc. 142. Bandar's mother was a servant in Sultan's household, and both of his parents were quite young when he was conceived. Bandar was initially treated as quasi-illegitimate before being accepted by his father's family; David B. Ottaway, *The King's Messenger: Prince Bandar Bin Sultan and America's Tangled Relationship with Saudi Arabia* (New York: Walker Books, 2008).

55. Jidda to State, September 30, 1970; Jidda to State, September 19, 1971, FN 15 SAUD 1/1/70, Box 945, SNF, RG 59, NARA.

56. Jidda to State, October 20, 1970, FN Saud 1/1/70, Box 945, SNF, RG 59, NARA.

57. Memcon, October 13, 1969, *FRUS* 1969–76, Vol. 24, Doc. 131.

58. *Foreign Assistance Act of 1969: Hearings on H.R. 11792 Before the Committee on Foreign Affairs, Part III*, 91st Cong. (1969), 584–85.

59. Jidda to State, May 6, 1970; Jidda to State, November 7, 1970, FN Saud 1/1/70, Box 945, SNF, RG 59, NARA; Sisco to Kearns, October 28, 1970, *FRUS* 1969–76, Vol. 24, Doc. 145, footnote 5.

60. Country policy statement on Saudi Arabia, November 21, 1969, *FRUS* 1969–76, Vol. 24, Doc. 133.

61. NIE 36-6-70, *FRUS* 1969–76, Vol. 24, Doc. 140.

62. Jidda to State and Defense, July 20, 1970, *FRUS* 1969–76, Vol. 24, Doc. 142.

63. Jidda to State, July 11, 1969; Jidda to State, July 22, 1970, DEF SAUD 1/1/70, Box 1792, SNF, RG 59, NARA; Jidda to State, April 16, 1970, E 2–4 SAUD 1/1/70, Box 779, SNF, RG 59, NARA. See also Jidda to State, January 26, 1970, DEF SAUD 1/1/70, Box 1792, SNF, RG 59, NARA.

64. Assessment of Saudi Internal Security Situation, January 23, 1970, POL 23 SAUD 1/1/70, Box 2586, SNF, RG 59, NARA.

65. Eilts, annual policy assessment for Saudi Arabia, March 31, 1970, POL 1 SAUD-US 3/3/70, Box 2587, SNF, RG 59, NARA.
66. Jidda to State, July 6, 1970, POL 15-1 SAUD 1/1/70, Box 2586, SNF, RG 59, NARA; Dhahran to State, June 13, 1970, POL 15-1 SAUD 1/1/70, Box 2586, SNF, RG 59, NARA.
67. Jidda to State, March 8, 1970, POL 23 SAUD 1/1/70, Box 2586, SNF, RG 59, NARA; Dhahran to State, March 9, 1970, POL 15-1 SAUD 1/1/70, Box 2586, SNF, RG 59, NARA; Jidda to State, April 18, 1973, POL 23 SAUD 1/1/70, Box 2586, SNF, RG 59, NARA; Eugene Bird, *Crossing Mandelbaum Gate* (New York: Scribner, 2010), 136–39.
68. State Department, Assessment of Saudi Internal Security Situation, January 23, 1970, POL 23 SAUD 1/1/70, Box 2586, SNF, RG 59, NARA.
69. NIE 36-6-70, April 7, 1970, *FRUS* 1969–76, Vol. 24, Doc. 140.
70. CIA memorandum, August 28, 1969, *FRUS* 1969–76, Vol. 36, Doc. 8.

4. MACHINES IN MOTION

1. Faisal's speech at the opening of the King Faisal Port in Jeddah, February 2, 1973, *WA* 1973, Doc. 38.
2. Faisal's speech in Jeddah, *WA* 1973.
3. PLO memorandum to the Seventh Annual Arab Petroleum Conference, Kuwait City, Kuwait, *WA* 1970, Doc. 96.
4. Katz to Trezise, July 28, 1970, *FRUS* 1969–76, Vol. 36, Doc. 51; Jidda to State, July 20, 1970, *FRUS* 1969–76, Vol. 24, Doc. 142.
5. On Libya's "exceptionally fortunate" combination of favorable "location and crude oil low in pollutants," see CIA memorandum, August 28, 1969, *FRUS* 1969–1976, Vol. 36, Doc. 8.
6. OECD mission to State, May 28, 1970, *FRUS* 1969–1976, Vol. 36, Doc. 46. See also Bureau of African Affairs memorandum, May 13, 1970; Katz to Trezise, July 28, 1970; Libya to State, September 23, 1970; NIE 20/30–70, November 14, 1970; Kissinger to Nixon, January 18, 1971, *FRUS* 1969–1976, Vol. 36, Docs. 45, 51, 55, 61, 73.
7. On the Libyan breakthrough, see Christopher R. W. Dietrich, *Oil Revolution: Anticolonial Elites, Sovereign Rights, and the Economic Culture of Decolonization* (Cambridge: Cambridge University Press, 2017), 191–227; Dirk Vandewalle, *A History of Modern Libya*, 2nd ed. (Cambridge: Cambridge University Press, 2012), 88–90; Steven A. Schneider, *The Oil Price Revolution* (Baltimore: Johns Hopkins University Press, 1983), 139–47; *MNC Report*, January 2, 1975 (Washington, DC: U.S. Government Printing Office, 1975), 121–25.
8. NSC staff to Kissinger, July 11, 1972, *FRUS* 1969–1976, Vol. 36, Doc. 127.
9. Richard H. K. Vietor, *Energy Policy in America Since 1945: A Study of Business-Government Relations* (Cambridge: Cambridge University Press, 1984), 194–98.
10. William Childs, *The Texas Railroad Commission: Understanding Regulation in America to the Mid-Twentieth Century* (College Station: Texas A&M University Press, 2005);

David Prindle, *Petroleum Politics and the Texas Railroad Commission* (Austin: University of Texas Press, 1981).

11. Preston Smith to Nixon, February 13, 1970, EX TA4/CM Tariff-Imports, 6 of 12 (Oil, February 1970), Box 26, CFSU TA (Trade), Subject Files, White House Central Files, RNL.

12. Thomas O'Toole, "Domestic Oil Gap Expected to Grow," *Washington Post*, November 27, 1972.

13. Rüdiger Graf, *Oil and Sovereignty: Petro-Knowledge and Energy Policy in the United States and Western Europe in the 1970s*, trans. Alex Skinner (New York: Berghahn Books, 2018), 57–59.

14. Oil production and consumption data are from BP, *Statistical Review of World Energy*, 2018, https://www.bp.com/en/global/corporate/energy-economics/statistical-review-of-world-energy.html. Population data are from the World Bank, https://data.worldbank.org. Per capita oil consumption was calculated from 1970 figures.

15. For a critique of the "love affair" trope, see Peter Norton, "Of Love Affairs and Other Stories," in *Incomplete Streets: Processes, Practices, and Possibilities*, ed. Stephen Zavestoski and Julian Agyeman (Abingdon: Routledge, 2015), 17–35.

16. "U.S. Traffic Chief Defends Roles of Railroads and Highways," *Christian Science Monitor*, June 6, 1968.

17. Carl-Henry Geschwind, *A Comparative History of Motor Fuels Taxation, 1909–2009: Why Gasoline Is Cheap and Petrol Is Dear* (Lanham, MD: Lexington Books, 2017).

18. Fuel consumption figures for 1973 model year vehicles provided by the Environmental Protection Agency, in 93 Cong. Rec. (1973), 40434–43.

19. "How Highway Lobby Ran Over Proposition 18," *Los Angeles Times*, December 27, 1970.

20. Raymond A. Mohl, "Stop the Road: Freeway Revolts in American Cities," *Journal of Urban History* 30, no. 5 (July 2004): 674–706; Raymond A. Mohl, "The Interstates and the Cities: The U.S. Department of Transportation and the Freeway Revolt, 1966–1973," *Journal of Policy History* 20, no. 2 (2008): 193–226.

21. Jane Jacobs, *The Death and Life of Great American Cities* (New York: Random House, 1961).

22. Zachary M. Schrag, *The Great Society Subway: A History of the Washington Metro* (Baltimore: Johns Hopkins University Press, 2006); Henri L. Stuart, *The Atlanta Plan: Rapid Transit for the People* (Atlanta: Metropolitan Atlanta Rapid Transit Authority, 1970).

23. Kim Phillips-Fein, *Fear City: New York's Fiscal Crisis and the Rise of Austerity Politics* (New York: Metropolitan Books, 2017).

24. Racialized criticism of MARTA as a black-run institution that would bring crime to white suburbs persisted for decades. Jason Henderson, "Secessionist Automobility: Racism, Anti-urbanism, and the Politics of Automobility in Atlanta, Georgia," *International Journal of Urban and Regional Research* 30, no. 2 (2006): 293–307.

25. Paul R. Ehrlich, *The Population Bomb* (New York: Ballantine Books, 1968); Donella H. Meadows and Club of Rome, *The Limits to Growth: A Report for the Club of Rome's Project on the Predicament of Mankind* (New York: Universe Books, 1972); E. F Schumacher, *Small Is Beautiful: A Study of Economics as If People Mattered* (London: Blond and Briggs, 1973). On the debate between pessimistic ecologists and optimistic economists over re-

source depletion in the 1970s, see Paul Sabin, *The Bet: Paul Ehrlich, Julian Simon, and Our Gamble Over Earth's Future* (New Haven, CT: Yale University Press, 2013).

26. Richard Fleischer, dir., *Soylent Green* (Metro-Goldwyn-Mayer, 1973).

27. At the time, the partisan divide on environmentalism was not as sharp as it is today. J. Brooks Flippen, *Nixon and the Environment* (Albuquerque: University of New Mexico Press, 2000); James Morton Turner and Andrew C. Isenberg, *The Republican Reversal: Conservatives and the Environment from Nixon to Trump* (Cambridge, MA: Harvard University Press, 2018).

28. Nixon, Special Message to the Congress on Energy Resources, June 4, 1971, APP. Economists refer to this idea as a tax on "negative externalities" or a "Pigouvian tax," after the British economist who developed the concept. See Arthur Pigou, *The Economics of Welfare* (London: Macmillan, 1920). On the application of that idea to environmental issues in the 1970s, see William J. Baumol, *The Theory of Environmental Policy: Externalities, Public Outlays, and the Quality of Life* (Englewood Cliffs, NJ: Prentice-Hall, 1975).

29. For an overview of U.S. energy policy during the period immediately before the embargo, see Meg Jacobs, *Panic at the Pump: The Energy Crisis and the Transformation of American Politics in the 1970s* (New York: Hill and Wang, 2016), 24–48.

30. Gene Smith, "Con Ed Warns of Blackout of Home Areas in Summer," *New York Times*, March 17, 1970; Lawrence Van Gelder, "City Feels Impact of Power Shortage," *New York Times*, July 29, 1970.

31. Lisa Cronin, "Natural Gas Deficiency Is Forecast: Long Term Needs," *Washington Post*, November 2, 1969; Richard Harwood, "Fuel-Short U.S. May Face Plant Closings, Rationing: Fuel Shortages May Force Plant Closings," *Washington Post*, August 17, 1970; Richard Halloran, "F.P.C.'s Head Warns Power Shortages Are Possible Next Winter," *New York Times*, 1970. On the way that various policy concerns were combined under the single label of the "energy crisis," see Timothy Mitchell, "The Resources of Economics: Making the 1973 Oil Crisis," *Journal of Cultural Economy* 3, no. 2 (2010): 189–204.

32. John Noble Wilford, "Nation's Energy Crisis: It Won't Go Away Soon," *New York Times*, July 6, 1971.

33. Nixon, Executive Order 11615—Providing for Stabilization of Prices, Rents, Wages, and Salaries, August 15, 1971, APP.

34. Jacobs, *Panic at the Pump*, 32–35; Daniel J. Sargent, *A Superpower Transformed: The Remaking of American Foreign Relations in the 1970s* (Oxford: Oxford University Press, 2014), 112–16; Allen J. Matusow, *Nixon's Economy: Booms, Busts, Dollars, and Votes* (Lawrence: University Press of Kansas, 1998), 149–81.

35. Nixon, Remarks on Transmitting a Special Message to the Congress on Energy Policy, April 18, 1973, APP; Jacobs, *Panic at the Pump*, 38–39.

36. Jidda to State, December 29, 1970, FN 16 SAUD 1/1/70, Box 945, SNF, RG 59, NARA. The 55 percent tax rate followed the Libyan precedent and OPEC's policy adopted at its December 1970 meeting in Caracas; see Giuliano Garavini, *The Rise and Fall of OPEC in the Twentieth Century* (Oxford: Oxford University Press, 2019), 196; Dietrich, *Oil Revolution*, 217.

37. Conversation between Piercy and Yamani, January 20, 1971, reported by Piercy to the London Policy Group, in *MNC Report*, 134.

38. State Department Bureau of Intelligence and Research memorandum, June 10, 1969; memorandum of conversation, December 2, 1971; State to Jidda, January 29, 1972; Jidda to State, February 17, 1972; Quandt and Saunders to Kissinger, December 26, 1972, *FRUS 1969–1976*, Vol. 36, Docs. 6, 96, 108, 112, 147.

39. Saudi Arabian Monetary Agency (SAMA), *Annual Report, 1392/93 A.H. (1973)* (Jeddah: SAMA, 1974), 25–27.

40. Jidda to State, September 19, 1971, FN 15 SAUD 1/1/70, Box 945, SNF, RG 59, NARA.

41. Jidda to State, July 26, 1971, DEF 6 SAUD 1/1/70, Box 1792, SNF, RG 59, NARA.

42. Jidda to State, March 18, 1971, E 5 SAUD 1/1/70, Box 779, SNF, RG 59, NARA.

43. SAMA *Annual Report, 1391/92 AH (1972)* (Jeddah: SAMA, 1973).

44. Economic Trends Report, August 23, 1971, FN 15 SAUD 1/1/70, Box 945, SNF, RG 59, NARA.

45. Saudi historical GDP in constant 2010 U.S. dollars; data provided by the World Bank, https://data.worldbank.org/indicator/NY.GDP.MKTP.KD?locations=SA.

46. Faisal speech, September 15, 1972, Faisal Doc. 152, Muqatel.

47. Interview with Faisal and Saud al-Faisal, *Al-Hawadith*, August 31, 1973, *WA 1973*, Doc. 298.

48. Address by Omar Saqqaf at Islamic foreign ministers' conference, March 3, 1972, *WA 1972*, Doc. 61. Saqqaf was referring to what would become the Islamic Development Bank headquartered in Jeddah. For later discussions on the project, see "Al-Yawm Taṣil ilā Jidda Wufūd al-Duwal Al-Islāmiyya li Dirasāt Mashrūʿa al-Bank Al-Islāmī" (Today, delegations from the Muslim countries arrive in Jeddah to study the project of an Islamic bank), *Al-Riyadh*, July 18, 1973.

49. SAMA, *Annual Report, 1392/93 A.H. (1973)*, 37–38.

50. Stans to Nixon, May 26, 1971, *FRUS 1969–76*, Vol. 24, Doc. 150.

51. Hume Horan interview, November 3, 2000, ADST.

52. James E. Akins, "The Oil Crisis: This Time the Wolf Is Here," *Foreign Affairs* 51, no. 3 (1973): 482.

53. Aramco visitor briefing materials, c. 1968–1973, included with a letter from Frank Jungers to Joe Johnston, July 24, 1973, in *MNC Hearings*, Part 7, 519; "Saudis Tie Oil to U.S. Policy on Israel," *Washington Post*, April 19, 1973. Production figures from BP *Statistical Review of World Energy*.

54. Memcon, July 26–31, 1972, *FRUS 1969–76*, Vol. 36, Doc. 134.

55. "The Saudi Oil Income Spending Machine," Jidda to State, August 26, 1972, FN Saud 1/1/70, Box 945, SNF, RG 59, NARA. See also materials in Writing—EHB, Saudi Spending Machine, Box 4, Eugene and Jerine Bird Papers, Princeton University Special Collections, Princeton, NJ.

56. *BP Statistical Review of World Energy*, 2018.

57. SAMA Yearly Statistics 2017, http://www.sama.gov.sa/en-US/EconomicReports/Pages/YearlyStatistics.aspx.

58. "The Saudi Oil Income Spending Machine," NARA.

59. Among other problems, the kingdom did not have the telex machines and other communications equipment necessary to monitor its investments overseas. Jidda to State, March 21, 1973, FN SAUD 1/1/70, Box 945, SNF, RG 59, NARA; Jidda to State, March 6, 1973, FN 16 SAUD 1/1/70, Box 945, SNF, RG 59, NARA.

60. For example, the 1973 International Industrial Conference in San Francisco included Rockefeller, Wriston, and Yamani. Milton Moskowitz, "A Business Summit by San Francisco Bay," *New York Times*, September 23, 1973.

61. Clyde H. Farnsworth, "Force on Monetary Scene: Oil Money from Mideast," *New York Times*, March 16, 1973.

62. Testimony by James Akins, *Foreign Policy Implications of the Energy Crisis: Hearings Before the Subcommittee on Foreign Economic Policy*, 92nd Cong. 205 (1972) (statement of James Akins). For more on the politics of "petrodollars," see David Wight, "The Petrodollar Era and Relations Between the United States and the Middle East and North Africa, 1969–1980" (PhD diss., University of California at Irvine, 2014).

63. *U.S. Interests in and Policy Toward the Persian Gulf: Hearings Before the Subcommittee on the Near East*, 92nd Cong. 140 (1972) (State Department prepared statement).

64. George Shultz, speech at American Bankers Association International Monetary Conference, June 6, 1973, Drawer 17, Folder 21, William Simon Papers (WSP), Lafayette College, Easton, PA.

65. PLO memorandum for the Arab Petroleum Conference in Kuwait, *W'A* 1970, Doc. 96.

66. "Naft al-'Arab . . . lil-Ma'raka" (Arab oil . . . to the battle), *Al-Hadaf*, June 10, 1972, Institute for Palestine Studies, Beirut, Lebanon.

67. Tariki, "Al-Naft Silāh fī al-Ma'raka" (Oil, a weapon in the battle), *Naft al-'Arab* (Arab oil), September 1972, from Abdullah Tariki, *'Abd Allāh Al-Ṭurayqī: Al-A'māl al-Kāmila* (Abdullah Tariki: Complete works) (Beirut: Markaz Dirāsāt al-Waḥda al-'Arabīyya, 1999), 753.

68. Resolution of the Kuwaiti National Assembly, January 7, 1973, *W'A 1973*, Doc. 8.

69. *FRUS* 1969–76, Vol. 25, Doc. 41, footnote 3.

70. Jidda to State, March 14, 1973, *FRUS* 1969–76, Vol, E-9, Part 2, Doc. 81.

71. Remarks by Salman, *Al-Bilad*, May 20, 1973, *W'A* 1973, Doc. 196.

72. The U.S. embassy in Saudi Arabia suspected that Saudi funding of the Palestinian movement was also intended to give the kingdom leverage over the PLO and prevent militant operations in Saudi Arabia. Jidda to State, August 10, 1972, FN SAUD-A 1/1/70, Box 945, SNF, RG 59, NARA.

73. Dhahran to State, December 2, 1970, POL 23 SAUD 1/1/70, Box 2586, SNF, RG 59, NARA.

74. Interview with Faisal, *Al-Sayyad*, July 12, 1973, *W'A 1973*, Doc. 261.

75. J. J. Johnson to Michael Ameen et al., May 3, 1973; W. J. McQuinn, "Meeting with King Faisal," May 23, 1973, *MNC Hearings*, Part 7, 504, 507–8.

76. Mobil Oil, "The U.S. Stake in Middle East Peace: I," Advertisement, *New York Times*, June 21, 1973, Box 2.207/E85, ExxonMobil Collection, Briscoe Center, University of Texas at Austin.

77. "Socal Chairman Cites 'Interests' of Israel," *New York Times*, August 8, 1973; "Jewish Veterans Call Oil Boycott," *New York Times*, August 8, 1973.
78. R. W. Powers to J. J. Johnson, August 18, 1973, *MNC Hearings*, Part 7, 512.
79. Jim Hoagland, "Faisal Warns U.S. on Israel," *Washington Post*, July 4, 1973.
80. NBC interview with Faisal, September 3, 1973; "King Faisal Warns U.S. of Oil Cut Off," *New York Times*, August 31, 1973.
81. David Ottaway and Ronald Koven, "Saudis Tie Oil to U.S. Policy on Israel," *Washington Post*, April 19, 1973.
82. Message to Richard Nixon, April 24, 1973; Jidda to State, May 17, 1973, *FRUS 1969–76*, Vol. 36, Docs. 181, 186. The likely delivery of the message via the CIA back-channel was corroborated by the author's interview with William Quandt, May 9, 2019.
83. Memcon, Jeddah, July 26, 1973, *FRUS 1969–76*, Vol. 36, Doc. 189. These messages, too, were probably delivered via the CIA, but the details of transmission are still classified.
84. Memcon, Jeddah, July 26, 1973, *FRUS 1969–76*, Vol. 36, Doc. 189.
85. Interview with Faisal and Saud al-Faisal, *Al-Hawadith*, August 31, 1973, *WA 1973*, Doc. 298.
86. Akins, "The Oil Crisis."
87. See the views of Adelman and Hunter in *Foreign Policy Implications of the Energy Crisis: Hearings Before the Subcommittee on Foreign Economic Policy, House of Representatives, September–October 1972* (Washington, DC: U.S. Government Printing Office, 1972), 152–77.
88. "Shultz Scores Arabs," *New York Times*, September 8, 1973.

5. THE CUTOFF

1. Telcon (Kissinger and Sisco), February 19, 1974, Box 25, Kissinger Telephone Conversation Transcripts (KTCT), RNL.
2. 119 Cong. Rec. 36587 (1973); 119 Cong. Rec. 37520 (1973); 120 Cong. Rec. 1119–21 (1974).
3. This conservative estimate was calculated using data provided by Robert Spiers, the historian for the Eighty-Ninth Airlift Wing of the U.S. Air Force, in an e-mail message to the author on February 26, 2019; and U.S. Energy Information Administration, *Monthly Energy Review*, January 2017, Table 3.7c, https://www.eia.gov/totalenergy/data/monthly/archive/00351701.pdf.
4. Telcon (Kissinger and Ziegler), February 14, 1974, Box 24, KTCT, RNL.
5. U.S. and Israeli officials saw their inability to predict the 1973 war as one of the worst intelligence failures in their history. Matthew T. Penney, "Intelligence and the 1973 Arab-Israeli War," from Central Intelligence Agency (CIA), the Richard Nixon Foundation, and the Richard Nixon Presidential Library and Museum, *President Nixon and the Role of Intelligence in the 1973 Arab-Israeli War*, 2013, https://www.cia.gov/library/publications/international-relations/arab-israeli-war/nixon-arab-isaeli-war.pdf, 7; CIA, "The Performance of the Intelligence Community Before the Arab-Israeli War of October 1973: A Preliminary Post-mortem Report" (December 1973), CIA Freedom of Information Act

Electronic Reading Room (ERR), http://www.foia.cia.gov/sites/default/files/document
_conversions/89801/DOC_0001331429.pdf; William Egan Colby and Peter Forbath,
Honorable Men: My Life in the CIA (New York: Simon and Schuster, 1978), 366; Uri
Bar-Joseph, "Israel's 1973 Intelligence Failure," *Israel Affairs* 6, no. 1 (September 1999):
11–35.

6. Telcon (Kissinger and Nixon), October 7, 1973, Box 22, KTCT, RNL.

7. Quandt to Scowcroft, October 10, 1973, *FRUS 1969–76*, Vol. 36, Doc. 210.

8. "Kalima Al-Riyāḍ: Amrīka wa al-Qaḍīa al-ʿArabīa" (*Al-Riyaḍ*'s View: America and the
Arab Cause), *Al-Riyadh*, October 7, 1973; "Min Ḥadīth al-Nās: Qad Yanfajir al-Burkān!"
(From the talk of the people: The volcano may erupt!), *Al-Riyadh*, October 7, 1973. Kiss-
inger's message is State to Amman and Jidda, October 6, 1973, *FRUS 1969–76*, Vol. 25,
Doc. 102.

9. Turki Abdullah al-Sudairi, "Liqāʾ" (Meeting), *Al-Riyadh*, October 7, 1973; Al-Sudairi,
"Liqāʾ: Mādhā Turīd Amrīkā bi-l-Ḍabṭ?" (Meeting: What does America want, exactly?),
Al-Riyadh, October 10, 1973. Al-Sudairi later served as the editor of the newspaper *Al-
Riyadh* (a semiofficial outlet for government opinion) and became perhaps the most famous and influential journalist in the kingdom, known for his opinion column "Liqāʾ"
that ran for more than four decades. Miriam al-Jaber, "Ṣuwar Turkī al-Sudayrī . . . Al-
Yatīm aladhī Aṣbḥa Malik al-Ṣiḥāfa" (Pictures of Turki al-Sudairi . . . orphan who became king of the press), *Al-Arabiya*, May 14, 2017, https://www.alarabiya.net/ar/saudi
-today/2017/05/14/صور-تركي-السديري-اليتيم-الذي-أصبح-ملك-الصحافة; "Turki al-Sudairi.. Malik al-Ṣiḥāfa
al-Saʿūdīa" (Turki al-Sudairi, king of the Saudi press), *Al-Jazeera*, May 14, 2017, https://
www.aljazeera.net/encyclopedia/icons/2017/5/14/الصحافة-ملك-السديري-تركي-السعودية.

10. "Oil Contingency Paper," October 7, 1973, CIA ERR, https://www.cia.gov/library
/readingroom/docs/1973-10-07B.pdf; Washington Special Action Group (WSAG) minutes, October 6, 1973, *FRUS 1969–76*, Vol. 25, Doc. 103; Dhahran to State, 1973DHAH-
RAN00794, October 8, 1973, Access to Archival Databases (AAD), National Archives
and Records Administration, aad.archives.gov; Kuwait to State, October 19, 1973, Kuwait, Vol. 1—Jan. 20, 1969–June 30, 1974 (1 of 2), Box 620, NSC Files, Country Files—
Middle East, RNL; Quandt and Stukel to Kissinger, October 7, 1973, WSAG Meeting
10/7/73, Box H-093, WSAG Meetings, RNL.

11. Jidda to State, 1973JIDDA04374, October 9, 1973, AAD.

12. WSAG minutes, October 6, 1973, and October 7, 1973, *FRUS 1969–1976*, Vol. 25, Docs.
103, 121.

13. Jamieson, Warner, Granville, and Miller to Nixon, October 12, 1973, *FRUS 1969–76*, Vol.
36, Doc. 212.

14. Telcon (Kissinger and Haig), October 13, 1973, Box 23, KTCT, RNL; WSAG minutes,
October 14 and 17, 1973, *FRUS 1969–76*, Vol. 36, Docs. 214, 219.

15. Telcon (Kissinger and Haig), October 7, 1973, Box 22, KTCT, RNL.

16. 119 Cong. Rec. 33291, 33717, 33837, 34209, 34424 (1973).

17. Telcon (Kissinger and Church), October 9, 1973, Box 22, KTCT, RNL; telcon (Kissinger
and Humphrey), October 12, 1973, Box 23, KTCT, RNL; telcon (Kissinger and Dinitz),
October 13, 1973, Box 23, KTCT, RNL.

18. William B. Quandt, *Peace Process: American Diplomacy and the Arab-Israeli Conflict Since 1967*, 3rd ed. (Washington, DC: Brookings Institution Press, 2005), 111.

19. Telcon (Nixon and Kissinger), October 14, 1973, Box 23, KTCT, RNL; telcon (Kissinger and Schlesinger), October 14, 1973, Box 23, KTCT, RNL.

20. Memcon, October 17, 1973, WSAG Meeting: Middle East, 10/17/73 (1 of 2), Box H-092, WSAG Meetings, RNL.

21. Telcon (Kissinger and Cromer), October 13, 1973, Box 23, KTCT, RNL.

22. WSAG meeting, October 17, 1973, *FRUS* 1969–76, Vol. 36, Doc. 219.

23. WSAG meeting October 16, 1973, *FRUS* 1969–76, Vol. 36, Doc. 217.

24. WSAG meeting, October 15, 1973, *FRUS* 1969–76, Vol. 36, Doc. 215.

25. Fuel consumption figures for Nickel Grass were made available to the author from the classified U.S. Air Force study *History, Military Airlift Command*, July 1, 1973–June 1974, Vol. 1, 153, by e-mail from Jeffrey Michalke, U.S. Air Force Air Mobility Command, February 25, 2019.

26. Author's telephone interview with William Quandt, March 14, 2019.

27. "Egyptian Envoy Still Touring Gulf States," *Kuwait Daily News*, October 14, 1973; for the details of Marei's proposals, see Mohamed Heikal, *The Road to Ramadan* (New York: Quadrangle/New York Times Book Co., 1975), 272.

28. "Force American Hand," *Kuwait Daily News*, October 14, 1973.

29. *MNC Hearings*, Part 5, 217.

30. Memorandum from Chairmen of Exxon, Mobil, Texaco, and Standard Oil Company of California, October 12, 1973, *FRUS* 1969–76, Vol. 36, Doc. 212.

31. State staff meeting, October 18, 1973, *FRUS* 1969–76, Vol. 36, Doc. 220.

32. Editorial note, *FRUS* 1969–76, Vol. 36, Doc. 216.

33. Editorial note, *FRUS* 1969–76, Vol. 36, Doc. 216.

34. Memcon, October 17, 1973, *FRUS* 1969–76, Vol. 25, Doc. 195; author's interview with Quandt, March 14, 2019. For Saudi reporting on Saqqaf's visit to the United States, see *Al-Riyadh*, October 20, 1973.

35. Telcon (Kissinger and Scowcroft), October 18, 1973, *FRUS* 1969–76, Vol. 25, Doc. 205; WSAG Meeting, October 17, 1973, Folder "WSAG Meeting: Middle East, October 2, 1973 to July 22, 1974 (2 of 3)," Box H-117, WSAG Meetings, RNL.

36. Telcon (Kissinger and Ziegler), October 18, 1973, Box 23, KTCT, RNL.

37. PLO statement, October 18, 1973, *WA* 1973, Doc. 329.

38. "Juhūd Saʿūdīa li Tʿadīl al-Mawqif al-Āmrīkī" (Saudi efforts to amend the American position), *Al-Riyadh*, October 20, 1973.

39. Embassy in Saudi Arabia Cable 4663 to State Department, October 23, 1973, National Security Archive Electronic Briefing Book, "The October War and U.S. Policy," https://nsarchive2.gwu.edu/NSAEBB/NSAEBB98/.

40. "Liqāʾ: Lā Bitrūl li Amrīkā" (Meeting: No oil for America), *Al-Riyadh*, October 21, 1973.

41. Robert Stobaugh, "The Oil Companies in the Crisis," in *The Oil Crisis*, ed. Raymond Vernon (New York: W. W. Norton, 1976), 179–202.

42. For more on the price controls, see Richard H. K. Vietor, *Energy Policy in America Since 1945: A Study of Business-Government Relations* (Cambridge: Cambridge University Press,

1984), chap. 9. For the political debate over the price controls, see Meg Jacobs, *Panic at the Pump: The Energy Crisis and the Transformation of American Politics in the 1970s* (New York: Hill and Wang, 2016).

43. Love to Nixon, "U.S. Domestic Response to Arab Oil Boycott," November 1, 1973, CM—Commodities, 29–35 (1971–1974), Box 4, White House Central Files, Subject Files: Confidential Files, RNL.

44. WSAG minutes, November 6, 1973, *FRUS 1969–76*, Vol. 36, Doc. 236.

45. Author's interview with Brent Scowcroft, Washington, DC, July 29, 2009.

46. Secretary of State's Staff Meeting, October 26, 1973, *FRUS 1969–76*, Vol. 36, Doc. 229.

47. Memcon, October 24, 1973, Box 2, National Security Advisor Memoranda of Conversation (NSAMC), Gerald Ford Library (GFL). Schlesinger also discussed the possibility of invasion with British officials, contacts that were reported in the press three decades later. See Lizette Alvarez, "Britain Says U.S. Planned to Seize Oil in '73 Crisis," *New York Times*, January 2, 2004.

48. Telcon (Kissinger and Haig), October 27, 1973, Box 23, KTCT, RNL.

49. Memcons, November 29, 1973, Box 2, NSAMC, GFL. Kissinger's and Schlesinger's comments are from two separate meetings on that date. For more on the U.S. invasion plans, see editorial note, *FRUS 1969–1976*, Vol. 36, Doc. 244; Andrew Scott Cooper, *The Oil Kings: How the U.S., Iran, and Saudi Arabia Changed the Balance of Power in the Middle East* (New York: Simon and Schuster, 2011), 128–34. Schlesinger seems to have had Abu Dhabi in mind as an invasion target, although some of the U.S. contingency planning during this period looked at Saudi Arabia instead.

50. Saunders to Kissinger, November 30, 1973, *FRUS 1969–76*, Vol. 36, Doc. 255.

51. The U.S. Naval Presence in Bahrain," July 15, 1973, Trucial States: Abu Dhabi, Bahrain, Oman, Qatar, Muscat 1969–1974, Box 632, NSC Files, Country Files—Middle East, RNL.

52. Memcon, January 22, 1974, Box 3, NSAMC, GFL.

53. Memcon, November 29, 1973, Box 2, NSAMC, GFL. For the later expansion of the U.S. military presence in the Gulf, see chapter 8.

54. Giuliano Garavini, *The Rise and Fall of OPEC in the Twentieth Century* (Oxford: Oxford University Press, 2019), 221–28; Tehran to State, December 23, 1973, 1973TEHRAN09031, AAD.

55. On U.S. unhappiness with the Shah's role in raising prices, see *FRUS 1969–76*, Vol. 27, Doc. 49. On the Shah's comments, see "Oil Price Doubled by Big Producers on Persian Gulf," *New York Times*, December 24, 1973. On Saqqaf's comments, see Jidda to State, December 30, 1973, *FRUS 1969–76*, Vol. 36, Doc. 276. For the Saudi-Iranian debate over oil prices, see Garavini, *The Rise and Fall of OPEC in the Twentieth Century*, 226–28; Cooper, *The Oil Kings*.

56. Secretary of State's staff meetings, October 24 and 26, 1973, *FRUS 1969–76*, Vol. 36, Docs. 226, 299.

57. Telcon (Nixon and Kissinger), February 18, 1974, Box 25, KTCT, RNL.

58. Author's interview with Donald Rumsfeld, Washington, DC, September 1, 2010.

59. Lodal and Sonnenfeldt to Kissinger, December 4, 1973, *FRUS* 1969–76, Vol. 36, Doc. 261; Memcon, February 10, 1974, *FRUS* 1969–76, Vol. 36, Doc. 315; telcon (Kissinger and Scowcroft), February 12, 1974, *FRUS* 1969–76, Vol. 36, Doc. 321. For more on Kissinger's strategy of using the oil crisis to bind the West together under U.S. leadership, see Daniel J. Sargent, *A Superpower Transformed: The Remaking of American Foreign Relations in the 1970s* (Oxford: Oxford University Press, 2014), 182–97.

60. For Kissinger's "step-by-step" diplomacy as a strategy for limiting pressure on Israel and delaying a more comprehensive settlement, see Salim Yaqub, *Imperfect Strangers: Americans, Arabs, and U.S.–Middle East Relations in the 1970s* (Ithaca, NY: Cornell University Press, 2016), 145–82.

61. Jidda to State, November 1, 1973 and November 26, 1973, Saudi Arabia, 5–12/73 (2 of 4), Box 630, NSC Country Files, RNL. Saqqaf's remarks foreshadowed the later Saudi-Egyptian split over the 1978 Camp David Accords, when Egypt broke with the rest of the world to make peace with Israel.

62. Faisal interview with *Al-Anwar*, November 22, 1973, *WA* 1973, Doc. 370.

63. For the evolving Saudi position on the embargo through the beginning of February 1974, see Saunders to Kissinger, February 6, 1974, Saudi Arabia, 1–4/74 (1 of 2), Box 631, NSC Country Files, RNL.

64. Faisal to Nixon, December 25, 1973, Saudi Arabia, 5–12/73 (4 of 4), Box 630, NSC Country Files, RNL.

65. Memcon (Kissinger and Schlesinger), November 29, 1973, Box 2, NSAMC, GFL.

66. Mendolia to Lawson, November 30, 1973, *FRUS* 1969–76, Vol. 37, Doc. 249, footnote 2.

67. Jidda to State, December 30, 1973; Jidda to State, January 21, 1974; Jidda to State, February 11, 1974; *FRUS* 1969–76, Vol. 36, Docs. 276, 283, 317; Jidda to State, January 21, 1974, Saudi Arabia, 1–4/74 (2 of 2), Box 631, NSC Country Files, RNL.

68. Jidda to State, April 20, 1974, Saudi Arabia 1/74–4/74 (1 of 2), Box 631, NSC Country Files, RNL. The shipment of Saudi oil to the U.S. military came to light years later. Naila Al-Sowayel, the daughter of the former Saudi ambassador, disclosed it in "An Historical Analysis of Saudi Arabia's Foreign Policy in Time of Crisis: The October 1973 War and the Arab Oil Embargo" (PhD diss., Georgetown University, 1991). Frank Jungers also discussed it in his interview on the PBS *Frontline* episode "House of Saud" (2005), and in author's telephone interview on May 31, 2011.

69. The U.S. press compared Yamani to Kissinger as global celebrities. Rüdiger Graf, *Oil and Sovereignty: Petro-Knowledge and Energy Policy in the United States*, trans. Alex Skinner (Berlin: Berghahn Books, 2018), 108.

70. Steffen Hertog, *Princes, Brokers, and Bureaucrats: Oil and the State in Saudi Arabia* (Ithaca, NY: Cornell University Press, 2010), 93.

71. Jidda to State, March 25, 1974, Saudi Arabia 1/74–4/74 (1 of 2), Box 631, NSC Country Files, RNL.

72. Jidda to State, February 2, 1974, Saudi Arabia 1/74–4/74 (2 of 2), Box 631, NSC Country Files, RNL.

73. Fahd interview with *Al-Anwar*, May 21, 1977, *WA* 1977, Doc. 163.

74. Jidda to State, January 21, 1974, *FRUS* 1969–76, Vol. 36, Doc. 284. See also State to Jidda, January 21, 1974, and Jidda to State, January 23, 1974, *FRUS* 1969–76, Vol. 36, Docs. 285, 290; Jidda to State, February 2, 1974, Saudi Arabia 1/74-4/74 (2 of 2), Box 631, NSC Country Files, RNL.

75. Jidda to State, December 27, 1973, Saudi Arabia, 5–12/73 (1 of 4), Box 630, NSC Country Files, RNL.

76. Jidda to State, March 25, 1974, Saudi Arabia 1/74-4/74 (1 of 2), Box 631, NSC Country Files, RNL.

77. Nixon, "White House Statement About House Action Overriding the War Powers Resolution Veto," November 7, 1973, APP; Nixon, "Address to the Nation About Policies to Deal with the Energy Shortages," November 7, 1973, APP.

78. Nixon, "Address to the Nation About Policies to Deal with the Energy Shortages," APP; Nixon, "Special Message to the Congress Proposing Emergency Energy Legislation," November 8, 1973, APP.

79. Energy Meeting with State and Local Elected Officials, November 7, 1973, President's Office Files, Box 93, RNL.

80. Memcon, May 28, 1974, Box 4, NSAMC, GFL.

81. Nixon, special message to the Congress, November 8, 1973, APP; veto of the Energy Emergency Bill, March 6, 1974, APP; Tyler Priest, "Shifting Sands: The 1973 Oil Shock and the Expansion of Non-OPEC Supply," in *Oil Shock: The 1973 Crisis and Its Economic Legacy*, ed. Elisabetta Bini, Giuliano Garavini, and Federico Romero (London: I. B. Tauris, 2016), 123.

82. On the cultural resonance of "energy independence," see Sebastian Herbstreuth, *Oil and American Identity: A Culture of Dependency and U.S. Foreign Policy* (London: I. B. Tauris, 2016); Melani McAlister, *Epic Encounters: Culture, Media, and U.S. Interests in the Middle East Since 1945* (Berkeley: University of California Press, 2005), 125–54; Natasha Zaretsky, *No Direction Home: The American Family and the Fear of National Decline, 1968–1980* (Chapel Hill: University of North Carolina Press, 2007), 71–104. On the politics of energy independence as a vital component of national sovereignty, see Graf, *Oil and Sovereignty*.

83. Nixon, "Address to the Nation," November 7, 1973, APP; Henry Kissinger, *Years of Upheaval* (Boston: Little, Brown, 1982), 873–74; Robert Dallek, *Nixon and Kissinger: Partners in Power* (New York: HarperCollins, 2007), 537.

84. Memcon, December 15, 1973, E 5 SAUD 1/1/70, Box 779, SNF, RG 59, NARA. Years later, Turki still remembered his dissatisfaction with Kissinger's answer, which "fuzzed" the basic question at stake: whether the United States would follow through on its promises to compel Israeli withdrawal from the occupied territories. Author's interview with Turki al-Faisal, Riyadh, January 8, 2011.

85. Memcon, December 14, 1973; Jidda to State, December 30, 1973; memcon, February 7, 1974, *FRUS* 1969–76, Vol. 36, Docs. 267, 276, 309.

86. Adham and Saud al-Faisal to Kissinger, January 22, 1974; editorial note, *FRUS* 1969–76, Vol. 36, Docs. 287, 292; telcon (Kissinger and Scowcroft), January 30, 1974, Box 24, KTCT, RNL.

87. Akins to Kissinger, February 5, 1974, *FRUS* 1969–76, Vol. 36, Doc. 303; Kissinger, *Years of Upheaval*, 893.

88. Memcons, March 2, 1974, *FRUS* 1969–76, Vol. 36, Docs. 331–332.

89. *Al-Ra'i al-Am*, March 10 and March 19, 1974.

90. Saqqaf's statement is from *Al-Riyadh*, March 17, 1974; the news of the embargo's end is from *Al-Riyadh*, March 19, 1974; Sultan's visit to Egypt was covered in *Al-Riyadh*, March 20, 1974. For other statements by Sultan on his trip to Egypt, see *WA* 1974, Docs. 90–91. For Arafat's visit and the Saudi press treatment of the end of the embargo, see Jidda to State, March 19, 1974, 1974JIDDA01361; Jidda to State, March 21, 1974, 1974JIDDA01400, AAD.

91. Jidda to State, March 11, 1974, 1974JIDDA01192, AAD.

92. Scowcroft and Cooper to Kissinger, March 1, 1974, *FRUS* 1969–76, Vol. 36, Doc. 330.

6. UNMOORED

1. The disarray at the Jeddah port was described by Robert Logan, who served as marine superintendent and later deputy harbor master at the port, in emails to the author, September 6–8, 2019.

2. Jidda to State, August 24, 1975, 1975JIDDA05883, AAD.

3. Author's telephone interviews with former Aramco employees Thomas Anderson, May 11, 2011, and Jennifer Simpson, April 14, 2011.

4. Author's telephone interview with Soliman Solaim, Riyadh, February 26, 2011; Logan emails.

5. Saudi Arabian Monetary Agency (SAMA) 43rd Annual Report (1428AH/2007CE) (Riyadh: SAMA, 2007), 332–33. Holding the value of the riyal constant at its 1999 level, Saudi GDP went from 148.039 billion riyals in 1970 to 516.337 billion riyals in 1980.

6. Saudi Ministry of Economy and Planning, *Achievements of the Development Plans: Facts and Figures*, 27th Issue, 1390–1431 AH (1970–2010) (Riyadh: Ministry of Economy and Planning, 2010).

7. UN Department of Economic and Social Affairs, *World Population Prospects*, 2019 revision, https://population.un.org/wpp/.

8. Interview with Fahd, *Al-Riyadh*, July 14, 1974.

9. "Takhfīḍ Jadīd fī As'ār al-Binzīn" (New reduction in gasoline prices), *Al-Riyadh*, September 15, 1974.

10. Interview with Fahd, *Al-Anwar*, October 25, 1974, *WA* 1974, Doc. 305. Fahd's remark was a remarkably forthright statement of the idea that oil wealth lets autocratic governments ignore demands for democratization. Political scientist Michael Ross has called this phenomenon the "rentier effect," arguing that "resource-rich governments use low tax rates and patronage to relieve pressures for greater accountability." Michael L. Ross, "Does Oil Hinder Democracy?," *World Politics* 53, no. 3 (2001): 325–61.

11. Steffen Hertog, *Princes, Brokers, and Bureaucrats: Oil and the State in Saudi Arabia* (Ithaca, NY: Cornell University Press, 2010), 84–136; Kiren Aziz Chaudhry, *The Price of*

Wealth: Economies and Institutions in the Middle East (Ithaca, NY: Cornell University Press, 1997), 139–92.

12. Author's telephone interview with Solaim.

13. Inflation data from the World Bank, https://data.worldbank.org/indicator/FP.CPI .TOTL?locations=SA. Cartoons in *Al-Riyadh*, January 19, 1974; August 15, 1974; "Kul Shi': Ramadan" (Everything: Ramadan), *Al-Riyadh*, September 22, 1974. For more on inflation, including the rapid increase in prices every year during the Ramadan holiday, see policy statement for Third Five Year Plan, Saudi Arabia Plan (2), Box 11, AJMP.

14. "Kul Shi': Ramadan" (Everything: Ramadan).

15. "The People's Concerns in an Open Letter to HH the Minister of Housing," *Al-Riyadh*, August 25, 1976; Muhammad Humaydah, "The Housing Problem in Medina and Proposals for Its Solution," *Al-Madinah*, May 30, 1975; "New Measures to Combat Inflation," *Al-Madinah*, June 17, 1976, U.S. Joint Publications Research Service.

16. Jidda to State, October 12, 1975, 1975JIDDA06888, AAD.

17. Ali Al-Naimi, *Out of the Desert: My Journey from Nomadic Bedouin to the Heart of Global Oil* (London: Penguin, 2016).

18. Pascal Menoret, "The Suburbanization of Islamic Activism in Saudi Arabia," *City and Society* 29, no. 1 (2017): 168–69.

19. Chaudhry, *The Price of Wealth*, 140–41, 156–63.

20. For the growth of Riyadh's slums in the 1970s, see Pascal Menoret, *Joyriding in Riyadh: Oil, Urbanism, and Road Revolt* (Cambridge: Cambridge University Press, 2014), 78, 87, 113. For the persistence of Saudi neighborhoods without electricity or clean water even in the early twenty-first century, see Rosie Bsheer, "Poverty in the Oil Kingdom: An Introduction," *Jadaliyya*, September 30, 2010, http://www.jadaliyya.com/Details/23527.

21. For an overview of Khashoggi's career in the mid-1970s, see Anthony Sampson, "Khashoggi—The 'Bridge' to Arab Deals," *New York Times*, July 3, 1977.

22. Jidda to State, April 2, 1975, To SECSTATE—NODIS (6); Box 29, Presidential Country Files for the Middle East and South Asia (PCF), GFL; State to Jidda, May 30, 1975, From SECSTATE—NODIS (3), Box 29, PCF, GFL; Juan de Onis, "Faisal's Killer Is Put to Death," *New York Times*, June 19, 1975.

23. State to Jidda, May 15, 1975, From SECSTATE—NODIS (3), PCF, GFL; "Saudi Prince's Girlfriend Denies That She Is Jewish," *New York Times*, April 10, 1975.

24. On U.S. perceptions that Fahd was a weaker leader than Faisal, see Kissinger's comments in memcon, March 25, 1975, Box 29, PCF, GFL. For Fahd's inability to exercise tight control over the royal family and other Saudi interest groups, see also Hertog, *Princes, Brokers, and Bureaucrats*, 91, 126.

25. Jidda to State, October 12, 1975, 1975JIDDA06888, AAD.

26. Planning for a new program of U.S.-Saudi cooperation was ordered in National Security Study Memorandum 198, March 12, 1974, RNL, https://www.nixonlibrary.gov/sites /default/files/virtuallibrary/documents/nssm/nssm_198.pdf. On the initial negotiations, see memorandum for Nixon, "Your Meeting with Prince Fahd of Saudi Arabia," June 5, 1974; Kissinger to Nixon, "Meeting with Saudi Prince Fahd," June 6, 1974; CO 128 Saudi Arabia (1971–1974), Box 8, WHCF, Subject Files: Confidential Files, RNL.

27. Bonnie Pounds, "The U.S.–Saudi Arabian Joint Commission: A Model for Bilateral Economic Cooperation," *American-Arab Affairs* 7 (Winter 1983–84): 60–68; U.S. General Accounting Office, *The U.S.–Saudi Arabian Joint Commission on Economic Cooperation: Report by the Comptroller General of the United States* (Washington, DC: U.S. General Accounting Office, 1979); Thomas Lippman, "Cooperation Under the Radar: The US–Saudi Arabian Joint Commission for Economic Cooperation (JECOR)," Middle East Institute, October 1, 2009, https://www.mei.edu/publications/cooperation-under-radar -us-saudi-arabian-joint-commission-economic-cooperation-jecor.

28. Fahd interview with *Al-Anwar*, October 25, 1974, *WA* 1974, Doc. 305.

29. Fahd interview with *Al-Anwar*, May 21, 1977, *WA* 1977, Doc. 163.

30. State to Tel Aviv, June 7, 1974, President's Middle East Trip, June 10–19, Folder 1, Box 1189, Saunders Files—Middle East Negotiations Files, NSC Files, RNL.

31. Stephen D. Hayes, "Joint Economic Commissions as Instruments of US Foreign Policy in the Middle East," *Middle East Journal* 31, no. 1 (Winter 1977): 16–30.

32. Memcon, September 10, 1974, Box 5, NSAMC, GFL.

33. Memcon, August 7, 1975, *FRUS* 1969–76, Vol. 37, Doc. 75. For other cynical U.S. views of JECOR as a source of leverage over Saudi Arabia and a way to use up Saudi revenues, see the comments of William Clements, deputy secretary of defense, in memcon, March 29, 1974, *FRUS* 1969–76, Vol. 36, Doc. 345, and Kissinger's comments in memcons, August 13, 1974 and August 17, 1974, *FRUS* 1969–76, Vol. 37, Docs. 1, 2.

34. Jidda to State, March 10, 1975, Saudi Arabia—State Department Telegrams, to SECSSTATE—EXDIS (2), Box 29, PCF, GFL.

35. David E. Spiro, *The Hidden Hand of American Hegemony: Petrodollar Recycling and International Markets* (Ithaca, NY: Cornell University Press, 1999), 99.

36. James Larocco interview, January 5, 2011, ADST, 45–47.

37. *The U.S.-Saudi Arabian Joint Commission on Economic Cooperation*, 14, 16.

38. Jack Schick to Cecil Thompson, May 20, 1976, Saudi Arabia (4), Box 21, NSC Operations Staff for Middle East and South Asian Affairs, Country File (Mirror), GFL.

39. David K. Harbinson, "The US–Saudi Arabian Joint Commission on Economic Cooperation: A Critical Appraisal," *Middle East Journal* 44, no. 2 (Spring 1990): 271–72.

40. James E. Akins, "The Oil Crisis: This Time the Wolf Is Here," *Foreign Affairs* 51, no. 3 (1973): 462–90.

41. Memcons, August 13, 1974; June 10, 1975; *FRUS* 1969–76, Vol. 37, Docs. 1, 65.

42. The NIEO has attracted growing interest from scholars in recent years. See, for example, Adom Getachew, *Worldmaking After Empire: The Rise and Fall of Self-Determination* (Princeton, NJ: Princeton University Press, 2019), 142–75; Vanessa Ogle, "State Rights Against Private Capital: The 'New International Economic Order' and the Struggle Over Aid, Trade, and Foreign Investment, 1962–1981," *Humanity: An International Journal of Human Rights, Humanitarianism, and Development* 5, no. 2 (2014): 211–34; Nils Gilman and Samuel Moyn, eds., "Special Issue: Toward a History of the New International Economic Order," *Humanity* 6, no. 1 (2015).

43. "Solemn Declaration" of the Conference of the Sovereigns and Heads of State of the OPEC Member Countries, Algiers, March 4–6, 1975, https://www.opec.org/opec_web /en/publications/347.htm.

44. The reference to the OPEC-NIEO "unholy alliance" was coined by German chancellor Helmut Schmidt at the November 1975 Rambouillet economic summit and approvingly quoted by Kissinger. Memcon, November 15–17, 1975, Box 16, NSAMC, GFL. Kissinger's wish to "divide these countries" is from memcon, May 26, 1975, *FRUS 1969–76*, Vol. 31, Doc. 294.

45. On the U.S. response to the NIEO and OPEC, see Daniel J. Sargent, "North/South: The United States Responds to the New International Economic Order," *Humanity* 6, no. 1 (2015): 201–16; Victor McFarland, "The New International Economic Order, Interdependence, and Globalization," *Humanity* 6, no. 1 (2015): 217–33; Christopher R. W. Dietrich, "Oil Power and Economic Theologies: The United States and the Third World in the Wake of the Energy Crisis," *Diplomatic History* 40, no. 3 (June 2016): 500–529.

46. Memcon, August 17, 1974, Box 5, NSAMC, GFL; memcon, March 13, 1976, *FRUS 1969–76*, Vol. 37, Doc. 95.

47. Memcon, November 16, 1974, Box 7, NSAMC, GFL. The best treatment of Kissinger's economic diplomacy during the mid-1970s is Daniel J. Sargent, *A Superpower Transformed: The Remaking of American Foreign Relations in the 1970s* (Oxford: Oxford University Press, 2014), 151–64, 175–97.

48. Faisal speech in Egypt, November 8, 1974; Faisal interview with Al-Hayat, October 12, 1974, *WA 1974*, Docs. 238, 294; Khalid statement, April 4, 1975, *WA 1974*, Doc. 120.

49. Memcon, June 15, 1974, DNSAMC, GFL.

50. Memcon, August 1, 1974, *FRUS 1969–76*, Vol. 21, Doc. 94.

51. On Kissinger's strategy of step-by-step diplomacy that avoided a final settlement and full Israeli withdrawal, see Salim Yaqub, *Imperfect Strangers: Americans, Arabs, and U.S.–Middle East Relations in the 1970s* (Ithaca, NY: Cornell University Press, 2016), 145–82.

52. Memcon, August 23, 1974, Box 5, NSAMC, GFL.

53. Memcon, August 13, 1974, *FRUS 1969–76*, Vol. 37, Doc. 1; memcon, September 6, 1974, Box 5, NSAMC, GFL; memcon, March 28, 1975, Box 1, NSC Meeting File, GFL.

54. Memcon, September 6, 1974, Box 5, NSAMC, GFL; memcon, December 7, 1974, Box 7, NSAMC, GFL; WSAG minutes, *FRUS 1969–76*, Vol. 37, Doc. 32.

55. For an assessment of the feasibility of such an operation, see Congressional Research Service, *Oil Fields as Military Objectives: A Feasibility Study* (Washington, DC: U.S. Government Printing Office, 1975).

56. Kissinger's December 23, 1974 interview with *Business Week* was published in the Department of State *Bulletin*, January 27, 1975. Schlesinger's comments were delivered in a January 14, 1975, press briefing. For an overview of the statements and the controversy surrounding them, see Bernard Gwertzman, "U.S. Avoiding Retraction of Threat of Force," *New York Times*, January 20, 1975.

57. Two of the most prominent were Robert Tucker, "Oil: The Issue of American Intervention," *Commentary* 59, no. 1 (1975): 21–31; and Miles Ignotus, "Seizing Arab Oil," *Harper's* 250, no. 1498 (March 1975): 45. Ignotus was the pseudonym of Edward Luttwak, a Pentagon analyst, although the article reportedly incorporated ideas from other defense analysts and Pentagon officials. Andrew Higgins, "In Quest for Energy Security, U.S. Makes New Bet: On Democracy," *Wall Street Journal*, February 4, 2004.

58. Jidda to State, January 5, 1975, Box 29, To SECSTATE—EXDIS (1), PCF, GFL; Jidda to State, January 7, 13, and 20, 1975, To SECSTATE—NODIS (3), Box 29, PCF, GFL; memcon, November 15–17, 1975, Box 16, NSAMC, GFL. See also editorial note, *FRUS 1969–76*, Vol. 37, Doc. 30; Yaqub, *Imperfect Strangers*, 192–94.

59. Jidda to State, January 4, 1975, To SECSTATE—EXDIS (1), Box 29, PCF, GFL; Akins to State, April 13, 1975; paper prepared in the Department of the Navy, n.d., *FRUS 1969–76*, Vol. 37, Docs. 52, 57; interview with Hume Horan, November 3, 2000, ADST, 82–84; interview with Charles Cecil, September 7, 2006, ADST, 79–80, 82–83.

60. Memcon, June 15, 1974, DNSAMC, GFL.

61. Memcon, June 15, 1974, GFL; Eugene Bird interview, January 6, 1994, ADST; Horan interview, ADST, 83; Robert D. Kaplan, *Arabists: The Romance of an American Elite* (New York: Free Press, 1995), 171–77. When I met Akins more than thirty years after the events in question, he was still furious at Kissinger. His respect for Faisal and Saudi Arabia was also obvious; Akins spoke admiringly of the former king, and his home was decorated with Saudi memorabilia. A portrait of Faisal, inscribed to Akins in Arabic, hung prominently on the wall. Author's interview with James Akins, Mitchellville, MD, June 30, 2009.

62. Ford reaffirmed his support for Project Independence in his speech to the Ninth World Energy Conference in Detroit, MI, September 23, 1974, APP. His advisers set energy independence goals for the coming decades at a December 14–15, 1974, meeting at Camp David, *FRUS 1969–76*, Vol. 37, Doc. 27, footnote 4.

63. Memcon, August 3, 1974, NSAMC, Box 4, GFL.

64. Memcon, August 12, 1974, NSAMC, Box 4, GFL; and memcon, September 17, 1974, NSAMC, Box 5, GFL.

65. For the proposed energy legislation, see Ford's letter to the Speaker of the House and president of the Senate, January 30, 1975, APP; for his speech promoting the plan, see Ford, Address Before the House Chamber of Commerce Conference on Energy and the Economy, Houston, TX, February 10, 1975, APP. For an overview of Ford's energy policies in 1974–1975, see "Energy and Environment 1974: Overview," "Energy and Environment 1974: Overview," *CQ Almanac 1974*, 30th ed. (Washington, DC: Congressional Quarterly, 1975), 723–26. For Ford's energy policy, see Yanek Mieczkowski, *Gerald Ford and the Challenges of the 1970s* (Lexington: University Press of Kentucky, 2005), 197–270; Meg Jacobs, *Panic at the Pump: The Energy Crisis and the Transformation of American Politics in the 1970s* (New York: Hill and Wang, 2016), 123–59.

66. Thomas O'Toole, "10 Governors Can't Budge Ford on Oil," *Washington Post*, January 24, 1975; Mieczkowski, *Gerald Ford and the Challenges of the 1970s*, 232–33.

67. Ford, Address to the Nation on Energy Programs, May 27, 1975; Veto of a Petroleum Price Review Bill, July 21, 1975, APP.

68. "Energy and Environment, 1975 Overview," *CQ Almanac 1975*, 31st ed. (Washington, DC: Congressional Quarterly, 1976), 173–76.

69. "Analysis of the Energy Policy and Conservation Act" by the American Petroleum Institute, undated, in material sent to John Marsh by Frank Ikard of the API, December 3, 1975, Energy—Energy Policy and Conservation Act: General 9/75–12/75, Box 13, John

Marsh Files, GFL; Republican Policy Committee, U.S. House of Representatives, State-ment #27: "S.622—Energy Bill: Bad Policy," December 11, 1975, Energy, Box H40, Ford Committee Records, GFL.

70. Glen Schleede to Jim Cannon, November 26, 1975, Energy—Energy Policy and Con-servation Act: General 9/75–12/75, Box 13, John Marsh Files, GFL.

71. Meeting with Republican congressional leadership, November 13, 1975, Congressional Leadership Meetings: GOP, 11/13/75, Box 2, Robert Wolthuis Files, GFL; meeting with Republican congressional leadership, December 10, 1975, Congressional Leadership Meetings: GOP, 12/10/75, Box 2, Robert Wolthuis Files, GFL.

72. Eric Zausner to Marsh, December 5, 1975, Energy—Energy Policy and Conservation Act: General 9/75–12/75, Box 13, John Marsh Files, GFL; Scowcroft to Ford, December 10, 1975, *FRUS* 1968–76, Vol. 37, Doc. 89.

73. Bo Callaway to Stu Spencer, Peter Kaye, and Fred Slight, January 29, 1976, Energy, Box H40, Ford Committee Records, GFL.

74. Joseph Lelyveld, "Ford's TV Ads on Superiority of U.S. Hint Gains by Reagan," *New York Times*, April 30, 1976.

75. "Reagan's Startling Texas Landslide," *Time*, May 10, 1976; Sean P. Cunningham, "The 1976 GOP Primary: Ford, Reagan, and the Battle That Transformed Political Campaigns in Texas," *East Texas Historical Journal* 41, no. 2 (October 2003): 18. Cunningham notes that anger at Ford's oil policy was only one factor behind Reagan's victory in Texas; others included Reagan's social conservatism and perceived strength on national defense.

76. The NSC concluded that if Ford had immediately lifted all price controls, U.S. imports would still be eight million barrels per day (mbd) after three years, as opposed to 9 mbd with the price controls still in place. Scowcroft to Ford, December 10, 1975, *FRUS*, 1969–77, Vol. 37, Doc. 89.

77. Robert Hormats to Brent Scowcroft, July 26, 1967, NSSM 237 and US Energy Policy (1), Box 41, Institutional Files—NSSMs, GFL.

78. Brent Scowcroft to Gerald Ford, "Saudi Arabia," June 7, 1976. The attached study by the NSC staff is "The Role of Saudi Arabia in the Middle East, OPEC and the Interna-tional Economy," June 1, 1976, Saudi Arabia (5), Country File (Mirror) Box 21, NSC Op-erations Staff for Middle East and South Asian Affairs, GFL.

79. Memcon, July 9, 1976, DNSAMC, GFL.

80. Mansouri noted, though, that his comments did not represent the official position of the Saudi government. Jidda to State, July 11, 1976, Saudi Arabia (5), Box 21, NSC Opera-tions Staff for Middle East and South Asian Affairs, Country File (Mirror), GFL. On the Lebanese Civil War as the beginning of a new era of violent conflict in the Middle East, often along sectarian lines, see Paul Thomas Chamberlin, *The Cold War's Killing Fields: Rethinking the Long Peace* (Harper, New York, 2018), 359–555.

81. CIA, "The Soviets in the Persian Gulf/Arabian Peninsula—Assets and Prospects," De-cember 1976, Remote Archives Capture (RAC), NLC-25-87-5-1-3, Jimmy Carter Presi-dential Library (JCL), Atlanta, GA.

82. See, for example, the Ford administration's request that the Saudis help Rhodesian op-position leader Joshua Nkomo, Telegram, State to Jidda, July 27, 1975, Saudi Arabia—State

Department Telegrams, From SECSTATE—NODIS (5), Box 29, PCF, GFL; and Kissinger's appeal to the Saudi intelligence chief Kamal Adham that Saudi Arabia consider aiding South Vietnam, February 19, 1975, Saudi Arabia—State Department Telegrams, From SECSTATE—NODIS (4), PCF, GFL.

83. Memcon, May 11, 1976, Box 2, NSC Meeting File, GFL.

84. Memcon, October 5, 1974, Box 6, NSAMC, GFL.

85. Patrick J. Sloyan and Joseph Treen, "Senate to Probe Saudi's Holdings," *Newsday*, May 9, 1975; Gaylord Shaw, "Corporate Slush Funds Probed: Pentagon Reviews Defense Contracts US Agencies Probing Corporate Slush Funds," *Washington Post*, May 11, 1975; Kenneth Bacon and Jerry Landauer, "Lockheed Says It Will Resist SEC Efforts to Block It from Paying Bribes Abroad," *Wall Street Journal*, August 6, 1975, William H. Jones, "SEC Seeks Agent's Data on Lockheed: Khashoggi's Records on Lockheed Sought," *Washington Post*, September 11, 1975.

86. Memcon, September 18, 1975, Box 15, NSAMC, GFL.

87. "Saudi Arabia Prohibits Commissions to Agents," *Los Angeles Times*, September 19, 1975.

88. Jidda to State, March 21, 1976, Saudi Arabia (2), Box 21, NSC Operations Staff for Middle East and South Asian Affairs, Country File (Mirror), GFL.

89. Memcon, March 3, 1975, Box 9, NSAMC, GFL.

90. Memcon, October 2, 1975, Box 15, NSAMC, GFL.

91. Laton McCartney, *Friends in High Places: The Bechtel Story: The Most Secret Corporation and How It Engineered the World* (New York: Simon and Schuster, 1988), 183–96; memcon, December 18, 1975, Box 17, NSAMC, GFL.

92. Scowcroft to Rockefeller, February 19, 1976, and Oakley to Scowcroft, February 12, 1976, Saudi Arabia (2), Box 21, NSC Operations Staff for Middle East and South Asian Affairs, Country File (Mirror), GFL.

93. Fahd interview with *Al-Anwar*, May 21, 1977, *WA* 1977, Doc. 163.

94. Memcon, August 30, 1976, Box 20, NSAMC, GFL.

95. Kenneth Reich, "Carter Says Ford Bows to Arabs," *Los Angeles Times*, October 1, 1976; Linda Charlton, "Mondale Scores Ford Arms Sales," *New York Times*, August 31, 1976.

96. Memcon, October 21, 1976, Box 21, NSAMC, GFL; "Bowing to Critics, U.S. Cuts Request on Saudi Missiles," *New York Times*, September 2, 1976.

97. Ford to Khalid, September 2, 1976, From SECSTATE NODIS (6), Box 29, PCF, GFL.

98. Abdullah Tariki, "Fawā'iḍ 'Awā'd al-Nafṭ wa kayf Nataṣrraf bi-hā bi-Ḥukma" (Surplus oil revenues and how we can act wisely), *An-Nafṭ Al-'Arab* (Arab Oil), October 1974, from Tariki, '*Abd Allāh Al-Ṭurayqī: Al-A'māl al-Kāmila* (*Abdullah Tariki: Complete Works*) (Beirut: Markaz Dirāsāt al-Waḥda al-'Arabīyya, 1999), 880.

99. Ahmed Hassan al-Bakr, "Min Risālatihi ilā al-Ra'īs al-Amrīkī Nīksūn ḥawla Azma al-Ṭāqa" (From his letter to the American president, Nixon, on the energy crisis); Saddam Hussein, "Min Ḥadīth Ṣaḥafī li Majala Bārī Mātsh" (From a press interview for *Paris Match Magazine*), *Al-Nafṭ wa al-Tanmiyya* (Oil and development) 1, no. 1 (October 1975), 4–5; "Al-Mukhaṭaṭ al-Amrīkī: Ashkāluhu wa Marāḥiluhu" (The American Plans: Their Forms and Stages), *Al-Nafṭ wa al-Tanmiyya* (Oil and development) 1, no. 12 (September 1976), 5–8.

100. Abdelrahman Munif, "Al-Khalīj al-ʿArabī Minṭaqa al-Ḥāḍir wa al-Mustaqbal" (The Arab Gulf, the present and future region, *Al-Nafṭ wa al-Tanmiyya* (Oil and development) 2, no. 2 (September 1976), 5–10.

7. TURNING RIGHT

1. Richard Harwood and Ward Sinclair, "Lobbying for Warplane Brings Saudis Out of Isolation," *Washington Post*, May 7, 1978.
2. Jewish Telegraphic Agency *Daily Bulletin*, May 16, 1978; Brzezinksi to Carter, May 5, 1978, NLC-1-6-2-19-2, RAC, JCL.
3. Jidda to State, January 23, 1977, *FRUS* 1977–80, Vol. 18, Doc. 145; Brzezinski to Carter, May 21, 1977, *FRUS* 1977–80, Vol. 18, Doc. 149.
4. Vance to Carter, February 2, 1978, NLC-128-13-5-1-9, RAC, JCL.
5. Steven V. Roberts, "Saudis Are Learning Public Relations Ways in U.S.," *New York Times*, May 12, 1978.
6. Daniel Southerland, "Saudis' Quiet Persistent F-15 Lobbying Effort," *Christian Science Monitor*, May 15, 1978.
7. Jidda to State, May 14, 1975, To SECSTATE—EXDIS (4), Box 29, PCF, GFL. Those numbers were exaggerated, and Saudi capacity never reached 16 mbd, but the kingdom still had a larger swing production capacity than any other OPEC nation.
8. David Crawford, "Saudi Oil Policy," February 6, 1976, Folder 27, Drawer 36, WSP.
9. Fahd interview with *Al-Hayat*, March 30, 1975, *WA* 1975, Doc. 115.
10. Jidda to State, February 19, 1975, To SECSTATE—NODIS (4); Jidda to State, March 9, 1975, To SECSTATE—NODIS (5), Box 29, PCF, GFL.
11. Adelman argued that the kingdom could not be trusted to keep its commitments on price and production levels, since over the long run, Saudi oil policy would always be determined by economic self-interest rather than promises to the United States. M. A. Adelman, "The Clumsy Cartel," *Energy Journal* 1, no. 1 (1980): 50–51.
12. State to Jidda, September 16, 1974; minutes of Rambouillet summit meeting, November 16, 1975; memcon, November 29, 1976; minutes of Bonn summit meeting, July 16, 1978, *FRUS* 1969–76, Vol. 37, Docs. 5, 88, 111, 157.
13. For example, Jidda to State, September 23, 1975, To SECSTATE—EXDIS (4), Box 29, PCF, GFL.
14. State to all posts, December 22, 1976; Ford to Khalid, December 29, 1976, *FRUS* 1969–76, Vol. 37, Docs. 113–114; Jidda to State, December 28, 1976, To SECSTATE—NODIS (15), Box 30, PCF, GFL.
15. Gonzalez to Burns, February 29, 1974, Oil, May–December 1974, Box B86, Arthur Burns Papers, GFL.
16. Ribicoff statement in *Recycling of Petrodollars*, Hearings Before the Senate Subcommittee on Investigations, October 16, 1974 (Washington, DC: U.S. Government Printing Office, 1974), 7.
17. Memcon, September 26, 1974, Box 6, NSAMC, GFL.

18. Sidney Lumet, dir., *Network* (MGM, 1976).

19. On the racialized fears of Arab oil wealth, see Edward Said, *Orientalism* (New York: Vintage Books, 1979), 287; Eqbal Ahmad and David Caploe, "The Logic of Military Intervention," *Race and Class* 17, no. 3 (1976): 328–29; Melani McAlister, *Epic Encounters: Culture, Media, and U.S. Interests in the Middle East Since 1945* (Berkeley: University of California Press, 2005), 125–64.

20. "Financial Consequences of OPEC Investment Funds," Willett to Volcker and Bennett, January 10, 1974, 1/74 Vol. I, Box 1, Action/Briefing Memos 1973–75, Office of the Assistant Secretary of International Affairs (OASIA), RG 56, NARA.

21. Jidda to State, September 13, 1974, To SECSTATE EXDIS (1), Box 29, PCF, GFL.

22. State to Jidda, December 3, 1974, 1974STATE265655, AAD. For more on the U.S. negotiations with SAMA, see Jidda to State, September 3, 1974, 1974JIDDA05070, AAD.

23. Alex Lang, Saudi Arabia: Dollar Deposits and Custodies Held at the FRBNY," June 13, 1978, SAMA, Box 557540, Paul Volcker Papers (PVP), Federal Reserve Bank of New York Archives (FRBNY), New York, NY.

24. "Summary of Some Draft Papers Already Prepared for Economic Mission to Saudi Arabia," n.d., December '73 Vol. II, Box 1, A/B Memos, OASIA, RG 56, NARA; Revey to Volcker, "The Question of Saudi Reserves," September 23, 1977, SAMA, Box 557540, PVP, FRBNY.

25. Jidda to State, December 4, 1974, NODIS (2), Box 29, PCF, GFL.

26. The option of purchasing Treasurys through the "add-on" arrangement was later extended to other countries, in addition to Saudi Arabia. On the special treatment of Saudi investments, see Andrea Wong, "The Untold Story Behind Saudi Arabia's 41-Year U.S. Debt Secret," *Bloomberg*, May 30, 2016, https://www.bloomberg.com/news/features/2016-05-30/the-untold-story-behind-saudi-arabia-s-41-year-u-s-debt-secret; David E. Spiro, *The Hidden Hand of American Hegemony: Petrodollar Recycling and International Markets* (Ithaca, NY: Cornell University Press, 1999), 105–26. For the Department of the Treasury's tight control over the relevant data, see House Committee on Government Operations, *Federal Response to OPEC Country Investments in the United States; Part I*, hearings held on September 22–23, 1981 (Washington, DC: U.S. Government Printing Office, 1981), 461–64; Spiro, 119–21.

27. Fahd interview with *Al-Anwar*, October 25, 1974, *WA* 1974, Doc. 305.

28. Simon to Ford, forwarded to Dick Cheney, January 15, 1975, Richard B. Cheney files, GFL, https://www.fordlibrarymuseum.gov/library/document/0005/1561375.pdf.

29. Greta R. Krippner, *Capitalizing on Crisis: The Political Origins of the Rise of Finance* (Cambridge, MA: Harvard University Press, 2011), 100–102.

30. Timothy D. Schellhardt, "Need a Home Loan? You Have a Friend in Saudi Arabia: Saudis Help Slumping U.S. Housing Market by Buying Debt Issues of Fannie Mae," *Wall Street Journal*, September 6, 1974.

31. "Financial Consequences of OPEC Investment Funds," NARA. The paper specifically suggested eliminating "the New York Stock Exchange rule prohibiting foreign membership." On the decline of the New York Stock Exchange's traditional gatekeeping role in American finance, and the troubling consequences of that decline, see Walter Mattli,

Darkness by Design: The Hidden Power in Global Capital Markets (Princeton, NJ: Princeton University Press, 2019).

32. Chase Manhattan Corporation, *1974 Annual Report* (New York: Chase Manhattan, 1975), 5–6. Chase's chairman David Rockefeller, however, argued that petrodollars could not be recycled by private banks alone, and that governments needed to play a larger role. See his comments in "Oil Money: A Crisis as the Billions Pile Up?," *U.S. News and World Report* 77, no. 7 (1974): 40–42.

33. "Attracting Petrodollars," *Wall Street Journal*, May 6, 1974.

34. Carter, "Address to the Nation on Energy," April 18, 1977, APP.

35. Author's interview with Cecil Andrus, Boise, ID, April 28, 2011.

36. Author's interview with Andrus.

37. For overviews of Carter's National Energy Plan, see Meg Jacobs, *Panic at the Pump: The Energy Crisis and the Transformation of American Politics in the 1970s* (New York: Hill and Wang, 2016), 161–90; Richard H. K. Vietor, *Energy Policy in America Since 1945: A Study of Business-Government Relations* (Cambridge: Cambridge University Press, 1984), 258–62; Jay Hakes, *A Declaration of Energy Independence: How Freedom from Foreign Oil Can Improve National Security, Our Economy, and the Environment* (Hoboken, NJ: Wiley, 2008), 45–53; Ian Ostrander and William Lowry, "Oil Crises and Policy Continuity: A History of Failure to Change," *Journal of Policy History* 24, no. 3 (2012): 391–92; W. Carl Biven, *Jimmy Carter's Economy: Policy in an Age of Limits* (Chapel Hill: University of North Carolina Press, 2002), 159–60; "Carter Energy Bill Fails to Clear," *CQ Almanac 1977*, 33rd ed., (Washington, DC: Congressional Quarterly, 1978), 708–45.

38. Jimmy Carter, diary entry for September 29, 1977, *White House Diary* (New York: Farrar, Straus and Giroux, 2010), 110.

39. Jimmy Carter, *Keeping Faith: Memoirs of a President* (New York: Bantam Books, 1982), 91, 123–24; Carter oral history interview, November 29, 1982, Miller Center, University of Virginia, http://millercenter.org/president/carter/oralhistory/jimmy-carter.

40. Carter, "Address to the Nation on Energy and National Goals," July 15, 1979, APP. See also Kevin Mattson, *"What the Heck Are You Up to, Mr. President?" Jimmy Carter, America's "Malaise," and the Speech That Should Have Changed the Country* (New York: Bloomsbury, 2009); Bruce J. Schulman, *The Seventies: The Great Shift in American Culture, Society, and Politics* (New York: Free Press, 2001), 121–43.

41. On the Bonn summit, see Biven, *Jimmy Carter's Economy*, 145–84; Robert D. Putnam and Nicholas Bayne, *Hanging Together: The Seven-Power Summits* (Cambridge, MA: Harvard University Press, 1984), 80–99.

42. State to various posts, November 4, 1977, *FRUS 1969–76*, Vol. 37, Doc. 136.

43. Carter, "Address to the Nation on Energy," April 18, 1977, APP.

44. Carter news conference, April 15, 1977, and question-and-answer session, April 15, 1977, APP. The CIA assessment was published as *The International Energy Situation: Outlook to 1985* (Washington, DC: U.S. Government Printing Office, April 1977). The CIA's forecast of a global oil shortage was based partly on the prediction that the USSR (which was, at that time, a major exporter) would become a net importer by the mid-1980s. See CIA, *Prospects for Soviet Oil Production* (Washington, DC: U.S. Government Printing

Office, April 1977); and *Prospects for Soviet Oil Production: A Supplemental Analysis* (Washington, DC: U.S. Government Printing Office, July 1977). The CIA's forecasts proved unduly pessimistic. For a critique of those forecasts and the policies adopted in response, see Roger J. Stern, "Oil Scarcity Ideology in US Foreign Policy, 1908–97," *Security Studies* 25, no. 2 (April 2016): 241–43.

45. Zbigniew Brzezinski, Weekly Report to President Carter, January 27, 1978, Weekly Reports, 10/77–1/78, Box 41, ZBM, JCL.

46. Turner to Schlesinger, August 14, 1978, *FRUS* 1969–76, Vol. 37, Doc. 158.

47. State Department Bureau of Near Eastern Affairs / Arabian Peninsula Affairs (NEA/ARP), "Background Facts for Saudi Arabia," December 12, 1977, NLC-4-6-6-3-2, RAC, JCL; Carter and Khalid remarks, January 3, 1978, APP.

48. Katz to Cooper, February 19, *FRUS* 1969–76, Vol. 37, Doc. 117; CIA, "International Oil Developments," July 27, 1977, NLC-31-69-4-11-6, RAC, JCL.

49. "Suggestions to Nazer" and "Memo to Hisham," Saudi Arabia Plan (2), Box 11, AJMP.

50. Roger Hansen of the NSC wrote in 1977 that Saudi Arabia was a "financial power" as well as a leading oil producer. Hansen to Brzezinski and Aaron, July 26, 1977, *FRUS* 1977–80, Vol. 3, Doc. 271.

51. On the 1977–1978 dollar decline and support package, see Biven, *Jimmy Carter's Economy*, 163–71; Daniel J. Sargent, *A Superpower Transformed: The Remaking of American Foreign Relations in the 1970s* (Oxford: Oxford University Press, 2014), 245–49.

52. Jidda to State, November 12, 1977, 1977JIDDA07765, AAD; Jidda to State, December 21, 1977, 1977JIDDA08702, AAD.

53. Clyde H. Farnsworth, "U.S. Will Intervene to Protect Dollar; Currency Rebounds: Warning by Saudi King Reported a Factor in Decision," *New York Times*, January 5, 1978; "Saudis Issue Dollar Warning," *Boston Globe*, March 23, 1978.

54. For more on Saudi influence on U.S. monetary policy in the late 1970s, based on U.S. Treasury Department records, see Evan A. North, "Saudi Arabia and the US Dollar Crisis of 1978–80" (unpublished paper, Georgetown University, 2008).

55. Bergsten and Solomon for Blumenthal, July 27, 1978, Box 2, Records of Assistant Secretary for International Affairs C. Fred Bergsten (CFB Records), RG 56, NARA. See also Bergsten to Miller, August 21, 1979, Meetings, Box 3, CFB Records, RG 56, NARA.

56. Jidda to State, July 25, 1978, 1978JIDDA05460, AAD.

57. Dhahran to State, June 13, 1978, 1978DHAHRA00751, AAD.

58. North, "Saudi Arabia and the US Dollar Crisis," 9–11.

59. State to Tehran, August 30, 1978, 1978STATE219928, AAD.

60. NSC meeting, September 21, 1978, *FRUS* 1969–76, Vol. 37 Doc. 161. The Treasury Department argued that while, in theory, an OPEC decision to price oil in a basket of currencies could have some advantages for the United States, it would be very dangerous if such a shift were made while the value of the dollar was under threat, as in mid-1978. See also Poats to Aaron, December 12, 1978, *FRUS* 1969–76, Vol. 37 Doc. 173.

61. Art Pine, "Carter Moves to Halt Decline of Dollar," *Washington Post*, November 2, 1978; "President Moves in to Strengthen Dollar," *Arizona Republic*, November 2, 1978.

62. Carter to Fahd, November 2, 1979, NLC-128-4-2-7-6, RAC, JCL.

63. Policy Review Committee meeting, November 9, 1978, *FRUS 1969–76*, Vol. 37, Doc. 168.

64. Stuart Eizenstat telephone interview with author, August 30, 2019.

65. Sam Jameson and David Holley, "Economy Will Slow, Chase Chairman Says," *Los Angeles Times*, November 14, 1978.

66. Memcon, November 19, 1978, Box 2, CFB Records, RG 56, NARA.

67. Jidda to State, December 18, 1978, 1978JIDDA08857, AAD.

68. Jidda to State, January 2, 1979, *FRUS 1969–76*, Vol. 37, Doc. 180.

69. Memorandum of conversation, January 27, 1979, CFB Records, Box 3, NARA.

70. "Al-Amwāl al-Muhājira" (Migratory funds), *Al-Riyadh*, February 26, 1979.

71. Paul Volcker, "Some Observations from My January 1979 Trip to the Middle East," February 9, 1979, Middle East Relations, Box 557545, PVP, FRBNY.

72. Murray Seeger, "Saudi Links Oil Price to Dollar Performance," *Los Angeles Times*, October 4, 1979.

73. David Lindsey, Athanasios Orphanides, and Robert Rasche, "The Reform of October 1979: How It Happened and Why," Federal Reserve Board, February 2005, https://www.federalreserve.gov/pubs/feds/2005/200502/200502pap.pdf.

74. Federal Open Market Committee Meeting transcript, October 6, 1979, https://www.federalreserve.gov/monetarypolicy/files/FOMC19791006meeting.pdf, 6.

75. See also Paul Volcker and Christine Harper, *Keeping at It: The Quest for Sound Money and Good Government* (New York: Public Affairs, 2018), 106–7.

76. Bonn summit minutes, July 16, 1978, *FRUS 1969–76*, Vol. 37, Doc. 157.

77. Paul Volcker, remarks to American Bankers Association, New Orleans, LA, October 9, 1979. See also Volcker's comment from his testimony to the House Budget Committee, September 5, 1979: "The desire of oil suppliers to recover losses in real income implied by rising prices of other goods and the weakness of the dollar appeared to be one factor contributing to the OPEC pricing decision." Both speeches are in Box 553650, PVP, FRBNY. This was a consistent theme for Volcker. As early as 1975, he argued that the oil price hikes of 1973 were caused in part by "the unrest in international financial markets, and particularly the weakness in the dollar." Since oil was priced in dollars, Volcker explained, inflation gave the producers an excuse "for acting aggressively." "Inflation, Gold and the US Dollar," speech at St. Louis University, February 21, 1975, Box 557538, PVP, FRBNY.

78. "Fāriq al-Siʿr Yaṣil ilā 1..% dākhil Madīna al-Riyāḍ" (Price disparity up to 100% in the city of Riyadh), *Al-Riyadh*, September 18, 1978.

79. "Sūʾ al-Takhṭīṭ: Min Aham Mā Tʿānīha Madīna al-Riyāḍ Tanāthir al-Aḥyāʾ wa Qilla al-Khidmāt" (Poor planning: Lack of services is one of the most important things suffered by the scattered neighborhoods of the city of Riyadh), *Al-Riyadh*, January 14, 1979.

80. "Maʿālī Wazīr al-Takhṭīṭ Yataḥadath li Al-Jazīra ʿan: Al-Mamlaka . . . wa al-Namū al-Iqtiṣādī, ʿabra al-Khuṭatayn.. al-Ūlā wa al-Thānīa" (His excellency the minister of planning talks with Al-Jazeerah about: The kingdom . . . and economic development through the two plans, the first and the second), *Al-Jazeerah*, March 21, 1980.

81. Saudi Ministry of Economy and Planning, *Achievements of the Development Plans: Facts and Figures* 27th Issue, 1390–1431 AH (1970–2010), Table 1–38: Government Subsidies (Disbursed), 195.

82. Saud al-Faisal interview with *Al-Hawadith*, March 2, 1979, *W'A* 1979, Doc. 56.

83. "Ta'kīdan li-Ma 'Alanaha al-Fahad qabla Shahrayn Amr Malakī bi-Tashkīl Lajna bi-Ri'āsa Nayif li-Istikmāl: al-Niẓam al-Asāsī li al-Ḥukm wa Niẓam Majlis al-Shūrā wa Niẓam al-Muqāṭāt" (Confirming what Fahd announced two months ago: The Basic Law of Governance and the Consultative Council and the system of provinces), *Al-Jazeerah*, March 19, 1980.

84. "Al-Amīr Nayif li 'Al-Sharq al-Awsaṭ': Li'anna Dustūr al-Sa'ūdīa Huwa al-Qur'ān" (Prince Nayef to *Asharq Al-Awsat*: Because the constitution of Saudi Arabia is the Quran), *Al-Muheet al-Saudi*, April 1980.

85. For Prince Mohammed's involvement with Mary Mohammad, an Arab American woman from Detroit, see chapter 2.

86. For a description of the incident that inspired *Death of a Princess*, see James West, Saudi Arabia—Preliminary Observations and Recommendations, August 1977, *FRUS 1977–81*, Vol. 18, Doc. 154.

87. For the "uproar" in Saudi Arabia on the British showing of the film, see Situation Room memorandum for Brzezinski, April 17, 1980, NLC-SAFE 17 E-27-3-3-6, RAC, JCL. For the French and Swedish decisions to prevent the film from being shown, see Christopher to Brzezinski, May 8, 1980, Saudi Arabia 5/80, Box 68, ZBM, JCL.

88. For Saudi protests to the Carter administration, see Situation Room checklist, May 5, 1980, NLC-1-15-3-32-6, RAC, JCL; Faisal Alhegelan to Christopher, May 7, 1980; Christopher to Brzezinski, May 8, 1980, Saudi Arabia 5/80, Box 68, ZBM, JCL. For the congressional debate, see 126 Cong. Rec. (1980), 10418, 10930.

89. Sultan interview with *Al-Bilad*, in *Al-Muheet al-Saudi*, April 1980.

90. Frank J. Prial, "Notes on People," *New York Times*, January 6, 1978.

91. "Southland," *Los Angeles Times*, January 10, 1978; Jacquelyn Powell, "Personalities," *Washington Post*, January 10, 1978.

92. CIA, "Human Rights Performance: January 1977–July 1978," September 1978, NLC-28-17-15-9-8, RAC, JCL.

93. Bloomfield to Brzezinski, January 16, 1981, NSC Accomplishments Human Rights, Box 34, ZBM, JCL.

94. James West, "Saudi Arabia—Preliminary Observations and Recommendations," August 1977, *FRUS 1977–80*, Vol. 18, Doc. 154.

95. "B'aḍ al-Jihāt Tarākhat fī Adā' Wājb al-Amr bi-l-M'arūf wa-l-Nahī 'an al-Munkar mimā Athār Qalaq al-Mas'ūlīn fī al-Mamlaka" (Some authorities slackened in the duty of promoting virtue and prohibiting vice, stirring the concern of the kingdom's officials), *Al-Muheet al-Saudi*, January 1980. See also "Taṭbīq al-Sharī'a al-Islāmīa fī al-Mamlaka J'alahā bi-Ma'aman min al-Jarīma" (The application of Islamic law in the kingdom made it safe from crime), *Al-Muheet al-Saudi*, April 1981.

96. Ellen to Mulligan, September 10, 1979, Box 11, Folder 28, WMP. In interviews with the author, Saudis (including both government officials and private subjects), as well as American expatriates living in the kingdom, remembered a sharp conservative turn by the Saudi government in the late 1970s and early 1980s. Standards for women's dress, tolerance of Western movies and other media, and the government's willingness to over-

look consumption of alcohol were all tightened. These observers saw the newly conservative policies as an attempt by the monarchy to counter challenges to its Islamic legitimacy from critics like al-Utaybi and the revolutionary Iranian government.

97. Vance to Carter, November 28, 1978, NLC-128-14-13-20-8, RAC, JCL; memo for Brzezinski, December 3, 1979, NLC-1-13-4-5-7, RAC, JCL. For more on the 1979 events, see Toby Craig Jones, " Rebellion on the Saudi Periphery: Modernity, Marginalization, and the Shi'a Uprising of 1979," *International Journal of Middle East Studies* 38, no. 2 (May 2006): 213–233.

98. Author's interview with Hassan al-Husseini, Dhahran, February 3, 2011.

99. Juhayman al-Utaybi, "Risāla al-Imāra wa-l-Bī'a wa-l-Ṭā'a" (The state, allegiance, and submission), http://www.ilmway.com/site/maqdis/MS_20536.html. For more on Juhayman's writings and ideological background, see Joseph A. Kechichian, "Islamic Revivalism and Change in Saudi Arabia: Juhaymān al-'Utaybī's 'Letters' to the Saudi People," *Muslim World* 80, no. 1 (January 1990): 1–16; Thomas Hegghammer and Stéphane Lacroix, "Rejectionist Islamism in Saudi Arabia: The Story of Juhayman Al-'Utaybi Revisited," *International Journal of Middle East Studies* 39, no. 1 (2007): 103–22. For Juhayman's father and the Ikhwan revolt, see Hegghammer and Lacroix, "Rejectionist Islamism in Saudi Arabia," 109.

100. For the mosque incident, see Yaroslav Trofimov, *The Siege of Mecca: The Forgotten Uprising in Islam's Holiest Shrine and the Birth of al Qaeda* (New York: Doubleday, 2007). Shorter treatments of the Meccan episode can be found in Robert Lacey, *Inside the Kingdom: Kings, Clerics, Modernists, Terrorists, and the Struggle for Saudi Arabia* (New York: Viking, 2009), 3–36, and Steve Coll, *The Bin Ladens: An Arabian Family in the American Century* (New York: Penguin, 2008), 225–29. For U.S. reactions, see memorandum, November 20, 1979, NLC-6-30-1-9-2, RAC, JCL; Vance to Carter, November 28, NLC-128-14-13-2-8, RAC, JCL; Odom to Brzezinski, November 28, 1979, NLC-12-22-2-17-4, RAC, JCL. For the death toll among Saudi security forces, see *Al-Riyadh*, January 10, 1980.

101. "Wāqi' al-Ṭalaba al-'Arab fī Amrīkā! Ittiḥād al-Ṭalaba al-Muslimīn fī Amrīkā wa-Kanadā Yuwājih Taḥdiyan Khaṭīran fī Nashāṭātihi" (The reality of Arab students in America! The Muslim Students' Union in America and Canada faces serious challenges in its activities), interview with Mohammed al-Rashdan, *Al-Riyadh*, March 8, 1979.

102. Memo to Hisham (III), n.d. but late 1970s, Saudi Arabia Plan (2), Box 11, AJMP.

103. "Ma'ālī Wazīr al-Takhṭīṭ Yataḥadath li Al-Jazīra" (His Excellency the Minister of Planning talks to *Al-Jazeerah*), *Al-Jazeerah*, March 21, 1980.

104. "Farīq 'Amal l-Dirāsa Ẓāhira Istiqdām al-Ajānib li-l-'Amal fī al-Dawā'ir al-Ḥukūmīa" (Working group to study the phenomenon of bringing foreigners to work in government departments), *Al-Muheet al-Saudi*, January 1980.

105. "'Aqūbāt Jadīda bi-Ḥaq al-Mutasatirīn 'alā al-Muqīmīn bi-Ṣūra Ghayir Niẓāmīa" (New penalties for hiding unauthorized residents), *Al-Muheet al-Saudi*, January 1980.

106. "Mukāfāt li-l-Lijān al-Idārīa bi-Silāḥ al-Ḥudūd" (Rewards for the administrative committees of the Frontier Forces), *Al-Muheet al-Saudi*, April 1981.

107. Nayef interview, *Al-Hawadith*, June 22, 1970, from *W'A* 1979, Doc. 174.

108. Stanford Research Institute, Saudi construction industry study, Saudi Planning Review Committee Materials, Box 9, AJMP.

109. Volcker speech to Commercial Club, January 29, 1980, and testimony before House Budget Committee, September 5, 1979, Box 553650, PVP, FRBNY.

110. Daniel Southerland, "Saudis' Quiet Persistent F-15 Lobbying Effort," *Christian Science Monitor*, May 15, 1978; Haynes Johnson, "Arms," *Washington Post*, May 17, 1978.

8. ASCENT

1. Memorandum for the record, n.d., *FRUS* 1977–80, Vol. 12, Doc. 269; CIA memorandum, June 11, 1980, *FRUS* 1977–80, Vol. 12, Doc. 288. Pakistan, too, was very sensitive to the risk of exposure and urged the United States to keep the operation secret. On the joint U.S.-Saudi sponsorship of the Afghan insurgency, including the eventual decision to supply more overt aid, see Steve Coll, *Ghost Wars: The Secret History of the CIA, Afghanistan, and Bin Laden, from the Soviet Invasion to September 10, 2001* (New York: Penguin, 2004); George Crile, *Charlie Wilson's War: The Extraordinary Story of the Largest Covert Operation in History* (New York: Atlantic Monthly Press, 2003); Odd Arne Westad, *The Global Cold War: Third World Interventions and the Making of Our Times* (Cambridge: Cambridge University Press, 2005), chaps. 8–10.

2. This chapter adds to earlier work that has identified the late 1970s as a critical turning point for U.S. military involvement in the Persian Gulf. Andrew J. Bacevich, *America's War for the Greater Middle East: A Military History* (New York: Random House, 2016), 3–49; Olav Njølstad, "Shifting Priorities: The Persian Gulf in US Strategic Planning in the Carter Years," *Cold War History* 4, no. 3 (April 2004): 21–55; William E. Odom, "The Cold War Origins of the U.S. Central Command," *Journal of Cold War Studies* 8, no. 2 (Spring 2006): 52–82. Adam M. Howard and Alexander R. Wieland argue that Carter's pivot to the Gulf marked a culmination rather than a sharp break with earlier trends in U.S. policy; Howard and Wieland, "Confronting the Arc of Crisis: The Carter Administration's Approach to Security Building in the 'Greater Gulf' Region, 1977–80," in *United States Relations with China and Iran: Toward the Asian Century*, ed. Osamah F. Khalil (London: Bloomsbury, 2019), 153–69. For an overview of recent literature on this subject, see Craig Daigle, "The American War for the Greater Middle East: From Diplomacy to Military Intervention," *International Journal of Middle East Studies* 49, no. 4 (2017): 757–65.

3. State to various posts, November 4, 1977, *FRUS* 1969–76, Vol. 37, Doc. 136. For Carter's approach to Middle East peace through the Camp David Accords and the 1979 Egyptian-Israeli treaty, see Seth Anziska, *Preventing Palestine: A Political History from Camp David to Oslo* (Princeton, NJ: Princeton University Press, 2018), 17–48; Salim Yaqub, *Imperfect Strangers: Americans, Arabs, and U.S.–Middle East Relations in the 1970s* (Ithaca: Cornell University Press, 2016), 239–75; William B. Quandt, *Peace Process: American Diplomacy and the Arab-Israeli Conflict Since 1967*, 3rd. ed. (Washington, DC: Brookings Institution Press, 2005), 177–243.

4. Fahd interview with *Al-Anwar*, May 21, 1977, *W'A* 1977, Doc. 163.

5. Saud al-Faisal interview with *Al-Nahar*, October 27, 1977, *W'A* 1977, Doc. 299.

6. Sadat's decision surprised both Saudi Arabia and the United States. On the reported Saudi shock at Sadat's visit to Jerusalem, see memcon, October 25, 1977, *FRUS* 1977–80, Vol. 8, Doc. 136.

7. On U.S. lobbying for Saudi support for the Egyptian-Israeli negotiations, see Vance to Fahd, November 18, 1977, NLC-1-4-5-3-8, RAC, JCL. On Saudi support for Camp David, see Analysis of Arab-Israeli Developments, August 14, 1978, NLC-SAFE 17 B-12-66-4-5, RAC, JCL; Tarnoff to Brzezinski, August 16, 1978, NLC-1-7-5-36-9, RAC, JCL; Vance to Carter, October 24, 1978, NLC-128-11-22-1-1, RAC, JCL.

8. On the failure of the Camp David Accords and 1979 Egyptian-Israeli peace treaty to achieve a comprehensive settlement and resolve the Palestinian issue, see Anziska, *Preventing Palestine*; Yaqub, *Imperfect Strangers*, 239–75.

9. Baghdad conference communiqué, March 31, 1979, *W'A* 1979, Doc. 94. An English translation was published as "Suspension of Relations with Egypt," Communiqué Issued by the Arab League Council, from *American Foreign Policy: Basic Documents, 1977–1980* (Washington, DC: U.S. Government Printing Office, 1983*)*, 687–90.

10. "Āmrīkā wa Istrātījiyya al-Ṣulḥ al-Munfarid" (America and the strategy of unilateral reconciliation) and "Liqā'" (Meeting), *Al-Riyadh*, May 5, 1979.

11. "Akthar min 7 . . . Milyūn Dūlār li-Miṣr mundhu 'Ām 1973" (More than 7 billion dollars to Egypt since 1973), *Al-Riyadh*, May 6, 1979; "Duwal al-Khalīj Qaddamat li-Miṣr Akthar min 13 Alf Milyūn Dūlār mundhu Ḥarb Aktūbar" (The Gulf countries have given more than 13 billion dollars to Egypt since the October War), *Al-Riyadh*, May 22, 1979.

12. Vance to Carter, May 10, 1979, NLC-128-14-7-7-0, RAC, JCL.

13. Among many examples of Saudi press attacks on Egypt at the beginning of the 1980s, see *Al-Jazeerah*, March 1 and 25, 1980; April 8, 1980; and January 21, 1981.

14. "Anti-Boycott Provisions of the Export Administration Amendments of 1977," BP-4 Briefing Memos, 4 of 4, Box 2, CFB, RG 56, NARA; "House Passes Anti-Arab-Boycott Bill," *Washington Post*, April 21, 1977; "Ban on U.S. Firms Supporting Boycott of Israel Is Enacted," *Wall Street Journal*, June 23, 1977.

15. Edward A. Gargan, "Compliance on Arab Boycott," *New York Times*, October 22, 1981.

16. Solomon to Miller, September 18, 1978, International Boycott Guidelines, Solomon Subject Files Box 2, NARA.

17. Bergsten to Blumenthal, February 17, 1978, BP-4 Briefing Memos, 4 of 4, Box 2, CFB, RG 56, NARA.

18. Brzezinski to Carter, March 15, 1978, NLC-1-5-5-63-1, RAC, JCL.

19. On the Middle East Force and Schlesinger's frustration with his limited military options in 1973, see chapter 5.

20. Roham Alvandi, *Nixon, Kissinger, and the Shah: The United States and Iran in the Cold War* (Oxford: Oxford University Press, 2014); Bacevich, *America's War for the Greater Middle East*, 8–10.

21. Quandt and Sick to Brzezinski, February 2, 1977; Bartholomew and Atherton to Vance, May 2, 1977, *FRUS* 1977–80, Vol. 18, Docs. 1, 5.

22. Presidential Review Memorandum/NSC-10: Comprehensive Net Assessment and Military Force Posture Review, February 18, 1977, pp. 21–22, JCL, http://www .jimmycarterlibrary.gov/documents/prmemorandums/prm10.pdf. PRM-10 is still heavily redacted, but some of its key conclusions are referenced in "Comprehensive Net Assessment 1978: Overview," forwarded to Carter by Brzezinski in his NSC Weekly Report of March 30, 1979, Weekly Reports 3/79–6/79, Box 41, ZBM, JCL. See also Zbigniew Brzezinski, *Power and Principle: Memoirs of the National Security Advisor, 1977–1981* (New York: Farrar, Straus and Giroux, 1983), 177; Njølstad, "Shifting Priorities," 26–27; Odom, "The Cold War Origins of the U.S. Central Command," 57–59.

23. Brzezinski weekly report March 18, 1977, from Weekly Reports, 2/77-6/77, Box 41, ZBM, JCL.

24. Presidential Directive/NSC-18: U.S. National Strategy, August 26, 1977, JCL, http:// www.jimmycarterlibrary.gov/documents/pddirectives/pd18.pdf. As with PRM-10, much of PD-18 is still classified, but the content of the redacted passages can be deduced from other evidence.

25. Letter from Nouri Ibrahim, March 20, 1976, to U.S. embassy in Jeddah, with enclosed message from Fahd, Saudi Arabia (3), Box 21, NSC Operations Staff for Middle East and South Asian Affairs, Country File (Mirror), GFL.

26. Kissinger to Porter, "Criticism of U.S. Policy in Saudi Arabia," May 7, 1976, NSC Middle East Staff Box 21, Folder: Saudi Arabia (2), GFL. For more on the Saudi offer, see the testimony of James Akins, May 4, 1976, in *Hearings Before the Subcommittee on Multinational Corporations of the Committee on Foreign Relations, United States Senate, Ninety-Fourth Congress, Second Session, on Lockheed Aircraft Corporation*, Part 14 (Washington, DC: U.S. Government Printing Office, 1976), 430–33.

27. Memorandum, April 19, 1977, NLC-1-1-5-54-5, RAC, JCL.

28. Nancy Mitchell, *Jimmy Carter in Africa: Race and the Cold War* (Stanford, CA: Stanford University Press, 2016), 281.

29. For more on the conflict in the Horn of Africa, see Westad, *Global Cold War*, 250–87; Piero Gleijeses, "Moscow's Proxy? Cuba and Africa 1975–1988," *Journal of Cold War Studies* 8, no. 4 (October 2006): 98–146.

30. Saunders and Bowdler to Vance, May 2, 1978, NLC-SAFE 17 B-10-52-5-1, RAC, JCL.

31. Author's interview with Turki al-Faisal, Riyadh, January 8, 2011.

32. Brzezinski, *Power and Principle*, 189.

33. For the Saudi role in encouraging the U.S. tilt toward Somalia, see Mitchell, *Jimmy Carter in Africa*, 264, 290–91, 293–94, 346, 380. On the U.S. move to the Berbera base in 1980, see Mitchell, 684.

34. "Transcript of Meeting Between East German Leader Erich Honecker and Cuban Leader Fidel Castro," East Berlin, April 3, 1977, from the Wilson Center Digital Archive, http://digitalarchive.wilsoncenter.org/document/111844.

35. Memorandum of conversation, German Democratic Republic Embassy in the USSR with S. J. Sinitsen of the Soviet MFA Third Department (Africa), February 16, 1978, Wilson Center Digital Archive, http://digitalarchive.wilsoncenter.org/document/110970.

36. Vance to President Carter, February 17, 1978, RAC, JCL.

37. Inamullah Khan, "Somalia and the World," *Muslim World League Journal* 7, no. 2 (December 1979): 33.

38. Sayyid Hasan Mutahar, "Somalia's Refugee Problem," *Muslim World League Journal* 8, no. 2 (December 1980): 4.

39. Testimony of John Ruszkiewicz, May 5, 1980, in *U.S. Interests in, and Policies Toward, the Persian Gulf, 1980*, Hearing before the Subcommittee on Europe and the Middle East of the Committee on Foreign Affairs (Washington, DC: U.S. Government Printing Office, 1980), 103–4.

40. For the 1962–1970 Yemeni Civil War and the border clashes with the PDRY, see chapters 2–3.

41. John West, "The Six Crises of Saudi Arabia in 1979," private message to Carter, undated but c. March 1980, RAC NLC-128-4-2-15-7, JCL.

42. Brzezinski to Carter, Weekly Report June 30, 1978, Weekly Reports 6/78–9/78, Box 41, ZBM, JCL.

43. Richard Burt, "Carter Will Speed Arms to Yemen, Bypassing Any Review by Congress," *New York Times*, March 10, 1979.

44. Brzezinksi, *Power and Principle*, 447; Richard Burt, "U.S. Sends Ships to Arabian Sea in Yemen Crisis," *New York Times*, March 7, 1979.

45. Burt, "Carter Will Speed Arms."

46. Discussion Paper, PRC Meeting on Saudi Arabia, April 27, 1979, NLC-25-140-8-1-0, RAC, JCL.

47. West, "Six Crises."

48. Ruszkiewicz testimony in *U.S. Interests in, and Policies Toward, the Persian Gulf, 1980*, 108.

49. Steven V. Roberts, Stephen Engelberg, and Jeff Gerth, "Prop for U.S. Policy: Secret Saudi Funds," *New York Times*, June 21, 1987.

50. Discussion Paper, PRC meeting on Saudi Arabia, April 27, 1979, NLC-25-140-8-1-0, RAC, JCL.

51. Current Reports, December 5, 1979, NLC-28-45-1-2-9, RAC, JCL. For more on Saudi intervention in Yemeni politics, see F. Gregory Gause, *Saudi-Yemeni Relations; Domestic Structures and Foreign Influence* (New York: Columbia University Press, 1990).

52. For the importance of the U.S.-Iranian relationship during the early 1970s, see Alvandi, *Nixon, Kissinger, and the Shah*. For the Iranian Revolution and the early years of the Islamic Republic, see Abbas Amanat, *Iran: A Modern History* (New Haven, CT: Yale University Press, 2017), 701–896; Ervand Abrahamian, *A History of Modern Iran* (Cambridge: Cambridge University Press, 2008), 155–95; Michael Axworthy, *Revolutionary Iran: A History of the Islamic Republic* (Oxford: Oxford University Press, 2013), 76–267. For U.S.-Iranian relations and the revolution, see Gary Sick, *All Fall Down: America's Fateful Encounter with Iran* (New York: Random House, 1985); James A. Bill, *The Eagle and the Lion: The Tragedy of American-Iranian Relations* (New Haven, CT: Yale University Press, 1988), 216–317; Andrew Scott Cooper, *The Fall of Heaven: The Pahlavis and the Final Days of Imperial Iran* (New York: Henry Holt, 2016).

53. Eizenstat to Carter, June 28, 1979, published in "Text of Eizenstat's Memorandum on Energy with Recommendations to Carter," *New York Times*, July 8, 1979. For the economic

impact of the 1979 oil shortage on the United States, and its political consequences for Carter, see Meg Jacobs, *Panic at the Pump: The Energy Crisis and the Transformation of American Politics in the 1970s* (New York: Hill and Wang, 2016), 203–70.

54. Brzezinski, Weekly Report June 1, 1979, Weekly Reports 3/79–6/79, Box 42, ZBM, JCL.

55. Brzezinski, Weekly Report December 2, 1978, Weekly Reports, 9/78–12/78, Box 42, ZBM, JCL. Brzezinski's alarming conclusions were quickly leaked to the press; see "Iran: The Crescent of Crisis," *Time*, January 15, 1979.

56. State/INR and CIA memorandum, February 20, 1979, NLC-24-102-3-3-6, RAC, JCL. For more on U.S. perceptions of a loss of Saudi confidence because of the United States' inability to prevent the Iranian Revolution, see Brown to Carter, undated but c. late January 1979; Policy Review Committee (PRC) meeting, June 21–22, 1979; report by West, July 15, 1979, *FRUS* 1977–80, Vol. 18, Docs. 15, 26, 196.

57. On the limited U.S. and Saudi support for the Afghan insurgents before December 1979, see Carlucci to Aaron, January 26, 1979; CIA memorandum, February 28, 1979; CIA cable, March 27, 1979; CIA paper, n.d.; NSC Special Coordination Committee (SCC) conclusions, June 26, 1979; Murray to McGiffert, September 21, 1979; SCC conclusions, October 23, 1979; Turner to Brzezinski, November 5, 1979, *FRUS* 1977–80 Vol. 12, Docs. 34, 38, 40, 45, 53, 66, 76, 80. For more on provision of U.S. aid to the Afghan mujahideen beginning by July 1979, see Odom, "Cold War Origins," 68; Robert M. Gates, *From the Shadows: The Ultimate Insider's Story of Five Presidents and How They Won the Cold War* (New York: Tombstone Books, 1997), 143–46.

58. Brzezinski to Carter, December 26, 1979, Southwest Asia/Persian Gulf—Afghanistan, December 26, 1979–January 4, 1980, Box 17, ZBM, JCL.

59. Editorial note, *FRUS* 1977–80, Vol. 12, Doc. 176.

60. Memcon (Brzezinski and Saud al-Faisal), March 17, 1979, Serial Xs 3/79, Box 36, ZBM, JCL; Memcon (Brzezinski and Khalid), March 17, 1979, Serial Xs 4/79, Box 36, ZBM, JCL.

61. "The 21st Session of the Rabita Council," *Muslim World League Journal* 7, no 1 (November 1979): 5.

62. Vance to Carter, January 29, 1980, NLC-25-99-18-7-0, RAC, JCL.

63. "Afghanistan: The Writing on the Wall," *Muslim World League Journal* 7, no. 4 (February 1980): 4.

64. For example, one Riyadh newspaper ran a cartoon featuring the Soviet leader Leonid Brezhnev as a giant ogre devouring innocent Afghans, who waved a flag labeled "Allahu Akbar" (God is great). *Al-Jazeerah*, January 1, 1981.

65. Saunders and Bowdler to Vance, May 2, 1978, NLC-SAFE 17 B-10-52-5-1, RAC, JCL.

66. Mohammed Yamani interview, June 18, 1980, *WA* 1980, Doc. 149.

67. Author's interview with Turki al-Faisal. This was a common theme for Turki; see his similar statement in Rachel Bronson, *Thicker Than Oil: America's Uneasy Partnership with Saudi Arabia* (Oxford: Oxford University Press, 2006), 130.

68. Memcon, March 17, 1979, Serial Xs 3/79, Box 36, ZBM, JCL.

69. Brzezinski to Carter, April 12, 1979, Weekly Reports 3/79–6/79, Box 41, ZBM, JCL.

70. Robert Hunter to Brzezinski, November 28, 1979, NLC-15-20-9-21-1, RAC, JCL.

71. Jimmy Carter, *Keeping Faith: Memoirs of a President* (New York: Bantam Books, 1982), 472.

72. Brzezinski to Carter, January 3, 1980, Southwest Asia/Persian Gulf—Afghanistan, 12/26/79–1/4/80, Box 17, ZBM, JCL.

73. Carter, State of the Union address, January 23, 1980, APP.

74. Vance to Carter, January 29, 1980, NLC-25-99-18-7-0, RAC, JCL.

75. Brzezinski to Carter, February 6, 1980, *FRUS* 1977–80, Vol. 12, Doc. 197.

76. SCC meeting, September 2, 1980, Southwest Asia/Persian Gulf 9/80, Box 16, ZBM, JCL.

77. Ermarth to Odom, March 17, 1980, Southwest Asia/Persian Gulf 3/80, Box 15, ZBM, JCL.

78. NSC meeting, September 12, 1980, Southwest Asia/Persian Gulf 9/80, Box 16, ZBM, JCL.

79. Discussion Paper, PRC meeting on Saudi Arabia, April 27, 1979, NLC-25-140-8-1-0, RAC, JCL.

80. Saud al-Faisal interview with *Al-Hawadith*, March 2, 1979, *WA* 1979, Doc. 56; Sultan and Fahd statements; Saud al-Faisal statement; Sultan interview with *Al-Bilad*, from *Al-Muheet al-Saudi*, October 1979, January 1980, and April 1980.

81. SCC meetings, September 2 and 5, 1980, Southwest Asia/Persian Gulf 9/80, Box 15, ZBM, JCL.

82. The State Department briefing paper "A Security Framework for Southwest Asia: Background for a Strategic Dialogue," March 13, 1980, noted: "The U.S. is committed to a sustained expansion of our capabilities to deploy forces in the region." Southwest Asia/Persian Gulf—3/80, Box 15, ZBM, JCL. See also Njølstad, "Shifting Priorities"; Odom, "Cold War Origins."

83. Kenneth H. Bacon, "President Requests 12% Increase in Defense Spending as Goal of Checking Soviet Aggression Chills Détente," *Wall Street Journal*, January 19, 1980; "American Military Strength Abroad," *CQ Researcher*, February 15, 1980.

84. Bacon, "President Requests 12% Increase."

85. "Poll Finds 64% Favor Sending Troops to Gulf," *Los Angeles Times*, February 4, 1980.

86. George F. Kennan, "On Washington's Reaction to the Afghan Crisis," *New York Times*, February 1, 1980.

87. "Kennedy and Brown Interviewed on Major Issues: Carter Declines Post Invitation," *Washington Post*, January 20, 1980; Kennedy address at Georgetown University, January 28, 1980, from *Washington Post*, January 29, 1980.

88. "Should the United States Use Force in the Persian Gulf?," *Washington Post*, February 13, 1980.

89. Saud al-Faisal interview with *Al-Hawadith*, February 3, 1979; Nayef interview with *Al-Hawadith*, June 22, 1979, *WA* 1979, Docs. 56, 194; Mohammed Yamani interview, June 18, 1980; *WA* 1980, Doc. 149.

90. Memo for Brzezinski, December 3, 1979, NLC-1-13-4-5-7, RAC, JCL.

91. Memorandum, Iran: Prospects for Retaliation Against Persian Gulf States, September 28, 1980, NLC-33-15-6-1-2, RAC, JCL.

92. "Chronology of Events," NLC-33-5-11-10-7, RAC, JCL; Brzezinski, *Power and Principle*, 452–54.

93. Brzezinski to Carter, September 27, 1980, Southwest Asia/Persian Gulf 9/80, Box 16, ZBM, JCL.

CONCLUSION

1. The details of the *Iddi*'s travels are from its voyage card at the Lloyd's Marine Collection, Guildhall Library, London. The ship's arrival in Queens was covered in Will Lissner, "Tanker Unloads a Huge Oil Cargo Here," *New York Times*, November 30, 1973.

2. Martin Skala, "New Ship-Subsidy Plan Piques Investor Interest," *Christian Science Monitor*, October 31, 1969; Werner Bamberger, "Shipbuilding Growing in Brooklyn Again," *New York Times*, November 22, 1970.

3. On the condition of the U.S. tanker industry and Seatrain's financial difficulties, see Gerald Parsky to William Simon, April 30, 1975, Energy Resources Council (ERC) 1975, Box 3, Records of the Assistant Secretary for International Affairs, 1973–76, RG 56, NARA. For the Energy Transportation Security Act of 1974, see H.R. 8193, 119 Cong. Rec. 41996 (1974); "Oil Imports on U.S. Flagships," *CQ Almanac*, 1974; Gerald Ford, *A Time to Heal: The Autobiography of Gerald R. Ford* (New York: Harper and Row, 1979), 226. For the layoffs at Seatrain, see Grace Lichtenstein, "Laid Off Seatrain Workers Angry at Company, Carey, Ford, Union," *New York Times*, January 24, 1975; and Peter Kihss, "Seatrain, Citing Brooklyn Loss, Lays Off 1,300," *New York Times*, May 9, 1979.

4. Anthony Solomon, Notes for Remarks at Central Bankers Luncheon, October 5, 1981, Foreign Central Bankers Luncheons, Box 553606, ASP, FRBNY.

5. Looking back on the 1970s, economist William Nordhaus writes: "The energy shocks were the earthquake, and the industries with the largest slowdown were near the epicenter of the tectonic shifts in the economy." Nordhaus, "Retrospective on the 1970s Productivity Slowdown," National Bureau of Economic Research Working Paper No. 10950, December 2004, https://www.nber.org/papers/w10950.

6. William H. Jones, "The Bottom-Line Details of the Chrysler Bailout," *Washington Post*, November 4, 1979.

7. "Braniff's Rainbow Ends, Leaving Void in Skies," *Wall Street Journal*, May 14, 1982.

8. Sternlight to Solomon, May 10, 1984, Continental Illinois, Box 553906, ASP, FRBNY; Macias and McNally to Schadrack, May 18, 1984, Continental Illinois, Box 553906, ASP, FRBNY; Permanent Assistance Program for Continental Illinois National Bank and Trust Company, July 26, 1984, Continental Illinois, Box 553906, ASP, FRBNY.

9. *The Operations of Federal Agencies in Monitoring, Reporting on, and Analyzing Foreign Investments in the United States: Hearings before a Subcommittee of the Committee on Government Operations*, 95th Cong. 140, 145 (1979) (statement of Munawar Hidayatallah).

10. Jerry Knight, "Arab Financier Questioned by SEC," *Washington Post*, October 19, 1978; "Fugitive Pharaon Is Fined $37 Million for Role in BCCI Case," *Wall Street Journal*, February 5, 1997.

11. U.S. Central Intelligence Agency (CIA), National Intelligence Daily, October 1, 1985, p. 10, from CIA FOIA Electronic Reading Room, http://www.foia.cia.gov/document /0005500140.

12. William Martin and Roger Robinson for Robert McFarlane, May 21, 1984, Persian Gulf 1984, Box 9, Near East & South Asian Affairs Directorate, National Security Council Records, Ronald Reagan Library (RRL), Simi Valley, CA; "Saudi Arabia and the World Oil Market," n.d. but c. April 1986, VP Trip (3), Box 3, Shirin Tahir-Kheli Files, RRL; "Is There a National Security Threat?," Appendix to DPC Memo to Reagan, April 27, 1987, 04/29/1987 Meeting RE Energy Security, Box 11, Beryl Sprinkel Papers, RRL.

13. Jeff Gerth, "New Report of Saudi Money for Contras," *New York Times*, January 13, 1987; Richard Berke, "McFarlane Said to Have Told of Saudi Offer to Aid Contras," *New York Times*, March 19, 1987; "Saudi Arabia and the Reagan Doctrine," *Middle East Report*, no. 155 (1988): 12–17; *Report of the Congressional Committees Investigating the Iran-Contra Affair*, 100th Cong. (1987).

14. Rachel Bronson, *Thicker Than Oil: America's Uneasy Partnership with Saudi Arabia* (Oxford: Oxford University Press, 2006), 158–162.

15. Richard Halloran, "2 Iranian Fighters Reported Downed by Saudi Air Force," *New York Times*, June 6, 1984.

16. On the war, see Pierre Razoux, *The Iran-Iraq War*, trans. Nicholas Elliott (Cambridge, MA: Belknap Press, 2015). On the initial U.S. reaction, see Hal Brands, "Saddam Hussein, the United States, and the Invasion of Iran: Was There a Green Light?," *Cold War History* 12, no. 2 (May 2012): 319–43. On the Carter administration's fear of an Iranian attack on the Arab Gulf states during the opening stages of the war, see Memorandum, Iran: Prospects for Retaliation Against Persian Gulf States, September 28, 1980, NLC-33-15-6-1-2; Chronology of Events, NLC-33-5-11-10-7, RAC, JCL; Zbigniew Brzezinski, *Power and Principle: Memoirs of the National Security Advisor, 1977–1981* (New York: Farrar, Straus and Giroux, 1983), 452–54.

17. On the CRAF, see "Mideast Crisis Spurs Largest U.S. Airlift Since Vietnam War," *Wall Street Journal*, August 13, 1990; Don Phillips, "Cheney Orders Airline Alert," *Washington Post*, January 19, 1991.

18. Letter by Rosemary Dempsey, November 29, 1990; Pam Hughes to NOW leadership, November 20, 1990; NOW press release, November 27, 1990; "Bring the Troops Home Now!," flyer by the National Campaign for Peace in the Middle East; Saudi Embassy Demonstration 1990, Box 341, Records of the National Organization for Women, Schlesinger Library, Radcliffe Institute, Harvard University. On the "gender apartheid" charge against Saudi Arabia, see Kelly Shannon, *U.S. Foreign Policy and Muslim Women's Human Rights* (Philadelphia: University of Pennsylvania Press, 2018), 79–97.

19. Abu Muhammad al-Maqdisi, *Al-Kawāshif al-Jaliyya fi Kufr al-Dawla al-Saʿūdiyya* (Clear proof of the Saudi state's disbelief), second printing, 1421 AH (2000/2001), http://www

.tawhed.ws, 13, 97, 100–116, 120. For more on Al-Maqdisi, see Thomas Hegghammer, *Jihad in Saudi Arabia: Violence and Pan-Islamism Since 1979* (Cambridge: Cambridge University Press, 2010), chaps. 3, 10.

20. For the diverse political discourses, incorporating Islamic themes and criticism of the government, that proliferated in the kingdom during and after the Gulf War, see Stéphane Lacroix, *Awakening Islam: The Politics of Religious Dissent in Contemporary Saudi Arabia*, trans. George Holoch (Cambridge, MA: Harvard University Press, 2011). For Bin Laden's political ideas in his own words, see Bruce Lawrence, ed., *Messages to the World: The Statements of Osama Bin Laden* (London: Verso, 2005). For Al-Qaeda's critique of the Al Saud's oil policies, see Bernard Haykel, "Oil in Saudi Arabian Culture and Politics: From Tribal Poets to Al-Qaeda's Ideologues," in *Saudi Arabia in Transition: Insights on Social, Political, Economic and Religious Change*, ed. Bernard Haykel, Thomas Hegghammer, and Stéphane Lacroix (Cambridge: Cambridge University Press, 2015).

21. For American views of Saudi Arabia between 1991 and 2019, see Gallup Country Ratings, https://news.gallup.com/poll/1624/perceptions-foreign-countries.aspx.

22. Polling conducted by Gallup and the Meridan International Center, "The 2010 U.S.–Global Leadership Project," https://news.gallup.com/poll/146561/2010-Global-Leadership-Project.aspx?utm_source=link_newsv9&utm_campaign=item_146771&utm_medium=copy.

23. Kathy Frankovic, "Americans Had Limited Trust in Saudi Arabia Even Before Khashoggi," YouGov, October 17, 2008, https://today.yougov.com/topics/politics/articles-reports/2018/10/17/america-had-limited-trust-saudi-arabia-even-disapp.

24. The United States is the world's largest arms exporter, and Saudi Arabia is the largest importer. More than 68 percent of Saudi arms imports came from the United States between 2014 and 2018. Data from the Stockholm International Peace Research Institute Military Expenditure Database, 1988–2018, https://www.sipri.org/databases/milex.

25. On the fracking revolution, see Russel Gold, *The Boom: How Fracking Ignited the American Energy Revolution and Changed the World* (New York: Simon and Schuster, 2014); Daniel Raimi, *The Fracking Debate: The Risks, Benefits, and Uncertainties of the Shale Revolution* (New York: Columbia University Press, 2017). For an optimistic view of its geopolitical consequences for the United States, see Meghan L. O'Sullivan, *Windfall: How the New Energy Abundance Upends Global Politics and Strengthens America's Power* (New York: Simon and Schuster, 2017).

26. Data from the Costs of War project, Watson Institute for International and Public Affairs, Brown University, https://watson.brown.edu/costsofwar/costs/economic.

27. Jeremy Leggett, "Global Warming: The Worst Case," *Bulletin of the Atomic Scientists* 48, no. 5 (June 1992): 28.

28. Riyadh Post, "Muḥammad Al Ṣabbān . . . wa al-Dars al-Saʿūdī f ī Idāra Laʿba al-Mufāwaḍāt'" (Mohammad Al Sabban . . . and the lesson in the art of the "game of negotiations"), May 26, 2019, https://riyadhpost.live/15447; Mohammad Al Sabban, Twitter post, May 26, 2019, https://twitter.com/sabbanms/status/1132741530467426304.

29. "Al-Saʿūdiyya Tadʿam Juhūd al-ʿĀlam li-Muʿālja al-Iḥtibās al-Ḥarārī" (Saudi Arabia supports global efforts to tackle global warming), *Al-Arabiyya*, September 23, 2014; Mohammad Al Sabban, "Al-Saʿūdiyya.. wa-Dhurwa al-Ṭalab ʿalā al-Nafṭ" (Saudi Arabia . . . and Peak Demand for Oil), *Okaz*, April 10, 2018, https://www.okaz.com.sa/articles/na/1631187. For government-sponsored sustainability campaigns, see "Al-Riyāḍ al-Khaḍrāʾ" (Green Riyadh), *Okaz*, March 19, 2019, https://www.okaz.com.sa/local/na/1713362; and the "Qatrah" (Drop) water-conservation program, https://www.qatrah.com.

BIBLIOGRAPHY

PRIVATE ARCHIVES

Eugene and Jerine Bird Papers, Princeton University Special Collections, Princeton, NJ.
ExxonMobil Historical Collection, Briscoe Center for American History, University of Texas, Austin, TX
Ford Foundation Archives, Rockefeller Archive Center, Sleepy Hollow, NY
Hoover Institution Archives, Stanford, CA
Albert J. Meyer Papers, Harvard University Archives, Cambridge, MA
William E. Mulligan Papers, Georgetown University, Washington, DC
William E. Simon Papers, Lafayette College, Easton, PA

U.S. GOVERNMENT ARCHIVES

Jimmy Carter Presidential Library, Atlanta, GA
Federal Reserve Bank of New York Archives, New York, NY
Gerald R. Ford Presidential Library, Ann Arbor, MI
John F. Kennedy Presidential Library, Boston, MA
National Archives and Records Administration (NARA), College Park, MD
Record Group 56, Records of the Department of the Treasury
Record Group 59, Records of the Department of State
Richard Nixon Presidential Library, Yorba Linda, CA
Ronald Reagan Presidential Library, Simi Valley, CA

OTHER ARCHIVES AND LIBRARIES

Institute for Palestine Studies, Beirut, Lebanon
King Abdulaziz University Library, Jeddah, Saudi Arabia
King Faisal Center for Research and Islamic Studies, Riyadh, Saudi Arabia
King Saud University Library, Riyadh, Saudi Arabia
Ministry of Petroleum and Mineral Resources, Riyadh, Saudi Arabia
Ministry of Planning, Riyadh, Saudi Arabia
Organization of the Petroleum Exporting Countries, Vienna, Austria
University of Jordan Library, Amman, Jordan

PRIMARY SOURCE COLLECTIONS

Al-Wathā'iq al-'Arabīyya (Arab political documents). Beirut: American University of Beirut.
American Presidency Project, University of California at Santa Barbara. http://www.presidency .ucsb.edu.
Association for Diplomatic Studies and Training, Oral History Interviews. https://adst.org/oral -history.
Central Intelligence Agency, Freedom of Information Act Electronic Reading Room. http:// www.foia.cia.gov.
Department of State, FOIA Reading Room. http://foia.state.gov.
Digitized National Security Adviser Memoranda of Conversations, Gerald R. Ford Library, https://www.fordlibrarymuseum.gov/library/guides/findingaid/Memoranda_of _Conversations.asp
Documents on the History of Saudi Arabia, vol. 3, edited by Ibrahim al-Rashid. Salisbury, NC: Documentary Publications, 1976.
Mu'asasa al-Malik Khālid (King Khalid Foundation), Wathā'iq (Documents). http://www .kingkhalid.org.sa.
Muqatel, Wathā'iq (Documents). http://muqatel.com.
National Archives and Records Administration, Access to Archival Databases, Record Group 59. https://aad.archives.gov.
U.S. Department of State, *Foreign Relations of the United States*. Washington, DC: U.S. Government Printing Office. http://history.state.gov/historicaldocuments.

INTERVIEWS

Nordine Ait-Laoussine (by telephone), March 1, 2011
James Akins (Mitchellville, MD), June 30, 2009
Michael Ameen (Kingwood, TX), May 28, 2011
Thomas Anderson (by telephone), May 11, 2011
Cecil Andrus (Boise, ID), April 28, 2011
Saeed Badeeb (Herndon, VA), May 26, 2011

Stuart Eizenstat (by telephone), August 30, 2019

Turki al-Faisal (Riyadh, Saudi Arabia), January 8, 2011

JoAnn Shaya Fidel (by telephone), June 10, 2019

Frank Fugate (Austin, TX) June 3, 2011

Hassan al-Husseini (Dhahran, Saudi Arabia), February 3, 2011

Mohammed Salih Jokhdar (Jeddah, Saudi Arabia), March 1, 2011; February 27, 2012

Frank Jungers (by telephone), May 31, 2011

Ali al-Khalifa Al Sabah (Kuwait City, Kuwait), March 11, 2011

Richard Lawrence (Austin, TX), June 3, 2011

Baldo Marinovic (Austin, TX), June 2, 2011

Abdullah Naibari (Kuwait City, Kuwait), March 12, 2011

William Quandt (Charlottesville, VA, and by telephone), January 26, 2008; February 9, 2019;
  March 14, 2019; May 7, 2019

Donald Rumsfeld (Washington, DC), September 1, 2010

Hal Saunders (Washington, DC), July 17, 2009

Brent Scowcroft (Washington, DC), July 29, 2009

Abdulrahman Saleh al-Shobaily (Riyadh, Saudi Arabia), February 22, 2012

Jennifer Simpson (April 14, 2011)

Soliman Solaim (by telephone), February 26, 2011

PUBLISHED SOURCES

Abd al-Mohsen al-Turki, Abdullah bin. *Al-Malik 'Abd al-'Azīz Āl Sa'ūd: Umma fī Rajul* (King
  Abdulaziz: A nation in a man). Riyadh: Wizāra al-Shu'ūn al-Islāmiyya wa al-Awqāf wa
  al-D'awa wa al-Irshād, 2000.

Abrahamian, Ervand. *The Coup: 1953, the CIA, and the Roots of Modern U.S.-Iranian Relations*.
  New York: New Press, 2013.

——. *A History of Modern Iran*. Cambridge: Cambridge University Press, 2008.

Adelman, M. A. "The Clumsy Cartel." *Energy Journal* 1, no. 1 (1980): 43–53.

——. *The Genie Out of the Bottle: World Oil Since 1970*. Cambridge, MA: MIT Press, 1995.

Ahmad, Edbal, and David Caploe. "The Logic of Military Intervention." *Race and Class* 17, no. 3
  (1976): 328–29.

Akins, James E. "The Oil Crisis: This Time the Wolf Is Here." *Foreign Affairs* 51, no. 3 (1973):
  462–90.

Al-Arian, Abdullah. "Seventy Years of the *New York Times* Describing Saudi Royals as Reformers." *Jadaliyya*, November 27, 2017. http://www.jadaliyya.com/Details/34727/Seventy
  -Years-of-the-New -York-Times-Describing-Saudi-Royals-as-Leading-Reform.

Al-Dajani, Amhed. *Khālid ibn 'Abd al-'Azīz: Sīra Mālik wa Nahḍa al-Mamlaka* (Khalid Bin Abdulaziz: A king's biography and a kingdom's renaissance). Riyadh: Maktaba al-Malik
  Fahd al-Wataniā, 2002.

Al Fahad, Abdulaziz H. "The 'Imama vs. the 'Iqal: Hadari-Bedouin Conflict and the Formation of the Saudi State." In *Counter-narratives: History, Contemporary Society, and Politics*

in Saudi Arabia and Yemen, edited by Madawi Al-Rasheed and Robert Vitalis, 35–75. New York: Palgrave Macmillan, 2004.

——. "Raiders and Traders: A Poet's Lament on the End of the Bedouin Heroic Age." In *Saudi Arabia in Transition*, edited by Bernard Haykel, Thomas Hegghammer, and Stéphane Lacroix, 231–62. Cambridge: Cambridge University Press, 2015.

Alireza, Marianne. *At the Drop of a Veil*. Boston: Houghton Mifflin, 1971.

Almana, Mohammed. *Arabia Unified: A Portrait of Ibn Saud*. London: Hutchinson Benham, 1980.

Al-Naimi, Ali. *Out of the Desert: My Journey from Nomadic Bedouin to the Heart of Global Oil*. London: Penguin, 2016.

Al-Rasheed, Madawi. *A History of Saudi Arabia*. 2nd ed. Cambridge: Cambridge University Press, 2010.

——. "Saudi Arabia and the 1948 Palestine War: Beyond Official History." In *The War for Palestine: Rewriting the History of 1948*, edited by Eugene Rogan and Avi Shlaim, 228–47. Cambridge: Cambridge University Press, 2007.

Al-Said, Nasir. *Tarīkh Āl Saud* (History of the Al Saud). Beirut: Ittiḥād Shaʻb al-Jazīra al-ʻArabiyya, 1985.

Altorki, Soraya, and Donald P. Cole. *Arabian Oasis City: The Transformation of ʻUnayzah*. Austin: University of Texas Press, 1989.

Alvandi, Roham. *Nixon, Kissinger, and the Shah: The United States and Iran in the Cold War*. Oxford: Oxford University Press, 2014.

Amanat, Abbas. *Iran: A Modern History*. New Haven: Yale University Press, 2017.

Anderson, Irvine H. *Aramco, the United States, and Saudi Arabia: A Study of the Dynamics of Foreign Oil Policy, 1933–1950*. Princeton, NJ: Princeton University Press, 1981.

Antonius, George. *The Arab Awakening: The Story of the Arab National Movement*. London: H. Hamilton, 1938.

Anziska, Seth. *Preventing Palestine: A Political History from Camp David to Oslo*. Princeton, NJ: Princeton University Press, 2018.

Axworthy, Michael. *Revolutionary Iran: A History of the Islamic Republic*. Oxford: Oxford University Press, 2013.

Bacevich, Andrew J. *America's War for the Greater Middle East: A Military History*. New York: Random House, 2016.

Balkhair, Abdullah. *ʻAbd Allāh Balkhayr Yatadhakkar* (Abdullah Balkhair remembers). Jeddah: ʻAbd al-Maqṣūd Muḥammad Saʻīd Khawjah, 1998.

Baltimore, Paul. "From the Camel to the Cadillac: Automobility, Consumption, and the U.S.-Saudi Special Relationship." PhD diss., University of California at Santa Barbara, 2014.

Barger, Thomas C. *Out in the Blue: Letters from Arabia 1937–1940*. Vista, CA: Selwa Press, 2000.

Bar-Joseph, Uri. "Israel's 1973 Intelligence Failure." *Israel Affairs* 6, no. 1 (September 1999): 11–35.

Baumol, William J. *The Theory of Environmental Policy: Externalities, Public Outlays, and the Quality of Life*. Englewood Cliffs, NJ: Prentice-Hall, 1975.

Berghahn, Volker R. "Philanthropy and Diplomacy in the 'American Century.'" *Diplomatic History* 23, no. 3 (July 1999): 393–419.

Berman, Edward H. *The Influence of the Carnegie, Ford, and Rockefeller Foundations on American Foreign Policy: The Ideology of Philanthropy*. Albany: State University of New York Press, 1983.

Bill, James A. *The Eagle and the Lion: The Tragedy of American-Iranian Relations*. New Haven, CT: Yale University Press, 1988.

Bin Abdul-Wahhab, Muhammad. *Kitab At-Tauhid: The Book of Monotheism*. Riyadh: Darussalam, 2011.

Bird, Kai. *The Chairman: John J. McCloy and the Making of the American Establishment*. New York: Simon and Schuster, 1992.

——. *Crossing Mandelbaum Gate: Coming of Age Between the Arabs and Israelis, 1956–1978*. New York: Scribner, 2010.

Biven, W. Carl. *Jimmy Carter's Economy: Policy in an Age of Limits*. Chapel Hill: University of North Carolina Press, 2002.

Black, Megan. *The Global Interior: Mineral Frontiers and American Power*. Cambridge, MA: Harvard University Press, 2018.

Blair, John. *The Control of Oil*. New York: Pantheon Books, 1976.

Borstelmann, Thomas. *The 1970s: A New Global History from Civil Rights to Economic Inequality*. Princeton, NJ: Princeton University Press, 2011.

Bradshaw, Tancred. *The Glubb Reports: Glubb Pasha and Britain's Empire Project in the Middle East, 1920–1956*. Basingstoke, Hampshire: Palgrave Macmillan, 2016.

Brands, Hal. "Saddam Hussein, the United States, and the Invasion of Iran: Was There a Green Light?" *Cold War History* 12, no. 2 (May 2012): 319–43.

Bronson, Rachel. *Thicker Than Oil: America's Uneasy Partnership with Saudi Arabia*. Oxford: Oxford University Press, 2006.

Brown, Anthony Cave. *Oil, God, and Gold: The Story of Aramco and the Saudi Kings*. Boston: Houghton Mifflin, 1999.

Brzezinski, Zbigniew. *Power and Principle: Memoirs of the National Security Advisor, 1977–1981*. New York: Farrar, Straus and Giroux, 1983.

Bsheer, Rosie. "A Counter-revolutionary State: Popular Movements and the Making of Saudi Arabia." *Past and Present* 238, no. 1 (February 2018): 233–77.

Carter, Jimmy. *Keeping Faith: Memoirs of a President*. New York: Bantam Books, 1982.

Chamberlin, Paul Thomas. *The Cold War's Killing Fields: Rethinking the Long Peace*. New York: Harper, 2018.

Chase Manhattan Corporation. *1974 Annual Report*. New York: Chase Manhattan, 1975.

Chaudhry, Kiren Aziz. *The Price of Wealth: Economies and Institutions in the Middle East*. Ithaca, NY: Cornell University Press, 1997.

Cheney, Michael Sheldon. *Big Oil Man from Arabia*. New York: Ballantine Books, 1958.

Childs, William R. *The Texas Railroad Commission: Understanding Regulation in America to the Mid-Twentieth Century*. College Station: Texas A&M University Press, 2005.

Citino, Nathan J. "Defending the 'Postwar Petroleum Order': The US, Britain and the 1954 Saudi-Onassis Tanker Deal." *Diplomacy and Statecraft* 11, no. 2 (July 2000): 137–60.

——. *Envisioning the Arab Future: Modernization in US-Arab Relations, 1945–1967*. Cambridge: Cambridge University Press, 2017.

——. *From Arab Nationalism to OPEC: Eisenhower, King Saʿūd, and the Making of U.S.-Saudi Relations.* Bloomington: Indiana University Press, 2002.

Colby, William Egan, and Peter Forbath. *Honorable Men: My Life in the CIA.* New York: Simon and Schuster, 1978.

Coll, Steve. *The Bin Ladens: An Arabian Family in the American Century.* New York: Penguin, 2008.

——. *Ghost Wars: The Secret History of the CIA, Afghanistan, and Bin Laden, from the Soviet Invasion to September 10, 2001.* New York: Penguin, 2004.

Commins, David. *The Mission and the Kingdom: Wahhabi Power Behind the Saudi Throne.* Rev. ed. New York: I. B. Tauris, 2016.

Congressional Research Service. *Oil Fields as Military Objectives: A Feasibility Study.* Washington, DC: U.S. Government Printing Office, 1975.

Cooper, Andrew Scott. *The Fall of Heaven: The Pahlavis and the Final Days of Imperial Iran.* New York: Henry Holt, 2016.

——. *The Oil Kings: How the U.S., Iran, and Saudi Arabia Changed the Balance of Power in the Middle East.* New York: Simon and Schuster, 2011.

Coppola, John. "A Pride of Museums in the Desert: Saudi Arabia and the 'Gift of Friendship' Exhibition." *Curator: The Museum Journal* 48, no. 1 (2005): 90–100.

Costigliola, Frank. *Awkward Dominion: American Political, Economic, and Cultural Relations with Europe, 1919–1933.* Ithaca, NY: Cornell University Press, 1988.

Cowie, Jefferson. *Stayin' Alive: The 1970s and the Last Days of the Working Class.* New York: New Press, 2010.

Crile, George. *Charlie Wilson's War: The Extraordinary Story of the Largest Covert Operation in History.* New York: Atlantic Monthly Press, 2003.

Cunningham, Sean P. "The 1976 GOP Primary: Ford, Reagan, and the Battle That Transformed Political Campaigns in Texas." *East Texas Historical Journal* 41, no. 2 (October 2003): 15–25.

Daigle, Craig. "The American War for the Greater Middle East: From Diplomacy to Military Intervention." *International Journal of Middle East Studies* 49, no. 4 (2017): 757–65.

——. *The Limits of Détente: The United States, the Soviet Union, and the Arab-Israeli Conflict, 1969–1973.* New Haven, CT: Yale University Press, 2012.

Dallek, Robert. *Nixon and Kissinger: Partners in Power.* New York: HarperCollins, 2007.

Daoudi, M. S., and M. S. Dajani. "The 1967 Oil Embargo Revisited." *Journal of Palestine Studies* 13, no. 2 (1984): 65–90.

DeGolyer, Everett. "Preliminary Report of the Technical Oil Mission to the Middle East." *Bulletin of the American Association of Petroleum Geologists* 28, no. 7 (July 1944): 919–23.

Dietrich, Christopher R. W. "Oil Power and Economic Theologies: The United States and the Third World in the Wake of the Energy Crisis." *Diplomatic History* 40, no. 3 (June 2016): 500–529.

——. *Oil Revolution: Anticolonial Elites, Sovereign Rights, and the Economic Culture of Decolonization.* Cambridge: Cambridge University Press, 2017.

Duguid, Stephen. "A Biographical Approach to the Study of Social Change in the Middle East: Abdullah Tariki as a New Man." *International Journal of Middle East Studies* 1, no. 3 (1970): 195–220.

Eddy, William Alfred. *F.D.R. Meets Ibn Saud*. New York: American Friends of the Middle East, 1954.

Ehrlich, Paul R. *The Population Bomb*. New York: Ballantine Books, 1968.

Eisenhower, Dwight D. *At Ease: Stories I Tell to Friends*. Garden City, NY: Doubleday, 1967.

Everly, Steve. "U.S., Britain Developed Plans to Disable or Destroy Middle Eastern Oil Facilities from Late 1940s to Early 1960s in Event of a Soviet Invasion (National Security Archive Briefing Book 552)." https://nsarchive.gwu.edu/briefing-book/iran-nuclear-vault /2016-06-23/us-britain-developed-plans-disable-or-destroy-middle.

Fahad, Khalifa. *Jaḥīm al-Ḥukm al-Saʿūdī wa Nīrān al-Wahhābiyya* (The hell of Saudi rule and the flames of Wahhabism). London: Al-Sīfa li al-Nashr wa al-Tawzʿīa, 1989.

Fandy, Mamoun. *Saudi Arabia and the Politics of Dissent*. Basingstoke, Hampshire: Macmillan, 1999.

Ferguson, Niall, Charles S. Maier, Erez Manela, and Daniel J. Sargent, eds. *The Shock of the Global: The 1970s in Perspective*. Cambridge, MA: Harvard University Press, 2010.

Ferris, Jesse. *Nasser's Gamble: How Intervention in Yemen Caused the Six-Day War and the Decline of Egyptian Power*. Princeton, NJ: Princeton University Press, 2013.

Field, Michael. *The Merchants: The Big Business Families of Saudi Arabia and the Gulf States*. Woodstock, NY: Overlook Press, 1985.

Fleischer, Richard. *Soylent Green*. Metro-Goldwyn-Mayer, 1973.

Flippen, J. Brooks. *Nixon and the Environment*. Albuquerque: University of New Mexico Press, 2000.

Ford, Gerald. *A Time to Heal: The Autobiography of Gerald R. Ford*. New York: Harper and Row, 1979.

Frank, Alison. *Oil Empire: Visions of Prosperity in Austrian Galicia*. Cambridge, MA: Harvard University Press, 2005.

——. "The Petroleum War of 1910: Standard Oil, Austria, and the Limits of the Multinational Corporation." *American Historical Review* 114, no. 1 (2009): 16–41.

Frydl, Kathleen J. *The G.I. Bill*. Cambridge: Cambridge University Press, 2009.

Garavini, Giuliano. *The Rise and Fall of OPEC in the Twentieth Century*. Oxford: Oxford University Press, 2019.

Gardner, Nikolas. "The Harold Wilson Government, Airwork Services Limited, and the Saudi Arabian Air Defence Scheme, 1965–73." *Journal of Contemporary History* 42, no. 2 (2007): 345–63.

Gates, Robert M. *From the Shadows: The Ultimate Insider's Story of Five Presidents and How They Won the Cold War*. New York: Tombstone Books, 1997.

Gendzier, Irene L. *Dying to Forget: Oil, Power, Palestine, and the Foundations of U.S. Policy in the Middle East*. New York: Columbia University Press, 2015.

Geschwind, Carl-Henry. *A Comparative History of Motor Fuels Taxation, 1909–2009: Why Gasoline Is Cheap and Petrol Is Dear*. Lanham, MD: Lexington Books, 2017.

Getachew, Adom. *Worldmaking after Empire: The Rise and Fall of Self-Determination*. Princeton, NJ: Princeton University Press, 2019.

Ghattas, Monika. *Los Arabes of New Mexico: Compadres from a Distant Land*. Santa Fe, NM: Sunstone Press, 2016.

Gilman, Nils, and Samuel Moyn, eds. "Special Issue: Toward a History of the New International Economic Order." *Humanity* 6, no. 1 (2015).

Gleijeses, Piero. "Moscow's Proxy? Cuba and Africa 1975–1988." *Journal of Cold War Studies* 8, no. 4 (October 2006): 98–146.

Glubb, John Bagot. *War in the Desert: An R.A.F. Frontier Campaign.* London: Hodder and Stoughton, 1960.

Gold, Russell. *The Boom: How Fracking Ignited the American Energy Revolution and Changed the World.* New York: Simon and Schuster, 2014.

Goralski, Robert, and Russell W. Freeburg. *Oil and War: How the Deadly Struggle for Fuel in WWII Meant Victory or Defeat.* New York: Morrow, 1987.

Graf, Rüdiger. *Oil and Sovereignty: Petro-Knowledge and Energy Policy in the United States and Western Europe in the 1970s.* Translated by Alex Skinner. New York: Berghahn Books, 2018.

Gregory, Ross. "America and Saudi Arabia, Act I: The Conference of Franklin D. Roosevelt and King Ibn Saud in February 1945." In *Presidents, Diplomats, and Other Mortals: Essays Honoring Robert H. Ferrell,* edited by J. Garry Clifford and Theodore A. Wilson, 116–33. Columbia: University of Missouri Press, 2007.

Gutfreund, Owen D. *Twentieth-Century Sprawl: Highways and the Reshaping of the American Landscape.* Oxford: Oxford University Press, 2004.

Habib, John S. *Ibn Sa'ud's Warriors of Islam: The Ikhwan of Najd and Their Role in the Creation of the Sa'udi Kingdom, 1910–1930.* Leiden: Brill, 1978.

Hakes, Jay. *A Declaration of Energy Independence: How Freedom from Foreign Oil Can Improve National Security, Our Economy, and the Environment.* Hoboken: Wiley, 2008.

Harbinson, David K. "The US–Saudi Arabian Joint Commission on Economic Cooperation: A Critical Appraisal." *Middle East Journal* 44, no. 2 (Spring 1990): 269–83.

Hart, Parker T. *Saudi Arabia and the United States: Birth of a Security Partnership.* Bloomington: Indiana University Press, 1998.

Hayes, Stephen D. "Joint Economic Commissions as Instruments of US Foreign Policy in the Middle East." *Middle East Journal* 31, no. 1, (Winter 1977), 16–30.

Haykel, Bernard. "Oil in Saudi Arabian Culture and Politics: From Tribal Poets to Al-Qaeda's Ideologues." In *Saudi Arabia in Transition: Insights on Social, Political, Economic and Religious Change,* edited by Bernard Haykel, Thomas Hegghammer, and Stéphane Lacroix, 125–47. Cambridge: Cambridge University Press, 2015.

Hegghammer, Thomas. *Jihad in Saudi Arabia: Violence and Pan-Islamism Since 1979.* Cambridge: Cambridge University Press, 2010.

Hegghammer, Thomas, and Stéphane Lacroix. "Rejectionist Islamism in Saudi Arabia: The Story of Juhayman Al-'Utaybi Revisited." *International Journal of Middle East Studies* 39, no. 1 (2007): 103–22.

Heikal, Mohamed. *The Road to Ramadan.* New York: Quadrangle, 1975.

Helms, Christine Moss. *The Cohesion of Saudi Arabia: Evolution of Political Identity.* Baltimore: Johns Hopkins University Press, 1981.

Henderson, Jason. "Secessionist Automobility: Racism, Anti-urbanism, and the Politics of Automobility in Atlanta, Georgia." *International Journal of Urban and Regional Research* 30, no. 2 (2006): 293–307.

Herbstreuth, Sebastian. *Oil and American Identity: A Culture of Dependency and U.S. Foreign Policy.* London: I. B. Tauris, 2016.

Hernandez, Kelly Lytle. *Migra! A History of the U.S. Border Patrol.* Berkeley: University of California Press, 2010.

Hertog, Steffen. *Princes, Brokers, and Bureaucrats: Oil and the State in Saudi Arabia.* Ithaca, NY: Cornell University Press, 2010.

Hicke, Carol, ed. *American Perspectives of Aramco, the Saudi-Arabian Oil-Producing Company, 1930s to 1980s.* Bancroft Library, University of California, Berkeley, 1995. https://archive .org/details/aramcooilproducoohickrich.

Howard, Adam M., and Alexander R. Wieland. "Confronting the Arc of Crisis: The Carter Administration's Approach to Security Building in the 'Greater Gulf' Region, 1977–80." In *United States Relations with China and Iran: Toward the Asian Century,* edited by Osamah F. Khalil, 153–69. London: Bloomsbury, 2019.

Huber, Matthew. *Lifeblood: Oil, Freedom, and the Forces of Capital.* Minneapolis: University of Minnesota Press, 2013.

Huxley, Aldous. *Brave New World.* London: Chatto and Windus, 1932.

Ignotus, Miles. "Seizing Arab Oil." *Harper's* 250, no. 1498 (March 1975): 45.

Jackson, Kenneth T. *Crabgrass Frontier: The Suburbanization of the United States.* Oxford: Oxford University Press, 1985.

Jacobs, Jane. *The Death and Life of Great American Cities.* New York: Random House, 1961.

Jacobs, Meg. *Panic at the Pump: The Energy Crisis and the Transformation of American Politics in the 1970s.* New York: Hill and Wang, 2016.

Jones, Toby Craig. *Desert Kingdom: How Oil and Water Forged Modern Saudi Arabia.* Cambridge, MA: Harvard University Press, 2010.

——. "Rebellion on the Saudi Periphery: Modernity, Marginalization, and the Shi'a Uprising of 1979." *International Journal of Middle East Studies* 38, no. 2 (2006): 213–33.

Kaplan, Amy. *Our American Israel: The Story of an Entangled Alliance.* Cambridge, MA: Harvard University Press, 2018.

Kaplan, Robert D. *Arabists: The Romance of an American Elite.* New York: Free Press, 1995.

Kechichian, Joseph A. "Islamic Revivalism and Change in Saudi Arabia: Juhaymān al-'Utaybī's 'Letters' to the Saudi People." *Muslim World* 80, no. 1 (January 1990): 1–16.

Kerr, Malcolm H. *The Arab Cold War: Gamal 'Abd Al-Nasir and His Rivals, 1958–1970.* 3rd ed. Oxford: Oxford University Press, 1971.

Kessler, Ronald. *Khashoggi: The Story of the World's Richest Man.* London: Bantam Press, 1986.

Khalil, Osamah F. *America's Dream Palace: Middle East Expertise and the Rise of the National Security State.* Cambridge, MA: Harvard University Press, 2016.

Kissinger, Henry. *Years of Upheaval.* Boston: Little, Brown, 1982.

Kolander, Kenneth. "Phantom Peace: Henry 'Scoop' Jackson, J. William Fulbright, and Military Sales to Israel." *Diplomatic History* 41, no. 3 (June 2017): 567–93.

Krippner, Greta R. *Capitalizing on Crisis: The Political Origins of the Rise of Finance.* Cambridge, MA: Harvard University Press, 2011.

Kruse, Kevin M. *White Flight: Atlanta and the Making of Modern Conservatism.* Princeton, NJ: Princeton University Press, 2005.

Kurpershoek, P. Marcel. *Bedouin Poets of the Dawasir Tribe: Between Nomadism and Settlement in Southern Najd*. Leiden: Brill, 1999.

Labelle, Maurice Jr. "'The Only Thorn': Early Saudi-American Relations and the Question of Palestine, 1945–1949." *Diplomatic History* 35, no. 2 (2011): 257–81.

Lacroix, Stéphane. *Awakening Islam: The Politics of Religious Dissent in Contemporary Saudi Arabia*. Translated by George Holoch. Cambridge, MA: Harvard University Press, 2011.

Lacy, Robert. *Inside the Kingdom: Kings, Clerics, Modernists, Terrorists, and the Struggle for Saudi Arabia*. New York: Viking, 2009.

Lauterpacht, E., C. J. Greenwood, Marc Weller, and Daniel Bethlehem. *The Kuwait Crisis: Basic Documents*. Cambridge: Cambridge University Press, 1991.

Lawrence, Bruce, ed. *Messages to the World: The Statements of Osama Bin Laden*. London: Verso, 2005.

Leggett, Jeremy. "Global Warming: The Worst Case." *Bulletin of the Atomic Scientists* 48, no. 5 (June 1992): 28.

Lerner, Mitchell B., and Andrew L. Johns. *The Cold War at Home and Abroad: Domestic Politics and US Foreign Policy Since 1945*. Lexington: University Press of Kentucky, 2018.

Lifset, Robert D. "A New Understanding of the American Energy Crisis of the 1970s." *Historical Social Research* 39, no. 4 (2014): 22–42.

Link, Stefan Johannes. "Transnational Fordism: Ford Motor Company, Nazi Germany, and the Soviet Union in the Interwar Years." PhD diss., Harvard University, 2012.

Lippman, Thomas. "Cooperation under the Radar: The US-Saudi Arabian Joint Commission for Economic Cooperation (JECOR)." Middle East Institute, October 1, 2009. https://www.mei.edu/publications/cooperation-under-radar-us-saudi-arabian-joint-commission-economic-cooperation-jecor.

——. *Inside the Mirage: America's Fragile Partnership with Saudi Arabia*. New York: Basic Books, 2004.

Little, Douglas. *American Orientalism: The United States and the Middle East Since 1945*. 3rd ed. Chapel Hill: University of North Carolina Press, 2008.

——. "Mission Impossible: The CIA and the Cult of Covert Action in the Middle East." *Diplomatic History* 28, no. 5 (2004): 663–701.

——. "The New Frontier on the Nile: JFK, Nasser, and Arab Nationalism." *Journal of American History* 75, no. 2 (1989): 501–27.

Logevall, Fredrik. "Politics and Foreign Relations." *Journal of American History* 95, no. 4 (2009): 1074–78.

Low, Michael Christopher. "Ottoman Infrastructures of the Saudi Hydro-State: The Technopolitics of Pilgrimage and Potable Water in the Hijaz." *Comparative Studies in Society and History* 57, no. 4 (2015): 942–74.

Mandani, Mahmood. *Good Muslim, Bad Muslim: America, the Cold War, and the Roots of Terror*. New York: Doubleday: 2005.

Mann, Joseph. "A Reassessment of the 1967 Arab Oil Embargo." *Israel Affairs* 19, no. 4 (October 2013): 693–703.

Matthiesen, Toby. "Migration, Minorities, and Radical Networks: Labour Movements and Opposition Groups in Saudi Arabia, 1950–1975." *International Review of Social History* 59, no. 3 (2014): 473–504.

———. *The Other Saudis: Shiism, Dissent and Sectarianism*. Cambridge: Cambridge University Press, 2014.

Mattli, Walter. *Darkness by Design: The Hidden Power in Global Capital Markets*. Princeton, NJ: Princeton University Press, 2019.

Mattson, Kevin. *"What the Heck Are You Up to, Mr. President?": Jimmy Carter, America's "Malaise," and the Speech That Should Have Changed the Country*. New York: Bloomsbury, 2009.

Matusow, Allen J. *Nixon's Economy: Booms, Busts, Dollars, and Votes*. Lawrence: University Press of Kansas, 1998.

Maxim, Hudson. *Defenseless America*. New York: Hearst's International Library Co., 1915.

McAlister, Melani. *Epic Encounters: Culture, Media, and U.S. Interests in the Middle East Since 1945*. Berkeley: University of California Press, 2005.

McCartney, Laton. *Friends in High Places: The Bechtel Story: The Most Secret Corporation and How It Engineered the World*. New York: Simon and Schuster, 1988.

McFarland, Victor. "The New International Economic Order, Interdependence, and Globalization." *Humanity* 6, no. 1 (Spring 2015): 217–33.

———. "The US Response to OPEC." In *Handbook of OPEC and the Global Energy Order: Past, Present and Future Challenges*, edited by Dag Harald Claes and Giuliano Garavini, 121–32. Abingdon: Routledge, 2020.

Meadows, Donella H., and Club of Rome. *The Limits to Growth: A Report for the Club of Rome's Project on the Predicament of Mankind*. New York: Universe Books, 1972.

Menoret, Pascal. *Joyriding in Riyadh: Oil, Urbanism, and Road Revolt*. Cambridge: Cambridge University Press, 2014.

———. "The Suburbanization of Islamic Activism in Saudi Arabia." *City and Society* 29, no. 1 (2017): 162–86.

Mieczkowski, Yanek. *Gerald Ford and the Challenges of the 1970s*. Lexington: University Press of Kentucky, 2005.

Miller, Aaron David. *Search for Security: Saudi Arabian Oil and American Foreign Policy, 1939–1949*. Chapel Hill: University of North Carolina Press, 1980.

Mitchell, Nancy. *Jimmy Carter in Africa: Race and the Cold War*. Stanford, CA: Stanford University Press, 2016.

Mitchell, Timothy. *Carbon Democracy: Political Power in the Age of Oil*. London: Verso, 2011.

———. "The Resources of Economics: Making the 1973 Oil Crisis." *Journal of Cultural Economy* 3, no. 2 (2010): 189–204.

Mohl, Raymond A. "The Interstates and the Cities: The U.S. Department of Transportation and the Freeway Revolt, 1966–1973." *Journal of Policy History* 20, no. 2 (2008): 193–226.

———. "Stop the Road: Freeway Revolts in American Cities." *Journal of Urban History* 30, no. 5 (July 2004): 674–706.

Moran, Theodore. "Managing an Oligopoly of Would-Be Sovereigns: The Dynamics of Joint Control and Self-Control in the International Oil Industry Past, Present, and Future." *International Organization* 41, no. 4 (Autumn 1987): 575–607.

Munif, Abdelrahman. *Cities of Salt*. Translated by Peter Theroux. New York: Random House, 1987.

———. *The Trench*. Translated by Peter Theroux. New York: Vintage, 1993.

Nasser, Gamal Abdel. *The Philosophy of the Revolution*. Washington, DC: Public Affairs Press, 1955.

National Highways Association. "United States Highways." 1915. https://collections.lib.uwm .edu/digital/collection/agdm/id/1476.

"Navy Purchases of Middle East Oil." Investigation of the National Defense Program: Additional Report. Washington, DC: U.S. Government Printing Office, 1948.

Njølstad, Olav. "Shifting Priorities: The Persian Gulf in US Strategic Planning in the Carter Years." *Cold War History* 4, no. 3 (April 2004): 21–55.

Nordhaus, William D. *The Climate Casino: Risk, Uncertainty, and Economics for a Warming World*. New Haven, CT: Yale University Press, 2013.

—— "Retrospective on the 1970s Productivity Slowdown," National Bureau of Economic Research Working Paper No. 10950, December 2004, https://www.nber.org/papers /w10950.

Norton, Peter. "Of Love Affairs and Other Stories." In *Incomplete Streets: Processes, Practices, and Possibilities*, edited by Stephen Zavestoski and Julian Agyeman, 17–35. Abingdon: Routledge, 2015.

Ochsenwald, William. "Islam and Loyalty in the Saudi Hijaz, 1926–1939." *Die Welt Des Islams* 47, no. 1 (2007): 7–32.

Odom, William E. "The Cold War Origins of the U.S. Central Command." *Journal of Cold War Studies* 8, no. 2 (Spring 2006): 52–82.

Offner, Amy C. *Sorting Out the Mixed Economy: The Rise and Fall of Welfare and Developmental States in the Americas* (Princeton, NJ: Princeton University Press, 2019).

Ogle, Vanessa. "Archipelago Capitalism: Tax Havens, Offshore Money, and the State, 1950s–1970s." *American Historical Review* 122, no. 5 (December 2017): 1431–58.

——. "State Rights Against Private Capital: The 'New International Economic Order' and the Struggle Over Aid, Trade, and Foreign Investment, 1962–1981." *Humanity: An International Journal of Human Rights, Humanitarianism, and Development* 5, no. 2 (2014): 211–34.

Orkaby, Asher. *Beyond the Arab Cold War: The International History of the Yemen Civil War, 1962–68*. Oxford: Oxford University Press, 2017.

Ostrander, Ian, and William Lowry. "Oil Crises and Policy Continuity: A History of Failure to Change." *Journal of Policy History* 24, no. 3 (2012): 391–92.

O'Sullivan, Meghan L. *Windfall: How the New Energy Abundance Upends Global Politics and Strengthens America's Power*. New York: Simon and Schuster, 2017.

Ottaway, David. "The King and Us: U.S.-Saudi Relations in the Wake of 9/11." *Foreign Affairs* 88, no. 3 (2009): 121–31.

——. *The King's Messenger: Prince Bandar Bin Sultan and America's Tangled Relationship with Saudi Arabia*. New York: Walker Books, 2008.

Painter, David S. "The Marshall Plan and Oil." *Cold War History* 9, no. 2 (2009): 159–75.

——. *Oil and the American Century: The Political Economy of U.S. Foreign Oil Policy, 1941–1954*. Baltimore: Johns Hopkins University Press, 1986.

——. "Oil and the Marshall Plan." *Business History Review* 58, no. 3 (1984): 359–83.

Parker, Chad H. *Making the Desert Modern: Americans, Arabs, and Oil on the Saudi Frontier, 1933–1973*. Amherst: University of Massachusetts Press, 2015.

Parmar, Inderjeet. *Foundations of the American Century: The Ford, Carnegie, and Rockefeller Foundations in the Rise of American Power*. New York: Columbia University Press, 2012.

PBS *Frontline*. "House of Saud." February 8, 2005.

Pennell, Joseph. *That Liberty Shall Not Perish from the Earth*. 1918. Library of Congress. https://www.loc.gov/resource/ppmsca.18343/.

Penney, Matthew T. "Intelligence and the 1973 Arab-Israeli War." In *President Nixon and the Role of Intelligence in the 1973 Arab-Israeli War*, 2013. By the Central Intelligence Agency (CIA), the Richard Nixon Foundation, and the Richard Nixon Presidential Library and Museum. https://www.cia.gov/library/publications /international-relations/arab-israeli-war /nixon-arab-isaeli-war.pdf.

Philby, St. John. "Pax Wahhabica." *English Review, 1908–1937* 62, no. 3 (1936): 309–22.

Phillips-Fein, Kim. *Fear City: New York's Fiscal Crisis and the Rise of Austerity Politics*. New York: Metropolitan Books, 2017.

Pigou, Arthur. *The Economics of Welfare*. London: Macmillan, 1920.

Pounds, Bonnie. "The U.S.–Saudi Arabian Joint Commission: A Model for Bilateral Economic Cooperation," *American-Arab Affairs* 7 (Winter 1983–84): 60–68.

Priest, Tyler. "Shifting Sands: The 1973 Oil Shock and the Expansion of Non-OPEC Supply." In *Oil Shock: The 1973 Crisis and Its Economic Legacy*, edited by Elisabetta Bini, Giuliano Garavini, and Federico Romero, 117–41. London: I. B. Tauris, 2016.

Prindle, David F. *Petroleum Politics and the Texas Railroad Commission*. Austin: University of Texas Press, 1981.

Putnam, Robert D., and Nicholas Bayne. *Hanging Together: The Seven-Power Summits*. Cambridge, MA: Harvard University Press, 1984.

Quandt, William B. *Peace Process: American Diplomacy and the Arab-Israeli Conflict Since 1967*. 3rd ed. Washington, DC: Brookings Institution Press, 2005.

Rahnama, Ali. *Behind the 1953 Coup in Iran: Thugs, Turncoats, Soldiers, Spooks*. Cambridge: Cambridge University Press, 2014.

Raimi, Daniel. *The Fracking Debate: The Risks, Benefits, and Uncertainties of the Shale Revolution*. New York: Columbia University Press, 2017.

Razoux, Pierre. *The Iran-Iraq War*. Translated by Nicholas Elliott. Cambridge, MA: Belknap Press, 2015.

Report of the Chief of the Motor Transport Corps to the Secretary of War. Washington, DC: U.S. Government Printing Office, 1920.

Riedel, Bruce. *Kings and Presidents: Saudi Arabia and the United States Since FDR*. Washington, DC: Brookings Institution Press, 2017.

Rihani, Ameen Fares. *Maker of Modern Arabia*. Boston: Houghton Mifflin, 1928.

Rockefeller, John D. *Random Reminiscences of Men and Events*. Garden City, NY: Doubleday, Page, 1913.

Rodman, David. "Phantom Fracas: The 1968 American Sale of F-4 Aircraft to Israel." *Middle Eastern Studies* 40, no. 6 (November 2004): 130–44.

Ross, Michael L. "Does Oil Hinder Democracy?" *World Politics* 53, no. 3 (2001): 325–61.

Rothstein, Richard. *The Color of Law: A Forgotten History of How Our Government Segregated America*. New York: Liveright, 2017.

Saba, Michael. *King Abdulaziz: His Plane and His Pilot*. Sioux Falls, SD: Gulf America Press, 2009.

Sabin, Paul. *The Bet: Paul Ehrlich, Julian Simon, and Our Gamble Over Earth's Future*. New Haven, CT: Yale University Press, 2013.

Safran, Nadav. *Saudi Arabia: The Ceaseless Quest for Security*. Ithaca, NY: Cornell University Press, 1988.

Said, Edward. *Orientalism*. New York: Vintage Books, 1979.

Samin, Nadav. *Of Sand or Soil: Genealogy and Tribal Belonging in Saudi Arabia*. Princeton, NJ: Princeton University Press, 2015.

Sampson, Anthony. *The Seven Sisters: The Great Oil Companies and the World They Shaped*. New York: Viking, 1975.

Sargent, Daniel J. "North/South: The United States Responds to the New International Economic Order." *Humanity* 6, no. 1 (2015): 201–16.

——. *A Superpower Transformed: The Remaking of American Foreign Relations in the 1970s*. Oxford: Oxford University Press, 2014.

Satia, Priya. "The Defense of Inhumanity: Air Control and the British Idea of Arabia." *American Historical Review* 111, no. 1 (2006): 16–51.

Saudi Arabian Monetary Agency (SAMA). *Annual Report, 1391/92 A.H. (1972)*. Jeddah, 1973.

——. *Annual Report, 1392/93 A.H. (1973)*. Jeddah, 1974.

——. *43rd Annual Report, 1428 A.H. (2007)*. Jeddah: 2007.

Sayf, Muhammad ibn ʿAbd Allah. *ʿAbd Allāh Al-Turayqī: Ṣukhūr al-Nafṭ wa-Rimāl al-Siyāsah* (Abdullah Tariki: The rocks of oil and the sands of politics). Beirut: Al-Muʾassasa al-ʿArabīyya li al-Dirāsāt wa-al-Nashr, 2007.

Scamehorn, H. Lee. *High Altitude Energy: A History of Fossil Fuels in Colorado*. Boulder: University Press of Colorado, 2002.

Schneider, Steven A. *The Oil Price Revolution*. Baltimore: Johns Hopkins University Press, 1983.

Schrader, Stuart. *Badges without Borders How Global Counterinsurgency Transformed American Policing*. Berkeley: University of California Press, 2019.

Schrag, Zachary M. *The Great Society Subway: A History of the Washington Metro*. Baltimore: Johns Hopkins University Press, 2006.

Schulman, Bruce J. *The Seventies: The Great Shift in American Culture, Society, and Politics*. New York: Free Press, 2001.

Schumacher, E. F. *Small Is Beautiful: A Study of Economics as If People Mattered*. London: Blond and Briggs, 1973.

Scott, James C. *Seeing Like a State: How Certain Schemes to Improve the Human Condition Have Failed*. New Haven, CT: Yale University Press, 1998.

Shannon, Kelly J. *U.S. Foreign Policy and Muslim Women's Human Rights*. Philadelphia: University of Pennsylvania Press, 2018.

Sick, Gary. *All Fall Down: America's Fateful Encounter with Iran*. New York: Random House, 1985.

Spiegel, Steven L. *The Other Arab-Israeli Conflict: Making America's Middle East Policy, from Truman to Reagan*. Chicago: University of Chicago Press, 1985.

Spiro, David E. *The Hidden Hand of American Hegemony: Petrodollar Recycling and International Markets*. Ithaca, NY: Cornell University Press, 1999.

Steil, Benn. *The Marshall Plan: Dawn of the Cold War*. New York: Simon and Schuster, 2018.

Stein, Judith. *Pivotal Decade: How the United States Traded Factories for Finance in the Seventies*. New Haven, CT: Yale University Press, 2010.

Stern, Roger J. "Oil Scarcity Ideology in US Foreign Policy, 1908–97." *Security Studies* 25, no. 2 (April 2016): 214–57.

Stobaugh, Robert. "The Oil Companies in the Crisis." In *The Oil Crisis*, edited by Raymond Vernon, 179–202. New York: W. W. Norton, 1986.

St. John, Rachel. *Line in the Sand: A History of the Western U.S.-Mexico Border*. Princeton, NJ: Princeton University Press, 2011.

Stuart, Henri L. *The Atlanta Plan: Rapid Transit for the People*. Atlanta: Metropolitan Atlanta Rapid Transit Authority, 1970.

Sugrue, Thomas J. *The Origins of the Urban Crisis: Race and Inequality in Postwar Detroit*. Rev. ed. Princeton, NJ: Princeton University Press, 2014.

Talmadge, Caitlin. *The Dictator's Army: Battlefield Effectiveness in Authoritarian Regimes*. Ithaca, NY: Cornell University Press, 2015.

Tariki, Abdullah. *'Abd Allāh Al-Ṭurayqī: Al-A'māl al-Kāmila* (Abdullah Tariki: Complete works). Beirut: Markaz Dirāsāt al-Waḥda al-'Arabīyya, 1999.

——. "Arab–Latin American Cooperation in the Energy Field." In *Arab–Latin American Relations: Energy, Trade, and Investment*, edited by Fehmy Saddy, 25–38. New Brunswick, NJ: Transaction Books, 1983.

Tooze, Adam. *The Deluge: The Great War, America, and the Remaking of the Global Order, 1916–1931*. New York: Viking, 2014.

——. *The Wages of Destruction: The Making and Breaking of the Nazi Economy*. New York: Viking, 2007.

Toprani, Anand. "The French Connection: A New Perspective on the End of the Red Line Agreement, 1945–1948." *Diplomatic History* 36, no. 2 (2012): 261–99.

——. "Oil and Grand Strategy: Great Britain and Germany, 1918–1941." PhD diss., Georgetown University, 2012.

Traboulsi, Fawwaz. "Saudi Expansion: The Lebanese Connection, 1924–1952." In *Kingdom Without Borders: Saudi Arabia's Political, Religious and Media Frontiers*, edited by Madawi Al Rasheed, 65–78. Oxford: Oxford University Press, 2008.

Trofimov, Yaroslav. *The Siege of Mecca: The Forgotten Uprising in Islam's Holiest Shrine and the Birth of al Qaeda*. New York: Doubleday, 2007.

Tucker, Robert. "Oil: The Issue of American Intervention." *Commentary* 59, no. 1 (1975): 21–31.

Tugwell, Franklin. *The Energy Crisis and the American Political Economy: Politics and Markets in the Management of Natural Resources*. Stanford, CA: Stanford University Press, 1988.

Turner, James Morton, and Andrew C. Isenberg. *The Republican Reversal: Conservatives and the Environment from Nixon to Trump*. Cambridge, MA: Harvard University Press, 2018.

Twitchell, Karl. *Saudi Arabia: With an Account of the Development of Its Natural Resources*. Princeton, NJ: Princeton University Press, 1947.

U.S. Bureau of Foreign and Domestic Commerce. *Commercial Relations of the United States with Foreign Countries*. Washington, DC: U.S. Government Printing Office, 1880.

U.S. General Accounting Office. *The U.S.-Saudi Arabian Joint Commission on Economic Cooperation: Report by the Comptroller General of the United States*. Washington, DC: U.S. General Accounting Office, 1979.

U.S. House of Representatives. *Report of the United States Revenue Commission on Petroleum as a Source of National Revenue*, 39th Cong., 1st Sess., Ex. Doc. 51, 3.

U.S. House of Representatives, Subcommittee on Foreign Economic Policy. *Foreign Policy Implications of the Energy Crisis: Hearings Before the Subcommittee on Foreign Economic Policy, House of Representatives*. Washington, DC: U.S. Government Printing Office, 1972.

U.S. Senate. *American Petroleum Interests in Foreign Countries*. Washington, DC: Government Printing Office, 1946.

U.S. Senate, Committee on Foreign Relations. *Executive Sessions of the Senate Foreign Relations Committee*, vol. 9. Washington, DC: U.S. Government Printing Office, 1979.

——. *The President's Proposal on the Middle East*. Washington, DC: U.S. Government Printing Office, 1957.

U.S. Senate, Committee on the Judiciary. *Protocols of the Elders of Zion: A Fabricated "Historic" Document*. Washington, DC: U.S. Government Printing Office, 1964.

U.S. Senate, Special Committee to Investigate Petroleum Resources. *Petroleum in War and Peace: Papers Presented by the Petroleum Administration for War Before the Senate Special Committee to Investigate Petroleum Resources*. Washington, DC: U.S. Government Printing Office, 1945.

U.S. Senate, Subcommittee on Multinational Corporations. *Multinational Oil Corporations and U.S. Foreign Policy: Hearings before the Subcommittee on Multinational Corporations*. Washington, DC: U.S. Government Printing Office, 1975.

U.S. Senate, Subcommittee on Multinational Corporations. *Multinational Oil Corporations and U.S. Foreign Policy: Report to the Committee on Foreign Relations by the Subcommittee on Multinational Corporations*. Washington: U.S. Government Printing Office, 1975.

U.S. War Department. "German Horse Cavalry and Transport." *Intelligence Bulletin*, March 1946, 53–66.

Vandewalle, Dirk. *A History of Modern Libya*. 2nd ed. Cambridge: Cambridge University Press, 2012.

Van Vleck, Jenifer. *Empire of the Air: Aviation and the American Ascendancy*. Cambridge, MA: Harvard University Press, 2013.

Vassiliev, Alexei. *The History of Saudi Arabia*. New York: New York University Press, 1998.

——. *King Faisal of Saudi Arabia: Personality, Faith and Times*. London: Saqi Books, 2013.

Vietor, Richard H. K. *Energy Policy in America Since 1945: A Study of Business-Government Relations*. Cambridge: Cambridge University Press, 1984.

Vitalis, Robert. *America's Kingdom: Mythmaking on the Saudi Oil Frontier*. Stanford, CA: Stanford University Press, 2007.

——. "Oil: The Stuff of Mass Delusion." *Jadaliyya*, March 9, 2016. https://www.jadaliyya.com/Details/33053.

——. "The Twentieth-Century Origins of a Twenty-First-Century Pseudo-science." *Montreal Review*, February 2013, http://www.themontrealreview.com/2009/America-s-Kingdom.php.

Volcker, Paul, and Christine Harper. *Keeping at It: The Quest for Sound Money and Good Government*. New York: Public Affairs, 2018.

Wahbah, Hafiz. *Arabian Days*. London: A. Barker, 1964.

——. *Jazīrat al-ʿArab fī al-qarn al-ʿishrīn* (The Arabian Peninsula in the twentieth century). 3rd ed. al-Qāhirah: Maṭbaʿat Lajnat al-Taʾlif wa-al-Tarjamah wa-al-Nashr, 1956.

Weingroff, Richard F. "Federal-Aid Highway Act of 1956: Creating the Interstate System," *Public Roads* 60, no. 1 (1996), 10–17, 45–51.

Wertheim, Stephen. "Tomorrow, the World: The Birth of US Global Supremacy in World War II." PhD diss., Columbia University, 2015.

Westad, Odd Arne. *The Global Cold War: Third World Interventions and the Making of Our Times*. Cambridge: Cambridge University Press, 2005.

Westgard, A. L. *Tales of a Pathfinder*. Washington, DC: Andrew B. Graham, 1920.

Weston, Mark. *Prophets and Princes: Saudi Arabia from Muhammad to the Present*. Hoboken, NJ: Wiley, 2008.

Wight, David. "The Petrodollar Era and Relations Between the United States and the Middle East and North Africa, 1969–1980." PhD diss., University of California at Irvine, 2014.

Wilford, Hugh. *America's Great Game: The CIA's Secret Arabists and the Shaping of the Modern Middle East*. New York: Basic Books, 2013.

Wilkerson, Isabel. *The Warmth of Other Suns: The Epic Story of America's Great Migration*. New York: Random House, 2010.

Wilkinson, John Craven. *Arabia's Frontiers: The Story of Britain's Boundary Drawing in the Desert*. London: I. B. Tauris, 1991.

Willis, John M. "Governing the Living and the Dead: Mecca and the Emergence of the Saudi Biopolitical State." *American Historical Review* 122, no. 2 (2017): 346–70.

Wong, Andrea. "The Untold Story Behind Saudi Arabia's 41-Year U.S. Debt Secret." *Bloomberg*, May 30, 2016. https://www.bloomberg.com/news/features/2016-05-30/the-untold-story-behind-saudi-arabia-s-41-year-u-s-debt-secret.

Wyrick, Traci. "Louis Schellbach's Log Books: Part IV." *The Ol' Pioneer: The Magazine of the Grand Canyon Historical Society* 22, no. 4 (Fall 2011): 14–15.

——. "Park Naturalist Louis Schellbach's Log Books." *The Ol' Pioneer: The Magazine of the Grand Canyon Historical Society* 22, no. 2 (Spring 2011): 11–12.

Yaqub, Salim. *Containing Arab Nationalism: The Eisenhower Doctrine and the Middle East*. Chapel Hill: University of North Carolina Press, 2004.

——. *Imperfect Strangers: Americans, Arabs, and U.S.–Middle East Relations in the 1970s*. Ithaca, NY: Cornell University Press, 2016.

Yergin, Daniel. *The Prize: The Epic Quest for Oil, Money, and Power*. New York: Free Press, 2008.

Yizraeli, Sarah. *Politics and Society in Saudi Arabia: The Crucial Years of Development, 1960–1982*. New York: Columbia University Press, 2012.

——. *The Remaking of Saudi Arabia: The Struggle Between King Saʿud and Crown Prince Faysal, 1953–1962*. Tel Aviv: Moshe Dayan Center, Tel Aviv University, 1997.

Zaretsky, Natasha. *No Direction Home: The American Family and the Fear of National Decline, 1968–1980*. Chapel Hill: University of North Carolina Press, 2007.

INDEX

Page numbers in *italics* refer to figures.

Jackson, Henry "Scoop," 90–91, 124, 129, 143, 253n9

Jacobs, Jane, 109

Jaheem al-Hukm al-Saudia (The Hell of Saudi Rule), 57

Japan, 36, 135, 141, 167

Javits, Jacob, 91, 128–29

Al-Jazeerah (newspaper), 206

JECOR. *See* Joint Commission on Economic Cooperation

Jeddah: conquest of, 20; as diplomatic capital, 158; infrastructure development, 29, 54, 102–3, 112; Nixon's visit to, 1–2, 5, 12; and oil boom of the 1970s, 1, 152–53, 158; and Operation Desert Shield, 243; port at, 1, 29, 102, *104*, 112, 152, *243*

Jerusalem, 90, 141, 167

Jews. *See* anti-Semitism; Israel; Zionism

jihadism, 9, 241

Johnson, Lyndon: and Arab–Israeli War of 1967, 84; and Egypt's blockade of Strait of Tiran, 88; Faisal and, 47; Nasser and, 74; sale of F-4 Phantom to Israel, 91; and tensions with Saudis over support for Israel, 92

Joint Commission on Economic Cooperation (JECOR), 142, 161–65, 180, 245

Jones, David, 228

Jordan: and Saudi desire for U.S. military assistance, 50; Saudi promotion of anticommunist regime, 9; Saudi subsidies to, 86, 97, 112–13, 174; Saudi troops in, 83. *See also* Arab–Israeli War of 1967; Arab–Israeli War of 1973

Jungers, Frank, 143, 169, 286n68

Kennan, George F., 231

Kennedy, John F.: Faisal and, 68, 71; and policy shift toward Egypt, 67; and proxy war in Yemen, 72–74; Saud and, 67–68, 271n92; and U.S.–Saudi relationship, 67–70

Kennedy, Ted, 231

Kenya, U.S. military facilities in, 229, 230

Khalid ibn Adulaziz (King Khalid): and arms sales, 177; ascension to throne after assassination of Faisal, 160; Carter and, 196, 198, 208; Ford and, 185; and ideological affinities of U.S. and Saudi Arabia, 224; Kissinger and, 169; preference for American aircraft, 9; and rightward turn of regime, 204; and Saudi control of oil prices, 185; and U.S. monetary policy, 196, 198; visit to the U.S. (1943), 16, 39; and Zionism, 167

Khartoum, embassy attack in, 117

Khashoggi, Adnan, 74–75, 154, 158, 165, 175–76, 240, 241

Kheirallah, George, 42

Khoja, Badulla Ahrar, 213–14

Khomeini, Ayatollah Ruhollah, 222, 232

Kissinger, Henry, 2, *162*; adversarial approach to diplomacy, 148–49, 165, 168–70; and airlift of arms for Israel, 134; and Arab–Israeli War of 1973, 126, 128–31, 133, 134; Arab resolve underestimated during oil crisis, 134–35; and arms sales, 177; and concerns about Saudi foreign aid, 186; empowered by oil crisis, 124–25; and energy conservation program, 131; Fahd and, 3, 8, 160; Faisal and, 169; and fears about another oil embargo, 167; and Israel, 167–68; and Jewish community in the U.S., 147–48; and Joint Commission for Economic Cooperation (JECOR), 161, 163, 165; Khalid and, 169; and military threats against Saudi Arabia, 168–70; and oil companies, 128; and oil embargo, 124–25, 138, 140–41, 146–49; and oil price increases, 132; and OPEC, 166–67; personal insulation from fuel shortages, 123, 140; and push for energy independence, 171; reputation of, 135; Saqqaf and, 10, 13, 167; and Saudi anti-Semitism, 176; and Saudi demands for Israel's

NOW. *See* National Organization for
Women
nuclear power, 146, 171, 191

October War. *See* Arab–Israeli War of 1973
Odom, William, 205
OECD. *See* Organization for Economic
Cooperation and Development
oil companies: anticompetitive practices, 48,
52; and antitrust violations, 11, 48, 51–52;
and Arab–Israeli War of 1973, 127–28,
132–33; consolidation of, 10–11, 48, 52–53;
European companies excluded from
richest oil-producing areas, 88; founding
of OPEC, 66–67; Iranian nationalization crisis of 1951–1953, 62, 89, 106;
nationalization of, 55, 62, 89, 111, 128, 136;
naval fuel scandal, 55; and oil embargo of
1973–1974, 136, 137; oil exploration in
Saudi Arabia, 30–31; origins of oil
concession, 29–31 (*see also specific
companies*); promotion of domestic
policies favoring increasing oil
consumption, 108; protected from
domestic oversight due to partnership
with U.S. national security state, 48, 52;
Seven Sisters, 52, 62, 66–67, 88, 89; ties
to U.S. banks, 46–47; U.S. companies in
the early 20th century, 32–33. *See also* oil
industry; oil prices; OPEC; *specific
companies*
oil crisis. *See* energy crisis; oil embargo of
1973–1974
oil embargo of 1967, 80, 84–89, 105
oil embargo of 1973–1974, 1–2, 5, 89, 103,
123–51, 237; embargo diplomacy, 140–45;
end of, 124, 148–50; and enhanced power
of Saudi monarchy, 125; and growth of
executive power in the U.S., 124–25,
145–48; impact of, 137–40, 237, 254n15;
and possibility of seizing oil fields by
force, 138–39, 150; prelude to, 119–22;
price increases and threat of the oil

weapon, 131–33, 139, 254n15; production
restrictions and embargo in response to
airlift, 133–36; Saudi violations of, 125,
142–43, 150, 254n15, 286n68; and
Watergate, 146–47
oil industry: and Arab–Israeli War of 1967,
105; Carter's foreign oil policy, 192–95;
congressional investigations during oil
embargo, 143; consumers' shift away
from OPEC, 240; declining American
production in the 1970s, 103, 107–8; and
energy crisis, 103, 110 (*see also* energy
crisis); fears about dwindling oil
supplies, 7, 193–94, 297n44; growth of
American oil consumption, 60–61, 103;
impact of fracking, 247–48; and
importance of border lands, 95;
increasing American dependence on
foreign oil, 103; increasing oil production
in Saudi Arabia, 111–12; influence in
Congress, 191; and Iranian Revolution,
222; and justifications for U.S.–Saudi
cooperation, 5–7, 49–50, 194; as key to
U.S. power during WWI and WWII,
32–33, 35–37; and Kissinger's strategy of
dividing OPEC and creating a consumer
alliance, 166–67; oil boom of the 1970s,
103, 112–15, 152–56; origins of oil
concession in Saudi Arabia, 29–31; rise
of Libya as oil producer, 105–6; rise of oil
industry in the U.S., 31–33; and rise of
the U.S. as a superpower in the 1940s, 16;
Saudi Arabia as "swing producer,"
183–85, 222, 241, 295n7; Saudi Arabia as
world's largest exporter, 253n10; Saudi
production capacity, 114, 183; shift in
balance of power between consumers, oil
companies, and oil-producing states,
106–7, 111–12; transformation of oil
market in the 1970s, 105–7, 111–12; U.S.
and Saudi push for global economy
based on oil, 248; U.S. as largest oil
producer in the early 20th century,

oil tankers, 105, 122, 235–38, *236*
O'Keefe, Richard, 50–51
Oman, 21, 95, 229
Onassis, Aristotle, 63
O'Neill, Thomas "Tip," 172, 191
OPEC: alliance with developing countries, 166; dominance threatened by new sources of production, 240; founding of, 66–67; and inflation and unemployment in the United States, 193; investments by members, 186; Kissinger's strategy of dividing OPEC, 166–67; and NIEO, 166, 291n44; and oil embargo of 1973–1974, 137–40; Saudi Arabia perceived as being the most responsible member, 8, 184, 194; Saudi Arabia's domination of, 183–84; and Saudi control of oil prices, 183–85, 254n16 (*see also under* oil prices); split between Saudi Arabia and price hawks, 254n16; and threat of changes to pricing arrangements, 197, 198; and U.S. monetary policy, 196–98
Operation Desert Shield, 242–43
Operation Desert Storm, 245
Operation Hard Surface, 73, 78
Organization for Economic Cooperation and Development (OECD), 106, 107
Organization of the Islamic Conference, 92–93, 225
Ottoman Empire, 19, 21

Pakistan, 223, 224, 226, 241, 248, 302n1
Palestine Liberation Organization (PLO), 105, 211; and civil war in Lebanon, 174; and oil embargo of 1973–1974, 136, 150; Saudi support for, 9, 113, 117, 281n72
Palestinians, 48, 50, 127; and Arab–Israeli War of 1973, 134; Faisal and, 4–5, 117–18; and Middle East peace process, 211, 212; poor treatment in Saudi Arabia, 118
Parsky, Gerald, 186
PAW. *See* Petroleum Administration for War

"Pax Wahhabica," 22–26
PD-18 (secret policy statement), 215–16, 229, 304n24
People's Democratic Republic of Yemen (PDRY; South Yemen): conflict with Saudi Arabia, 93–95, 101; conflict YAR, 219–21
petrodollars. *See* investments, Saudi; oil revenue
Petroleum Administration for War (PAW), 36–37
Pharaon, Gaith, 240
Philby, Harry St. John Bridger ("Jack"), 23–24, 26, 29, 35
Piercy, George, 111
PLO. *See* Palestine Liberation Organization
Population Bomb, The (Ehrlich), 109
Porter, William, 174, 185, 216–17
ports, 29, 103–4, *104*; bottlenecks at, 1, 152–53, 156, 165; development of, 102, 112; and Operation Desert Shield, 243
Powell, Adam Clayton, 65
Price, Melvin, 128–29
Princeton University, 43, 68
Project Independence, 170–73, 292n62
Proposition 18 (California), 108
Protocols of the Elders of Zion, 92
Proxmire, William, 124
public (Saudi Arabia): anti-American sentiment, 91–92, 245–47; and Arab–Israeli War of 1967, 79–80; and climate change, 249; dissidents (*see* dissidents); domestic discontent, 99–100, 153, 157, 165, 200–205; expectations for continuing benefits, 156; gender segregation, 203, 243–44; al-Hasa protests (1979), 204, 205, 232; high cost of living, 157, 165, 201; housing, 155, 157, 158, 201; and human rights, 202–3; immigrants (*see* immigrants to Saudi Arabia); and inequality, 83, 153, 157–58, 161, 165; lack of political freedoms, 155–56, 201–4; material benefits of oil boom, 153–56; negative

consequences of oil boom, 153, 156–59; opposition to non-Muslims in the kingdom, 246; opposition to U.S. military presence in Saudi Arabia, 245–47; protests during Arab–Israeli War of 1967, 83–84; public anger at government mismanagement and lack of social liberalization, 99, 201; and *shura*, 155; state employees, 155, 156; subsidies for food, water, electricity, etc., 155, 201; suppression of dissent, 48, 56, 100, 204; uprisings of 1980, 201; workers (*see* labor). *See also* Bedouin; immigrants to Saudi Arabia; Shia community in Saudi Arabia

public (U.S.): and behind-the-scenes recruitment of Saudi investments, 188; concerns about Arab investments, 185–96; divisions over extending military protection to Saudi Arabia, 243–45; growth of American oil consumption, 60–61; and Gulf War, 244; negative views of Saudi Arabia, 47, 63–65, 243–47; opposition to sale of F-15 to Saudi Arabia, 181; percentage favoring protecting the Gulf in the event of a Soviet invasion, 231; U.S. as car-centric society, 33–35, 60–61, 108

Qaddafi, Muammar, 106
al-Qaeda, 246
Qatar, 21, 135
Quandt, William, 134
Quraishi, Abdulaziz, 187, 197–99

Al-Ra'i al-Am (newspaper), 149
railways, 53, 54
Rangel, Charles, 124
Rapid Deployment Joint Task Force (RDJTF), 215, 229
Al-Rashdan, Mohammed, 205–6
Rashidi dynasty, 19
Rayner, Charles, 38
Raytheon, 74, 175–76

RDJTF. *See* Rapid Deployment Joint Task Force
Reagan, Ronald, 193; and Afghanistan, 241; and AWACS aircraft sale, 242; and Iran-Contra scandal, 241–42; and Iran-Iraq War, 242; primary battle with Ford, 173, 293n75; and U.S.–Saudi relationship, 241–42
Real Estate Development Fund, 157
real estate speculation, 31, 157
recession, 198
religious discrimination, 204. *See also* anti-Semitism; Shia community in Saudi Arabia
rentier effect, 288n10
Revey, P. A., 187
Ribicoff, Abraham, 185, 213
Riesel, Victor, 64
Rihani, Ameen, 23, 29
Riyadh, 158
Al-Riyadh (newspaper), 4, 136, 156–57, 199, 201, 206, 283n9
Rockefeller, David, 46, 116, *162*, 198, 297n32
Rockefeller, Nelson, 47
Rockefeller family, 46
Rockefeller Foundation, 76
Roosevelt, Franklin, 35, 37–44
Roosevelt, Kermit, 72, 74
Rub al-Khali desert, 95
Rumsfeld, Donald, 141
Rush, Kenneth, 127
Rustin, Bayard, 181
Ruszkiewicz, John, 220–21

Al Sabah, Ali Khalifa, 197
Sabbagh, Isa, 71, 72, 271n92
al-Sabban, Mohammad Salim, 248–49
al-Sabban, Mohammed Sorour, 92
Sadat, Anwar, 101, 131–32, 211–12
al-Said, Nasir, 48, 50, 80, 87
Saleh, Ali Abdullah, 220
Salman, Prince, 117, 160

corporations doing business with Israel); blurred lines between public and private interests, 53; critics' fears about growing Saudi influence in American economy, 116; difficulties for Saudis in maintaining relationship while also maintaining credentials as a supporter of the Arab cause against Israel, 117–22, 212; difficulties for Saudis in maintaining relationship while also maintaining popular support, 49–50, 93; difficulties for Saudis in maintaining relationship while also maintaining relations with other Arab nations, 73, 78, 117; and economic turmoil of the 1970s, 164–65 (*see also* oil revenue); ideological and cultural differences, 243–44; opposition to alliance in Saudi Arabia, 4, 48, 87, 91, 93, 117, 126–27, 154, 165, 178–79, 188–89, 245–47; opposition to alliance in the Middle East, 4, 124; opposition to alliance in the U.S., 4, 43–45, 47–48, 63–65, 153–54, 175–77, 203, 243–47; political purposes of military coopera-tion, 50, 94, 97; and rivalries within the Saudi government, 144–45; and Saudi anti-Semitism (*see* anti-Semitism); Saudi royals favored over educated technocrats by the U.S., 144–45; and Saudi struggle to maintain Arab nationalist credentials, 81, 84–85; tensions downplayed by both sides, 84, 142; tensions over Israel, 40, 43–44, 47, 49–51, 78, 117–19, 126–27, 167, 176–77, 179 (*see also* Arab–Israeli War of 1967; Arab–Israeli War of 1973); and U.S. leverage over Saudi Arabia, 165–68; and U.S. military threats against Saudi Arabia, 168–70; and U.S. pressure for reform, 68–72

U.S.–Saudi alliance, components of: arms sales (*see* arms sales); behind-the-scenes diplomacy, 39, 47–48, 77, 120–21, 143–44, 184, 186, 209–10, 213; close relationship

between Saudis and White House and executive branch, 12–13; education of Saudi elites in the U.S., 3, 8, 42–43, 68, 205–6; lack of formal alliance treaty, 3–4; military assistance, 3–4, 81, 93–97 (*see also* U.S.–Saudi military coopera-tion); provision of American technical expertise, 3, 8, 16, 38–39, 76–77; royal family treated as elites in the U.S., 40–42; sales of American goods and technology to Saudi Arabia, 3, 8, 16–17, 113–14, 152–53, 178–79 (*see also* arms sales); Saudi funding for covert U.S. actions, 241–42; Saudi investment in U.S. financial markets, 3, 8, 11, 104, 116, 178, 186–90, 214, 239–40; Saudi investment in U.S. mortgage market, 189, 239; Saudi investors shielded from oversight, 11, 187–89, 239–40; security relationship, 3, 210, 214–16 (*see also* U.S.–Saudi military cooperation); ties between U.S. executive, Saudi elites, and American corporations, 12–13, 45–48, 116; U.S. commitment to defending Saudi Arabia against regional threats, 3, 51, 101, 227, 233, 242–47; U.S. commitment to survival of the monarchy, 77–78, 100; U.S. concerns about democracy, human rights, gender equality, and religious freedom disregarded, 7, 202–3, 243–44, 256n22

U.S.–Saudi alliance, consequences of, 9–14, 247–49; consolidation of American corporations, 10–11, 48, 52–54; entrench-ment of royal power, 10, 13, 39, 45, 77, 100; financialization of U.S. economy, 10, 11, 189–90, 239–40; growth of executive power in the U.S., 10, 13, 45, 124–25, 145–48; Saudi influence on U.S. economic policy, 196–97, 210; Saudi influence on U.S. foreign policy, 12–14, 175, 180–82, 210, 216–33, 241–42; Saudi influence on U.S. monetary policy, 11–12, 196–200, 208, 238

Printed in the USA
CPSIA information can be obtained
at www.ICGtesting.com
JSHW021545110724
66271JS00003B/46